Kaiser Wilhelm II, Queen Victoria's eldest grandchild, took over the running of the powerful German Reich from Bismarck and within a couple of decades had led it into world war and collapse. How did the Kaiser come to have so much power? Why was there no-one to help him steer a less disastrous course? This book analyses these crucial questions with the help of a wealth of new archival sources.

The book begins with a character-sketch of the Kaiser which provides new and alarming insights into his personality. It then looks, crucially, at the Kaiser's friends and favourites, at the neo-absolutist culture of the court and of Berlin court society, and at the nature of his relationship with the court on the one hand and with the administrative 'pyramid' in Prussia and the Reich on the other. The book makes clear that these bureaucrats and diplomats had neither the means nor the will to oppose the overwhelming determination of the Kaiser and his close friends and advisers in directing the policies of the most dynamic and volatile state in Europe. The dangerous consequences of this situation led to the brink of world war as early as December 1912. A final chapter reveals for the first time the appalling extent and nature of the exiled Kaiser's anti-semitism.

JOHN C. G. RÖHL is Professor of History at the University of Sussex.

The Kaiser and his Court

The Kaiser and his Court

Wilhelm II and the Government of Germany

John C. G. Röhl

Professor of History,
University of Sussex

Translated from the German by Terence F. Cole

CAMBRIDGE
UNIVERSITY PRESS

Published by the Press Syndicate of the University of Cambridge
The Pitt Building, Trumpington Street, Cambridge CB2 1RP
40 West 20th Street, New York, NY 10011-4211, USA
10 Stamford Road, Oakleigh, Melbourne 3166, Australia

Originally published in Germany as *Kaiser, Hof und Staat: Wilhelm II.*
und die deutsche Politik
by Verlag C. H. Beck, Munich 1987
and © John C. G. Röhl 1987
First published in England by Cambridge University Press 1994
as *The Kaiser and his Court. Wilhelm II and the Government of Germany*
English translation © John C. G. Röhl 1994
Reprinted 1995
First paperback edition published 1996
Reprinted 1997

Printed in Great Britain at the University Press, Cambridge

A catalogue record for this book is available from the British Library

Library of Congress cataloguing in publication data
Röhl, John C. G.
The Kaiser and his Court. Wilhelm II and the Government of Germany /
by John C. G. Röhl: translated from the German by Terence F. Cole.
     p.   cm.
Includes bibliographical references.
ISBN 0 521 40223 9
1. William II. German Emperor, 1859–1941. 2. Germany – Politics and
government – 1888–1918. 3. Germany – Kings and rulers – Biography.
4. William II, German Emperor, 1859–1941 – Views on Jews.
I. Title.
DD229.R6413 1995
943.08'4'092–dc20
[B]   94–6 CIP

ISBN 0 521 40223 9 hardback
ISBN 0 521 56504 9 paperback

For my daughter
Stephanie

Contents

Preface to the English edition

When this book on the political role played by Kaiser Wilhelm II and his court was published in Germany in 1987, it quickly went through three editions, selling over 15,000 copies in the space of a few years. This fact alone suggests that its subject, which had for decades been marginalised by professional German historians, was held to be of some interest and importance by a wider German public. Very few people in the English-speaking world will share or even understand the view which until recently predominated in German historical circles that Wilhelm II was a mere 'shadow emperor' who played no part in shaping the policies of the Kaiserreich, and that the Imperial court, too, could safely be ignored when analysing German decision-making in the crucial quarter-century between Bismarck's dismissal and the First World War. There (and elsewhere outside Germany) the reverse assumption has always prevailed that 'the Kaiser' (as he is known *tout court*) was an aggressive autocrat who must bear a large degree of responsibility for plunging the Old Europe into war and catastrophe. Some readers of the English edition of this book, while finding such assumptions largely confirmed, may therefore be especially interested to see how frighteningly chaotic and corrupt behind the resplendent façade the governmental system of imperial Germany really was.

For this edition, those chapters not originally written in English have been faithfully translated from the German by Terence F. Cole, himself an expert on the history of the Second Reich. The final chapter, which reveals for the first time the dreadful extent of Wilhelm II's anti-semitism, was written at the Woodrow Wilson International Center for Scholars in Washington DC in the summer of 1990 and did not therefore form part of the original German edition. With this one exception, I have by and large resisted the temptation to add new material to old and established texts except where important new evidence on very specific points has come to light. Since I began to study the history of the Kaiser's Germany as a doctoral student at Cambridge in 1961, the scholarly literature on the period has grown to the point where it is almost impossible for one person to absorb; I have not tried to bring up to date the references to all such work in the footnotes.

JOHN RÖHL
Sussex, November 1993

Introduction

The eight studies collected together in this book were written at various times and in a variety of contexts over a period of some twenty-five years. They are nevertheless all concerned with the same fundamental theme, the system of government of the German Reich under Kaiser Wilhelm II. The book opens with a character-sketch of this remarkable ruler, who was not merely some exotic 'Fabulous Monster', as one British writer dubbed him,[1] but who in a number of ways embodied the split personality of that 'transitional generation'[2] which bridged the old Prussian world of Wilhelm I and Bismarck on the one hand and the 'modern' world of mass industrial society on the other. It ends with an investigation into the nature and extent of the Kaiser's anti-semitism which enables us to see how close he came, in the bitterness of exile, to the *Weltanschauung* of Adolf Hitler. Most of the studies in this book, however, are not primarily concerned with the Kaiser. Their main focus is, first, on the mentality of the Kaiser's friends and advisers; second, on the structural foundations on which his so-called 'personal rule' was first erected and then sustained, including the court and court society, the higher civil service and the diplomatic corps; and third, and above all, on the interdependent relationship between the Kaiser, his court and the state. The book is therefore predominantly a work of cultural and social history. It sets out to analyse the structure and the mentality of the German ruling elite in the era of Kaiser Wilhelm II.

The studies are all based closely on original sources. Rather than providing a sweeping essayistic interpretation, each chapter is perhaps more like a pointillist painting, or like a photomontage composed of several individual photographs. Each of these pictures is an independent composition which originated as such and which can therefore be read and judged on its own merits. These individual pictures, however, can and should also be seen as facets of a larger totality. If I may stay with the artistic analogy for a moment longer, this means that the book works in the same way as a Cubist painting in which an object can be seen in several different perspectives simultaneously.

This larger picture has not always been correctly understood by my critics. As these studies appeared as individual contributions in a variety of publications over a quarter of a century, what was an examination of one feature of a topic has occasionally been regarded as a full-scale treatment of the entire complex, with the result that one study has been criticised as being too 'psychological' or 'personalistic', another as perhaps usefully 'multibiographical' but nevertheless too 'impressionistic', a third as exaggeratedly statistical, structuralist or sociological. Only now, when the individual studies are brought together in one book, is it possible to see the connections between them; only here is it possible to offer something approaching a comprehensive answer to the question which informs all eight studies: how adequate was the decision-making process, how good the quality of government in the German Empire under Kaiser Wilhelm II? (Even so, however, there are many aspects of the problem which are dealt with here all too briefly, the army and the navy being two striking examples.)

Why do I speak of the 'quality of government', and why has this question pursued me like a recurrent nightmare for more than three decades? Friedrich Stampfer, the editor of the Social Democratic newspaper *Vorwärts*, delivered the retrospective judgment in the Weimar Republic that the German Kaiserreich had been the most economically successful and the best administered but the 'worst governed' country in Europe before 1914. Max Weber wrote, some years before the outbreak of the First World War, that he sometimes had the feeling that Germany was being governed by a 'herd of lunatics'. And Friedrich von Holstein, the 'grey eminence' of the German Foreign Office whose political correspondence must rank as one of the greatest literary achievements of the Wilhelmine era, warned as far back as the winter of 1894 that the young Kaiser's mode of governing was an 'operetta régime, but not one that a European nation at the end of the nineteenth century will put up with'. Holstein warned that he could not exclude the possibility that 'the reign of His Majesty Wilhelm the Second' might form 'a transition' either to a dictatorship or else to a republic.[3]

Faced with such acute judgments, the observer interested in the historical past (or indeed concerned for the future) finds himself confronting a multiplicity of questions – questions which have if anything grown in their explosive potential in the seventy-five years since the Kaiser's abdication. Was the much criticised 'personal rule' of Kaiser Wilhelm II really as bad, as anachronistic, as insane, as the judgments of Stampfer and Weber referred to above would suggest? How was it possible for such a highly developed European people as the Germans to tolerate such an 'operetta régime' until well into the twentieth century, indeed not just tolerate but in many cases support it with great enthusiasm? What is the relationship between the ridiculous but also terrifying incompetence of this régime and the unleashing of the First World War, that basic catastrophe of our century in whose beginning – as Thomas Mann so presciently wrote at the beginning of his novel *The Magic Mountain* in 1924 – 'so much began which has scarcely yet left off beginning'? What place should we assign to Kaiser Wilhelm II, and to the thirty-year epoch that bears his name, in the brief and cataclysmic history of the German nation-state from 1871 to 1945? What inferences should we draw from the evidence – clearly discernible during the Wilhelmine era itself – that the deployment of the phenomenal power created by modern industrial technology depends in the final analysis on the decisions of a small number of not always very competent 'statesmen'?

So far as the first question is concerned, it would clearly be absurd to claim that Kaiser Wilhelm II ever established full-scale autocracy. When contemporaries spoke critically of his 'personal rule', they were expressing disapproval of his too frequent and too sudden interference in the affairs of state, of the emphasis he placed on his Divine Right, which was perceived as an insult to the nation, of the speeches and interviews which had such a disastrous impact on the foreign policy and the international standing of the German Reich. Wilhelm II might have dreamed of establishing absolute rule for himself, but it remained no more than a dream. Even his severest critics did not believe that he ever practised such a form of rule. As this point occasions so much misunderstanding in the present day, it would perhaps be wiser, wherever possible, to avoid the use of the Wilhelmine polemical term 'personal rule' and to deploy in its stead the more neutral concept of 'kingship mechanism' elaborated by the sociologist Norbert Elias. The use of this concept should help to distract attention from the deeds and misdeeds of 'Wilhelm the Sudden', thus enabling us to concentrate on the more significant and interesting question of the interplay of the Kaiser, his court and the state bureaucracy in the exercise of power in Wilhelmine Germany.[4]

All the same, the central thesis of this book is that the political system of the German Kaiserreich is to be understood in essence as a *monarchy*, and that consequently the Kaiser, the royal family, the Kaiser's circle of friends, the Imperial entourage and the court form the heart of this system on which the very highest officials of the Reich and state bureaucracy (as well as the leaders of the army and navy) were psychologically and politically dependent. In this crucial sense the system of government under Wilhelm II can be distinguished from Bismarck's Chancellor-dictatorship, even though no constitutional changes giving formal recognition to the new situation were effected after Bismarck's dismissal in March 1890. Such constitutional changes were in fact not necessary as Bismarck, despite his monopolistic exercise of power, had consistently maintained the fiction – the word is used here in both its meanings – that in Prussia the King gave the orders and the ministers obeyed. 'In this country . . . the King himself governs', Bismarck proclaimed in a speech in the Reichstag in 1882. 'Ministers no doubt edit [*redigieren*] what the King has ordered, but they do not govern [*regieren*].'[5] After Bismarck's dismissal, all that Kaiser Wilhelm II needed to do was to transform Bismarck's political fiction into fact, though this could not be accomplished overnight, nor without severe internal crisis. Yet in the course of the 1890s a new system of power relationships *was* created, a genuinely monarchical régime in which the Kaiser and his court, rather than the Chancellor and 'his men', exercised political power and decision-making authority and thus laid down the fundamental guidelines of domestic, foreign and armaments policy. Kaiser Wilhelm II created this system on the basis of his constitutional authority as King of Prussia, which gave him unrestricted power of command in all military matters, and on his right to appoint, promote and dismiss all officials in both Prussia and the Reich – a right of which he made the fullest use. In the years after Bismarck's fall and with the help first and foremost of his best friend Count Philipp zu Eulenburg, and also with the aid of the chiefs of his three Secret Cabinets for Military, Naval and Civil Affairs, Wilhelm was in fact able to construct a system of what Bernhard von Bülow called 'personal rule in the good sense'. In this system the Reich Chancellor, as Bülow revealingly expressed it in 1896, would simply regard himself as 'the executive tool of His Majesty, so to speak his political Chief of Staff'.[6] This was the system which produced the decisions and the avoidance of decisions which led, via *Weltmachtpolitik* and Tirpitz's gigantic battleship programme, to internal crisis and external isolation, until at the last this tiny elite, increasingly dominated by military elements at court, came to regard a short, sharp, 'fresh and joyful war' as the only exit from the blind alley into which it had manoeuvred itself.

For these reasons the reign of Kaiser Wilhelm II should be seen as a discrete epoch in the constitutional history of the German nation-state, one with its own distinctive power structures and behaviour patterns. It cannot be understood, as Hans-Ulrich Wehler has claimed, as the mere continuation of the 'Bonapartist Chancellor-dictatorship' of Bismarck by 'the anonymous forces of authoritarian polycracy'. Seen in this light, as a new and unique system of rule, the fierce campaign against the new régime by the Bismarckian 'fronde' after the dismissal of the 'Iron Chancellor' becomes readily understandable. Given that Bismarck's successful 28-year period of office could not be obliterated from the memories of the German people overnight, and that on the contrary with each foolish new act on the part of the Kaiser it shone more gloriously than ever, the Bismarckian campaign constituted a dire threat to the Hohenzollern monarchy. Bismarck's system had, it is true, been established in the 1860s against the 'spirit of the times', but the restoration under Kaiser Wilhelm II of a genuinely functioning monarchy claiming legitimation by Divine Right one hundred years after the French Revolution was even more forced, artificial, anachronistic, reactionary, grotesque. Despite its populist and plebiscitary elements, it was bound to lead to severe tensions in a country where there was universal male suffrage and in which increasingly the dominant forces shaping society and its attitudes were urbanisation, industrialisation and democratisation. Historically speaking this attempt by the Wilhelminians to introduce, on the threshold to the twentieth century, a monarchy by the grace of God with a neo-absolutist court culture can probably be compared only with the absolutist designs of Charles I of England, who was beheaded in the middle of the Civil War in January 1649, or with Charles X of France, who had to flee abroad after the bloodless revolution of July 1830, however wanting such comparisons are bound to be.

By emphasising the unique character of the Wilhelmine system of government as the re-establishment of a pre-Bismarckian monarchical régime in the era of mass industrial society, I do not wish to preclude consideration of the question of continuity in the history of the German nation-state between 1871 and 1945: quite the reverse. But the question of continuity turns out to be more complicated – and more open – than first appears to be the case. Certainly the appointment of Bismarck as Prussian Minister-President and Minister for Foreign Affairs in the autumn of 1862 was a decisive turning-point which had implications for the Wilhelmine period and far beyond it. Yet, however significant the events of 1862 to 1871 were for the future development of Germany, the role of chance, of personality, of political decision-making in the broader course of German history should not be underestimated. What would have happened, for instance, if Kaiser Wilhelm I had died when he was seventy or eighty rather than when he was over ninety years of age? Without doubt a reign of ten or twenty years by the liberal-minded Kaiser Friedrich III and his English wife, Queen Victoria's eldest child (with or without Bismarck as Chancellor), would have fundamentally re-orientated the system of government along the lines of a constitutional or even parliamentary monarchy. It would have created a situation which their son Wilhelm II would have found difficult if not impossible to reverse.

Furthermore the Wilhelmine era itself cannot be seen simply as the forerunner of the Third Reich, at least not without severe qualification and differentiation. Certainly features exist in the personality and in the *Weltanschauung* of Kaiser Wilhelm II which anticipate many terrible things which were to come much later. These include not only the 'world power' strategy with its battlefleet programme directed against Britain, and the war aims in the First World War so tellingly analysed by Fritz Fischer, but also demands to 'gun down' such 'unpatriotic fellows' as the Social Democrats and the Catholics, to 'sweep away' that 'pigsty', the Reichstag, to defend the 'peoples of Europe' from the 'yellow peril', to have German troops behave as mercilessly 'as the Huns' towards the rebellious Chinese, to bring about the 'final struggle between the Slavs and the Teutons', to drive 90,000 Russian prisoners of war to death by starvation, and even – this soon after the First World War – to 'wipe out from German soil and exterminate' those 'parasites', the hated 'tribe of Juda', 'this poisonous mushroom on the German oak-tree'.[7] And much, much more besides. Yet increasingly, and especially among contemporary critics of the form of rule practised by Wilhelm II and among the opponents of such appalling aggression, we find those forces – liberal political commentators, Catholic Centre party members, Social Democrats and others – which were to establish the rich political culture of the Weimar Republic, for a while at least, until the great silence descended.

What should have happened, what could have been done, to avoid the unspeakable catastrophes which lay in wait? At first sight, the astonishing answer is: nothing. If Germany had not opted for war in 1914, there would have been no war, because Austria-Hungary would certainly not have dared risk a war without Germany's support, and the Triple Entente would not have attacked the Central Powers then, nor three years later (nor indeed later still). Imperial Germany would have continued its unprecedented economic, scientific and cultural progress, and soon, in its own right and without war, it would have become the natural leader among the European powers. The dissolution of the Habsburg Empire, that 'prison of the nations', was almost certainly inevitable by then, but did that constitute a reason for Germany to 'leap into the dark' in an act of Dark Ages tribal fidelity? Was there no conceivable 'diplomatic revolution' which, without war, could have provided the German Reich with the requisite 'security and guarantees' which Reich Chancellor Theobald von Bethmann Hollweg sought to enforce in his infamous 'September programme' of 1914 by means of annexations, revolutionisation and economic measures? An understanding with the British Empire could have been achieved up until the last moment. The British War Minister Lord Haldane had offered Germany an agreement as late as the spring of 1912. The price? Berlin was to slow down – not stop entirely – the rate of battleship construction, which made no strategic sense in any case,[8] and it had to promise not to attack France or Russia. Reich Chancellor Bethmann Hollweg, the 'responsible leader' of German policy and 'first adviser to the Crown', wanted to accept. But, even in this most critical question, he was overruled; the Kaiser listened to Tirpitz and abruptly rejected the proposal. In this light it is not surprising that, only ten months later, Bethmann was excluded from a 'military-political discussion' at the royal palace in Berlin, at which the highest-ranking generals and admirals discussed, under the direction of the Kaiser, the question whether a world war against Britain, France and Russia should be unleashed immediately (by urging Austria to attack Serbia), or whether it would be more advantageous to 'postpone the great fight for one and a half years', i.e. until the Kiel Canal was finished in the summer of 1914.[9] Prince Lichnowsky, the last Imperial German ambassador in London, understood clearly what was happening and warned against it. No-one listened. This German patriot and citizen of the world was forced to observe, with a bleeding heart, how a handful of men in Berlin, without valid reason, without really understanding what they were doing, hurled the old Europe into the abyss.

It is for this reason that I write 'at first sight', for in the last analysis a peaceful policy could not have been ensured by doing nothing, but only by a change of personnel and of structure at the top, and neither Lichnowsky nor anyone else had the intention, far less the power, to bring about such a drastic transformation. By 1914 it was in any case already far too late for that. But did the opportunity present itself at any time during the era of Wilhelm II to bring about significant changes in the system of government, was there an historical turning-point at which history failed, in fact, to turn? Perhaps in 1888, if Kaiser Friedrich III had not been so terribly weakened by cancer when he mounted the throne, if he had reigned longer than ninety-nine days, there could have been a move in a liberal direction, but this was only a very fleeting possibility. If Bismarck had succeeded in 1890 in making himself indispensable by deliberately provoking domestic and foreign crises, and thus checkmating the young Kaiser, German history would also have taken a different course, though whether it would have been a better one in the long term is more than doubtful. If Friedrich von Holstein had succeeded in 1895 and 1896 in persuading Reich Chancellor Prince Chlodwig zu Hohenlohe-Schillingsfürst and the Prussian Ministers of State to establish a determined and solid opposition to the ever-growing power of the Kaiser and his courtiers, an eleventh-hour move in the direction of constitutional government might still have been possible. But Hohenlohe, the Kaiserin's uncle, was too old, too soft and too venal, and the ministers had the instincts of public officials rather than politicians, with the result that very few among them could stand up to the elemental will-power of the Kaiser and the lures of the 'kingship mechanism'. If the army had managed to push through its plans for a *coup d'état* in 1890, 1894 or 1897, political power would have slipped into the hands of the generals much sooner, but that would only have meant, as Holstein rightly observed, 'an early war'.[10] In 1897 and 1900 there were repeated rumours to the effect that the federal princes – the rulers of the individual German States –

together with the Reichstag and even some members of the Kaiser's family, wanted to force the abdication of the Kaiser in the national interest, but nothing came of these moves. Then came the single and, as it turned out, last real chance to introduce a system of government fitted to the needs of the times, one which would have been able to deal with the dangers facing the Reich. This was when in November 1908, following the painful revelations arising from the Eulenburg–Harden trials and the publication of a typical series of indiscretions by the Kaiser in the *Daily Telegraph*, the Reichstag unanimously demanded that the monarch should behave in a more constitutional fashion. But there it remained: a change in the system was neither seriously desired nor effected, and behind the scenes the same old operetta régime was allowed to continue.

The First World War did not have to come. While the dreams of 'world power' among wide sections of the German population must not be ignored nor made to sound harmless, the fact of the matter is that the people, the parties, the pressure groups could not have *forced* the government to unleash a world war. In Berlin, as in other capitals, there were enthusiastic demonstrations in favour of war, but there were equally large street processions demanding peace. Both took place towards the end of July 1914, in other words, when the die had long since been cast. And even if this pressure from below in favour of war had been much stronger, the obvious truth has to be remembered that the German Kaiserreich was not a plebiscitary democracy forced to accede to the demands of an angry crowd! Nor was it a parliamentary monarchy in which the government depended on the will of a majority in the Reichstag! No: the decision for war against the three world empires of France, Russia and Britain was taken by a tiny group of men who seem to have had hardly any idea of the shattering consequences that their decision would have for Germany, for Europe and for the world, right down to the present day. I am convinced that a constitutional monarchy with a collective cabinet responsible to parliament and the public would not have acted in such isolation and ignorance and, for this reason alone, would have decided differently. The German people did not unleash the First World War, but they did tolerate an absurd 'operetta régime' which in 1914 could think of nothing better than by unsheathing the sword to solve all the internal and external problems which had piled up over a quarter of a century, not least as a result of their own misjudgments and omissions. In this 'unpolitical' acceptance, in this blind faith in the authoritarian state – still being celebrated by Thomas Mann in his *Betrachtungen eines Unpolitischen* in 1918 – lay the fault and the tragic fate of the German people.

I   Kaiser Wilhelm II: a suitable case for treatment?

I have the feeling that we are being governed by a herd of lunatics

Max Weber

At the outbreak of war in 1914, a Prussian officer in Brazil wrote to a friend in Germany that people were at last attributing to Kaiser Wilhelm II 'more greatness than Bismarck and Moltke put together, a higher destiny than Napoleon I', seeing in him the *Weltgestalter* – the 'shaper of the world'.

Who is this Kaiser [the officer exclaimed], whose peacetime rule was so full of vexation and tiresome compromise, whose temperament would flare up wildly, only to die away again? ... Who is this Kaiser who now suddenly throws caution to the winds, who tears open his visor to bare his Titanic head and take on the world? ... I have misunderstood this Kaiser, I have thought him a waverer. He is a Jupiter, standing on the Olympus of his iron-studded might, the lightning-bolts in his grasp. At this moment he is God and master of the world.

Even if Germany were to lose the war, the officer predicted, 'the figure of Wilhelm II will stand out in history like a colossus'.[1] He was mistaken. To this day not a single full-scale biography of Kaiser Wilhelm II has come from the pen of a German historian in a university position. Worse still, the prevailing tendency of historical research among the younger generation in Germany precludes any treatment of him – or indeed of the role of any individual in history. That, they declare, is *Personalismus*, the relapse into a 'personalistic' historical methodology which has long since been superseded. The 'new orthodoxy' insists on writing the history of the Kaiserreich without the Kaiser, that of Wilhelminism without Wilhelm.[2]

And yet, for a number of reasons, there could hardly be a more suitable case for treatment than 'The Incredible Kaiser', the 'Fabulous Monster', this 'most brilliant failure in history'.[3] For one thing, the Kaiser's curious character poses a fascinating riddle in its own right, as we shall see in a moment. Second, it must be remembered that Wilhelm ruled not over Bayreuth, Bremen or Bückeburg, but over the most powerful, dynamic and volatile state in Europe, and he did so for no less than thirty crucial years, from 1888 to 1918 – that is to say for even longer than Bismarck, and two

9

and a half times as long as Hitler. And while no-one would wish to claim that his power quite matched that of the Iron Chancellor or the Führer, it is absurd to suppose that the complex decision-making process in this 'heroic-aristocratic warrior state'[4] can be understood without paying due attention to the monarch who was in theory and in practice the pivot of the whole system of government, to the man who was *summus episcopus*, who had absolute powers of command in the military sphere and total control over all official appointments. His contemporaries, in stark contrast to historians writing later, were at any rate agreed in seeing the Kaiser as 'the most important man in Europe'.[5] 'There is no stronger force in the Germany of today than Kaiserdom', wrote Friedrich Naumann in 1900.[6] Two years later Maximilian Harden, one of Wilhelm's fiercest critics, stated that 'the Kaiser is his own Reich Chancellor. All the important political decisions of the past twelve years have been made by him.'[7]

A third justification for undertaking a study of the Kaiser lies in the extraordinary extent to which Wilhelm personified and symbolised the political culture of his epoch. He was a monarch by Divine Right yet always the parvenu; a medieval knight in shining armour and yet the inspiration behind that marvel of modern technology, the battlefleet; a dyed-in-the-wool reactionary yet also – for a time at least – 'the Socialist emperor'. Like the society over which he ruled, he was at once brilliant and bizarre, aggressive and insecure. Wilhelm was what most Germans at that time wanted him to be. During the Silver Jubilee celebrations of his reign in June 1913, Friedrich Meinecke declared before the assembled members of the University of Freiburg: 'We need a Führer ... for whom we can march through flames.'[8]

Even beyond the span of his reign, Wilhelm can be seen as a 'key figure' for understanding the hubris and the nemesis of the German nation-state as a whole. His life spans, almost exactly, the history of the German Reich from its unification by Bismarck to its self-destruction under Hitler. His love–hate for his mother, Queen Victoria's eldest daughter, exactly mirrors the Anglo-German antagonism which culminated in the naval arms race and the terrible European civil war of 1914–18. Defeat, revolution and abdication in 1918–19 produced in Wilhelm a fanatical radicalisation of his hatred for his enemies, real and imagined, at home and abroad, which left little to choose between his attitudes and the supposedly more revolutionary anti-semitism and racial nationalism of Adolf Hitler. If Wilhelm had lived only a few weeks longer he would undoubtedly have sent the Führer an enthusiastic congratulatory telegram to mark the attack on Russia, just as he had after Germany's victory over Poland in 1939 and France in 1940.

The best reason of all for studying the Kaiser, however, is simply that the archives of Europe are full to bursting with letters from him, to him and about him – letters which for the most part no-one has ever looked at. The historian has more than a *right* to examine and assess this abundant source: he has the duty. For otherwise the myths put out by propagandists and wishful thinkers will continue to go unchallenged.[9] In this short character-sketch I hope to be able to convey a little of my excitement at, say, breaking the seal in an East German archive on a package of sixty-one letters from Queen Victoria to her grandson Willie; or of my bewilderment and distress on reading, high in a turret of the Hohenzollern ancestral castle in Swabia, the exiled Kaiser's anti-Jewish diatribes.

Who, then, was this Kaiser, who in 1888 at the age of twenty-nine years inherited 'the mightiest throne on earth'? Bernhard von Bülow wrote in 1898, when he was already Foreign Secretary and about to become Reich Chancellor:

> I grow fonder and fonder of the Kaiser. He is so important!! Together with the Great King and the Great Elector he is by far the most important Hohenzollern ever to have lived. In a way I have never seen before he combines genius – the most authentic and original genius – with the clearest *bon sens*. His vivid imagination lifts me like an eagle high above petty detail, yet he can judge soberly what is or is not possible and attainable. And what vitality! What a memory! How quick and sure his understanding! In the Crown Council this morning I was completely overwhelmed![10]

That the Kaiser possessed some of the impressive qualities invoked by Bülow is not in doubt. The trouble is that these qualities went hand-in-hand with more alarming traits which, though mostly kept from the public, were bound to discourage even the most optimistic of those who worked closely with him. Not even Bülow's faith could survive contact with reality for long.

What was that reality? Let me begin by enumerating six of the characteristics which struck close observers most about the Kaiser.

1. Any sketch of his character must begin with the fact that he never matured. To the end of his thirty-year reign he remained the 'young' emperor with the 'childlike genius'.[11] 'He is a child and will always remain one', sighed an astute court official in December 1908.[12] Wilhelm seemed incapable of learning from experience. Philipp Eulenburg, who knew him better than anyone, remarked in a letter to Bülow at the turn of the century that Wilhelm had, in the eleven years since his accession to the throne, 'become very much quieter as far as his outer being is concerned ... Spiritually however there has not been the slightest development. He is unchanged in his explosive manner. Indeed even harsher and more sudden as his self-esteem has grown with experience – which is no experience. For his "individuality" is stronger than the effect of experience.'[13] More than thirty years later, when both Eulenburg and Bülow were dead and the Kaiser exiled and seventy-two years old, his adjutant Sigurd von Ilsemann wrote in his diary at Doorn:

I have now almost finished reading the second volume of the Bülow memoirs and am struck over and over again by how little the Kaiser has changed since those times. Almost everything that occurred then still happens now, the only difference being that his actions, which then had grave significance and practical consequences, now do no damage. The many good qualities, too, of this strange, peculiar person, of the Kaiser's so very complicated character, are repeatedly stressed by Bülow.[14]

Why? In her study of the Kaiser's entourage, the American historian Isabel Hull has suggested that his notorious restlessness – his endless travelling, his craving on those journeys for an unceasing stream of stories and jokes, his inability to listen to others, his insistence on turning every 'conversation' into a hectic monologue, his need to have people about him all the time, even when he was reading, the great speed with which he ate – was but a 'conspiracy against self-understanding', a defence mechanism to enable him to avoid confronting his own personality.[15] That is surely the case. At the very least one must admit that such a restless lifestyle must have severely inhibited the process of maturation towards what psychologists call personal autonomy and ego integrity.

2. However, another of Wilhelm's character traits, his notorious over-estimation of his own abilities, dubbed by contemporaries 'caesaromania' or *folie d'empereur*,[16] similarly inhibited his responsiveness to constructive criticism. For how could the monarch learn from experience if he despised his ministers, rarely received them and seldom listened to what they had to say; if he was convinced that all his diplomats had so 'filled their pants' that 'the entire Wilhelmstrasse stank' to high heaven;[17] when he addressed even the War Minister and the Chief of the Military Cabinet with the words 'you old asses',[18] and announced to a group of admirals: 'All of you know nothing; I alone know something, I alone decide'?[19] Even before coming to the throne he had warned, 'Beware the time when I shall give the orders.' Even before Bismarck's dismissal he had threatened to 'smash' all opposition to his will.[20] He alone was master of the Reich, he said in a speech in May 1891, and he would tolerate no others.[21] To the Prince of Wales he proclaimed at the turn of the century: 'I am the sole master of German policy and my country must follow me wherever I go.'[22] Ten years later he explained in a letter to a young Englishwoman: 'As for having to sink my ideas and feelings at the bidding of the people, that is a thing unheard of in Prussian history or traditions of my house! What the German Emperor, King of Prussia thinks right and best for his People he does.'[23] In September 1912 he chose Prince Lichnowsky to be ambassador in London against the advice of Chancellor Bethmann Hollweg and the Foreign Office with the words: 'I will only send an ambassador to London who has *My* trust, obeys *My* will and carries out *My* orders.'[24] And during the First World War he exclaimed: 'What the public thinks is totally immaterial to me. I decide

according to my conviction, although I do then expect my officials to do what they can to correct the false opinions of the public by whatever means seem appropriate.'[25] Small wonder, after such a catalogue of self-glorification, that the Viennese should joke that Wilhelm insisted on being the stag at every hunt, the bride at every wedding, and the corpse at every funeral!

3. Third, the Kaiser had an extraordinary capacity for seeing the world, not as it was, but as he wished it to be. In the summer of 1903 Philipp Eulenburg wrote to Reich Chancellor Bülow from on board the Imperial yacht:

Being in contact with the beloved master for weeks on end opens the eyes of even the less initiated – and he too is then shocked by the fact, which becomes more apparent all the time, that H.M. sees and judges *all* things and *all* men purely from his personal standpoint. Objectivity is lost completely, and subjectivity rides on a biting and stamping stallion.[26]

In 1927 the Crown Princess wondered how it was possible that such a clever man 'could lose all sense of proportion and say the most fantastic things and even believe them. At a certain moment there is absolutely nothing more to be done with the Kaiser, he closes his eyes to every reality and then believes in the most impossible connections. He is and remains a riddle.'[27]

A graphic example of Wilhelm's propensity for literally swearing that black was white if it suited his psychological requirements is his verdict in 1923 that he had been wrong to warn Europe against the 'yellow peril'.

At last I know (he said) what the future holds for the German people, what we shall still have to achieve! . . . We shall be the leaders of the Orient against the Occident! I shall now have to alter my picture 'Peoples of Europe'. We belong on the other side! Once we have proved to the Germans that the French and English are not Whites at all but Blacks . . . then they will set upon this rabble.[28]

A man who could categorise the English and the French as negroes of course had little difficulty in designating Jesus of Nazareth as a 'non-Semite' nor in claiming that the latter 'had never . . . been a Jew'.[29]

4. The Kaiser raged against all those who would not do his bidding, and plotted to avenge himself on those he thought had betrayed him. In 1900 Eulenburg observed that Wilhelm II regarded the murder of the German envoy to China by the Boxer rebels as 'a *personal* insult', and that he was determined to 'send troops to take *revenge*!!'[30] The Kaiser accordingly sent Bülow a telegram demanding that Peking be destroyed: 'The German envoy must be avenged by my troops. Peking must be razed to the ground.'[31] A few weeks later, in what is probably his most shocking speech, he ordered German troops on their way to China to behave like Huns:

You must be examples of manliness and discipline, but also of self-denial and self-control. You will be fighting against a well-armed power, but at the same time you must avenge the death not only of the envoy but of many other Germans and Europeans. When you come before the enemy, you must defeat him, pardon will not be given, prisoners will not be taken. Whoever falls into your hands will fall to your sword. Just as a thousand years ago the Huns under their King Attila made a name for themselves for ferocity which tradition still recalls; so may the name of Germany become known in China in such a way that no Chinaman will ever again dare to look a German in the eye even with a squint.[32]

This was no mere slip of the tongue. In the early stages of the First World War Wilhelm shocked his entourage by commanding one division to take no prisoners. After the battle of Tannenberg in September 1914 he proposed to kill 90,000 Russian prisoners of war by driving them onto the barren spit of land in the Baltic Sea known as the Kurische Nehrung, and letting them starve and thirst to death.[33]

Things were no better with regard to home affairs. In 1899 the Kaiser declared: 'Matters will not improve until the troops drag the Social Democratic leaders out of the Reichstag and gun them down.'[34] During a strike of tram workers in Berlin in 1900, he telegraphed the Commanding General: 'I expect when the troops move in at least 500 people to be gunned down.'[35] And on the North Sea cruise of 1903 the Kaiser outlined how he would deal with the coming revolution. He would, he said, mow down all the Social Democrats, 'but only after they had first plundered the Jews and the rich'. His plan was to 'take revenge for 1848 – revenge!!!'[36]

His desire for revenge naturally became more dominant still after the revolution of 1918 had ousted him from the throne. By the early 1920s Wilhelm had evolved a full-scale world conspiracy theory according to which the Freemasons, Jesuits and Jews were plotting to take over the world and destroy all 'German' (he meant monarchical) values. His friends in Germany and America were regularly bombarded with twenty- to thirty-page letters warning against this Jewish world conspiracy in terms so Ludendorffian or even Hitlerian that, as I read them, I began to dread the moment, which seemed to be approaching with increasing certainy, when I would discover the unspeakable. And sure enough before long I discovered the following passage in a letter from the Kaiser:

The lowest, most abject outrage ever to be perpetrated by any nation in history, that is what the Germans have done unto themselves. Egged on and misled by the tribe of Juda whom they hate, who were guests among them! That was the thanks they got! Let no German ever forget this, nor rest until these parasites have been wiped out from German soil and been exterminated! This poisonous mushroom on the German oak-tree![37]

These words were written in the Kaiser's own handwriting and were dated 2 December 1919.

It was not only against the so-called 'enemies of the Reich' – the

Socialists, Catholics, Jews and Freemasons – that the Kaiser raged, however, but against anyone who opposed his will. After Hindenburg's death in the summer of 1934 he declared, expecting an imminent return to the throne: 'Blood must flow, much blood, [the blood] of the officers and the civil servants, above all of the nobility, of everyone who has deserted me.'[38] It was, as Eulenburg had realised in 1901, as if 'certain feelings which we take for granted in others were suddenly simply not there'.[39]

Even Wilhelm's family and relations were not exempt. In 1887 he threatened, for example, to 'put a bullet through the head' of that 'damned Pollack' Prince Alexander of Battenberg and to 'club the Battenberger to death'.[40] During Queen Victoria's visit to Berlin in the following year, he said that it was high time that the old woman – his grandmother – died.[41] He now referred to her as the 'empress of Hindustan', to his mother and sisters as the 'English colony', to the doctors in attendance on his father as 'Jewish louts', 'scoundrels' and 'Satan's bones'. All, he said, were inspired by 'racial hatred' and 'anti-Germanism even at the edge of the grave'.[42] During the tragic 99-day reign of his father, Wilhelm wrote to Eulenburg:

What I have endured here in the last 8 days simply defies description and even mocks the imagination! The sense of deep shame for the sunken prestige of my once so high and inviolable House – that is the strongest feeling. I see it as something sent to try me and all of us, and am attempting to bear it with patience. But that our family shield should be besmirched and the Reich brought to the brink of ruin by an English princess who is my mother – that is the most terrible thing of all.[43]

One year before his accession, Wilhelm had declared 'One cannot have enough hatred for England', and had warned that England had better watch out when he took over.[44]

5. A fifth point is that Wilhelm's 'sense of humour' frequently took an offensive, sometimes even a sadistic turn. While his left arm was weak due to damage at birth, his right hand was strong in compensation, and he found amusement in turning his rings inwards and then squeezing the hand of visiting dignitaries so hard that tears came to their eyes.[45] King Ferdinand of Bulgaria left Berlin 'white-hot with hatred' after the Kaiser had slapped him hard on the behind in public.[46] Grand Duke Vladimir of Russia was hit over the back by Wilhelm with a field-marshal's baton.[47] The Duke of Saxe-Coburg-Gotha, another of Queen Victoria's grandsons, was pinched and pummelled by the Kaiser in the library to such an extent 'that the poor little Duke received a proper beating up', as the Court Marshal wrote in his diary.[48] Even after the duke had ascended the throne the Kaiser on one occasion made him lie on his back and then proceeded to sit on his belly.[49] The Kaiser's entourage were treated in much the same manner. One diplomat noted in his diary during the North Sea cruise of 1894:

In the mornings we all do exercises together with the Kaiser ... It is a curious sight: all those old military fogeys having to do their knee-jerks with strained faces! The Kaiser sometimes laughs out loud and eggs them on with a dig in the ribs. The old boys then pretend that they are particularly delighted over such a favour, but in fact they clench their fists in their pockets and afterwards grumble among themselves about the Kaiser like a lot of old women.[50]

Philipp Eulenburg was also shocked by the 'quite disgusting spectacle' of 'all the old excellencies and dignitaries having to assemble for gymnastics to the accompaniment of shouts and jokes'.[51] After one particularly enervating day on board the *Hohenzollern*, when Eulenburg had sought the refuge of his cabin, he suddenly heard at midnight 'the loud, laughing, shouting, pealing voice of the Kaiser outside my door: he was chasing the old excellencies Heintze, Kessel, Scholl, etc., through the corridors of the ship to *bed*'.[52] This, too, did not change with the passing of the years. At the height of the Second Moroccan Crisis in 1911, Admiral von Müller recorded in his diary with dismay: 'At gymnastics this morning great tomfoolery. H.M. cuts through [General von] Scholl's braces with a penknife.'[53]

6. Finally, the Kaiser loved uniforms, historical costumes, jewellery and gems, most of all childish pranks in all-male company. One of his closest friends, Count 'Em' Görtz, who was on the plump side, could 'dance like a howling dervish and do all kinds of nonsense' for the Kaiser.[54] One of his favourite tricks was to roll backwards down the hillside 'like a hippopotamus that has gone berserk'.[55] On another occasion Görtz and the future Foreign Secretary Alfred von Kiderlen-Wächter 'did the Siamese twins' for Wilhelm by tying themselves together with a large sausage.[56] For the hunt at Liebenberg in 1892, Georg von Hülsen proposed to Görtz:

You must be paraded by me as a circus poodle! – That will be a 'hit' like nothing else. Just think: behind *shaved* (tights), in front long bangs out of black or white wool, at the back under a genuine poodle tail a marked rectal opening and, when you 'beg', *in front* a fig-leaf. Just think how wonderful when you bark, howl to music, shoot off a pistol or do other tricks. It is simply *splendid!!* ... In my mind's eye I can already see H.M. laughing with us ... I am applying myself with real relish to this 'work' in order to forget that my beloved sister – the dearest thing I have on earth – is at this moment dying in Breslau ... I feel like the clown in Knaus's picture '*Behind* the Scenes'. No matter! – H.M. shall be satisfied!![57]

In 1908, Georg von Hülsen's brother Dietrich – the head of the Military Cabinet – died of a heart attack at Donaueschingen while dancing for the Kaiser in a large feather hat and a tutu.[58]

Our catalogue of the Kaiser's peculiarities has so far produced a highly unedifying portrait, one which is far removed from the picture painted by most of his biographers. But was all this perhaps only a façade? Was there, behind this hard, fearsome exterior, a softer, nicer Wilhelm, as Rathenau –

for one – supposed?[59] To discover the answer we shall have to delve a little more deeply into his private life.

At first glance there seems little to relate. Prior to his accession, throughout his long reign and also thereafter, Wilhelm was praised as a paragon of marital virtue, as the embodiment of 'German' or 'Christian' morality.[60] His biographers have agreed. Michael Balfour, for example, writes that the Kaiserin 'represented a point of stability in his restless life', that she managed to increase her hold over him 'by her ability to satisfy his sexual appetites', and that 'the complete lack of worthwhile evidence of his ever having been unfaithful is certainly remarkable when one considers how many people would have liked to catch him erring'.[61]

But life, as the French say, is more like a novel than a novel is like life. Within a year of his marriage in February 1881, Wilhelm wrote a letter 'quite officially, without disguising his handwriting' to a well-known Viennese procuress by the name of Frau Wolf. Through her good offices he made the acquaintance of Ella Somsics (or Sommssics), an Austrian girl who came to live in the Linkstrasse in Berlin, where the prince visited her 'very frequently' over a number of years. In October 1887, when his father lay dying of cancer, Prince Wilhelm travelled to hunt in Austria and Ella Somsics followed with a friend called Anna (or Marie) Homolatsch. The three young people met in the village of Mürzsteg, first in the Catholic cemetery and then at the only inn. But since Wilhelm was unwilling to pay the women their rail fare, they departed in anger – though only after Ella had stolen Wilhelm's monogrammed cuff-links adorned with the Prussian crown, to display them in triumph around Vienna. After several urgent pleas from Wilhelm, Ella and Anna eventually joined him in Eisenerz, at the 'Gasthaus zum König von Sachsen'. A policeman was on the point of sending them away when one of Prince Wilhelm's servants appeared and explained that the ladies were 'for his master'. When the Prince joined them both in one room in the middle of the night, the noise was so great that all the other guests were awakened.[62]

By an extraordinary stroke of good fortune, a Viennese archivist recently discovered a letter from Crown Prince Rudolf which gives a full description of Prince Wilhelm's pillow talk with Ella Somsics and Anna Homolatsch. According to Rudolf's letter to the Austrian military attaché, Wilhelm

spoke not very respectfully of our Kaiser [Franz Joseph], very detrimentally about me, likening me to his father as a conceited popularity-seeker under Jewish influence . . ., without character, without ability, etc., etc. Then he said things were going well only in Prussia; in Austria the entire state was rotten, close to dissolution. It would soon collapse, leaving the German provinces to fall like ripe fruit into Germany's lap; they would come as an insignificant Archdukedom into a position more dependent on Prussia than is Bavaria. The Kaiser of Austria can, if he so wishes, eke out his life as an insignificant monarch in Hungary ... He said, moreover, that he liked to hunt with us, we were all pleasant people, but useless pansies and gourmands, no longer fit for life. In politics there is no such thing as sympathy. His task will be to enlarge Germany at our expense. After he had praised his grandfather and even more himself, and complained in the most cynical way about his parents and his wife, he closed this enchanting conversation with these two unclean females. I could not write everything down [said Rudolf], I could only recount this ... [But] I was not in the least surprised.[63]

Certainly there is little sign here of a softer, nicer Wilhelm; only the same self-satisfied, malicious tone which was apparent in the letters, speeches and marginal comments which we already know.

Whatever pleasure Wilhelm got out of such risky escapades must have seemed even less worthwhile when the women involved began to blackmail him. Nine months after her memorable night in the 'König von Sachsen', Anna Homolatsch gave birth to a daughter and claimed that the child was Wilhelm's. In the end a substantial sum of money was paid over by Wilhelm's private correspondence secretary, Privy Councillor Miessner.[64] Another woman, whose professional name was Miss Love, also had a daughter by Wilhelm and was similarly silenced by the expedient of handing over money.[65] One of the women with whom Wilhelm was involved in the mid-1880s accidentally left five of his letters in the safe of the Persian Legation in Berlin, where she worked for a time. In 1956, incredibly, these letters were discovered in Teheran, and facsimiles of some of them were published in a popular German magazine. In one of them he wrote: 'Chère Comtesse, you have indeed a difficult life behind you. Oh ma chère adorée, how great are you in my estimation! You sacrificed your love out of patriotism! That is magnificent! You refused your former husband everything, would you refuse me, adorée, everything too, if we should one day be together? If I knelt before you and begged?'[66]

After his accession to the throne in 1888, the risks involved in such adventures became too great for Wilhelm. He did continue to flirt with women he found attractive, especially on his journeys away from Berlin. Eulenburg was shocked, for example, when, on one North Sea cruise, the Kaiser kissed the hand of a certain Mrs Gould from New York – especially when it emerged that the lady had once earned her living by lying on her back in a nightclub and firing off rifles with her big toe. 'What would ... the German say if he were to learn of that??', asked Eulenburg in horror.[67] But despite all the rumours to the contrary, it would appear that Wilhelm did not dare enter into any more love-affairs after 1888.

One wonders, however, what such self-restraint may have cost the Kaiser. The indications are that, despite his very active sex-life in the 1880s, his attitude towards women was ambivalent throughout his life. Wilhelm once wrote in English of his dislike of the women of Berlin who talked only of clothes and love-affairs. 'I hope that you know me well enough to know that I am a serious enemy of such kind of ladies, who want to be flirted with. I think that is something beneath a real man and gentleman, especially I think beneath myself, don't you think so too?'[68] That was in 1879, when he was twenty. Thirty-three years later, in a letter to a young English lady, he expressed the view that 'women were to marry, love their husbands, have lots of babies, bring them up well, cook well and make their husbands' home comfy for them'.[69] He was clearly fascinated and at the same time somewhat alarmed at the evidently rather advanced ideas of his young correspondent on free love:

I have also to thank you for a very long letter ... which I read through several times ... It was most interesting. It contained much information about the opinions and actions of the independent English girl, which were wholelly [sic] new to me. Especially regarding the relations to the other sex, and the position held vis à vis to them in case of inability to marry whom one wants to. I was very much surprised at the way of thinking, and must agree with you entirely, when you say, that I have not the slightest notion, of what girls think, or fancy they are entitled to do? I own, after what I read, that I am totally at loss, and sadly in want of experience in English girls ... At all events I fancy that their view of life and actions springing from it, will certainly lead to very tragic developments and cause much disillusions and unhappiness.[70]

All in all, the new evidence on Kaiser Wilhelm's relationships with women, though demonstrating that he was far more 'the slave of his sexual drives'[71] than contemporary admirers and later biographers imagined, offers few clues to the causes of his agitated restlessness and his savage anger. If anything, we only see here once again that his 'individuality' was stronger than experience. No, Wilhelm seems to have found his point of repose not in the company of women in the Linkstrasse or in Eisenerz, but among his regimental comrades and even more so in the so-called 'Lieben-berg Circle' led by Count Philipp zu Eulenburg. 'I never feel happy, really happy at Berlin', he wrote in his idiosyncratic English. 'Only Potsdam that is my 'el dorado' ... where one feels free with the beautiful nature around you and soldiers as much as you like, for I love my dear Regiment very much, those such kind nice young men in it.'[72] In his regiment, as he confided to Eulenburg, he found his family, his friends, his interests – everything which he had previously missed. Over were 'the terrible years in which no-one understood my individuality'.[73] On his accession, Wilhelm was able to appoint many of his former regimental comrades as adjutants. And with them he could indulge his 'disturbing bent for the obscene',[74] treat every complex political issue as a straightforward 'purely military question', and receive enthusiastic encouragement in his absolutist strivings. Bismarck remarked in his memoirs on Wilhelm's preference for 'tall chaps', such as his ancestor the Sergeant King had liked to have around him.[75] Eulenburg, who knew a lot about such things, once sighed that the 'adjutants – and in particular a certain type' – had 'unfortunately become a problem *in their own right* ... in the life of our dear master'.[76] It is indeed disturbing to reflect that the generals who took Germany and Europe into the Armageddon of 1914 not infrequently owed their career to the Kaiser's admiration for their height and good looks in their splendid uniforms.

The voluminous political correspondence of Philipp Eulenburg leaves no scope for doubt that he (Eulenburg) and the other members of the influential 'Liebenberg Circle' who in the 1890s stood at the very centre of the political stage in the Kaiser's Germany were indeed homosexual, as their destroyer, Maximilian Harden, believed.[77] This of course raises the question of where to place the Kaiser on the 'heterosexual–homosexual continuum'. If he ever did have anything approaching a homosexual experience, it almost certainly occurred in the mid-1880s, in the same period, that is, as his numerous extra-marital affairs with women. After interviewing Jakob Ernst, the Starnberg fisherman whose testimony in 1908 damaged Eulenburg's case irreparably, Maximilian Harden became convinced that he was in possession of evidence which, if laid before the Kaiser, would suffice to cause him to abdicate. What information Harden received from Jakob Ernst, we can only guess at. In several letters written at this time, Harden linked Wilhelm II not only with Jakob Ernst but also with Eulenburg's private secretary, Karl Kistler.[78] But these are only straws in the wind, not proof. On the evidence presently available to us, it is probably wiser to assume, as Isabel Hull has written, that Wilhelm remained unconscious of the homoerotic basis of his friendship with Eulenburg and thus failed to recognise the homosexual aspects of his own character.[79]

In the late 1970s and early 1980s, this interpretation of Wilhelm II as a repressed homosexual seemed for a time to be gathering support as the Eulenburg correspondence and similar new evidence was being evaluated. It is now becoming clear, however, that no matter how much it might help us to explain some of his character traits – his restlessness, his friendships, his love of childish games, of rings and bracelets, of dressing up in all-male company, perhaps even the softness of his skin and hair, which made such an impression on Rathenau,[80] repressed homosexuality was not the 'fundamental fact' of Wilhelm's life. The disturbance lay deeper, at a more primitive level. This becomes clear when we examine the fears concerning his mental state shared by his family, his friends and those who worked most closely with him.

The constant worries of Wilhelm's parents throughout his childhood about his health were significantly strengthened in 1878 when his right ear not only became chronically infected, but worrying growths and suppurating discharges were detected in the inner ear. The doctors warned explicitly that 'the position of the infection in the depths of the head, separated from the brain only by a not very thick wall of bone, [and] the direct relationship that exists between the deeper parts of the ear and the brain . . ., could well lead to a rapid spreading of the infection into the brain'.[81]

From this time on, numerous medical authorities warned that Wilhelm 'was not, and never would be, a normal man', that 'he would always be subject to sudden accesses of anger' and would, at such times, be 'quite incapable of forming a reasonable or temperate judgment', and that, though he would probably not become clinically insane, 'some of his actions would probably be those of a man not wholly sane'. They expressly warned that Wilhelm's accession to the throne could be 'a danger to Europe'.[82] In a very similar vein Sir Felix Semon, the German-born throat specialist working in London, characterised 'the restlessness of the present Kaiser as the precisely definable first stage of a psychiatric condition, but one which in the beginning should be considered and treated from the physiological rather than from the psychological standpoint'.[83] In 1895 a diplomat at the British Embassy in the German capital reported to Lord Salisbury that there were 'curious rumours going about Berlin as to the Emperor's health'. It would indeed be a serious matter, he wrote, 'if a Sovereign who possesses a dominant voice in the foreign policy of the Empire is subject to hallucinations and influences which must in the long term warp his judgment, and render Him liable at any moment to sudden changes of opinion which no-one can anticipate or provide against'.[84]

Lord Salisbury, who was informed in 1887 and 1888 of the doctors' worries, repeatedly expressed the fear that the Kaiser was 'not quite normal'.[85] A later British Prime Minister, Asquith, said in 1911, after reading the report of a strange conversation between the Kaiser and Prince Louis of Battenberg: 'One is almost tempted to discern in some of the things he [Wilhelm II] said to Prince Louis the workings of a disordered brain; but (even if that were so) they are none the less dangerous.'[86] The liberal Foreign Secretary Sir Edward Grey also expressed the view that the Kaiser was 'not quite sane, and very superficial'.[87] The German emperor reminded him, Grey said, of 'a battleship with steam up and screws going, but with no rudder', and he warned that the Kaiser could well 'cause a catastrophe' some day.[88]

In the spring of 1892 the French Foreign Ministry also came to the conclusion, on the basis of reports it had received from Berlin, that 'the German Kaiser is mentally ill' and 'temporarily of unsound mind'.[89] At the same time Grand Duke Sergius of Russia, who was married to Wilhelm's cousin (and first love) Princess Ella of Hessen-Darmstadt, was saying that the Kaiser was 'mentally ill'.[90] The long-serving Austro-Hungarian Military Attaché Freiherr von Klepsch-Kloth, also concluded that Wilhelm was 'not quite sane' and had, 'as one says, a screw loose'.[91]

In 1895 Friedrich von Holstein complained that the Kaiser's 'glow-worm character' constantly reminded Germans of King Friedrich Wilhelm IV of Prussia and King Ludwig II of Bavaria, both of whom had gone mad.[92] Early in 1896, after a violent row with the Kaiser, the Prussian War Minister, General Bronsart von Schellendorf, said 'that H.M. did not appear to be quite normal and that he [Bronsart] was deeply concerned about the future'.[93] In the following year Holstein wrote that the Conservative party thought the Kaiser was 'not quite normal', that the King of Saxony had declared him to be 'not quite stable' and that the Grand Duke of Baden had spoken 'in a very worrying way about the psychological side of the matter, about the loss of touch with reality'.[94] Reich Chancellor Prince Hohenlohe also once earnestly asked Bülow whether he 'really believed that the Kaiser was mentally normal'.[95]

Such views became commonplace after the Kaiser's notorious speech of February 1897, in which he referred to Bismarck and Moltke as 'lackeys and pygmies'. Count Anton Monts, the Prussian Envoy to Bavaria, wrote from Munich that the emperor was clearly no longer of sane mind. 'I gather from the hints of the doctors that the Kaiser can still be cured, but that the chances grow dimmer with each day.'[96] Monts wrote to Eulenburg that the mood in southern and western Germany was now beyond redemption.

Our numerous enemies here are triumphant and are quietly preparing for the disintegration of the Reich. Our friends are dismayed by the Kaiser. The resentment goes deeper than ever before ... Many are saying secretly that H.M. is insane, already there are hints to this effect in the press ... What I think of H.M. I dare not even say, but I fear that he is completely finished now, here in the south. Perhaps the masses will still shout hurrah during the manoeuvres, but the hearts of the patriotic middle classes are now surely lost to him forever. People here are talking very seriously about the possibility of a coup d'état in the Reich ... What is the point of all this work and effort. Nobody believes one when one describes the Kaiser as he was, for example, on his visit here, so simple, understanding, clear, moderate and quiet. – It is as if from time to time the lord were seized by an evil spirit, benighting his mind and compelling him to make speeches which insult the nation to the quick.[97]

Bismarck now told a number of followers that he had only wanted to stay in office in 1890 because he had known of Wilhelm's 'abnormal mental condition' and had wished to save the nation from catastrophe. He informed a Bavarian writer that he had realised as early as 1888 that Wilhelm was 'hereditarily burdened from both the English and Russian sides'. But, Bismarck warned, it would be far more difficult to remove Wilhelm II from the middle of all his generals than it had been to secure the abdication of King Ludwig II.[98] In 1900, soon after assuming the Chancellorship, Bülow had to tell Eulenburg that one more false move by Wilhelm would result in the formation of a coalition of the German princes and the Reichstag against him to have him declared unfit to rule.[99] After the *Daily Telegraph* crisis of 1908, the Kaiser's own sister came to the conclusion that the only salvation for Germany and Europe lay in the institution of a 'collective regency' of all the German princes to constrain the monarch.[100]

The most devastating evidence on the Kaiser's disturbed psychological condition, however, comes from the man who knew him best and loved him most: Philipp Eulenburg. In 1897, when so many people in Germany had come to believe that Wilhelm was not quite right in the head and ought to be 'put into care', Eulenburg assured Bülow that all was well. 'The Kaiser was quieter, clearer, cleverer and kinder than ever', he wrote. 'What disgusting cheek to represent Him as over-excited or even mad!'[101] But soon he had to change his mind. In July 1900 he reported from the North Sea cruise that the Kaiser had had an attack of rage so violent that it had frightened him (Eulenburg) and filled him with grave concern. 'H.M. is no longer in control of himself when He is seized by rage. I regard the situation as highly dangerous and am at a loss to know what to do.' The Kaiser's doctor was also 'utterly perplexed', Eulenburg said. 'He sees a sort of weakening of the nervous system in this condition, but *decidedly* rejects any fears concerning changes in [the Kaiser's] mental state.' Eulenburg himself had the feeling of 'sitting on a powder-keg'. 'These things', he admitted poignantly, 'cut me *to the quick*. I have had so much faith in the Kaiser's abilities – and in the passage of time! – Now *both* have failed, and one sees a person suffering whom one loves dearly but cannot help.'[102]

In the summer of 1903, Eulenburg reported more fully still on what proved to be his last cruise with the Kaiser. He now noticed a significant change in the nature of the monarch's emotional turmoil. Three years earlier, he wrote, the problem with the Kaiser's behaviour stemmed from the way in which he tended to be 'completely obsessed' by one thought. 'Everything which touched on that thought, no matter how remotely, took on a nervous, convulsive form. Side by side with that, however, in the things of everyday life, he would be friendly, not obstinate, and relatively easy to be with and to handle.' Now matters had changed for the worse. 'He is no longer painfully obsessed with any *one* thing which weighs down on him and refuses to let Him rest; he is difficult to handle and complicated in *all* things, no matter how trivial. *No-one* can make even the most harmless remark . . . without provoking a violent objection, an insulting response or even an outburst of rage.' Eulenburg was distraught to see the Kaiser's *'earnestness'* as he 'builds his card houses and – constantly contradicting himself – violently abuses people and things'. Wilhelm wandered about the ship 'as if in a dream-world', constantly 'boosting his ego into an ever-greater phantom'. Eulenburg felt the tears well up in him as he heard the Kaiser 'excessively railing against all manner of windmills', and saw 'his face completely distorted with rage'. 'There can no longer be any question of self-control', he wrote. 'Sometimes he appears to have lost discipline over himself *entirely*.' For hours on end the Kaiser would walk about alone with a 'distracted look' on his face. 'Pale, ranting wildly, looking restlessly about him and piling lie upon lie he made such a terrible impression on me that I still cannot get over it', Eulenburg said. It was quite beyond doubt that 'a slow transformation of the mental and emotional condition of our dear master' was taking place and was sure to lead to a crisis. But that crisis, whenever it came, Eulenburg predicted, would 'not take on the form of a mental disturbance', but rather of a 'breakdown of the nerves'. 'The crisis will take on the *appearance* of abnormality without actually being that', he told Bülow. Nevertheless, the Kaiser would 'suffer dreadful convulsions when the total breakdown occurred'.[103]

In fact, Kaiser Wilhelm never did have the 'total breakdown' which his best friend predicted. The man who once denied having a little cold because everything about him had to be great,[104] nevertheless only had little breakdowns. In September 1918 he actually admitted to having had a 'little nervous breakdown' – but he 'put himself to bed, slept for 24 hours and was now as good as new'.[105] Even so, these interludes of weakness and embarrassment were by no means politically insignificant, for, as Eulenburg later recorded, it was precisely at such moments, which occurred 'several times a year', that Wilhelm II was particularly susceptible to the influence of others.[106]

This, then, is some of the evidence currently available to the biographer of Kaiser Wilhelm II. What are we to make of it? Naturally we must be cautious in labelling someone who cannot be interrogated and cannot answer back. For no-one more than for the biographer is Heraclitus's saying valid, that 'the soul of man is a far country, which cannot be approached or explored'. And yet, in the case of Kaiser Wilhelm, two factors enable the historian to give at least a tentative and approximate answer. First, the direct evidence is so very colourful and strong, and second, the biographer of Kaiser Wilhelm II has the inestimable advantage that among the latter's contemporaries were the founding fathers of modern psychiatry and psychology, who left on record their own diagnoses of this most prominent figure of their time.

From 1914 onwards, a stream of books appeared in America, Britain, France, Italy, Russia and Switzerland on the subject of the Kaiser's troubled psyche, and after 1918 a wave of similar works appeared in Germany itself. In 1914 the Swiss psychiatrist Dr Neipp diagnosed Wilhelm as suffering from 'maniaco-depressive' psychosis, and this view received considerable backing in Germany itself, even before the war ended. Dr Paul Tesdorpf, a psychiatrist living in Munich, wrote to the Reich Chancellor in 1916 that he had been convinced 'for decades' that Wilhelm was a manic-depressive. It was certain, Tesdorpf claimed, that 'the mental illness known by the name of "periodic disturbedness" ... is the cause of the numerous words and actions which have emanated for decades now from the All-Highest, which are inexplicable except in psychiatric terms, and which have determined the fate of the German Reich and those who belong to it'.[107] In fact the clinical description of manic-depressive mental illness fits so perfectly with what we know of the Kaiser's state of mind that it is not surprising that Emil Kraepelin and Robert Gaupp, the leading psychiatrists of their time, had also long expounded the view that Kaiser Wilhelm II was 'a typical case of periodic disturbedness'.[108]

Whether or not one accepts this kind of psychiatric labelling, two further elements – one physical and the other psychological – must be kept in mind if we are to understand the 'character neurosis' developed by Wilhelm II, and they must be seen both separately and in their interaction. It is well known that Wilhelm suffered organic damage at birth, although the full extent of the damage is still not fully appreciated. Apart from his useless left arm, which was eventually about fifteen centimetres too short, he also suffered from the alarming growths and inflammations in the inner ear already referred to. As a result of this condition he underwent a serious operation in 1896 which left him deaf in the right ear. The possibility that he also suffered brain damage at the time of his birth cannot be ruled out. In Germany in 1859, the year in which Wilhelm was born, no fewer than 98 per cent of babies in the breech position were stillborn. The danger was of course greatest in young mothers having their first child, and it stemmed above all from the possibility of suffocation as the baby's head squeezed the umbilical cord running up alongside it. If the air supply was cut off for longer than, say, eight minutes, the baby was sure to die. And indeed, the royal baby with which we are concerned was 'seemingly dead to a high degree', as the doctor's report put it, when he came into the world on the afternoon of 27 January 1859, over ten hours after the waters had broken.[109] Whatever damage was done to Wilhelm's brain in those hours, it is certain that the left arm was crippled not locally, as the doctors assumed, but rather as a result of damage to the brachial plexus, that is to say the nerves which ensure the innervation of the shoulder, arm and hand muscles were torn from the vertebral column in the neck during the final stages of the delivery.[110]

The entire experience was a ghastly one for Vicky, the Princess Royal. Despite the fact that she inhaled chloroform for hours on end, the birth was extremely painful. She had married only a year before at the age of seventeen. During the long, complicated birth of her first child, 'poor Dr Martin' had to work under her long flannel skirt so that royal decency prevailed. Vicky's response to giving birth to a crippled boy was, it would seem, ambivalent. If *she* had been male, as the first child of Queen Victoria she would have been able to stay in her beloved England and in due course become its sovereign. As things stood, however, all that was open to her was to bear a son, and through him to do what she could to remodel the country into which she had married along the lines of the country of her birth. But this son had a crippled arm, he was not particularly talented, and he exhibited from a very early age a stormy, hyperactive temperament which gave growing cause for concern. Her moment of triumph had turned into failure. Sigmund Freud himself put his finger on Vicky's sense of narcissistic injury as one of the root-causes of Wilhelm's later psychological disturbance. In 1932 he wrote:

It is usual for mothers whom Fate has presented with a child who is sickly or otherwise at a disadvantage to try to compensate him for his unfair handicap by a super-abundance of love. In the instance before us, the proud mother behaved otherwise; she withdrew her love from the child on account of his infirmity. When he had grown up into a man of great power, he proved unambiguously by his actions that he had never forgiven his mother.[111]

Once the doctors were set loose on the young Wilhelm with their 'animal baths', their electric-shock treatment and their metal contraptions and leather straps for stretching his arm and his neck, once his education was placed in the hands of the unsmiling, never-praising Calvinist Hinzpeter, whatever slender hope there still remained for his emotional and mental stability lay in his mother's hands. But she was unable to establish that bond of unconditional love and trust which he so desperately needed. Small wonder, then, that he felt drawn precisely to those elements who deprecated his mother above all else – to Bismarck, to the 'kind nice young men' of the Potsdam guards regiments, to the Byzantine 'Liebenberg Round Table'; small wonder that he felt one could not have enough hatred for England. When he came to the throne, at the age of twenty-nine, Wilhelm could use the whole apparatus of the army, the navy and the state, the whole arena of world politics, to prove his worth. He could knock over admirals and generals doing their physical jerks, he could cut through their braces with a penknife and chase them with loud shouts to bed. Until it was too late.

In the winter of 1918, when the political barometer had swung from

Weltmacht to *Untergang*, a German admiral in the Crimea wrote of Kaiser Wilhelm II: 'Everything which I predicted, not just in the last few weeks but for much, much longer, has come true. What Germany has sinned in the last three decades it must now pay for. It was politically paralysed through its blind faith in, [and] its slavish submission to, the will of a puffed-up, vainglorious and self-overestimating fool.'[112]

Philipp Eulenburg,
the Kaiser's best friend

In a man's letters his soul lies naked   Ben Jonson (1572–1637)

The name of Philipp, Count zu Eulenburg, later Prince zu Eulenburg-Hertefeld (1847–1921) is associated so closely with the history of the Wilhelmine period that one could call him the Wilhelminian[1] *par excellence* if that were not at best only a half-truth. It is certainly correct that Eulenburg, perhaps more than any other individual, acted as crisis manager for the Prussian-German monarchy in the long governmental crisis following Bismarck's fall; that he prevented a reversion to the *status quo ante* 1866, and averted the twin dangers threatening the Reich's future, namely a dictatorship of either a military or Bismarckian character, or else parliamentarisation; and that he was the intellectual founder of the so-called 'personal rule' of Kaiser Wilhelm II, established in 1897 on the basis of *Sammlungspolitik* and *Weltpolitik*.[2] On the other hand it is equally true not only that this system soon became trapped in a blind alley under the pressure of massive armaments costs,[3] but also that, just ten years after the victory of his strategy, Philipp Eulenburg suffered human and political destruction at the hands of a second generation of Wilhelminians. However, this bourgeois, liberal-imperialist generation[4] (Albert Ballin was born in 1857, Friedrich Naumann in 1860, Maximilian Harden in 1861, Bernhard Dernburg in 1865 and Walter Rathenau in 1867) similarly failed to achieve decisive influence for themselves. They intensified the expansionist tendencies in the Kaiserreich by means of their economic might and their 'world power' aspirations without being able to break the power of the court and, most important, of the generals who stood behind it. On the contrary, they paved the way for an increase in the political influence of the military by overthrowing Eulenburg and by seriously undermining confidence in the Kaiser in the *Daily Telegraph* crisis of 1908, and in this sense they aided the self-destruction of the Prussian-German monarchy as well as the collapse of the old order throughout Europe.

Philipp Count zu Eulenburg stood out in contrast to this second Wilhelmine generation by virtue of his age and also his social standing. He was

born in Königsberg on 12 February 1847, the first son of an officer of one of
the oldest aristocratic clans of East Prussia. The sociologist Karl Mannheim
has pointed out that generations in the public sphere do not differentiate
themselves from each other purely genealogically, as they do within individual families. He advanced the thesis that they are formed by a 'decisive
experience' falling in the particularly receptive years of a person's development between the ages of about seventeen and twenty-five.[5] Even if this
thesis undervalues the importance of unconscious and socially determined
factors in the formation of fundamental political attitudes, it nonetheless
seems to offer instructive insights into Eulenburg's political development.
Philipp Eulenburg was fifteen years old when his father's elder brother,
Count Fritz Eulenburg, was appointed to the key position of Minister of the
Interior in Bismarck's government at the time of the Prussian constitutional
conflict.[6] He was nineteen when, because of the Austro-Prussian war, he
was forced to leave the Vitzthum grammar school in hostile Dresden. He
was twenty-three when, as a lieutenant in the famous Gardes du Corps
Regiment, he accompanied a horse detachment to Paris. He was twenty-six
at the outbreak of the *Kulturkampf*, in which his uncle Fritz again played a
leading role. Philipp Eulenburg's political vision was permanently dominated by the fear that the newly united Protestant, Prussian-dominated
Lesser German Reich could disintegrate, as well as by the conviction that
only the hegemony of Prussia, underpinned by the executive authority and
military command power of the King of Prussia unfettered by any form of
parliamentary control, could guarantee the continued existence of this new
German Reich in the face of the alliance of its numerous internal and
external enemies. Perhaps this perception also explains his attraction to the
racial theories of Wagner, Gobineau and Houston Stewart Chamberlain, as
well as his contempt for the 'open' social and political order prevailing
among the western powers. At any rate Philipp Eulenburg was a central
European, continental man, whose outlook was much more closely attuned
to Bismarck, with his nightmare vision of a ring of enemies – his *cauchemar
des coalitions*[7] – than it was to a Max Weber, who in his famous inaugural
lecture of 1895 condemned the establishment of the Reich as the youthful
prank of an old man unless it were to prove itself to be the springboard for
further vigorous expansion.[8] If despite all this Philipp Eulenburg participated in the inauguration of *Weltpolitik* and the battleship programme in
the Bülow era by means of his influence on ministerial appointments, he did
so for quite different reasons.

   Until the beginning of the 1880s Eulenburg's life appeared to run along
quite normal lines, even if the conspicuously frequent and erratic changes in
his career intentions betrayed an inner restlessness. It was on 4 May 1886,
with the formation, in Prökelwitz in East Prussia, of an ardent friendship

with Prince Wilhelm of Prussia, who was twelve years his junior, that he was to be drawn into the world of high politics for which his background and his gifts seemed to mark him out.

Neither his father, Philipp Konrad, nor his mother, Baroness Alexandrine von Rothkirch und Panthen (from Schön-Ellguth near Breslau) were wealthy, so that to begin with the family (Philipp had one brother and one sister) depended on their father's salary as captain and later major in the cavalry. Their fortunes were decisively altered in February 1867, however, when their mother inherited from her uncle Karl, Baron von Hertefeld, the Liebenberg estate in the Ukermark, and Hertefeld on the Dutch border, with the result that Philipp's father was able and indeed obliged to resign his army commission. From then on this line of the Eulenburgs counted as one of the richest families of Prussia, and the proximity of Liebenberg to Berlin, the family's close relationship with the Prussian government ministers Fritz and Botho Eulenburg and the court official August Eulenburg, as well as their long-standing friendship with the Bismarcks, seemed to guarantee the elder, highly gifted son a brilliant career in state service. The improvement in the family's financial circumstances, however, came too late to have any influence on his father's outlook. He had, as Muschler writes, 'peered too deeply into the countenance of wretchedness in his youth ever to be able to forget the dreadful time of privation and nagging anxiety'.[9] The children suffered greatly, as we shall see, from the Junker parsimony of the austerely Prussian patriarch.

Philipp Eulenburg's father's frequent moves (in 1853 he was appointed personal adjutant to Wrangel in Berlin, in 1860 cavalry captain in Nauen, in 1865 major in Potsdam) and the complications associated with the wars of unification, meant that Philipp Eulenburg's schooling was interrupted on a number of occasions. In 1859 he went to the French grammar school in Berlin. Thereafter he received private tuition in Nauen, and from 1863 to 1866 he was at the Vitzthum grammar school in Dresden. At the outbreak of war in 1866 he passed his ensign examination in the company of his boyhood friends, Eberhard Count von Dohna-Schlobitten and Edgard von Wedel, and entered the Gardes du Corps regiment. In the following year he went with Dohna to the war academy in Kassel, and there he formed a close and fateful friendship with the similarly musical Kuno Count von Moltke. In November 1867 he passed his officer examination and returned to Potsdam as a lieutenant.

Despite the fact that these early phases of Philipp Eulenburg's military career had apparently passed off successfully and had been strongly supported by his father, in 1869 he decided to lay aside his lieutenant's uniform to return to school at the age of twenty-three in order to complete his final examinations in the tiny Hessian town of Weilburg an der Lahn.

When war with France broke out, Eulenburg hurried to rejoin his regiment in Potsdam, and was ordered to lead a horse transport to Paris, for which he was decorated with the Iron Cross. Garrison life after the war, however, was not congenial to him, and thanks to the intervention of his uncle Fritz and his cousin August he was appointed Adjutant to the General Government in Strassburg. In the autumn of 1871 he procured his father's consent to his final departure from the army 'though only on condition', as he later wrote, 'that I devoted myself first to a legal and then to a diplomatic career'.[10]

Following a trip to Palestine and Egypt, which had to be terminated prematurely because he became ill with typhus,[11] Eulenburg took up his law studies in the winter semester of 1872 at the University of Leipzig (this too being laid down by his father). Here began what was subsequently to be for him an important friendship with Axel Baron von Varnbüler, son of the former Minister-President of Württemberg and brother of Baroness Spitzemberg, now famous for her illuminating diaries.[12] Varnbüler was to recall in his memoirs, written some sixty years later, how Philipp Eulenburg was 'the most versatile, easily the most brilliant and therefore the leading spirit' in their circle of friends in Leipzig, and, when the two friends transferred to Strassburg in the following year, Eulenburg there again became the 'intellectual and artistic focus' of the group.[13] In Strassburg the circle of friends was enlarged to include Konstantin von Dziembowski (who took his own life in 1885),[14] Karl von Dörnberg (who died in St Petersburg in 1891)[15] and Alfred von Bülow (a son of the then Foreign Secretary and brother of the later Reich Chancellor).[16] An important reason for the transfer to Strassburg was Eulenburg's wish to take private tuition from Dr Paul Kayser, who was a judge in the district court there, a man who had 'drummed' knowledge into the two Bismarck sons, and who later – despite his Jewish origin – became Colonial Director in the Foreign Office and (with Eulenburg's help) was eventually promoted to be President of the Reich Court at Leipzig. After a first unsuccessful attempt in January 1875, Eulenburg passed the junior barrister examination in Kassel on 12 July; a few days later he was awarded a doctorate (for the same piece of work) at the University of Giessen with the grade 'magna cum laude'.

At the completion of his studies Philipp Eulenburg travelled to Stockholm, where he married the Swedish Countess Augusta Sandels, whom he had known for some years. In the summer of the following year, after a lengthy honeymoon in the south of Italy, Eulenburg took up residence with his wife and his two friends, Dörnberg and Alfred Bülow, in a small country house at Wulkow close to Liebenberg, where he set about completing his practical legal training under the supervision of Laemmel, the judge of the district court of Neu-Ruppin, another man who was to play a significant role at a later stage of Eulenburg's life. In March 1877 they received Count Arthur Gobineau in Wulkow for a visit lasting several days.

By the time his uncle Fritz Eulenburg was dismissed as Prussian Minister of the Interior in April 1878, to be replaced by Philipp's cousin Botho, Philipp Eulenburg had already transferred from the legal to the diplomatic phase of his career, working under Philippsborn in the trade department of the Foreign Office in Berlin. Soon his first 'foreign' missions followed: in the winter of 1878 he was attached to the German legation in Stockholm, and in August 1879 he was sent to Dresden to represent Count Dönhoff while the latter was on vacation. (Dönhoff's Italian wife divorced him some years later to marry Bernhard von Bülow.) Finally, in the autumn of 1880 Eulenburg passed his diplomatic examinations, though again not without some difficulty,[17] and was appointed Third Secretary in the German Embassy in Paris on 1 January 1881. The German Ambassador there, Prince Chlodwig zu Hohenlohe-Schillingsfürst, was advanced to the office of Reich Chancellor in October 1894 through Eulenburg's influence; the Second Secretary, Bernhard von Bülow, became Secretary of State in the Foreign Office in 1897 and Reich Chancellor in 1900; the First Secretary, Baron Max von Thielmann, became Secretary of State at the Reich Treasury in 1897.

The year 1881, which had begun so promisingly, was however to be overshadowed by more than one tragic event, which provoked in Eulenburg a *dégoût de la vie* leading him to turn his back on politics in favour of his artistic leanings, which he had hitherto repressed. The illness and death of Fritz Eulenburg, who had been ostracised by Bismarck, the abrupt dismissal of Botho Eulenburg, the tragic love affair between Philipp's friend Herbert Bismarck and Princess Elisabeth Carolath, whose marriage was prevented by the Reich Chancellor's threat to commit suicide[18] – all these events would without doubt have sufficed to convince the finely strung, sensitive Philipp Eulenburg that he was not equipped for the merciless world of politics, dominated as it was by a ruthless figure like Bismarck. What affected him most deeply, however, was the death of his little diabetic daughter, Astrid, on 23 March 1881. Eulenburg left Paris two days later to accompany the coffin to Liebenberg. He asked Herbert Bismarck to send him as Prussian Secretary of Legation to Munich as soon as possible, as he would find it intolerable to stay in Paris any longer. On 1 July 1881 his wish was granted.

As Eulenburg slowly began to recover in Starnberg and Munich, it was the arts which attracted him more and more, while for the court and political life of the Bavarian capital he felt only contempt and hatred. Now he wrote the first of the Nordic ballads: the *Atlantis* Cycle, *Gorm*, *Frühlingsmacht*, *Altnordisches Wiegenlied*, the *Märchen von der Freiheit*, the first *Skaldenge-*

sänge. Margot, the play he wrote in 1883/84, was first performed in March 1885 in the Residenztheater in Munich;[19] a second play, *Der Seestern*,[20] excited even more interest when it was performed in Berlin in 1887. Eulenburg's 'Nordic-mystical' enthusiasm was reinforced not only by his acquaintance with Gobineau, who died in October 1882 and about whom he wrote an article in 1884/1885 for the Wagnerian *Bayreuther Blätter*,[21] but by his connections with the Wagner circle in general.[22] His mother had after all played the piano *à quatre mains* back in the 1850s with Cosima Wagner (then still the wife of Hans von Bülow). His superior in the Prussian Legation, Count Werthern, also supported him in this, as did his Munich friends, Count Ferdinand Sporck, Count Stanislaus Kalckreuth, Lady Charlotte Blennerhassett (née Countess Leyden) and Jan von Wendelstadt. It is quite possible that the name of Philipp Eulenburg, like that of Ernst von Wildenbruch, who was a Councillor in the Foreign Office, would have entered German history as that of a writer, had he not received an invitation from his boyhood friend Eberhard Dohna on 19 April 1886 to hunt at Prökelwitz with the future Kaiser Wilhelm II.[23] In March 1888, when Wilhelm was already Crown Prince, Eulenburg could still write to his mother: 'I am very aware of the fact that it is, and always will be, a question [for me] of either state service or art.'[24] In his letters of the 1880s the same *Leitmotiv*, that he had 'completely missed his vocation'[25] and was remaining in state service solely for financial reasons, is repeatedly struck. Indeed as late as October 1888, by which time his friend had sat for four months on 'the mightiest throne on earth'[26] and had, against Bismarck's wishes, wanted to appoint him Prussian envoy in Munich, Eulenburg hinted in a letter to his mother that he himself would view such an exceptional promotion as an opportunity above all to give freer expression to his artistic talents.

I do not leave go of the thought expressed here, and in my fairly regular letters to him [Kaiser Wilhelm II] I return to it! It would be a very wonderful thing for my future to get such an appointment. For apart from the agreeable material aspects, I would hope that no-one would then ask *more* of me than this, and I could devote myself in peace to the things to which I am *really* attached.[27]

It is striking and of great psychological interest that Eulenburg repeatedly identified his 'real' self with his mother, while the state service he hated so much he identified with his father, though the latter died in 1889. His very first literary publication was undoubtedly an autobiographical story entitled 'Aus der Art. Eine märkische Geschichte', which appeared at the beginning of 1884 in a journal edited by Paul Lindau called *Nord und Süd*.[28] In it, as the title suggests, Eulenburg made clear how little he felt he stood in the family tradition, how much he blamed his father, with his concentration on purely materialistic considerations, for the suppression of his poetic talents. In a retrospective essay, 'Leid', Eulenburg wrote of his father: 'He was suffused with the prosaic ethos of Prussia, and inevitably he sought to steer me in a similar direction, when so much inspiration lay dormant in my imagination.'[29] In the same memoir he wrote that his soul belonged completely to his mother: 'My mother, whom I deeply adored, the ideal figure who filled my whole being with boundless love, fired my inspiration. Music, painting, poetry occupied her thoughts, and she practised the arts with talent and with understanding, and they took full possession of me as well.'[30]

Bismarck also recognised Philipp Eulenburg's deep antipathy to everything political; it was precisely for this reason that he opposed the wish of the young Kaiser to appoint him to the important position of Prussian envoy in Munich. In a letter to his son Herbert, who was by this time Foreign Secretary, Bismarck emphasised that he had kept a close eye on Eulenburg's development 'because I like him personally; he is amiable, but politically he has little sense of what is important and what is not; he allows himself to be influenced by carping gossip, passes it on and in this way needlessly puts people's backs up'. Eulenburg could 'with pleasure' be appointed Prussian envoy in Oldenburg, Braunschweig and Lippe, a post of political insignificance, but for the crucial Munich position he was 'impossible'. Bismarck declared that he was unable 'to fly in the face of the experience in these matters which I have accumulated over forty years', nor could he 'abandon, in the last act of my drama, the good conscience which I have insisted on maintaining towards the country in hard battles fought with the old master [Kaiser Wilhelm I], despite my love for the latter'.[31]

One would not wish to deny Bismarck's harsh judgment a certain degree of justification in view of the fact that Eulenburg tended to see the domestic and foreign policy of the Reich through the spectacles of his Munich experiences. The close kindred relationships between the Bavarian and Austrian courts convinced him of the approaching danger of a Catholic family league between the two, whose 'spearhead would be directed against Protestant Kaiserdom in Berlin'. When Franz Ferdinand became emperor of the Danube Monarchy, Eulenburg warned, he would form an alliance against the German Reich in league with Russia, France and the Curia, and with the help of his brother-in-law, the future King of Bavaria, his two cousins on the thrones of Dresden and Stuttgart, the Catholic Church and the Centre party throughout Germany, he would attempt to return to the pre-1866 order.[32] In view of this danger, the Reich government in Berlin should regard its foremost domestic aim as being the maintenance of the pro-Prussian Liberal government in Bavaria, and its most important aim in foreign policy should be the maintenance of the Triple Alliance with Austria and anti-clerical Italy. With the fall of the Liberal cabinet in Munich, Catholic–aristocratic forces there would seize control and attempt to promote Bavaria as 'the Catholic hegemonial power in the Reich'[33] and in this way inaugurate the policy of the 'family league' in Vienna. This meant, however, that the Reich government must never establish any form of alliance with the Centre party in the Reichstag because that 'would be synonymous with the inauguration of the "family league" by Berlin itself'. Only if 'quick financial credits' were needed 'to start an immediate war, to undertake a *coup d'état* etc.' would a temporary arrangement with the Centre party be acceptable. As the Prusso-German Reich would consequently be dependent on a government in Bavaria 'which rested on the support of the national, liberal parties in that state', the government in Berlin could similarly 'not dispense with the political party of the national-German liberals'. For this reason, however, the moderate conservative tendency must always rule both in Prussia and in the Reich, since reactionary policies would be a provocation to the National Liberal forces in south Germany and in the new Prussian provinces. In August 1892 Eulenburg wrote in his essay 'Deutsche Politik':

The difficulty of this policy for the leading state, Prussia, lies in the fact that, if necessary, it must champion an apparently revolutionary movement. It will be able to keep things in balance by ruling on a moderate conservative basis in Prussia itself. The organs of the Prussian executive must never become extreme conservative, however, as the national parties in the Reich would then lose faith in the objectivity of the Reich government.[34]

As late as 1896 he was writing that he thought 'the sorest spot of the new German Reich' was that the 'old Prussian tradition' had to make concessions to 'the liberalism of the German Philistine'.[35] In this way he came to the conclusion – on the basis of tactical considerations rather than inner conviction – that the German Reich was governable only 'by relying on the support of the middle parties'.[36]

Before we reject these views as those of a hopelessly unpolitical dilettante, we should remember that they were shared by Bismarck himself during the 1870s, as the *Kulturkampf* and the famous dictation of Bad Kissingen show, and that very similar views were held until well beyond the turn of the century by a large and influential circle of political personalities. In Munich Eulenburg received confirmation of his views not only from the liberal ministers of the cabinets of Lutz and Crailsheim, but also from his 'anti-Catholic, even anti-Christian'[37] superior at the Prussian Legation, Count Georg von Werthern, and from political outsiders such as the fanatically anti-Austrian Count Fritz Yrsch. Eulenburg's depiction of the dangers of Ultramontanism was decisively supported by the Freiburg Professor Franz Xaver Kraus[38] and by the circle around Lady Charlotte Blennerhassett, the

Grand Duke of Baden, the moderate leader of the Conservative party, Otto von Helldorff-Bedra, the Baden Envoy and later Foreign Secretary Adolf Marschall von Bieberstein, the friend and ambassador Bernhard von Bülow and the former tutor Dr Paul Kayser. For the history of Germany, however, the most significant voice of assent which Eulenburg's views encountered was that of the 'all-powerful' Privy Councillor in the Political Department of the Foreign Office, Friedrich von Holstein.

Philipp Eulenburg's association with Holstein[39], which dated from June 1886, was, after his friendship with Wilhelm II, the second precondition for the political influence he was to wield in the following twelve years. The Privy Councillor's acute intellect and unrivalled intelligence network – Holstein wrote his first letter to Eulenburg on 13 June 1886, two days after Prince Wilhelm had asked Eulenburg for 'detailed information' about the abdication crisis in Bavaria![40] – combined with Eulenburg's emotional penetration, narrative talents and 'boundless love' for Wilhelm of Prussia in such a way that the inherited power of the latter could, in certain circumstances, be directed against the Reich Chancellor himself. At the latest by the time of the young Kaiser's accession to the throne on 15 June 1888, the Holstein–Eulenburg–Wilhelm II combination was proving itself stronger than Bismarck, who had accumulated his power over a quarter of a century, even though by this time the founder of the Reich was clearly ageing rapidly.

The first example of how effectively the Holstein–Eulenburg–Wilhelm II system functioned can be seen in the summer of 1889 with the beginning of the crisis over Bismarck's dismissal. In the previous year Bismarck had signalled a willingness to allow the return of the Redemptorists to Germany, an Order which was closely associated with the Jesuits. He had done this under the influence of his son-in-law, Count Kuno Rantzau, whom Bismarck had appointed Prussian Envoy in Munich against repeated attempts to prevent it on the part of Eulenburg and Holstein. They interpreted this policy as an attempt on Bismarck's part to make himself indispensable in the realm of both domestic and foreign policy by bringing about the disintegration of the 'Kartell' in the Reichstag comprising the Conservative and the National Liberal parties, the collapse of Lutz's pro-Prussian Liberal cabinet in Munich and the awakening of mistrust on the part of the anticlerical government of Italy. By doing this, they calculated, Bismarck would have placed the young Kaiser in a 'position of constraint'. The Chief of the General Staff Count Waldersee, who at that time was still closely associated with Holstein and Eulenburg, no doubt spoke for the whole group when he wrote in 1889:

Once we have a bad House, we shall not be able to rectify the situation without either great successes in war or very serious fights at home. The Chancellor would still be able to cope with such a situation, but he would be the only one, and in that case he would have the Kaiser in the palm of his hand.[41]

As soon as Holstein learned of Bismarck's intentions with regard to the Redemptorists, he warned Eulenburg that the Kartell would suffer heavy losses in the forthcoming Reichstag elections unless the Kaiser himself made clear his sympathies for the moderate parties. It was without doubt due to Eulenburg's influence that, just a few days later, Kaiser Wilhelm II assured the Kartell of his support in a statement in the official gazette, the *Reichsanzeiger*. When Holstein perceived that Bismarck and Rantzau were taking no notice of this statement, he prompted Eulenburg to write twice to the Kaiser, who was then in Constantinople. Eulenburg also persuaded the Grand Duke of Baden to send a letter to the Kaiser. The result of this operation was that on 6 November 1889 the Reich Chancellor suddenly received an imperial telegram from Constantinople telling him that 'under no circumstances and in no way whatsoever can and will His Majesty permit the return of the Redemptorists to Germany'. Eulenburg and Holstein were nevertheless unable to prevent Bismarck from destroying the Kartell by other means, that is by introducing a more extreme Anti-Socialist Bill into the Reichstag, and this despite the intervention of the Kaiser's former tutor Hinzpeter and the transmission by Eulenburg of Paul Kayser's detailed social reform plans to Wilhelm II. The result was that the middle parties did indeed suffer serious losses in the elections of 20 February 1890, just as Holstein had predicted. Following Bismarck's continuation of his policy of provocation by the planned introduction of a new Anti-Socialist Bill and a massive new Army Bill, by his celebrated interview with the Centre party leader Ludwig Windthorst, and finally by the working out of plans for a *coup d'état*, the crisis came to a head in the middle of March 1890, and once again Philipp Eulenburg found himself in the key position of mediator between the Holstein group and the Kaiser. On 11 March 1890 Holstein wrote to Eulenburg that he himself, Marschall and the Grand Duke of Baden felt Eulenburg's immediate presence in Berlin to be absolutely essential. Every hour was of crucial importance for the Kaiser.[42] Bismarck, Marschall warned on the following day, was openly steering towards 'chaos at home' in order to put himself forward in the eyes of the propertied classes as the 'only saviour in their hour of need'.[43] Paul Kayser, too, let Eulenburg know that the 'great turning-point' had arrived.[44] It is true that Eulenburg only decided to travel to Berlin on 16 March, after he had also received a pressing invitation from General Waldersee. Despite this he had already played a significant role in Wilhelm's final decision to dismiss Bismarck by passing on Marschall's letter to the Kaiser on 14 March. The letter would have arrived on the same day or the following morning. Early on 15 March 1890 Wilhelm II dragged the seventy-five year old Reich Chancellor out of bed and, after a violent quarrel, demanded that he tender his resignation.

What role Philipp Eulenburg played in the choice of the new men in 1890 is unclear, but we are unlikely to be seriously wide of the mark if we assume that here too he was more the messenger than the driving force. General Leo von Caprivi had already belonged to the Holstein group in the 1880s when he was Chief of the Admiralty; Marschall, who worked extremely closely with Holstein throughout the crisis surrounding Bismarck's dismissal, knew as far back as January 1890 that Caprivi was likely to be appointed as Bismarck's successor.[45] When Philipp Eulenburg called on Caprivi in Hanover on 6 March 1890, he did so probably at Holstein's suggestion. Eulenburg later claimed that, if the Kaiser had asked for his opinion, he would never have recommended Caprivi, but this explanation seems unreliable for a number of reasons, and it no doubt arises from a retrospective attempt at self-justification, much as does Eulenburg's claim that he tried to prevent the non-renewal of the Reinsurance Treaty with Russia by means of a telegram to the Kaiser.[46] What is clear is that the new Secretary of State in the Foreign Office, Adolf Baron Marschall von Bieberstein, was Holstein's candidate, and that Eulenburg persuaded the Kaiser to agree to Marschall's appointment after all his exertions to retain his friend Herbert Bismarck in office had failed.[47]

With the end of the great crisis of March 1890 Eulenburg could hope that in future his life would be less eventful. And the years 1890 and 1891 were indeed less crisis-ridden than the years before and after. But at the same time Eulenburg's role as mediator between the so-called 'responsible government' and the Kaiser's court was called on frequently in order to avert crises. In September 1890, for instance, when the Kaiser clashed with Caprivi and the whole Prussian Ministry of State over the ratification of the re-election of the Left Liberal politician Max Forckenbeck as Lord Mayor of Berlin, only Eulenburg's letters persuaded Wilhelm to give way.[48]

By no means everything which the remarkably liberal 'Chancellor-General' set in motion met with Eulenburg's approval, however. As early as March 1891 the latter became seriously concerned about the hatred of the former Kartell parties towards Caprivi, and he declared that it would be necessary 'to rally the propertied classes, big business etc., so as to provide Caprivi with a solid parliamentary base'. He advocated the appointment of Jencke, the manager of the Krupp works at Essen, as Prussian Minister of Public Works 'in order to reassure the big industrialists' without bothering about the fact that Caprivi had already expressed his determined opposition to Jencke's appointment.[49] When the Kaiser informed his friend on the North Sea cruise in 1891 of his intention to carry through a *coup d'état* in association with a great Army Bill within three years, Holstein had to conceal Eulenburg's letters from Caprivi so that the latter would not get too discouraged.[50]

Even Eulenburg's appointment in the spring of 1891 to 'that post ...

which he had yearned for above all others for ages',[51] namely to the Prussian Legation in Munich, occurred as a result of a direct deception of the Reich Chancellor. During a visit to Munich in November 1890, Caprivi asked Crailsheim, the Bavarian Minister-President, to invite Kaiser Wilhelm II to the Bavarian army corps manoeuvres. Crailsheim feared that the invitation of the Kaiser could annoy Prince Regent Luitpold of Bavaria, and he asked Eulenburg, who by that time was Prussian envoy in Stuttgart, in the strictest confidence whether and how the Kaiser's visit might be averted. When Holstein and Marschall learned from Eulenburg of Crailsheim's letter, they strongly advised him to reply rejecting the request as impossible, and they warned that Caprivi should not be told of the letter. By some unexplained route Caprivi did nevertheless hear of these irregular negotiations going on behind his back and angrily demanded an explanation from Crailsheim. Eulenburg stated in response to an alarmed inquiry from Crailsheim that he had, as promised, made no mention of Crailsheim's letter to anyone; the latter thereupon solemnly swore to Caprivi that he did not know what he was referring to. That would no doubt have brought the incident to a close had not Eulenburg used it to prove to the Kaiser that Count Rantzau no longer enjoyed the confidence of the Bavarian government. On this basis Wilhelm II reached the decision to send Bismarck's son-in-law to The Hague, and to secure the post of Prussian envoy in Munich for his best friend, Philipp Eulenburg. When Eulenburg informed the Bavarian Minister-President of the happy outcome of the affair, the latter was astounded and demanded to know how it could have come about if Eulenburg had really not reported anything of the secret request of the Bavarian government to the authorities in Berlin!

The worst clash between Eulenburg and Caprivi, however, occurred early in 1892, when the Reich Chancellor, together with the extreme Conservative Prussian Minister of Education Count Zedlitz, set out to introduce a School Bill in the Prussian Landtag which would have secured the support of the Centre party in the Reichstag for the great Army Bill which the Kaiser had demanded. As in the Bismarck crisis of 1889–90, Holstein again opposed this 'black–blue' policy, going so far as to consider the merits of Caprivi's dismissal as a way of securing for the Kaiser the lifelong 'confidence of the groups loyal to the Reich'.[52] Philipp Eulenburg wrote to the Kaiser on 21 January 1892 of the need to carry the School Bill through 'in league with the middle parties' so that the 'anger of the liberals' would not be directed at the person of the monarch. On receipt of this letter the Kaiser called together the leaders of the Kartell parties, and in their presence he told the Education Minister that he would 'never' consent to a School Bill based on a Conservative-clerical majority. Even Eulenburg was alarmed that his letter had 'worked like a bomb'. He nevertheless wrote once again to the Kaiser on this matter, strongly recommending that the Bill be altered so as to make it acceptable to the Kartell parties. He warned, however, that the situation 'required boundless discretion if we are not to cause Caprivi's fall'. One week later, on 17 March, the Kaiser declared in a meeting of the Crown Council that he would only consent to an amended Bill. On the following day, exactly two years after Bismarck's dismissal, and in very similar circumstances, both Caprivi and Zedlitz submitted their resignation. Once again the Holstein–Eulenburg–Wilhelm II combination had proved itself stronger than the 'responsible government'.[53]

Following the 'halving' of the post of Chancellor brought about by Caprivi's surrender of the Prussian Minister-Presidency to Eulenburg's cousin Botho – and the choice really seems not to have been the result of Philipp's work, even though it soon led to severe difficulties in his relations with Caprivi, Holstein and Marschall – the Holstein group's attempts to use the power vacuum and Philipp Eulenburg's friendship with the Kaiser for their own (predominantly personnel) purposes became even more marked. When for example the important ambassadorial post in St Petersburg became vacant in October 1892, the Kaiser, the Chancellor and the departing Ambassador General Lothar von Schweinitz were agreed that Count Friedrich von Alvensleben would be the most suitable candidate. But Holstein and Kiderlen-Wächter did not share this view, and they asked Eulenburg to 'place obstacles' in Alvensleben's path. Eulenburg accordingly worked via the Russian envoy in Munich, Count Osten-Sacken, to bring about a direct request from the Tsar that General Bernhard von Werder should be appointed successor to Schweinitz. Eulenburg had given the Russians to understand that this was the Kaiser's secret wish – and was deeply discomfited when the Kaiser threatened to ignore the Tsar's express desire! In 1893 Holstein and Kiderlen concocted a plan to bribe the Pope to persuade the Centre party to support the Army Bill. As it was clear from the outset that both the Reich Chancellor and the Foreign Secretary would reject the plan, the only route was through Eulenburg. He was to persuade the Kaiser to tell the Chancellor 'that He wished the [bribery] attempt to be made'. Should Caprivi inquire where the idea had originated, the Kaiser was to name Prince Hohenlohe, the Statthalter of Alsace-Lorraine, since 'if His Majesty mentions our names to the Reich Chancellor', Kiderlen wrote, 'he will inevitably think that we are engaged in some dark intrigue'.[54] Eulenburg was able to report within two days that the Imperial command had been despatched to the Foreign Office. The only practical result of this operation, however, was a crisis of confidence between Caprivi and Hohenlohe and – over and beyond that – an overall dissolution of the 'close bonds between the men of the New Course'.[55] Certainly occasions still arose – such as Bismarck's visit to the Berlin Schloss at the end of January 1894 – when

Philipp Eulenburg's mediation was called upon both by the court and the Wilhelmstrasse; times, such as in the crisis between the governments of Prussia and Bavaria over the differential rail tariff in February 1894, when the Foreign Secretary, on hearing that Eulenburg had written to the Kaiser, could sigh with relief: 'Then the battle is won.'[56] But when Marschall refused to order an inquiry into who was behind the campaign beginning in December 1893 in the satirical magazine *Kladderadatsch* against the trio Holstein–Kiderlen–Eulenburg, the latter was not alone in thinking that the attacks were possibly not wholly unwelcome to the Secretary of State; and the Reich Chancellor was reported to have said shortly before his resignation in October 1894 'that he was master of his own house and would not tolerate the activity of shady intriguers'.[57]

With regard to the future development of the crisis of government following Bismarck's fall, it is almost impossible to exaggerate how important it was that in the course of 1893, thanks to his relations with the Foreign Office on the one hand and the Kaiser on the other, Philipp Eulenburg was able to strengthen his own position to the point where, from the beginning of 1894 onwards, he was able to pursue policies not only independently of Holstein but even in opposition to him. Eulenburg's cousin August, whose inconspicuous influence on German politics until the fall of the monarchy in 1918 has hitherto gone largely unremarked, was with Philipp's assistance raised to be Liebenau's successor as Oberhofmarschall (High Marshal of the Court) in the summer of 1890.[58] His other cousin Botho – August's brother – had become, as we have seen, Prussian Minister-President in the spring of 1892 and Minister of the Interior in the summer of the same year. In the spring of 1893 Count Kuno Moltke was appointed aide-de-camp to Kaiser Wilhelm II, certainly not without Eulenburg's involvement; at any rate Eulenburg wrote to Varnbüler, their common friend in Vienna: 'Kuno as aide-de-camp!! The Kaiser telegraphed it to me full of joy. It is good to have him in Berlin.'[59] During his time in Stuttgart (1890–1) Eulenburg had arranged, together with another friend from their student days, Boris Wolff, for Varnbüler to be made Württemberg Envoy in St Petersburg.[60] When this post was dissolved at the beginning of 1893, Eulenburg appears to have played a part in Varnbüler's transfer to Vienna, although he modestly explained to Varnbüler that he deserved 'little credit' for this success. But Varnbüler's appointment to the politically important post of Württemberg Envoy and Federal Council Plenipotentiary in Berlin, which he occupied from April 1894 until the November revolution in 1918, was entirely due to Eulenburg's efforts. The sources demonstrate unambiguously that Eulenburg sought to bring about the fall of the Württemberg Minister-President Mittnacht and his replacement by the Berlin envoy Moser, so freeing this post for Varnbüler. As early as April 1893 Eulenburg wrote to Varnbüler that things would 'not last much longer' with Mittnacht, and as a consequence Moser would soon be appointed Minister-President in Stuttgart and Moser's post would 'inevitably fall into the lap' of Varnbüler.[61] On 27 August 1893 Eulenburg wrote to Kaiser Wilhelm II: 'It's time for Moser to take over – and then for Axel [Varnbüler] to come to Berlin. King Wilhelm [of Württemberg] has long since had enough of Mittnacht.'[62] In October 1893 Kuno Moltke told Varnbüler that 'the bomb . . . is ready to explode'. 'At a briefing from Phili' at Rominten the Kaiser had decided on the recall of Moser and his replacement by Varnbüler. 'Phili asks you to keep the matter strictly secret', Moltke continued, 'as your immediate fatherland [Württemberg] has no knowledge of the bomb which is being primed.'[63] Faced with such statements, it is necessary to ask whether the violent crisis between Caprivi and the government of Württemberg over the manoeuvres in the autumn of 1893 would have taken on the proportions that it did, had it not been for Eulenburg's wish to see Varnbüler appointed to the Württemberg Legation in Berlin. At any rate Moser's recall provoked nothing but outrage, even on the part of Varnbüler's sister, Baroness Spitzemberg,[64] and it led directly to the veiled attacks by two Foreign Office officials in the satirical magazine *Kladderadatsch* on Holstein ('Oyster friend'), Kiderlen ('Spätzle') and Eulenburg ('Troubadour'), who were depicted as looking for a fourth player (i.e. Varnbüler) for the game of skat.

The most powerful element in Philipp Eulenburg's political activity in the following few years, however, was his co-operation with Bernhard von Bülow. Their friendship, which had begun in 1881 in Paris, and which had seen Eulenburg playing a decisive role as early as 1884–6 in Bülow's controversial marriage to the divorcee Countess Marie Dönhoff, deepened significantly after 1892. Axel Varnbüler recounts in his memoirs how, in his time in Vienna (April 1893 to April 1894), he had often acted as 'confidant' and 'chaperon' to Prince Karl Max Lichnowsky, the later ambassador to London, at that time First Secretary in the German Embassy in Vienna, in relation to the latter's 'tender relationship with Marie Bülow'. On one occasion Philipp Eulenburg had also been present, and Varnbüler had later developed the 'suspicion that at these *parties fines* a conspiracy had been woven, providing mutual reinsurance: Bülow ambassador in Rome, Phili in Vienna, Lichnowsky Director of Personnel in the Foreign Office'.[65] Eulenburg's correspondence makes it possible to reconstruct this 'plot' in almost every detail, and it leaves no room for doubt that Varnbüler's 'suspicion' was very much on target. Similarly to Werder's appointment to St Petersburg, Bülow's appointment as ambassador in Rome was the work of Holstein and Eulenburg. Holstein was primarily motivated by the wish to obstruct Engelbrecht, the military attaché, whom the Kaiser was considering promoting to the ambassadorship. He therefore advised Eulenburg to persuade Bülow's influential mother-in-law Donna Laura Minghetti to ask the King of Italy to make a direct request for Bülow's appointment. King Umberto was unwilling to become involved in this intrigue because he was convinced that Germany was dominated by the military. Both Caprivi and Marschall opposed Bülow's appointment until Holstein was able to prove to the Chancellor that Engelbrecht was intriguing against the Foreign Office. Thereafter Caprivi was prepared to support the transfer of Bülow from Bucharest to Rome, though he feared that the Kaiser would refuse his consent. Eulenburg was then able to overcome the Kaiser's opposition with the argument that Caprivi would resign if the Kaiser did not respect his wishes! Caprivi was pleasantly surprised when Wilhelm made no difficulties. 'No doubt Eulenburg had prepared the ground', Caprivi remarked afterwards to Holstein; the Privy Councillor thought it best to say nothing as it did not seem useful to let the Chancellor know just how much 'preparation' Eulenburg had undertaken. What little self-confidence the Reich Chancellor still possessed had to be maintained, he declared. 'Marschall also knows nothing.'[66] This incident clearly shows the extent to which power had shifted from those who were constitutionally 'responsible' for the direction of policy to the Holstein–Eulenburg cabal. When Caprivi learned soon after Bülow's move to Rome that the ambassador was corresponding directly with the Kaiser, a serious clash occurred between the Chancellor and Bülow, just as it had in the case of Prince Hohenlohe over the plan to bribe the Pope.[67]

Bernhard and Marie Bülow and Prince Lichnowsky then returned the favour by proceeding to smoothe Eulenburg's path to Vienna.[68] Caprivi was already considering the possibility of sending Eulenburg to Vienna in 1892 – Holstein and Kiderlen suspected that the Chancellor wished to remove him from Munich because of his activity in the School Bill crisis – but a suggestion to this effect encountered the opposition of the Kaiser, who thought Eulenburg 'was indispensable in Munich given the circumstances there'. During the North Sea cruise in July 1892 Eulenburg asked the Kaiser not to send him 'too far away', should his name arise again in connection with an ambassadorial post. With that the matter was put on ice for the time being. But the recall of the long-serving ambassador, Prince 'Septi' Reuss, could only be a matter of time, in view of his disloyal behaviour during Bismarck's 'grand tour' of Austria and southern Germany in the summer of 1892 and also the fanatical devotion of Princess 'Sitta' Reuss to Bismarck. Bülow and Lichnowsky recommended Eulenburg to the Austro-Hungarian Foreign Minister, Count Gustav Kálnoky, as the most suitable successor, while Holstein also supported Eulenburg's candidacy, once again in order to prevent the appointment of an aide-de-camp, in this case Count Carl von Wedel. When Holstein suggested that Eulenburg should go with the Kaiser to Vienna in the autumn of 1892, in order that he could make himself known in official circles there, Eulenburg begged that Kiderlen should accompany the Kaiser instead. 'You would not believe how repugnant it is to me to be spoken of as a favourite, intriguer etc. Such talk may well be widespread already, but I can assure you that I have not provoked it.' The behaviour of Princess Reuss in Vienna so annoyed the Kaiser that he told Kiderlen: 'Reuss can't stay here much longer; Phili will have to come.' Bülow now urged Eulenburg to do more to secure his own appointment. 'Overcome your deep-rooted repugnance of anything which could possibly smell of pushing for advantage', he wrote in October 1892, 'and ponder the fact that amongst people who are mostly as thick-skinned as hippopotami, a finely constructed character is compelled, under certain circumstances, to get tough in the interests of serving the Kaiser.'[69] In the meantime Bülow had settled on a plan whereby, in the event of Reuss's resignation, Vienna would make a direct request for Eulenburg as his replacement. In 1893 the question was put into a different perspective when Eulenburg began to be increasingly spoken of as a future Foreign Secretary, something which for a variety of reasons he wished to avoid: he lacked, as he confessed to Holstein, amongst other things, '1. a willingness to do so much paperwork, 2. the nerves for the job, 3. good knowledge of English, 4. parliamentary experience, 5. the desire to take it on.'[70] In the summer of 1893, when he accompanied the Kaiser to Britain, yet another 'danger' arose: he made such an excellent impression at the Court of St James that the Kaiser offered him the London ambassadorship in the event of Hatzfeldt's resignation.[71] And so in order to avoid both Berlin and London, from the middle of 1893 onwards Eulenburg actively set about obtaining the embassy in Vienna. When Princess Reuss was careless enough to write him a letter which proved that she was a 'rabid follower of Bismarck' and 'totally impossible as the wife of the Kaiser's ambassador',[72] Eulenburg did not neglect to place this letter before the Reich Chancellor. Bülow and Lichnowsky decided that the time had come to arrange a dinner, which took place on the 16 December 1893 in Vienna, at which Eulenburg would be able to get to know the Austro-Hungarian Foreign Minister socially. Bülow then reported to the Kaiser that Kálnoky had said that he liked Eulenburg 'enormously' and that he would suit Vienna very well. On 17 December 1893 a lengthy political discussion between Eulenburg and Kálnoky took place, which had been arranged on Bülow's initiative and for which Eulenburg was extremely well prepared by confidential briefings from Holstein on matters of so-called 'grand policy'. During his return journey to Munich Eulenburg put together a comprehensive report for the Foreign Office, a copy of which he also included in his next letter to the Kaiser. On the official document the Kaiser wrote: 'The first sensible and interesting report to come out of Vienna for a long time.'[73] With that, the decision had in effect been made: the Kaiser informed the Wilhelmstrasse that he wished to announce Eulenburg's appointment as ambassador in Vienna on his coming birthday. Guided by this statement and at Holstein's insistence, Bülow and the Consul-General in Budapest, Count Anton Monts, advised Prince Reuss to bow to the inevitable. They also suggested that he should propose Eulenburg as his successor in his resignation letter, which was dispatched on 31 December 1893. Thus Bülow had indeed 'succeeded in his efforts to prevent any discordant note' and had 'brought everything to a harmonious conclusion', even if the change, much to Eulenburg's relief, was pushed back until the beginning of May 1894.

The collaboration between Eulenburg and Bülow had even weightier consequences, however, than their respective promotions to ambassadorships. It created the conditions for Eulenburg's increasing political independence from Holstein and therefore for Caprivi's fall from office in October 1894, as well as for the great re-shuffle of Secretaries of State in the Summer of 1897 which would bring about not only the appointment of Bülow and Tirpitz to top positions in Berlin but also the establishment of the 'personal rule' of the Kaiser, *Weltpolitik* and the battleship plan, and a re-orientation of domestic policy along Prussian-Conservative lines.

If we compare the innumerable letters written by Holstein and Bülow to Eulenburg, the difference in tone is always unmistakable, and it suggests that here too personal inclinations and disinclinations were very closely intertwined with political developments. In spite of Eulenburg's occasional attempts to introduce a warmer tone,[74] Holstein's letters remained sober and factual. The contrast with Bülow's extravagant protestations of friendship could hardly be greater. 'My innermost thoughts hasten towards you', Bülow declared for instance in a letter of 1 January 1894, which was completely attuned to Eulenburg's mystical and romantic inclinations.[75] 'We must surely have already known and loved each other somewhere in the endless stream of time, for in my soul there is only affinity and friendship for you.'[76] When in March 1893 Eulenburg addressed Bülow in the familiar '*Du*' form, the latter replied in terms which were intended to indicate not just the extent to which the two men were 'kindred spirits', but also how Bülow saw himself as Philipp Eulenburg's political *alter ego*, as the executor of his ideals.

As sisters our souls once arose from the mysterious spring of Being; we were simply given different shells and differently coloured wings. As the heavenly beings have granted you the magic gift of a rich and brilliant artistic talent, I cannot stand productively by your side in this regard, though I can certainly be gladdened when experiencing what you can give, enjoying your spirit and marvelling at you. I, by inclination and upbringing more dependent on historical, legal, economic studies, may be able to pass over to you from the storeroom which I am slowly stocking up, many a piece for the edifice which you, having been thrown into the political struggle against your own inclinations, are nevertheless constructing with a felicitous and certain touch for the benefit of our Kaiser and country.[77]

The seemingly boundless admiration which Eulenburg and Bülow had for the Kaiser formed the cornerstone of their co-operation, and at the same time the main reason for the growing tension with Holstein. If a calculating figure from the world of heavy industry like Stumm-Halberg could arrive at the view as early as 1882 that in the face of intensifying class conflict 'our kings will be absolutely unable to avoid throwing themselves into the battle against the forces of dissolution',[78] then in Bülow's case the additional calculation was presumably at work that he himself might succeed in scaling the highest office in the land if he managed to manipulate Eulenburg's enthusiastic feelings of friendship towards Wilhelm II, particularly in the light of Eulenburg's known aversion to the glare of publicity. At any rate we find in Bülow's letters as early as 1892 statements such as these: 'The leading ideas of our Imperial Master are mostly undoubtedly correct; all that is needed is that they should in future be defended and executed with greater skill and tact', or 'The grand aims of our Most Gracious Master can only be attained if those who have the task of executing the Kaiser's plans possess the ability to do so.'[79] It is not difficult to guess the identity of the person being lined up as executor of the Kaiser's will and architect of the new strategy of stabilisation. When at the end of 1895 Kaiser Wilhelm II told Eulenburg that Bülow was to be his 'Bismarck', the two Ambassadors met secretly in Merano, and afterwards Eulenburg reported to the Kaiser: 'If the majority of politicians had heard our conversation, they would not have believed their ears ... For how, in this complicated world, could they have understood this personal, human love for the best of all Kings and our natural, heartfelt friendship for one another?'[80] When Bülow thought in the summer of 1896 that his time had come, he announced that as Chancellor he would strive to ensure 'that the entire prestige and the whole plenitude of power of His Majesty, which were taken away in 1890, are fully restored in the eyes of the Army and the country'. He, Bülow, would be

a different kind of Chancellor from my predecessors. Bismarck was a power in his own right ... Caprivi and Hohenlohe regarded or regard themselves as the representatives of the 'Government' and to a certain extent of the Parliament against His Majesty. I would regard myself as the executive tool of His Majesty, so to speak his political Chief of Staff. With me, personal rule – in the good sense – would really begin.[81]

Holstein was outraged at this attitude towards the Kaiser. He, like the Superior of the great seminary in Strassburg, Dacheux, a friend of Hohenlohe's, characterised the situation as a struggle between the 'système de

Louis XIV' and the twentieth century which was fast approaching.[82] The Kaiser, according to Holstein, was behaving as though he lived in the absolutist era before 1848; soon he would be 'far more of an autocrat' than the Tsar.[83] It was becoming clearer all the time that the reign of Kaiser Wilhelm II would constitute the transition either to a dictatorship or to a republic, because what the Kaiser was permitting himself amounted to 'an operetta government but not one that a European people at the end of the nineteenth century will put up with'.[84] He, Holstein, was in favour of 'a moderate use of a practicable system of constitutional co-operative government which, with the exception of St Petersburg and Constantinople, is in operation in the rest of the European and civilised world'. Eulenburg, on the other hand, inclined, so Holstein felt, 'instinctively ... to an autocratic régime no matter whether it be Russian patriarchal or *despotisme éclairé* on the French model'. Eulenburg belonged to those who believed that 'every political, military, and legal question is best decided directly by the Kaiser'.[85] Prophetically Holstein warned Eulenburg: 'See to it that world history does not some day picture you as the evil spirit who was at the side of the imperial traveller when he chose the false path.'[86]

Eulenburg's mystical reaction to this accusation proves that Holstein's supposition was only too justified: 'I am convinced that the Guiding Hand of Providence lies behind this elemental and natural drive of the Kaiser's to direct the affairs of the Kingdom in person', wrote Eulenburg to Holstein in December 1894. 'Whether it will ruin us or save us I cannot say. But I find it difficult to believe in the decline of Prussia's star.'[87] Eulenburg wrote to Bülow, enclosing copies of his correspondence with Holstein, to say that he could leave the Privy Councillor in no doubt that he would go 'through thick and thin' with the Kaiser. If he sought to modify some of the monarch's actions, he did so purely out of a desire to help his Imperial friend and not to exploit a 'liberal system' against him. In this, concluded Eulenburg, lay the real difference between Holstein and himself. 'The Holstein of 1888, with his old-Prussian loyalty to the monarch, has certainly not turned in 1896 into an anti-monarchist, but he has become a parliamentarian.' Holstein would never understand the feelings of friendship that he, Eulenburg, had for the Kaiser. 'Sympathy and that feeling that a friend has when his friend encounters misfortune ... was something that played no part for him.' Eulenburg was, as he said himself, 'hardly the man to do violence to the Kaiser'.[88]

Philipp Eulenburg went even further, however, by consciously elevating the Kaiser's supposed character traits into being the foundation of his political faith. The most conspicuous of the Kaiser's characteristics, he claimed, was 'the knightly – reminiscent of the finest time of the Middle Ages, with all its piety and mysticism'; he combined this knightliness with a modern outlook, though the latter was certainly subordinate. As long as Germany remained a monarchy, 'we must take into account the King's own character', Eulenburg declared. Therefore, if he now transferred 'the effect of the Kaiser's personality onto politics', he, Eulenburg, necessarily came to the conclusion that the Kaiser 'must have his natural support among the Conservatives'. He was convinced that 'the Kaiser's individuality would find its equilibrium in politics on a sensible Conservative basis. The whole of the Kaiser's vital, dynamic being stands in such remarkable contradiction to the predominance of Liberal-Progressive or Liberal-Catholic (Centre) ideas that this has been one of the main reasons for the feeling of unsteadiness about which the whole of Germany is complaining.' If 'sensible Conservative' Prussian values were to be brought to bear in the Wilhelmstrasse again, even the Kaiser's military entourage would soon become friendly towards the ministry, and it would be 'quite immaterial if people then talked about a victory of the entourage'.[89] Such were Eulenburg's guiding principles in the three years 1894–7, a period during which, as Johannes Haller correctly states, he frequently advised the Kaiser to show caution and smoothed away the ever-recurring crises, but in which he also undermined the authority of the Chancellors Caprivi and Hohenlohe, making possible the ultimate establishment of the 'Bülow system' in the summer of 1897.

In a memorandum of 20 March 1894 drawn up for the Kaiser,[90] Eulenburg for the first time set out his plan for the fundamental reorganisation of the German government, which he followed systematically over the next three years. The Secretary of State in the Foreign Office, Marschall, would have to be removed, for after his clash with Kuno Moltke and August Eulenburg over Bismarck's visit to Berlin at the end of January 1894, the Kaiser's entourage would never trust him again. Bülow alone came into question as the new Foreign Secretary; if Holstein were not willing to accept him, he too would have to go. Bülow would begin by completing the reconciliation with Friedrichsruh by appointing Herbert Bismarck as ambassador to London. Caprivi too would soon have to depart because, given that 'His Majesty takes no notice whatever of the Reich Chancellor' and regarded his 'ability to direct domestic and foreign policy as non-existent', it was unlikely that he would ever 'fully recover' his confidence in Caprivi. The new Reich Chancellor would have to be Botho Eulenburg, with all his political and parliamentary experience, while the Finance Minister, Miquel, would form the 'connecting link' between the government and the increasingly militant agrarians. The combination Botho Eulenburg–Miquel–Bülow would, Philipp Eulenburg believed, be greeted in most quarters with surprisingly little suspicion.

The fact that Caprivi's dismissal was decided on in Liebenberg, where the

Kaiser had assembled (as Caprivi himself registered) 'together with all the Eulenburgs'[91] to hunt at the end of October 1894, was therefore no accident: we may see it as the direct result of Philipp Eulenburg's memorandum of 20 March 1894. In August of that year, following the North Sea cruise, Eulenburg told the Kaiser that he must now choose between Botho Eulenburg and Miquel on the one hand, and Caprivi and Marschall on the other. The choice of the first pair would entail a *coup d'état* policy with a change in the Reichstag electoral law, which the Kaiser was advocating. But Botho was 'the most important statesman Your Majesty possesses' and he would know how to manage the crisis.[92] On Philipp Eulenburg's advice a secret meeting took place between Wilhelm II and Botho Eulenburg on 1 September 1894, at which the Kaiser informed the Prussian Minister-President that he could regard himself as the next Reich Chancellor.[93] At the end of the day Holstein and Marschall were incapable of preventing Caprivi's fall, but they did succeed in forcing the resignation of Botho Eulenburg, too, with the result that Philipp Eulenburg was for the moment unable to create his 'grand combination'.

It was Eulenburg, however, who, while they were still in Liebenberg, suggested to the Kaiser the elderly Prince Chlodwig zu Hohenlohe-Schillingsfürst, who had also been recommended by the Grand Duke of Baden, as a transitional Chancellor.[94] His ultimate aim nevertheless remained, now as before, the creation for his friend Bülow of the *joyeuse entrée* into the Reich Chancellor's palace. When a new clash between Marschall and the Kaiser's entourage occurred in February 1895, Eulenburg in no way sought to retain the Foreign Secretary. On the contrary he suggested the dismissal of both Marschall and Holstein, the appointment of Bülow as Foreign Secretary with Anton Monts as Under-Secretary and – in accordance with the March memorandum – the dispatch of Herbert Bismarck to London. For 'Bernhard is the most valuable servant Your Majesty possesses, the predestined Reich Chancellor of the future', who must not be shipwrecked by a Bismarckian feud. The Kaiser would be able to work 'easily, comfortably and surely' with Bülow because he, Eulenburg, knew with certainty of Bülow's 'glowing admiration for Your Majesty and his absolute subordination to his lord's wishes'. Eulenburg even managed to convince Hohenlohe of the need for these fundamental personnel changes, so that the Kaiser would, he thought, be able to effect Bülow's appointment as Foreign Secretary calmly and without a Chancellor crisis.[95]

The next two years were nonetheless to prove much more crisis-ridden than Eulenburg had foreseen. In the Köller crisis of November and December 1895 the members of the Prussian Ministry of State brought about by their combined actions the resignation of one of their colleagues who enjoyed the Kaiser's particular confidence. When Eulenburg joined the

Kaiser's special train in Breslau and learned how decisively the Prussian Ministry of State had 'behaved like a Cabinet in a parliamentary state', he advised the dismayed monarch to allow Köller to fall and then to dismiss the 'ringleaders of the ministerial revolt', Boetticher, Marschall and the War Minister Bronsart, at the appropriate time. Hohenlohe should, however, remain in office until he died so that he could cover Bülow's rise with his name, 'which has so soft a tone'. Entirely in agreement with Eulenburg's suggestions, the Kaiser informed Hohenlohe when he returned to Berlin that Bernhard Bülow was to be his successor as Reich Chancellor. In the following spring, however, Boetticher would have to be replaced by Posadowsky and Marschall by Bülow, the latter being appointed at the same time Vice-President of the Prussian Ministry of State.[96] Soon after the receipt of this news Bülow and Eulenburg met in Merano, and Eulenburg was able to inform the Kaiser that Bülow would present himself 'whenever, however and wherever' the Kaiser wished, 'without hesitation and full of joy and gratitude'.

These apparently perfected plans for an early reorganisation of the government were thrown into disarray in March 1896 by a 'conspiracy' on the part of Holstein, Marschall and Bronsart, who wanted to force Hohenlohe into taking a firm stand with the Prussian Ministry of State against the Kaiser. In pursuit of their objective they intended to exploit the popular Courts Martial Bill, which sought to admit the public and the press to military trials and to which the Reich Chancellor had given his personal support. The purpose of the conspiracy, according to Eulenburg, was to provoke 'a decisive crisis which will destroy His Majesty's authority and deliver him bound hand and foot'.[97] The dismissal of Marschall under these circumstances would have severe consequences, Eulenburg realised, and would certainly make it impossible for Bülow to assume office in the Wilhelmstrasse in an inconspicuous manner. The latter consequently begged Eulenburg to have his appointment to Berlin delayed until the storm had died down.

Eulenburg's main concern in this very changed situation was to take the wind out of the sails of the 'conspiracy' by quietly bringing about the removal of the Prussian War Minister. A close confidant of the Reich Chancellor recognised Eulenburg's decisive influence as crisis manager to the Kaiser when he wrote in March 1896: 'I think H.M. will give way ... It is a pity that Eulenburg has arrived at the wrong moment.'[98] Eulenburg worked for a postponement of the crisis until the summer. As Hohenlohe's resignation had to be regarded as probable because of his commitment to the Courts Martial Bill, Eulenburg revived his earlier idea of making his cousin Botho Eulenburg Chancellor, so that Bülow would gain time as Foreign Secretary to familiarise himself with the situation in Berlin. This solution had the further advantage that Holstein would depart while Bülow would not have to take the blame for his dismissal. At the same time, however, Eulenburg did not lose sight of the possibility of advancing Bülow directly to the Chancellorship. For, as Eulenburg recognised, the Kaiser was 'tired of crises' and no longer wanted a transitional Chancellor, but one who would stay 'for twenty years or more'. The best solution of all in Eulenburg's view, however, remained Bülow's appointment as Foreign Secretary under Hohenlohe. 'It would be a blessing for you', he wrote to his friend in Rome, 'to be able to work with Hohenlohe for some time.'[99]

During the North Sea cruise in 1896 Eulenburg and the Kaiser had plenty of opportunity to work out an astonishingly detailed plan, one which covered every possibility, for the final resolution of the government crisis.[100] According to Eulenburg, the best thing would be for Hohenlohe to accept the dismissal of Bronsart, Marschall and Boetticher, thus respecting the 'principles and prestige' of the Kaiser. Bülow could then be appointed to the Foreign Office, taking over as Reich Chancellor on Hohenlohe's death. If, on the other hand, Hohenlohe should declare himself in solidarity with Marschall, Bronsart and Boetticher over the issue of public military trials, then they could all be dismissed and Botho Eulenburg would be appointed Chancellor with Bülow as Foreign Secretary and Vice President of the Prussian Ministry of State. In this combination, as Eulenburg explained in the programme approved by Wilhelm II and Bülow, the most versatile statesmen in the realms of domestic and foreign policy would stand together. It would indicate a 'Prussian' but nevertheless moderate direction with a bias against 'the revolution' (i.e. socialism), but not against the constitution and the Reichstag. Botho Eulenburg would exhaust his usefulness after a few years and then Bülow, richer by then in parliamentary experience, would be able to step into his position. If, as a third possibility, the Kaiser decided in favour of a *coup d'état* to change the constitution, a political general such as Waldersee would have to be appointed Chancellor. In this case Bülow would have to be kept in reserve because, after the 'violent struggles' of the *coup d'état*, new men would be needed.

Thus Philipp Eulenburg was prepared for all eventualities when, at the beginning of August 1896 in Alt-Aussee, he made his final attempt to persuade the elderly Chancellor, dependent as he was on the material advantages of office,[101] to abandon his principles – which really meant to abandon his most able and most loyal advisers. As Hohenlohe finally came to terms with the dismissal of Bronsart in the summer of 1896 and the removal of Marschall and Boetticher in the following year, and remained in office until October 1900 as (to use his own words) a 'straw doll' and a 'façade',[102] Bülow was in fact able to climb smoothly to the Reich Chancellorship, the solution which Eulenburg had consistently regarded, ever since March 1894, as the most advantageous for both the Kaiser and Bülow.

Let us now summarise the main features of Eulenburg's political activity in the years 1886–97 as we have outlined them above.

1. The *sine qua non* of Eulenburg's political influence was his friendship – which was inherent in the monarchical system in general – with Prince Wilhelm of Prussia, the future Kaiser Wilhelm II. This friendship began in May 1886.

2. Until the beginning of 1894 Eulenburg placed his incomparable (and irresponsible) influence mainly at Holstein's service. He thereby played a significant role in the dismissal of Bismarck and also in the resolution of the numerous government crises of the Caprivi period.

3. In the years 1893–4 Eulenburg used his influence from time to time to advance the cause of his friends, by which means he was able to increase his own power. It was above all his co-operation with Bülow which enabled him to assert himself increasingly against Holstein.

4. Eulenburg's independent political activity was confined to the years 1894–7, and its aim was, despite all the unforeseen 'conspiracies' and delays, to secure the Chancellorship for Bülow in as smooth a way as possible. One must characterise the 'Bülow system' as Eulenburg's chief political accomplishment. If we compare it with the hasty, impulsive decisions which led to the appointment of Caprivi, Hohenlohe and later Bethmann Hollweg, Bülow's stands out as the only carefully planned and prepared Chancellor appointment in the entire Wilhelmine era.

5. Even if Eulenburg's personal liking for Bülow played an undeniable role in this activity, the 'Bülow system' was not an end in itself, but the means to a higher end, namely the establishment of the 'personal rule' of Kaiser Wilhelm II on Conservative-imperialistic foundations.

6. After Bülow's appointment as Foreign Secretary in the summer of 1897, and even more so after he entered the Reich Chancellor's palace in October 1900, Philipp Eulenburg withdrew more and more from politics. In 1902 he gave up the post of ambassador in Vienna, and in the following years, as his letters to the Kaiser show, he played nothing like the role in German politics which his enemies (perhaps recalling his activity in the years 1894–7) were inclined to assume.

There were several reasons for Eulenburg's withdrawal from the political battlefield. With the transfer of Bülow to Berlin and the circumscription of the independent authority of the 'responsible' government with which it was associated, the crisis of government which had begun soon after Wilhelm II's accession to the throne and which Philipp Eulenburg had been reluctantly drawn into, had for the time being come to an end. Eulenburg described the 'great turning-point' of the summer of 1897 with the words:

'No more bomb-like despatches, no more wild letters from Holstein, no more lamentations from Marschall!!', and he continued: 'I feel that after nine years of frightening storms I have finally succeeded in steering the ship of the Kaiser's government – the governmental machine – into a tolerably safe harbour ... The matter is now in the able hands of Bülow, whom the Kaiser thinks of as "his Bismarck".'[103] For the time being at least, Eulenburg really could regard the 'Bülow system' as the realisation of his own ideals, making any further intervention in affairs of state superfluous. Bülow was able to strengthen him in the belief that he was the *spiritus rector* of the new order. 'I say, write, do nothing political without thinking of you', he told Eulenburg in December 1897. 'Everything which happens for the dear, dear Kaiser, happens as you would wish, and he stands constantly before me, he is for me the motive and the aim, the *raison d'être* in all things.'[104] Health problems, which would become really serious for the first time in the years 1902–4, were a further reason for Eulenburg's political restraint.[105] The most important cause, however, seems to have lain in a tangible cooling in his personal relations with the Kaiser, which hitherto had formed the basis of his political influence. This development is difficult to comprehend and to penetrate, but it is very likely that the reasons for this cooling lay in that intimate realm which, from the autumn of 1906, made headlines in the world's press and which has to a large extent moulded Philipp Eulenburg's historical reputation to the present day.

On 8 May 1908 Prince (as he had become) Philipp zu Eulenburg-Hertefeld was arrested at Schloss Liebenberg on suspicion of homosexuality and, as he was seriously ill, placed in the Charité hospital in Berlin. The trial was suspended on 17 July 1908 after eighteen days without a verdict because of the incapacity of the accused to continue with the trial. The resumption of proceedings in the following year was similarly inconclusive as Eulenburg collapsed after a few hours.

If we feel obliged here to clarify as far as possible the questions which the trials left open, we do so not just because they dominate the memoir literature and much of the historical writing on Philipp Eulenburg, over-shadowing his political activity, and because this situation will continue until these questions have received a satisfactory scholarly answer. Rather we devote particular attention to these questions of homosexuality and the occult – the two being closely associated in the eyes of contemporaries – because they illuminate the nature of the so-called 'Liebenberg round table' and above all of the friendship between Eulenburg and Wilhelm II, which, as we have shown, formed the basis of Eulenburg's political activity in the first decade of the Wilhelmine era. These questions can also convey important insights into the outlook of the All-Highest Person (whose key position owed so much to Eulenburg's influence) and of his immediate entourage.

Naturally this complex of questions requires particularly careful and circumspect treatment if for no other reason than that Philipp Eulenburg's correspondence with almost everyone named in the trial has been lost. For some unknown reason the Prussian Ministry of Justice itself destroyed all the material relating to the Eulenburg trial in 1932[106] – including, one supposes, Eulenburg's incriminating letters to the Starnberg fisherman and chief witness, Jakob Ernst.[107] It is not known whether Eulenburg's correspondence with his friend Jan Freiherr von Wendelstadt, in whose castle Neubeuern in the Bavarian Alps he had so frequently recovered from ill health, was disposed of in a similar fashion; all we know is that the letters were seized at Neubeuern by a judicial commission on 27 May 1908, and that Wendelstadt collapsed and died soon after being cited as a witness in Eulenburg's trial.[108]

We know for certain that Eulenburg himself took care to destroy other letters. At the beginning of 1885, when he was preparing an article on his relations with the racialist writer Count Gobineau for the journal *Bayreuther Blätter*,[109] he wrote to the editor that he had 'looked wistfully through the forty-five to fifty letters which this unforgettable friend had written me. On doing so it has become clear to me that they touch on so many intimate matters that I cannot extract much from them which is of general interest.' Elsewhere Eulenburg writes, concerning Gobineau's letters: 'They contain too much of an intimately personal nature.'[110] Not a single one of these letters is to be found in the Eulenburg Papers, though it is true that the family archive suffered serious fire damage in 1945.[111] Only a handful of letters from Eulenburg to Gobineau and to the Countess de la Tour are contained in the Gobineau Papers in Strassburg.[112] Maximilian Harden pointed in considerable detail to the homoerotic character of the correspondence between Fritz von Farenheid-Beynuhnen and Philipp Eulenburg, which the latter had privately published in 1897.[113] When the attacks on him began in 1906, Eulenburg had the book removed from the bookshops; and yet the originals of this correspondence have also been lost without trace. The French Secretary of Embassy Raymond Lecomte, who was a close friend of Eulenburg's from the early 1880s and whose invitation (together with Wendelstadt) to hunt with the Kaiser in Liebenberg in November 1906 was the final provocation for Harden's attack, destroyed his own papers after the catastrophe.[114] Most telling of all, however, is the fact that in 1907 Eulenburg and Kuno Moltke, as the former admitted in a sentence which was later struck from his *Aufzeichnungen*, destroyed 'the originals of our correspondence ... almost without exception, in the face of an absolutely devilish misinterpretation which was then being placed on everything which I and Moltke had ever written'.[115]

In view of these gaps in the record, we shall want to subject those items
which have survived to especially careful inspection. Particularly interesting in this regard is a letter which Eulenburg wrote after a long silence to his
friend Nathaniel Rothschild in Vienna on 17 September 1904. 'I look back
on the last few years – since our parting – as on a bad dream', he remarked.

Men, just like women, go through a period of bodily change in certain years of their
life. I believe that those men who, because of their sensitivity and their finer
disposition, possess a kind of feminine sensibility alongside their masculine activity,
are condemned to suffer a great deal more in this period than the male – cannons. I
seek to console myself with these 'period thoughts', and on your behalf I make
similar and consoling thought-excursions ... God be praised that we have an
awareness of our souls locked together in solidarity, that we can think back to our
similarly formed, sensitive natures and console each other.[116]

Less direct but much more extensive is the thirty-page memorandum
which Philipp Eulenburg wrote in 1900 on his brother Friedrich's divorce
in consequence of the latter's homosexuality. The memorandum was
intended for his close circle of friends, and Eulenburg placed a copy in the
'Liebenberg secret files'. We do not need to pay much attention to Philipp
Eulenburg's elaborate proofs of his brother's 'innocence', since he later
demonstrated what he thought of the credibility of the case he had made
when he sought to deflect the accusations against himself by claiming that
the witnesses must have confused him with his brother.[117] What is of
interest is the striking way in which the memorandum makes it clear that
Philipp Eulenburg himself felt seriously threatened by the accusations
against his brother. 'The events' of those weeks in September and October
1897 were, as he wrote, 'written in my wounded heart in flaming characters'.
When Eulenburg joined the Kaiser's special train in Vienna to accompany
him to Hungary, 'the Kaiser suddenly said to me that he had been told of my
sister-in-law's appalling accusations'. Eulenburg was 'as if struck by lightning; for I perceived at once the danger which was engulfing my unfortunate
brother'. 'Now began for me', Eulenburg continues, 'a terribly distressing
time of suffering. I sought to save what it was still possible to save because I
felt strongly that the evil spirits would hold the field of battle'. Attempts to
send Klara Eulenburg into a lunatic asylum if she refused to withdraw her
allegations foundered, and by this time would hardly have helped anyway,
for the 'rolling ball' could no longer be stopped. The Chief of the Military
Cabinet, General von Hahnke, declared that it was impossible for him to
influence proceedings in such a serious case. At the beginning of October in
the Kaiser's hunting lodge at Rominten, Eulenburg learned that the military authorities had begun taking statements from the servants. Friedrich
Eulenburg's legal adviser visited Philipp Eulenburg in East Prussia and
explained 'that he felt my brother was lost'. This conversation 'shattered me

so deeply that I almost broke down'. Eulenburg now set about doing everything possible to ensure that the trial would not be before a Court Martial because in such military courts 'extreme and merciless elements' were to be found. After a discussion with his brother's commanding officer, Colonel von Falkenhayn, Eulenburg advised his brother 'with a heavy heart' to submit his resignation from the army. After that he asked the President of the Court Martial, General Count Wartensleben, 'not to convene the Court Martial – which would mean *scandal* – but to regard the matter as closed'. But Wartensleben explained that an officer against whom proceedings were pending could not resign. Eulenburg was 'dumbstruck – and only my heart beat fit to burst'. He at once travelled to see the Kaiser in Hubertusstock – the date was 11 October 1897 – and persuaded him to issue an order stopping the convening of the Court Martial. Wartensleben, however, also made a report to the Kaiser on the matter. And in military affairs the Kaiser was acknowledged to be 'blind'. For Wilhelm II the president of a military court had an almost sacred position of total impartiality. As a result Philipp Eulenburg soon afterwards received a letter from the Kaiser informing him 'that my poor dear brother was without doubt at least partially guilty'. At the end of this remarkable memorandum appear the words: 'I know only too well, what people keep from me, what will be associated with this ... spectacular dismissal! And I do not *wish* to know it. I fear that I may boil over with wrath at this tragedy, which broke my poor old mother's heart.' And finally, directed at the reader:

Farewell, my friend! Are you certain that you have understood the story *correctly*? Please read it once again! I beg you! So that you understand completely that the path of our lives is crossed by terrible demons, and that we should raise our hands to God in supplication, begging him, begging him *fervently* to defend us from them, to defend our loved ones from them![118]

We possess further indications of the homoerotic inclinations of Philipp Eulenburg and Kuno Moltke as a result of the aristocratic-Bohemian untidiness of Axel Varnbüler. Alone among the members of the so-called 'Liebenberg round table', Varnbüler maintained relations with both friends even after the catastrophic scandals of 1908. Had he taken more care over the destruction of his correspondence with Eulenburg and Moltke, we would have been dependent on his candid but not always truthful memoirs alone for our picture of the type of friendship which existed between these three men. In the latter Varnbüler not only sought to deflect any suspicion of homosexuality from himself by comprehensive descriptions of his numerous romantic escapades with women, but, in relation to Philipp Eulenburg, he explicitly states:

Never and in no way, throughout our intimate acquaintance in all kinds of situations, did I detect a trace of homosexual perversity or depravity. There was to be sure an intense side to his male friendships which I found alien – and from which was later woven the hangman's noose. But this sprang from his intense nature in general, it manifested itself equally in the love of women – in the many flames I know he had, and in my own as well, where he was my confidant, my companion and my helpmate, and showed the finest sensitivity and understanding for the eternal-feminine which exalts us.[119]

In another place in his memoirs, Varnbüler describes the Swedish countess whom his 'multifaceted' and 'brilliant' friend Eulenburg took as his wife in 1875, and continues:

With Phili himself the hoped for 'release' from demonic forces did not last long – then and later he fell victim to sensual passion for beautiful women. He freed himself from them and recovered again in highly idealised and often enraptured male friendships – Honi soit qui mal y pense. With Gobineau, Farenheid amongst others – especially with the Kaiser, who drew him completely into politics and away from family life.[120]

However, fragments of correspondence with Eulenburg and Moltke discovered in Varnbüler's castle, Schloss Hemmingen, point to the fact that these passages in his memoirs served more to justify himself in the eyes of posterity than to aid the discovery of uncomfortable truths.

On 15 February 1891 the death occurred in St Petersburg of Karl Freiherr von Dörnberg, known to most as 'Chacha' or simply 'the little one'. On 31 March 1891 Kuno Moltke wrote to Varnbüler:

My old Dachs! I am just getting ready for the journey to Stuttgart, I'm longing for old Philine ..., have to see her [sic!] because of the feeling that now this gap [Dörnberg's death] has opened up in our beloved circle, we must hold on to each other doubly, more firmly ... Then I'll move over to Munich with P. on the 8th – the family will not follow till later.[121]

There can be no doubt who the name 'Philine' refers to: on 8 April 1891 the Prussian envoy in Stuttgart, Count Philipp Eulenburg, travelled to Munich with his friend Count Kuno Moltke, to present himself to Prince Regent Luitpold on 10 April as the new Prussian Envoy in Bavaria.[122]

When in the spring of 1898 the marriage of Kuno Moltke, by that time military attaché at the German Embassy in Vienna, collapsed as a direct result of his close relations with Philipp Eulenburg, the ambassador, Axel Varnbüler wrote Moltke a letter which not only alluded unmistakably to Moltke's 'peculiarity', but which raises the question whether Varnbüler did not himself have an androgynous personality. On 15 April 1898 he wrote to Moltke:

I know now, through Philly, what I long saw coming – had to see, my Dachs, however much I tried to close my eyes, because I felt that you did not wish to confess it to me – and understood and appreciated this proud silence, this brave lonely suffering, even in relation to your best friend ... Had you really succeeded in transforming your innermost being, renouncing the ideals which you have held high throughout your life, to step down from this exalted purity and to feel comfortable in the dull atmosphere of ordinariness – then, old Dachs, only then would you have lost yourself and I would have lost you. You could not do that, you could not allow yourself to do that – and I thank God that the excessive weight of intolerable burdens led you to a realisation and a liberation before you had injured your innermost being. And now, my Dachs, now that you are free – now come back to me, to my wide-open heart – without mistrust, without hesitation, without false shame. I will not hurt you – with questions – I do not want to know any of the details. You do not need to say a word, it is just as it always was – only that I love and treasure and admire you even more, if that is at all possible.

As the letter unfolds, Varnbüler likens his friend Moltke to Dostoyevsky's *Idiot*[123] and then continues:

Perhaps you smile, my Dachs, if you can smile again at all, at the erroneous translation of this word, which we both understood so very well, even though we cannot speak Russian. Yes, the majority of people, what we might call the world, smiles condescendingly at such figures, because it does not understand them. You too have never been fully accepted by many people ... You were not manly enough for them, not dashing enough, not worldly-wise enough.

Similarly many foolish people had 'shrugged their shoulders in pity' at Dr Albert Moll, who had published several books on homosexuality (and who was later to be called as an expert witness at the Moltke–Harden trial).[124] But at the same time there were others who understood only too well. 'They are not that few in number – not just the thinned-out ranks of the circle of friends. Think too of the departed, whose souls I feel myself so close to here [in Silesia].' Indeed even the Kaiser, according to Varnbüler, would understand him better than he perhaps thought:

And also the One, my Dachs – I'm sure I am not mistaken in thinking that your pain is sharpened because you cannot hide, keep at bay, all this ugliness from him, from the *Liebchen*. But do not torment yourself unnecessarily about this – he is man enough to put a stop to nasty gossip – and he knows and loves you too well in your peculiarity [*Eigenart*] to allow even the shadow of blame to fall upon you.[125]

When the 'nasty gossip' was published in the *Zukunft* and subsequently brought to his attention, the '*Liebchen*' – this was the Liebenbergers' term of endearment for the Kaiser – turned out not to be man enough after all to protect his old friends. The Chief of Cabinet of the King of Württemberg, Baron Soden, spoke no doubt for many when he wrote to Varnbüler in November 1907: 'The Kaiser's disfavour makes it difficult for one to believe in the innocence of E[ulenburg] and M[oltke] – especially when a man like Krupp, who was most certainly unclean in sexual matters, found favour!'[126] Possibly the Kaiser felt under too great a threat himself in this case – in contrast with the Krupp case in 1902 – to act differently. And besides, Krupp had committed suicide as soon as the rumours about him had become public. Axel Varnbüler expected nothing less of Philipp Eulenburg in the wake of the Harden case against the Munich publisher Anton Städele in April 1908!

As early as May 1906, when Holstein sought to provoke Eulenburg to a duel by means of an unmistakably libellous letter,[127] Varnbüler as Eulenburg's second had taken the view 'that only by a duel to the death can this *personal* insult be put aside', while Eulenburg declared that he would be satisfied with an exchange of letters.[128] Two years later, when Harden's attacks were laid before the Kaiser, the monarch commanded: 'Axel Varnbüler must take the matter in hand.' The Württemberg envoy was then received by Bülow, who told him of the 'incriminating evidence . . . being reported to him from all sides . . . but also of the secret reports of the political and vice police in Vienna, Munich, Berlin which were held in the Foreign Office safes'. This evidence was 'supposedly so overwhelming that it would be virtually hopeless for Phili to contest it in open court, and that at the very least it would mean a disastrous scandal for the Kaiser, as his friend, and for the well-being of the state'. Bülow begged Varnbüler to persuade Eulenburg to go on 'sick leave' abroad until the storm had died down, but Varnbüler objected that Eulenburg 'would be admitting his guilt urbi et orbi by fleeing abroad, and in this way would really compromise his friend the Kaiser'. Varnbüler was – at any rate according to his memoirs – 'not wholly without doubt' whether his old friend was 'guilty' or 'not guilty'; he therefore asked Eulenburg's legal adviser, Laemmel, as a precaution to accompany him on subsequent visits to Liebenberg. From these visits the two gained the clear impression that Eulenburg was innocent. They based their conviction on the fact that 'Phili, though physically a nervous wreck and lying in bed, was nevertheless able, with complete clarity of mind, without hesitation or reflection, to explain away, refute, render absurd all the new incriminating material which, at Bülow's repeated request, we placed before him.'[129]

All the greater, then, was Varnbüler's dismay when on 22 April 1908, once again in Silesia, he read in the newspapers the statements which the two Starnberg fishermen, Georg Riedl and Jakob Ernst, had made concerning their sexual relations with Eulenburg in the Harden versus Städele trial in Munich.[130] Severely shaken, Varnbüler wrote to Laemmel:

I have now read the devastating testimony of the witnesses in Munich – and, alone as I am here, without the opportunity to speak my mind on the matter, I direct my thoughts to you, who will be very deeply shaken, just as I am. Or do you retain the slightest glimmer of hope, the merest doubt even, which one could cling to? I do not, I see nothing but the inexorable, irrevocable fact: he is irretrievably lost.

Eulenburg's oath would not prevail against the testimony of the two
witnesses, of which Jakob Ernst's at least was 'unobjectionable', even if

he should not be further weakened in the course of the proceedings by *letters* – (what
else could have led to these witnesses?) – which *now* cannot be interpreted innocently. But that means the complete collapse of his whole existence ... But still more
dreadful than this outward catastrophe is the inward collapse of belief in one's
friend. That he lied to us, swore to us falsely – that could be forgiven as an act of
desperation by a man hounded almost to death, if he does it not just on his own
behalf, but also to save the honour of his family, of his name. But then he would be
compelled to pass sentence on himself before being judged by others – inconspicuously departing this life, as his illness would make possible.

Perhaps, thought Varnbüler, Eulenburg had intended to do this in the
extreme case, and had now been caught out 'like all of us, by the devilishly
skilful surprise attack of his opponent'.

But E. should not have allowed everything to depend on such a possibility – *he* knew
the danger, he *alone* should not have played va banque ... Endless sympathy – how
could one not feel that for one who has fallen so low – but that is too little for him –
for him to go on living, relinquishing life is even now the most merciful course of
action, even if it can no longer save him and his family from disgrace ... And yet
doubts at least could remain – gradually solidifying into *belief* amongst those around
him ... And at least it would be a tragic end – an end at last to all this nauseating
filth.

Varnbüler seriously asked himself 'whether it was not his ultimate duty as
his friend' to persuade Eulenburg to commit suicide. 'And if I were standing
before him at this moment – God knows, I would say it to him.' He could
not write, as a member of the family might open the letter for Eulenburg.
'And going to see him, that is something I cannot do any more, I cannot take
that responsibility vis-à-vis my official position nor my family.' Varnbüler
therefore asked Laemmel to go to Liebenberg and advise Eulenburg to take
his life. 'In my name as well, I empower you to do this, you may even read
this letter out to him. It is a terribly heavy responsibility, but I would carry
it – before God and my conscience. However hard and cruel it may seem, it
would still be the greatest act of compassion.'[131]
    On the following day Varnbüler telegraphed to Laemmel that he had
written in his first surge of agitation; Laemmel should not act on the letter
for the time being.[132] When the castle where for twenty years the Kaiser had
stayed with his retinue fell silent, when 'all members of court and military
circles avoided [Eulenburg] as though he were a criminal and a leper',[133]
when old friends like Alfred von Bülow failed 'the test of friendship'[134] and
members of Eulenburg's family 'shamefully distanced themselves from
Liebenberg',[135] when even Moltke declined repeated invitations to Liebenberg, Axel Varnbüler was alone among Eulenburg's old friends to remain

faithful to him. But this in no way meant that he had altered his judgment on Philipp Eulenburg. In a letter to Kuno Moltke of 24 October 1912, a letter which combined human compassion with a devastating indictment of Eulenburg, Varnbüler explained why he still visited Liebenberg:

He [Eulenburg] adheres to the fiction that he is innocent and that I believe this – and I accept the fiction even though I do not believe it. With the *single* reproach: 'Why do *you* not fight your trial through to its bitter end as a matter of life or death' – one could destroy the whole theatrical pathos of his accusations and protestations. But this pose, before his family and a few friends whom he hopes to hold on to in this way, is his very last support – I do not have the heart to destroy it for him. And neither do you.[136]

Statements such as these from the authentic correspondence between these two best friends, which has, it must be remembered, come down to us only in very fragmentary form, leave no room for doubt. Philipp Eulenburg was, if not homosexual in the narrower sense of the term, certainly homoerotically inclined and therefore – since he was also drawn towards women – bisexual.[137] It is now generally recognised that people cannot be classified as *either* hetero- *or* homosexual, as in the past even self-styled progressive spokesmen such as Harden axiomatically assumed. Instead there are various intermediate stages between these extremes into which Philipp Eulenburg and some of his friends surely fitted. Eulenburg fathered eight children, he led in many ways an exemplary family life and besides this, as Varnbüler and others attest, he conducted occasional adulterous affairs with other women.[138] Kuno Moltke's marriage may have rapidly foundered, but there is also unambiguous proof that Eulenburg's beautiful cousin, Gisela von Hess-Diller, wanted to get divorced in order to marry Moltke.[139] Axel Varnbüler on the other hand made many enemies because of his adulterous love-life, and yet we have been able to notice homoerotic tendencies in his case too.[140] Such fine distinctions perished, however, in an intellectual climate in which, following the teachings of the Heidelberg psychiatry professor, Emil Kraepelin, 'contrary sexual proclivities' were classified along with 'idiocy', 'cretinism' and 'congenital feeblemindedness' as a form of 'lunacy'.[141] In consequence, Eulenburg and Moltke would almost certainly have been convicted in their trials had the former not been declared unfit to be questioned[142] and the latter not sought an out-of-court settlement involving the payment of 40,000 marks 'damages' to Harden.[143]

This observation necessarily leads to the question whether Kaiser Wilhelm II really knew 'nothing of the whole business' and 'considered it a crime'.[144] It does indeed seem implausible, even given the Kaiser's proverbial lack of human understanding. As early as the autumn of 1888 Herbert Bismarck was told by a court official 'that H.M. loves Ph. Eulenburg more than any other living being'.[145] What Chancellor Bismarck thought of the relationship between the young Kaiser and Eulenburg, he did 'not wish to commit to paper'; therefore, as he wrote in a letter to his son, 'I will not *write down* very much that I want to talk to you about.'[146] Eulenburg's letters to the Kaiser, above all in these early years of their friendship, exhibit – as do Bülow's letters to Eulenburg – a degree of enthusiasm which seems remarkable, at any rate to modern sensibilities: 'Your Majesty has thrown me into transports of joy with his gracious letter with its rich contents, and I must take the greatest care to control myself so that I do not write four pages expressing my gratitude! Your Majesty knows very well – without my saying it – what feelings gripped me when I saw the beloved handwriting!'[147] Certainly within the close circle of friends the nature of the relationship between Eulenburg and the monarch was no secret. In November 1890 Varnbüler reported to Kuno Moltke on the 'half embarrassed joy and enthusiasm' with which Eulenburg had shown him and Karl Dörnberg 'the innumerable photographs that Kistler had taken on the North Sea cruise. Your beloved Kaiser and he always in innermost union. H.M., as Dörnberg says, alas looks for the most part fat and common – but I could not bring myself to say this to Philly.'[148] When after 1897 one crisis followed another, the Kaiser, too, became aware of the danger of a scandal. Eulenburg expressed his 'deepest, most heartfelt gratitude' for the 'tender, the indescribably friendly, self-suffering way in which He wrote to me' that the charges against his brother Friedrich had been partly substantiated.[149] When a year after Friedrich Eulenburg's divorce, Moltke's marriage came to an end, Kaiser Wilhelm II learned the first details from Axel Varnbüler. 'The *Liebchen* accosted me in the Tiergarten the day before yesterday', Varnbüler wrote to Moltke on 4 June 1898. 'After he had duly admired my yellow boots and colour co-ordinated riding costume, he asked me: "Don't you know anything about Kuno? I can't get anything out of either him or Philly."' In the course of the conversation the Kaiser made use of some 'unrepeatably energetic expressions' which convinced Varnbüler 'that he was extremely well informed and no longer retained any illusions'.[150] In spite of the cooling off in the relationship between Wilhelm II and Philipp Eulenburg which set in around the turn of the century – probably directly because of the threat of disclosures – even foreigners continued to be struck by the intimacy between the two men.[151] The pain which Eulenburg nonetheless felt because of the way in which the monarch increasingly distanced himself can be seen from a letter which he wrote to Varnbüler soon after he had, with great difficulty, resolved his libel affair with Holstein in May 1906: 'I had a long, very heated discussion with H.M. about Hol[stein], and very disagreeable it was for me. He will not forgive me, if he should later hear anything concerning my affairs, that I have said not a word to him about what has taken place.'[152] Those whom kings love they also cast down with ease.

Wilhelm II's reaction to the news that the Eulenburg trial had been broken off on 17 July 1908 remains incomprehensible. He telegraphed Bülow in an excited tone, saying that he was 'very unpleasantly surprised' at the 'sudden calamitous decision' of the court. 'The whole business has been in vain, and the *Schweinerei* will start all over again! . . . On the one hand the doctors declare him unfit to give evidence, on the other he gives a long speech in his defence! How can these two things go together? The trial should have continued, even if E[ulenburg] is consumed by the flames.'[153] In his agitated state the Kaiser had clearly not perceived that he himself, together with a row of other highly placed persons,[154] including perhaps even the Reich Chancellor,[155] might also have been consumed by the flames if the Eulenburg trial had continued. For Harden believed that he had in his possession additional incriminating material about the All-Highest Person, and he would certainly not have been afraid to exploit it as a last resort. He had in any case come to the conclusion during the course of the trial that the root of the evil lay not just in the influence of a clique of irresponsible advisers but in the character and the 'personal rule' of Kaiser Wilhelm II.

On 15 November 1908, at the height of the *Daily Telegraph* crisis, Harden wrote to Holstein that if Bülow fell and Marschall von Bieberstein became Chancellor the 'united fairies' would be able to breathe again.

But they do not know what I know, and that is that I am firmly determined this time to protect no-one. I mention the [Eulenburg] 'affair' because it seems to me the fundamental cause of the present crisis. Since then, complete loss of balance at the top. One thing after another . . . [The Chancellor] knows, of that I am convinced, that his evaluation in history depends upon his conduct during the present days. But he is perhaps making the mistake of thinking that the possibilities of intimidation by the Liebenberg party are the greater as long as my trump card is held back. I no longer have any confidence in promises and reservations; this monarch will *never* change, and is simply in the hands of blackmailers . . . To clear ourselves of shame and ridicule, we will *have* to go to war, soon, or face the sad necessity of making a change of imperial personnel on our own account, even if the strongest personal pressure had to be brought to bear. (Or I could say: even if we had to do things in 'Earnest').[156]

How accurately Harden had hit the target with this last sentence can be seen from a letter which Philipp Eulenburg wrote to Wilhelm in May 1888, only days before the latter's accession to the imperial throne: 'Yesterday I rowed on the Starnbergersee to Berg, with that certain fisherman Jakob, and thought back to our excursion in 1886. Jakob still pays homage to the old principles.'[157] Following the November crisis of 1908 and the sudden death of the Chief of the Military Cabinet while he danced for the amusement of the Kaiser, if the news had broken that Wilhelm II had once rowed on the Starnbergersee, however innocently, with Jakob Ernst, the chief witness against Philipp Eulenburg, the effect would have been devastating and might well have led to the Kaiser's abdication.

The correspondence between Eulenburg and Kaiser Wilhelm II does not, then, permit a wholly unambiguous answer to the question to what extent the Kaiser was aware of the homoerotic basis of his friendship with Eulenburg. That correspondence does, on the other hand, provide a clearer picture of the role played by spiritism in their friendship, at any rate in its early stages.

Philipp Eulenburg has possibly suffered even longer from accusations of spiritism than from those concerning 'abnormal sexual tendencies'. At the time of Harden's attacks, the assertion that Liebenberg was a 'nest of spiritism' was not without a certain justification. Led by Edmund Jaroljmek, whom the family had taken over as private tutor from Countess Stubenberg, the mother-in-law of Eulenburg's eldest son, the Eulenburg children organised, as Varnbüler reports in his memoirs, 'secret spiritist seances, in a darkened chamber lined in black, with fraudulent apports and incarnations'.[158] It was the youngest son Karl, according to his godfather Varnbüler, who more than any of the others 'sank deep into mystical occultism, tried for days on end in a darkened room to cut off all conscious thoughts and, following Rudolf Steiner's theosophic prescription, make himself receptive to higher inspirations and perceptions'.[159] Karl Eulenburg left the family home together with his sister 'Lycki' (Augusta) when the latter married Jaroljmek against her father's wishes. During the trials the family were in constant anxiety lest Jaroljmek should appear as a prosecution witness against Philipp Eulenburg.[160] He did not do so, but Eulenburg nevertheless pursued him for the rest of his life with a hatred which bordered on the pathological. 'There is no more evil or *dangerous* force than hatred', Adine, his eldest daughter, wrote in August 1912. 'Papa is in the grip of such a force, his hatred for J[aroljmek].'[161]

The most gifted of Eulenburg's sons, the composer Sigwart, who was to be killed in action in Galicia in 1915, also succumbed to the attractions of spiritism, in this case embodied in Axel Varnbüler's Russian wife Natasha. In his memoirs Varnbüler writes that his wife 'bewitched [Sigwart] upstairs in her spiritual tower during my long absences in Berlin'.[162] According to Varnbüler, 'the most active of this clique' who, following the current fashion, gradually moved from spiritism to Rudolf Steiner's anthroposophy, was Eliza (Lissa) von Moltke, the Swedish wife of the 'unfortunate Chief of the General Staff'. In striking parallel to events in the Eulenburg and Varnbüler households, Helmuth von Moltke's daughter bore the child of her music teacher, an ardent spiritist, who divorced in order that he could marry her. 'Helmuth [Moltke], who had fallen for the swindle, was from then on a broken man, but could nonetheless not free himself from Lissa's spell, and he followed her as she moved from spiritism to the theosophy and anthroposophy of Rudolf Steiner, whose disastrous influence still worked on him during the world war, all the way to the battle of the Marne.'[163] With so much smoke in the air, it was not surprising that contemporaries tended to believe Harden when he shouted 'fire'.

Varnbüler nevertheless claimed emphatically that Philipp Eulenburg held himself completely aloof from his children's spiritist activities: he was 'only rarely in Liebenberg, was completely uninvolved in them [and] hardly knew of their existence'.[164] This statement seems suspect, however, if for no other reason than because from 1902 onwards, that is, during the years when the seances were taking place, Eulenburg was almost exclusively in Liebenberg. Direct proofs of his continued interest in spiritism (or 'spiritualism'[165]) and in 'faith healing' are, it is true, sparse. Countess Mathilde Stubenberg recounts in a memoir of January 1915 how she discovered her clairvoyant powers around 1904 when she was moved to say three times to Eulenburg, who had for months lain ill in bed, 'Stand up and walk' – whereupon the prince had been cured of his malady.[166] When Eulenburg had recovered, he wrote the letter already partially quoted to his friend Nathaniel Rothschild in Vienna, in which he seemed to believe in the reincarnation of 'similarly inclined' beings.

During my illness I preserved this sense [of solidarity] in my mind as a superior good; at one moment almost painfully yearning, at another more peaceful, looking out over distant clouds in which souls attuned to each other meet to undertake new – more beautiful – tasks. For only in this way can we understand the *completely immaterial* sense of belonging which people in certain groups have for each other. Otherwise what meaning would this *purely spiritual* process have in which very clear traces of a pre-existence of perfect harmony are to be found?[167]

Reports from the late 1880s and early 1890s are much more concrete and numerous. In March 1892, for instance, Eulenburg recommended the hypnotist Gössel to the sceptical Holstein. Gössel possessed 'a quite extraordinary excess of animal magnetism' and at the same time an '*undeniable* gift of clairvoyance', Eulenburg claimed, which enabled him to recognise diseases and, 'by the application of his magnetic powers', with great regularity to cure them.[168] One year earlier, in April 1891, Eulenburg had himself been examined by a clairvoyante in the presence of Kuno Moltke, this time with evidently less successful results, for Moltke reported soon after to Varnbüler: 'Philine writes to me that he feels absolutely dreadful – in spite of the clairvoyante who felt him in the rectum and gave him such helpful guidelines for his behaviour.'[169] It is a striking fact that at this time Eulenburg's spiritist experimentations always met with rejection even amongst his family and close friends, with the sole exception of his aunt, Klara Baroness Esebeck.[170] In the summer of 1888 Varnbüler wrote to

Kuno Moltke that Eulenburg's cousin Gisela von Hess-Diller had found the 'spiritism staged by Philly with wobbling tables . . . clearly horrifying'.[171] If even his mother, who in almost all other matters was so close to him, condemned these practices,[172] it is no wonder that Bismarck's son-in-law, Count Kuno Rantzau, could write soon after Eulenburg's transfer from Munich to Oldenburg: 'I wish Eulenburg all the best, but I am heartily glad that he can now play his spiritist mumbo-jumbo in a different setting.'[173] Similarly it was not surprising that rumours continuously circulated, to the effect, for instance, that 'Herr von Varnbüler and also Count Philipp Eulenburg are spiritists, and the Prussian Envoy in Munich [Eulenburg] stands high in the estimation of H.M. precisely because of this intellectual tendency.'[174] This was claimed by the National Liberal Reichstag deputy Prince Heinrich von Schönaich-Carolath, a nephew of the Silesian magnate Guido Count Henckel von Donnersmarck, on the eve of the *Kladderadatsch* campaign which began in December 1893. Almost a decade later, when even the Kaiser felt obliged to 'warn [Eulenburg] about [his] spiritism' because the Social Democrats were waiting 'to make things unpleasant [for him] in public over this matter', Eulenburg replied:

Your Majesty will have realised that, since Your accession, I have never spoken of supernatural things on a spiritist basis and, when asked, have given only an evasive answer. I wish to have a clear conscience about not having led the Kaiser to views or experiments which could mean that in the eyes of the public he could be labelled as a spiritist.[175]

Against this it must be said that spiritism was a significant element in the friendship between Eulenburg and Prince Wilhelm from the beginning, that this interest was at times deliberately fanned by Eulenburg in order to strengthen the friendship while it was still in its early stages, and that this theme continued to play a not unimportant part in the correspondence between the two friends for at least eighteen months after Wilhelm's accession to the throne on 15 June 1888.

The first discussion of spiritist questions evidently took place at the beginning of August 1887, when Prince Wilhelm visited the Eulenburg family in Starnberg. On the following day Eulenburg sent the prince a comprehensive account of a seance which had been held at the home of the invalid Prince Rudolf Liechtenstein. In an accompanying letter Eulenburg wrote: 'I was overjoyed that we find ourselves in agreement in this area as well, and it has shown me clearly yet again how *very* lucky I have been to meet Your Royal Highness! To be understood in all things *so* well, that is *true* happiness!' At the same time Eulenburg felt obliged, in this first written communication about 'supernatural' questions, to warn Prince Wilhelm earnestly about the dangers of a premature public utterance on the subject:

With reference to our discussion yesterday about 'things eternal', I should like to urge Your Royal Highness once more to exercise the greatest caution. Many people – indeed the majority of our most splendid fellow citizens – totally lack any appreciation of the miraculous ... So if Your Royal Highness were openly to speak his *true* opinions on this subject, many would withdraw their respect for Your Royal Highness, or at the least a contemptuous regret would creep in. But hostile elements would trumpet forth that Your Royal Highness had joined the spiritists.

There was, however, Eulenburg asserted, 'a strong current' running in favour of spiritism, with the result that within a few years the government would be forced to take a position on the subject. 'And then the time will come', Eulenburg continued, 'when Your Royal Highness will be able to contribute his views in a most telling way.'[176] After his royal friend had become Crown Prince, Eulenburg wrote to him that he had 'experienced the most amazing things ... in the realm of spiritism, genuine things that convince me *totally* of the continued existence of the individual after death'. On this subject he had 'much to tell – but *when* will, when can that be?'[177] On 16 December 1888, by which time Wilhelm had already been German Kaiser for seven months, Eulenburg had an hour-long private audience with him, during which spiritism was discussed 'in detail'.[178]

Some weeks before this discussion took place, Eulenburg had again written of the danger which the Kaiser would face if he were to fall into the hands of spiritist mountebanks. 'The humbug in this area is terrible', he warned; 'I respectfully request that Your Majesty only avails himself of *my* mediation in these sensitive and exciting matters.'[179] When in February 1889 Eulenburg's sister felt obliged to advise her brother not to engage in further discussions on questions such as these with the Kaiser, Eulenburg reacted irritably: 'Your concern about the Kaiser's spiritism is quite unnecessary', he replied. 'When he was still Prince Wilhelm, we spoke about these matters – just as you speak about everything to the person who is your friend. How can the Kaiser now suddenly stop talking about them?' But Eulenburg sought to mollify his sister with the argument that he was far from wanting to 'influence' the Kaiser in such a direction. 'I cannot help the fact that, by the time I got to know him, Prince Wilhelm already *firmly* believed in ghosts and other such things; it is a part of his mystical inclination.' His sister should completely calm herself, since 'I shall certainly not take upon myself the colossal responsibility of influencing the character of this splendid Kaiser in a disconcerting way.'[180] Only a few months later, however, when he was arming himself for his first North Sea cruise with his 'splendid Kaiser', Eulenburg provided himself with spiritist material with the aim of entertaining the Kaiser when the time was right. In June 1889 he wrote to the Munich spiritist Bernhard Forsboom: 'I have set aside things to tell my friend [Wilhelm II] when we are living side by side on board ship, and they will interest him enormously ... So much in life depends on the "right timing". He who understands how to exploit this will always come out on top.'[181]

In December of the same year, Eulenburg noted in his diary that once again he, together with Forsboom and another expert on spiritism, Professor du Prel, had heard 'the most extraordinary things' from the mouth of a certain Frau Schremmel, 'amongst other things the contents of the Kaiser's last letter to me'.[182] In the light of evidence such as this, it is not possible to dismiss the following well-known entry of 18 November 1891 in Count Waldersee's diary as 'a lot of rubbish', as Johannes Haller tries to:

In the highest place it is believed that it is possible to rule alone, to understand *everything*, to know *everything* best, while in reality no aim is clearly understood, nothing is properly understood ... Is that really too bleak a view? Only today I have learned the following for the first time. Philipp Eulenburg was earlier strongly urged not to strengthen the Kaiser in his spiritist leanings. During the first North Sea cruise he kept to this, as I was able to observe in detail. Apparently things had already changed by the time of the second cruise. During his last visit to Munich the monarch was brought into direct contact with a female spiritist by Eulenburg, I guess in the Legation hotel. While she was in a trance she was asked by the Kaiser, of whose presence she was allegedly unaware, what he was to make of a friend in Russia – obviously an allusion to the Tsar. If the lord can be influenced in this way, the well-being of the Fatherland lies irretrievably in the hands of swindlers. Friedrich Wilhelm II and Bischoffwerder![183]

Whatever abhorrence we may feel for Maximilian Harden's persecution of homosexuals and whatever sympathy we may have for a man who with his family was tragically thrown down from the highest summit into the abyss, the political motive behind Harden's campaign against the Eulenburg 'Camarilla' must be seen to have had some justification. In a monarchical system of government such as that practised in Prussia-Germany, where the tradition of absolutism had not been broken but merely overlaid with constitutional forms, the character traits of the Kaiser were, as Eulenburg himself recognised, of central political significance. Amongst the crowned heads of modern Europe, Kaiser Wilhelm II stands out as a monarch who was imbued to an almost pathological degree with the 'will to power', as well as with an indefinable sense of mission. Because at the same time he was highly impulsive and easily influenced, those who came into regular contact with him or who for other reasons enjoyed his confidence were able not only to exercise an often decisive influence over the domestic and foreign policy of the Reich, but also to mould the personality of the Kaiser in an enduring way. The fact that Wilhelm II surrounded himself almost exclusively with military people, for instance, explains in part the 'autistic' nature of German armaments policy before 1914 to which Volker Berghahn has drawn attention.[184] Similarly, the inability of the tiny group of leaders headed by the Kaiser to collect realistic information about the domestic and foreign position of the Reich, and to arrive at rational political decisions on the basis of that information, is no doubt connected with the fact that for almost two decades the Kaiser's most intimate friends were convinced that they were different and indeed transcendentally superior. Especially in the years 1888–97 they frustrated every attempt by the 'responsible government' to go over to a more open, more constitutional system by invoking their 'friendship' and 'love' for the Kaiser. Phenomenologically speaking, therefore, the Harden–Holstein campaign of 1906–8 should be seen as an attack on favouritism, which is symptomatic of monarchical systems in the stage of decay. The events of 1908 did not bring about a fundamental change – rather, as Count Zedlitz-Trützschler noted in his diary, they led to an intensification of military influence over the Kaiser.[185] But this was due less to the fact that Reich Chancellor Bülow played, for whatever reason, a remarkably ambiguous role in these events, and allowed many people (such as the Chief of the General Staff von Moltke) *still to remain* in the most senior positions',[186] than to the fact that the opponents of the 'Liebenberg round table', while they wanted to make the old system work better, were not willing to draw the Reichstag and the public into the process of political decision-making. And so even after 1908 the 'mightiest throne on earth' remained the heart of the German system of government, and it continued to be dominated by forces who had no better answer to the new challenges arising from modern industrial society than the old Prussian-militaristic prescription of a short, victorious war. In so far as these challenges drove the old ruling elite more tightly than ever into a corner without undermining its real power, the Eulenburg and Moltke trials, just like the *Daily Telegraph* crisis, were in fact, as the Kaiser said in 1927 in Holland, a 'first blow' against the monarchy, the shock of which was absorbed by Philipp Prince zu Eulenburg-Hertefeld as the 'sacrificial martyr'.[187]

3   The Kaiser's court

As Germany under Kaiser Wilhelm II approached the apogee of its industrialisation, there simultaneously occurred a 'monstrous'[1] blossoming of a court culture of a kind not seen before in the whole of its history. Whether they enthused over the 'splendour of the Crown'[2] in that 'magnificent imperial epoch',[3] or alternatively complained about the 'bombastic character, the showy glitter and ostentation'[4] of this phenomenon, contemporaries were united in their view that, alongside its rise to preeminence as an industrialised Great Power, alongside the universally admired organisation of its state and military institutions, the Wilhelmine Reich was characterised by the efflorescence of a sumptuous neo-absolutist court culture. Yet this key aspect of German history has until recently barely been touched upon by historians of the period.

The reasons for this neglect can be indicated only briefly here. After both 1918 and 1945 there were weighty political motives behind the attempts to trivialise the role of the Kaiser and of his court. During the Weimar Republic the historical profession was preoccupied by the war guilt question and by the trauma of 1918. To the historians of the time, who were almost without exception of a 'patriotic' disposition,[5] it seemed wiser, for reasons both of domestic and of foreign policy, to concentrate on Frederick the Great and Bismarck as formative historical influences and to pass over in silence not only the widespread aspirations to 'world power' but also the absolutist speeches and marginalia of Wilhelm II, the scandal-ridden court society and the gradual corruption of the old Prussian civil service and officer corps by the Byzantinism of the Kaiser's court. To this 'national' historiographical tendency was added after 1945 a new preoccupation with the southern, Catholic tradition, and with the liberal and social democratic impulses of the German past, and these needless to say also distracted attention from the Hohenzollern court. Those historians who did concern themselves with the state organs of the Kaiserreich were inclined to paint a one-sidedly bureaucratic or legalistic picture. A preference was shown for the history of official institutions and of the constitution, politics was confused with administration, the written constitution with constitutional reality, the political structure of the Reich – even after Bismarck's fall from power – was seen as a hierarchy of officialdom headed by the Reich Chancellor. The Kaiser and his court remained outside the field of vision or at the most they received mention as unexplained factors suddenly disrupting the political process.[6]

When at the end of the 1960s this narrow approach began to be widened, it was primarily the abstract explanatory models of Max Weber – further wrung dry of their original historical content by American sociologists – which attracted adherents in Germany.[7] However necessary and fruitful these new investigations into the interrelationship of state and society, of administration and economy, may have been, they distracted attention still further away from the political and social role of the court. Weber's interpretation of modern history as the process of 'rationalisation' and 'demystification' could not further an understanding of the significance of court ceremonial and dynastic ritual. The reception of the 'structuralist-functionalist' approach in Germany would not have been so all-embracing, however, if, on the one hand, all forms of anthropology had not been discredited by the excesses of the Third Reich, and, on the other, the psychoanalytic element of historiography had not been literally wiped out by the persecution of the Jews under National Socialism. It can only be a question of time, however, before the anthropological and psychological impulses, which have already produced such rich fruit in American, British and French historiography,[8] are also applied in the German context. The works of Norbert Elias,[9] Jürgen Freiherr von Kruedener[10] and Nicolaus Sombart[11] are harbingers of this development.

The need for a serious investigation of the Wilhelmine court is also becoming clearer as a result of empirical research. Three major editions of documents have recently provided the historian with unprecedented insight into the decision-making mechanisms, the attitudes and the behavioural patterns of the Wilhelmine *classe politique*. The four-volume edition of the 'secret papers' of Friedrich von Holstein,[12] the three-volume edition of the political correspondence of the Kaiser's best friend, Philipp Eulenburg,[13] and the four volumes of Badenese documents on imperial politics from 1871 to 1907,[14] all demonstrate unmistakably how the Hohenzollern court continued to be the focus of political and social life in Germany down to the outbreak of war in 1914, and indeed how it grew in size and significance during the Wilhelmine period. These sources enable us to understand the central historical significance both of the power struggle of the 1890s between the court and the state which led to the 'Bülow system' with its total dependence, in the final analysis, on the Kaiser,[15] and also of the rivalries among the various groups at court, which, as Isabel Hull has shown in her perceptive study of the Kaiser's entourage,[16] ended in 1908 with the triumph of the military retinue.

Although these research findings have now been documented in the finest detail, they nevertheless encounter scepticism and rejection in certain quarters and in particular among German social and structural historians. Perhaps it is unavoidable that historians whose primary concern is with the theoretical relationship between the state and society, or those who wish to demonstrate the dependence of the organs of the Reich and the state on industrial and agrarian interest groups, are unable to show much understanding of the role played by the Kaiser and his court in the formation of German policy. By virtue of their approach they are almost necessarily forced to view the complex decision-making mechanisms of the German Reich from the outside and from below. Occasionally they fall prey to the temptation to project 'modern' concepts into the past and thus overlook the extent to which the remarkably undeveloped Wilhelmine state structure had *not yet* been penetrated by the 'principle of state omnipotence' which would ultimately, as Bülow recognised in 1899, 'negate monarchy by the grace of God, undermine the whole monarchical principle and pave the way for a republic'.[17] To illustrate the political and social significance of the Prusso-German court under Kaiser Wilhelm II even to these sceptics, the following analysis will employ those methodologies favoured by social historians. We shall examine the financial and bureaucratic foundations which underlay the so-called 'personal rule' of Kaiser Wilhelm II. In the first section we shall analyse the financial disbursements of the Prusso-German state for the Wilhelmine court in an attempt to provide a quantified answer to the question whether the Kaiser's court should be seen as the 'swansong' of absolutism or as a 'late blossoming' of an old culture which was nipped in the bud by the coming of the war.[18] In the second section, the internal administrative structure of the court, and in the third the size, social composition and behaviour patterns of court society will be examined. In the concluding section we shall make some brief general observations on the role of the court in an era of rapid industrialisation and growing state power.

The trend which set in towards the end of the nineteenth century in all developed states, of increasing state expenditure, is undoubtedly one of the most powerful formative developments of the modern epoch. In all the countries of Europe – and particularly in Germany, where parliamentarism can hardly be said to have put down deep roots – the relative power of the legislature lessened while that of the executive increased. In Germany at the beginning of the 1870s annual Reich expenditure amounted to 813 million marks; by 1908 this had nearly doubled, to 1,503 million marks.[19] Prussian state expenditure rose during the first twenty years of the reign of Kaiser Wilhelm II from an annual 318 million marks to an annual 798 million marks.[20] Expenditure on the army and navy cost the Reich and the federal states 440 million marks in the year 1881, and this had risen to 1,056 million marks by the year 1907.[21] The question now arises whether expenditure on the Kaiser's court fell as a proportion of expanding state expenditure, stayed approximately the same, or increased. This question can be answered relatively unambiguously on the basis of the civil list. The first Prussian civil list, the *Krondotation* or Crown Endowment, was set at an annual rate of 2,500,000 talers (equivalent to 7,719,296 marks) by an ordinance of 17 January 1820. The Prussian Landtag later increased this sum four times in all: in 1859 by 1.5 million marks; in 1868 by 3 million marks; on 20 February 1889 by 3.5 million marks and on 17 June 1910 by a further 3.5 million marks.[22] During the reign of Wilhelm II the Prussian civil list therefore rose from 12.2 million marks to 19.2 million marks, i.e. by more than 50 per cent. The German Kaiser did not receive civil list payments as such, but from 1874 onwards the Reichstag granted him an 'Allerhöchster Dispositions-fonds' which at first amounted to only 300,000 marks annually but between 1889 and 1918 climbed to no less than 3 million marks per year.[23] Represented as a curve on a graph[24] these increases show that the noticeable growth in civil list payments of the period 1859–68 continued throughout the Wilhelmine epoch. With an income from state revenues of 22.2 million marks annually, the court of Kaiser Wilhelm II cost more than the Reich Chancellor, the Reich Chancellery, the Foreign Office (including the whole of the diplomatic corps and consular service), the Colonial Office and the Reich Justice Administration put together.[25] Measured in terms of the civil list, then, the Prusso-German court grew constantly between the Napoleonic War and the First World War, even if at not quite the same rate as state expenditure in general began to grow towards the end of the nineteenth century.[26]

The civil list is certainly an interesting criterion for measuring the size and significance of the court, but it is not of course a very complete one. Two elements which were an essential feature of the Prusso-German court hardly figured in these statistics at all: the three politically important Secret Cabinets (for civil, military and naval matters respectively) were financed separately; and only 50,000 marks annually appeared in the Crown accounts for the ever-present 'military retinue' because the army and navy officers serving in the Kaiser's entourage were (like the various medical personnel) deemed to be 'on secondment' to the court.[27]

There was another important group at court for whose support the state did not need to find all the resources, namely the extended Hohenzollern family itself. Alongside the civil list, in which the appanages for each member of the family were set down,[28] there existed a very substantial house entail (*Hausfideikommiss*) which had been established by King Friedrich Wilhelm I on the basis of properties he had acquired. There was

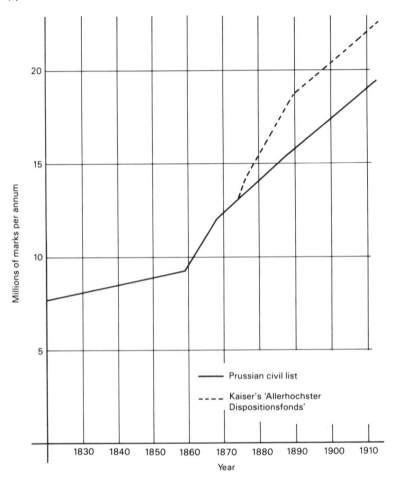

Figure 1 The growth in the Hohenzollern monarchy's civil list, 1820–1910.

furthermore the Crown Treasury (*Krontresor*), established by King Friedrich Wilhelm III. These funds were originally endowed with 18 million marks, but they were constantly enlarged, for example from French war reparations after 1815 and 1871. In 1873, a state endowment of 4.5 million marks was added to them.[29] Prince Friedrich Leopold of Prussia, cousin of Wilhelm II and brother-in-law of the empress, was among the richest members of the Hohenzollern family, even though his appanage in the civil list amounted to only 30,000 marks per annum, and this was because he possessed beneficiary rights in the family entail fund established in 1854.[30] Prince Heinrich, the Kaiser's brother, was also able increasingly to meet the costs of his household from the benefits he enjoyed from the Opatow-Swiba entail and from Burg Rheinstein. As a result of the resources of this estate, Prince Heinrich was able to 'join the ranks of those princes . . . who are not wholly dependent on their civil list appanages for their livelihood', as the Minister of the Royal Household, Count August zu Eulenburg, informed the Kaiser in 1909.[31] From 1884 onwards, the Crown Prince of Prussia-Germany was able to call on the income from the fifteen properties of the Oels estate in Silesia (10,000 hectares) which he had inherited from the Duke of Brunswick on the latter's death. The income of Ernst Günther, Duke of Schleswig-Holstein, brother of the Empress, was considered 'not overly large, but sufficient'. He received 300,000 marks annually from state resources and had in addition a private income amounting to around 200,000 marks. Even so, at the time of his sister's marriage to Wilhelm II he received an endowment of 1 million marks from the German Reich.[32] Normally a woman marrying into the Hohenzollern family would bring with her a significant dowry. Millions of marks could, furthermore, be inherited.[33] The Empress Frederick excited considerable envy in February 1891, for example, when she inherited several millions from the Duchess de Galiera which she used to finance the building of Schloss Friedrichshof in Kronberg.[34] The Prussian princes were appointed to various state and army positions for which they also received remuneration.[35]

The Kaiser himself was one of the richest people in Germany. His enormous private means were administered at first by Privy Councillor Miessner, and after his death in 1909 by the banker Ludwig Delbrück.[36] It is even more difficult for us to estimate the size of his fortune than it was for contemporaries. Rudolf Martin, the well-informed ex-official of the Reich Office of Interior, wrote in 1913, no doubt broadly accurately, in his *Jahrbuch des Vermögens und Einkommens der Millionäre in Berlin*:

Kaiser Wilhelm II is, with a fortune of 140 million marks and an income of 22 million marks, by far the richest person in the city of Berlin. In the Kingdom of Prussia, however, his fortune puts him in fifth place, even though his annual income is not equalled by anyone . . . The Kaiser's wealth does not increase at the same rapid rate as does that of Frau Bertha Krupp von Bohlen und Halbach or of Prince Henckel von Donnersmarck . . . But the Kaiser's wealth is by no means static; it is in constant upward motion and increases from year to year. The value of his unusually extensive properties in town and country is constantly and uninterruptedly growing.

Thus, according to Martin, the Kaiser received, alongside his civil list payments which had only just been raised in 1910, additional income 'stemming from his properties and his capital' which could be expected to go on increasing 'due in particular to the increasing profitability of agriculture'. The Kaiser's primary holdings consisted of 119,826 hectares with a value of more than 70 million marks and an annual net income of around 3.4 million marks. Officially the Kaiser also possessed fifty-three castles, though some of these buildings 'were not in the Kaiser's ownership but in that of the state or other people' and had been placed at his disposal 'only in return for the assumption of the costs of upkeep by the Crown entail fund in 1868'. This was the case in particular with regard to the much-used castles in the newly conquered provinces including Bad Homburg, Wiesbaden, Hanover, Celle, Osnabrück and Kassel with Schloss Wilhelmshöhe.

But the Kaiser personally owns three castles in Berlin, thirteen in Potsdam and environs and in all more than forty castles ... which together represent a very high value. The Royal Schloss in Berlin, together with its furnishings and including its valuable paintings and collections, is worth at least 20 million marks alone ... All forty castles owned by the Kaiser have with their furnishings a value of at least 40 million marks.

Besides these the Kaiser owned numerous buildings in Berlin whose value, excluding the three castles there (Königliches Schloss, Bellevue and Monbijou), was estimated at some 18 million marks. Martin put the Kaiser's liquid assets at around 20 million marks and the bank interest in the Crown Treasury on this sum at 900,000 marks per annum. He therefore came to the conclusion that the Kaiser's total wealth could be estimated at more than 140 million marks, and his annual income (including the civil list but excluding the upkeep of the royal theatres and the *Allerhöchster Dispositionsfonds*) could be estimated at around 20 million marks.[37]

This intermixing of state monies and private wealth, which is typical of the central European courts,[38] makes any international comparison difficult. In Britain a relatively clear division between the civil list and the Crown's private income had been introduced after Queen Victoria's accession. Edward VII, too, gave up his hereditary income to the Exchequer, where it was added to the 'consolidated fund'. In this way the civil list in Britain was – notionally at least – a substitute for the private income of the Crown, even if the latter remains to the present day the second greatest landowner in the country (after the state and ahead of the Anglican Church) and continues to have control of monies through the Duchy of Cornwall and the Duchy of Lancaster which do not appear in the civil list.[39] In absolutist Russia, on the other hand, there was no such thing as a civil list; all the expenses of the court and the royal household were supplied from the private means of the Crown, the extent of which remained completely unknown to the public. Only Austria-Hungary had the interlocking of state and private means which was so typical of Germany. Indeed, the family assets of the Habsburgs were even greater than those of the Hohenzollerns.[40] A further complication arises from the varying functions which had to be financed from the civil list in the different courts. The British monarch, for instance, did not have to pay for royal hunts after 1901; external upkeep of the great palaces was taken over by the state; many of the monarch's travelling expenses were met from the public purse.[41] By contrast, until 1910 17 per cent of the Prussian Crown Endowment (*Krondotation*) was earmarked for the upkeep of the royal theatres in Berlin, Hanover, Kassel and Wiesbaden.[42] Despite these difficulties, however, an international comparison of the various civil lists is instructive. Only such a comparison will make clear just how weighty an element the court was in the Wilhelmine Empire.

It was the Social Democrat Adolph Hoffmann who pointed out in 1910 that the Prussian Crown Endowment was double the size of the British civil list, even though the King of England was 'not the man to worry about every last penny' and 'despite the fact that his country is somewhat larger and also richer' than the Reich.[43] Taking into account the appanages for various princes and princesses, the British Crown under Edward VII received the equivalent of 11.6 million marks per annum.[44] By comparison, the King of Prussia and German Kaiser received, after the increase in the Crown Endowment in 1910 and including the Kaiser's *Dispositionsfonds*, the sum of 22.2 million marks, as we have seen. Only the Emperor of Austria and King of Hungary received, with 19.2 million marks, comparable support from state sources. The King of Italy received 12.8 million, the Spanish court 7.1 million marks, and the remaining non-German courts of Europe much less: Belgium 2.8 million, Portugal and Sweden 1.8 million each, Holland 1.5 and Denmark 1.2 million marks.[45] But within the borders of the German Empire could be found around twenty other courts, some of which completely overshadowed the smaller courts of Europe. The Bavarian court with its civil list of 5.4 million marks[46] stood at eighth place in the world, directly after Japan, and the Saxon court with a civil list of 4.2 million marks stood at ninth place. The courts of Württemberg and Baden and the Hessen court at Darmstadt could all stand comparison with the influential Danish court. Even Saxony-Weimar had a civil list of 1 million marks per annum.[47] The Crown Endowments of the non-Prussian courts of the German Empire together amounted to approximately 20 millions marks per annum of state subsidies. When this sum is added to the 22.2 million marks allocated to the Prusso-German court, we arrive at a grand total of over 42 million marks per annum from tax revenues for the upkeep of the courts within the territory of the German Empire, which is around four times the amount set aside for this purpose in Britain at the same time. Measured in this way, the Wilhelmine Reich was the country which, by some margin, paid most to uphold the institution of monarchy. (And this calculation takes no account whatever of the more than one hundred 'mediatised' noble families of the old Holy Roman Empire, whose equal birth and right of intermarriage with the reigning sovereign houses of Europe was recognised, and who often continued to be revered as sovereign by their own 'subjects'.) It would surely be mistaken to argue that this pre-eminence of monarchy and court society in Germany had no effect on the mentality of the middle and lower strata of the population. On the contrary, we can safely assume that both the 'caesaro-papist' and the 'hierocratic' structures[48] of the German courts – and in particular of the imperial court – percolated down to become a constituent element of the German national identity, especially as these values were vigorously propagated in the schools, the churches, the army and the universities. At the same time, however, it is also a characteristic feature of the Wilhelmine epoch that Wilhelm II himself and the archaic ceremonial and extravagant pomp of the Berlin court provoked increasing criticism on all sides.

It is not surprising that the Social Democrats in the Prussian House of Deputies voted against the increase of the Crown Endowment.[49] They calculated that, even before 1910, the Crown received 43,000 marks *daily*, the equivalent of 5,383 marks per hour, while a good worker hardly earned 1,000 marks in a year.[50] In popular parlance the *Zivilliste* was known as the *Zuvielliste*, the 'too-much list', as Hoffmann complained.[51] While the workers were abjured to practise 'hard work, fear of God, sobriety, contentment', while officers were enjoined to be 'frugal' and 'austere', while the Prussian Minister of Education could announce in the Landtag that it was questionable whether in the long run the universities could continue to be supported from public funds,[52] the Kaiser could buy a palace on Corfu for 600,000 marks, and thousands of marks could be spent 'simply on lighting up the rose bushes with electric bulbs'.[53] Economies could be introduced, according to Hoffmann, on travel, castle construction and monuments without the prestige of the German Empire suffering any damage: 'Indeed I am of the opinion that it would in fact gain in prestige by such measures'.[54] Less expected than this Social Democratic criticism but just as significant is the fact that in quite different circles there was also growing unease with the 'fripperies' of Wilhelmine court culture, as General Helmuth von Moltke termed it in 1905. In the crisis year of 1908 a newspaper close to the Catholic Centre party pointed to the fact that

the old Kaiser, even at a time of genuine splendour at the Berlin court, when Berlin was the political focus of Europe, managed to create a most worthy impression on 12,500,000 marks. His grandson draws more than a quarter more. The cost of living has not risen by a quarter since the days of the old Kaiser. If our court were conducted in a less ostentatious and less extravagant way, this would be no loss, if for no other reason than for the example it would set for the nation as a whole.[55]

At the same time a critical Junker who was standing in the Berlin municipal elections and who had examined the electoral lists wrote that he had been genuinely shocked 'at the multitude of court officials I discovered there. Page after page contained nothing but silverware servants and chamber servants, footmen and senior footmen, royal polishers and royal roast basters'. In horror he posed the question whether 'so many court officials are really necessary ... How many are employed in the royal stables alone! ... Could the numbers of horses and men not be reduced without damage to the national interest?'[56] The following section will attempt to address these questions.

The size and the complex structure of the Prusso-German court can best be illustrated by referring to the *Handbuch über den königlich-preussischen Hof und Staat*, which was published annually as an indispensable guide through the labyrinth of the vast court and state bureaucracy.[57] In the first part the members of the royal house themselves are listed. At the turn of the century they consisted of: the Kaiser, the Empress, the Kaiser's mother, the Kaiser's seven children, the Kaiser's brother and four sisters together with their spouses and children, his Aunt Luise of Baden, the widow of Prince Friedrich Karl with her children and grandchildren, the Prince Regent Albrecht of Brunswick with his sister and three children, and finally the childless, mentally disturbed Prince Georg of Prussia, born in 1826, a cavalry general. In a second section are listed the members of the Catholic line of the house of Hohenzollern. A third section contains the Principal Chamberlain's Office (Oberst-Kämmerer-Amt), which was situated at 73 Wilhelmstrasse, and the Ministry of the Royal Household, located in the same building. Alongside the two chiefs of these offices, Friedrich Count (later Prince) zu Solms-Baruth and House Minister Wilhelm von Wedell-Piesdorf, are listed a director (who was a count), three noble councillors (Vortragende Räte), a Curator of Accounts (a commoner) with the rank of Councillor (Third Class) as well as eight private secretaries, accountants, registrars and Privy Chancellery inspectors. The first department within the Ministry of the Royal Household was the Office of Heralds, responsible for matters concerning noble rank and privilege. It was headed by General Count von Schlieffen, whose deputy was Master of the Heralds von Borwitz und Harttenstein, who was ranked a Councillor (Second Class).[58] The second department was the Royal House Archive which had a noble director and employed three non-noble archivists with doctorates. The third department of the Ministry of the Royal Household was the very large Court Chamber for the administration of the royal family's estates, the *Hofkammer für die Verwaltung der Königlichen Familiengüter*. Its president, von Stünzner, carried the rank (and received the salary) of a Regierungspräsident; beneath him was a council consisting of eight Court Chamber councillors and two assistants, a secretariat with eleven accountants and

Court Chamber secretaries, a Court Chamber receiver of revenue with two further secretaries, and nine provincial buildings inspectors.[59] In addition there were in all almost one hundred leaseholders of the farms, forestries, freehold estates, throne holdings and family endowment estates belonging to the Crown.

Then the handbook takes us from the household to the court, from deep in the provinces back to the centre, from the simple leaseholder Schulz in the Jarotschin district, from the registrar Krause on the Flatow-Krojanke estate, to the noblest and richest families in the land. This next section on the Kaiser's court opens with the highest honorary posts in Prussia, with the Principal Chamberlain (Oberst-Kämmerer) Count zu Solms-Baruth, the Principal Marshal (Oberst-Marschall), the Principal Master of the Hunt (Oberst-Jägermeister) Prince von Pless, the Principal Cupbearer (Oberst-Schenk) Prince von Hatzfeldt-Trachenberg and the Lord High Steward (Oberst-Truchsess) – and Ambassador in St Petersburg – Prince Hugo von Radolin. Then follow the Senior Court Officials: first the Senior Chamberlain of the Robes (Ober-Gewand-Kämmerer) His Excellency General Count Friedrich von Perponcher-Sedlnitzky, who ranked immediately below the Prussian Ministers of State; His Excellency General Count August zu Eulenburg occupied the positions both of Senior Marshal of the Court and the Household (Ober-Hof- und Haus-Marschall) and of Senior Master of Ceremonies (Ober-Zeremonienmeister), and by virtue of his salary for the former post alone, of 18,000 marks per annum, he was on an equal footing with the Under-Secretaries of State in the Prussian ministries. The same salary was paid to the General Intendant of Royal Theatres, the hereditary Member of the Prussian House of Lords Bolko Count von Hochberg, and also to the Senior Master of the Horse (Ober-Stallmeister), Count Ernst von Wedel. The two Senior Masters of the Hunt (Ober-Jägermeister) enjoyed a position equivalent to Regierungspräsident and were therefore paid at this time a salary of 12,000 marks per annum. After these Senior Court Officials come the four Deputy Senior Court Officials, namely the Kaiser's Marshal of the Household (Haus-Marschall) Maximilian Baron von Lyncker and the Marshal of the Court (Hof-Marschall) Heinrich Baron von und zu Egloffstein, plus the two Deputy Senior Masters of Ceremonies (Vize-Ober-Zeremonienmeister) Count Kanitz and Bodo von dem Knesebeck, the latter being at the same time on attachment as Chamberlain to the Empress, Secretary to the High Order of the Black Eagle and Usher to the Diplomatic Corps at court.[60] Then follow the ordinary Court Officials: first the twenty-one Castle Governors (Schlosshauptleute), then the nine Masters of Ceremonies (Zeremonienmeister) and the six Masters of Court (Hofmeister). The next category consisted of the Gentlemen of the Court, the Kammerherren, who by the end of 1899 numbered 283; then come the twenty-nine Gentlemen of the Bedchamber (Kammerjunker) listed according to the date of their commission, all of them aristocratic gentlemen from the best families in Prussia. Then follow the Kaiser's two personal physicians, Dr Rudolf – already dignified by the addition of the aristocratic 'von' – Leuthold and Dr (not yet 'von') Ilberg. Under the title 'Keeper of the Privy Purse and Treasury' (Schatull-Verwaltung und Privat-Kanzlei) to the Kaiser we find the name of Privy Councillor Miessner, who handled much of the Kaiser's most delicate correspondence and who ended his career with a salary of over 12,000 marks, including personal allowances and an accommodation supplement for Councillors (Second Class).[61] He was assisted by a treasury accountant and a treasury secretary.

Only at this point do we reach the Ober-Hof-Marschall-Amt, the Office of the Senior Marshal of the Court which, with an establishment of no less than 510 officials, counted as 'the oldest and largest of the court authorities'.[62] From the accession of Wilhelm II this central court office was headed by a Senior Marshal of the Court and Household (Ober-Hof- und Haus-Marschall), a Marshal of the Household (Haus-Marschall), a Marshal of the Court (Hof-Marschall) as well as a Director with the rank of Councillor (Second Class).[63] Immediately under this four-man directorate the handbook lists the Institute of Court Pages, led by a Governor of Pages and consisting at any one time of two Pages in Ordinary (Leibpagen) and twenty-four Court Pages. The names which appear under these headings are exclusively noble, and some of them, such as those of Kurt von Schleicher and Franz von Papen, for example, were to crop up again in a different context later in Germany's history. The following First Department of the Office of Senior Marshal of the Court, consisting of eleven Court Secretaries and three Secretaries of the Office of Senior Marshal of the Court, was by contrast exclusively manned by commoners,[64] as was the Second Department, which consisted of the Castle Buildings Commission (nine officials), the administration of the Hohenzollern Museum in Schloss Monbijou, the Justiciary, the administration of art treasures and of the Castle and House libraries, and finally the five court doctors in Berlin and Potsdam. The Third Department represented the Court Garden Intendancy with a total of fifty court gardeners, senior gardeners and park supervisors.[65]

Only now do we come upon the names of the exotic-sounding servants whom Hellmut von Gerlach discovered on the Berlin electoral lists: three rifle loaders (Büchsenspänner) at the immediate service of His Majesty the Kaiser and King, six court furriers who supervised the servants, three kitchen masters, two cellar masters, three silverware superintendents, four linen supervisors and a manager of the laundry in Potsdam. After them come the fifty-eight stewards and castle administrators, then the small but important Principal Royal Office of Ceremonies, the Royal Stables,[66] the Royal Court Office of Hunts,[67] the Institute of Hunting, the pheasantries, the swan-breeding stations at Spandau and Potsdam, and the Coursing and Hunting Dress department under Ober-Piqueur Palm at the hunting manor at Klein-Glienicke.

If the reader should imagine that, with the named listing of an Ober-Piqueur at Potsdam, the gazetted list of court appointments and officials would have come to an end, he would be sadly mistaken. In a further lengthy section are listed the administrators and artists of the Royal Theatres. After the head, Count Hochberg, and his Director of Theatre Intendancy Pierson (who was to take his own life following a scandal in February 1902),[68] there follow the twenty-two Secretaries of the Intendancy Office[69] and the eight technical-artistic officials; then the nine producers and directors, the male and female actors of the Royal Theatre in Berlin, the singers of the Opera House, the solo dancers of the ballet (the females among them listed – exceptionally – with their Christian names), the conductors (including, of course, a certain 'Herr Strauss') and the musical directors of the orchestra,[70] and finally the directors of the drama academies. Then follow the list of personnel at the 'outward' theatres in Hanover, Kassel and Wiesbaden, which were taken over by the Prussian Crown in 1866. Next come the court pianists and royal singers. In total many more than a thousand people were employed at the various theatres and opera houses run by the Kaiser's court.[71]

The next section in the handbook lists the household of the other members of the royal family, starting with that of the Empress. At the head we find the names of the three so-called 'Hallelujah Aunts', Countess Brockdorff, Countess Keller[72] and Fräulein von Gersdorff. Then the Senior Master of the Court Baron von Mirbach, who had the personal rank of an Ober-Hofcharge and the title of Wirklicher Geheimer Rat;[73] the Deputy Senior Master of the Court Baron von Ende; three Kammerherren in Waiting[74], two Pages in Ordinary (Walther von Brauchitsch[75] and Friedrich Baron von Wilmowski[76]), the personal physician Dr Zunker, three Secretaries of the Privy Purse and four grooms of the chamber. As the six sons of the Kaiser had not yet come of age, they were under the supervision of senior and military governors and house tutors. The household of the next member of the family was that of the Empress Frederick, the Kaiser's mother, which had a similar composition, then the household of Prince and Princess Heinrich in Kiel, that of the widowed Princess Friedrich Karl, the extremely turbulent household of Prince Friedrich Leopold and his family[77], the equally scandal-ridden household of the Prince Albrecht line (including the young Count Robert von Zedlitz-Trützschler whose diary was to cause such a furore when it was published in the 1920s[78]) and four further households. On the death of a member of the family, the personnel were normally divided up amongst the younger princes whose needs were constantly growing.

The influence of the next group listed in the handbook can scarcely be exaggerated.[79] At the apex of the Military Retinue stood General Wilhelm von Hahnke in his capacity as Reporting Adjutant-General. No less influential was General Hans von Plessen, the Adjutant-General in Waiting and Commandant of the 'Headquarters of His Majesty the Kaiser and King', established on 7 July 1888. The members of the Headquarters were in 1900 General à la suite of the Kaiser in Waiting and Commandant of the Life Gendarmerie Major-General von Scholl plus the five Adjutants in Waiting von Mackensen,[80] von Jacobi, von Boehn, the Commandant of the Castle Guard Company Baron von Berg and, as the sole commoner in this almost exclusively noble circle, Corvette Captain Grumme. These officers, who were chosen mainly for their stature and appearance,[81] performed the general court duties for the Kaiser.[82] As the Master of Ceremonies to Kaiser Wilhelm I, Rudolf Count von Stillfried-Alcantara, wrote so perceptively in his *Ceremonial-Buch für den Königlich-Preussischen Hof*, this was a very characteristic feature of the Prussian military monarchy:

Looking back into the past one finds again and again at the Royal Prussian court a preference for simple forms on the part of the rulers, inspired by the spirit of militarism which suffused them and which made the Prussian Kingdom into a military state. There was, however, frequently a need to stage large, glittering festive occasions, with the result that both the austere and thrifty King Friedrich Wilhelm I and his wise and parsimonious great-grandson King Friedrich Wilhelm III were unable to resist a certain opulence in court style by calling upon an enlarged household to help provide the much needed effect of splendour on these occasions. And so it came about that in Prussia, more than in most other courts, the King's aides-de-camp [Flügel-Adjutanten] are also his Chamberlains in Waiting, and that the military disposition can be seen in more than one place in the ceremonial of the Prussian court. The Prussian national character is clearly reflected in court life as well as elsewhere.[83]

At least two equerries (Flügeladjutanten) were attached to the Kaiser at any one time, and during these periods they had to be at his service 'without interruption'.[84] In this way a personal bond – Admiral von Müller describes it as 'nothing short of a religious relationship'[85] – was established between Wilhelm and his Flügeladjutanten, which continued after their period of service at court had ended. The Flügeladjutanten often advanced to the highest positions in the army and navy, but remained a part of the Kaiser's military retinue. In 1900 there were twenty-six Adjutants-General, Generals or Admirals à la suite and Flügeladjutanten who had been posted elsewhere. The court thus became a temporary posting for these officers, and one through which the army could exert its notorious influence on the politics of the Prusso-German military monarchy. In June 1896 Philipp Eulenburg expressed his concern on the matter: 'People are speaking of the political influence of the Flügeladjutanten *far* more than H.M. realises. In *all* strata of the population this matter is under discussion. People are coming to the conclusion that the Kaiser allows himself to be completely *led* by his military entourage.'

If Eulenburg at this time still believed that the 'myth of aides-de-camp politics' could in due course be dispelled since 'the new era [by which he meant a future government under Bülow] will live in peace with the Flügeladjutanten because it will broadly share the political attitudes of H.M.'s entourage',[86] by 1899 he was forced to admit that it was 'more difficult to keep the Flügeladjutanten ... out of the game of politics than to solve the most complicated problem'.[87]

Nothing symbolises the character of Prussia as a 'heroic-aristocratic warrior state'[88] better than the next court group listed in the handbook, namely the High Order of the Black Eagle, founded on 17 January 1701 by the Elector Friedrich III on his acceptance of the Prussian Crown and in conscious imitation of the traditions of the German Knights of the Cross. As the highest honour in Prussia, it was bestowed not only on members of the royal family and on the other sovereign families both inside and beyond the Reich's boundaries, but increasingly too on 'domestic' notables who enjoyed the Kaiser's trust. In 1887 there were twenty-five, in 1889 forty-three and in 1912 there were fifty-five such domestic members of the Chapter. Since, according to the Court Order of Precedence of 1878, they ranked *ahead of* the heads of the most high-ranking princely families of Prussia,[89] the investiture of the Order of the Black Eagle represented a classic method by which the monarch could break through the traditional hierarchy by applying the principle of the 'proximity to the throne'.[90] As we shall see, the occupants of the Great Offices of Court and the Hereditary Offices in the Prussian provinces also bore a favoured rank, according to the Court Order of Precedence.

The last two posts referred to in the first part of the *Handbuch über den königlich-preussischen Hof und Staat* are the Secret Cabinets of the Kaiser and King, one for Civil and the other for Military Matters. The Naval Cabinet, established in 1889, counted as a Reich department and was therefore not mentioned in the Prussian handbook, even though its political operations were often of decisive significance.[91] These three Cabinets formed the connecting link, so to speak, between the court and the state. Thus the monarch's instructions to state and Reich departments were called *Allerhöchste Kabinetts-Ordres* (All-Highest Cabinet Orders), while those to the household or court administration were not issued via the Cabinets and were simply called *Allerhöchste Ordres*, All-Highest Orders. In 1900 the personnel of the Civil Cabinet consisted of the Chief, His Excellency Dr Hermann von Lucanus,[92] a Vortragender Rat Rudolf von Valentini,[93] an Office Director, two Secret Cabinet Secretaries and ten Secret Registrars. They dealt with an annual flow of around 80,000 documents.[94] The Military Cabinet was still larger and more influential. Under its chief, General Wilhelm von Hahnke, its establishment in 1900 consisted of six further noble officers as well as, temporarily, a non-noble Major from Württemberg, six non-noble secretaries and accountants and fourteen registrars. In the 1880s, under the leadership of its 'all-powerful' Chief, General Emil von Albedyll, the Military Cabinet had made itself increasingly independent of the Prussian War Ministry.[95] The socio-political influence of the Military Cabinet becomes clear when it is remembered that there was hardly a highly placed family in Prussia which did not have at least one son in the officer corps. As all promotions, transfers and all other signs of the Kaiser's favour or displeasure went through the Military Cabinet, there was no such family in the land which did not have something to hope for or to fear from its chief.[96] Even the Kaiser's uncle by marriage, Grand Duke Friedrich I of Baden, was not in a position to effect the transfer of his eldest son to Baden.[97] As we have seen, the influence of the Military Cabinet – and of the military elements at court in general – grew more powerful still after the destruction in 1908 of the only serious contenders for the Kaiser's favour, the Liebenberg circle around Philipp Eulenburg.[98]

Needless to say, an analysis of the structure of the Wilhelmine court administration based, as has been undertaken here, on the *Handbuch über den königlich-preussischen Hof und Staat* has many omissions. However extensive and complicated this structure may already appear, it must be stressed that only a small proportion of the 2,320 officials who made up the court administration[99] find a mention in this official handbook. The lower servants (the coachmen, grooms, gardeners, castle domestics, etc.) and the innumerable daily workers paid from Section 14 of the Household Budget 'for castle cleaning'[100] naturally do not feature. Including them and the officials of the princely households, the Prusso-German court employed in total at least 3,500 people.[101] Conditions for the lower servants at the Hohenzollern courts were of course very different from those enjoyed by the higher office-holders and officials. 'The lower court officials', wrote a critical contemporary, 'were appointed to their positions as a rule as young chaps directly from military service, enticed by the glitter of life at court. And then they remained in post by force of habit, by the needs of marriage and children, by the attraction of an existence free of worry and the prospect of a pension.'[102] Since the 1870s it had been the deliberate policy of the

Ministry of the Household to provide appropriate accommodation for as many as possible of the servants at court,

and especially the unmarried persons among them, in the interests of the service and in order to achieve better control, and the lower categories had to agree to share quarters with two or more other people . . . In general it will not be a matter of choice for the individual whether he accepts the accommodation offered or instead claims the rental supplement as laid down in the official tariff.

Apart from the theatres, married women could not as a rule be employed at court anyway: 'In Your Majesty's household', according to a Ministry of the Household memorandum from the year 1873, 'female servants must give up their position as soon as they marry.'[103]

Just as the number of court officials increased in the course of time, so a significant 'expansion of the household in general' became necessary, not least as a result of the restless style in which Kaiser Wilhelm II conducted his reign. As early as 1890 additional appointments were necessary: 'two men accustomed to the sea, a royal cook and a personal attendant', plus two polishers, five porters, one cellarman and two court quartermasters.[104] After the turn of the century it was the growing needs of the Kaiser's six princely sons and their families which accounted for the expansion of the court administration. Thus the salaries budget of the Crown Prince's household had to be increased by 36,000 marks in 1909 because, as August Eulenburg discovered, the household administration had 'increased the original complement of officials by a string of new posts which they believed were necessary for a comprehensive household and which in part they had already filled'. Eulenburg was not disposed to dispute the need for the additional posts. 'Amongst them are for instance a special physician for the Crown Princess, a second chauffeur and two attendants for car journeys, a second wardrobe attendant, etc.'[105] Even after 1918, both the Kaiser and the Crown Prince retained a sizeable court administration.[106] On the other hand, with the collapse of the monarchy hundreds of lower servants were thrown onto the streets without compensation or pension, because neither the Hohenzollern family nor the state bothered what happened to them. It was, as Kurt Heinig has written, 'the saddest and most bitter chapter in the dissolution of the Imperial Hohenzollern household as it hit almost all the lower sections of what had been the court personnel'. The embitterment of those affected was sharpened still further when they learned that the state had awarded a 23-year-old lady-in-waiting with only three years' service at court half pay at the rate of 10,000 marks per annum for five years and then 7,500 per annum for the rest of her life.[107]

What was the role of this expensive court apparatus in the Wilhelmine period? Some of its functions have already become clear in our examination of its inner structure: the Ministry of the Household, the personal physicians, the administration of the privy purse, the Kammerherren and Flügeladjutanten cared for the comfort of the various members of the imperial house; the Court Chamber, the stables, the master of the hunt, the stewards, castle agents, house archivists, museum and garden inspectors administered their numerous possessions; the theatre intendancy organised the royal drama, opera, orchestras, ballets and choirs; the 'Imperial Head-quarters' together with the Military Retinue, the Military Cabinet, the Commanding Generals and the Flügeladjutanten formed the link between the Supreme Warlord and the army, just as the Naval Cabinet provided the link with the navy and the Civil Cabinet with the civilian administration. But the court also had a further ritualistic function which, while it is not easy to define, should not be underestimated. It formed the focus of Prusso-German court society which, since the proclamation of the Court Precedence Regulation of 19 January 1878, was ranked in the following order:

1. The Principal Chamberlain [Der Oberst-Kämmerer]
2. The General-Field-Marshals
3. The Minister-President [and Reich Chancellor]
4. The Principal Marshal [Der Oberst-Marschall]
5. The Lord High Steward [Der Oberst-Truchsess]
6. The Principal Cupbearer [Der Oberst-Schenk]
7. The Principal Hunt-Master [Der Oberst-Jägermeister]
8. The Knights of the High Order of the Black Eagle
9. The Cardinals
10. The Heads of the Princely families and of the formerly Imperial Count families in the order listed below:

    Arenberg
    Salm-Salm
    Fürstenberg
    Thurn und Taxis
    Solms-Braunfels
    Isenburg-Birstein
    Croy-Dülmen
    Hohenlohe-Oehringen
    Hohenlohe-Waldenburg-Schillingsfürst
    Wied
    Solms-Lich und Hohensolms
    Sayn-Wittgenstein-Berleburg
    Sayn-Wittgenstein-Hohenstein
    Bentheim-Bentheim und Bentheim-Steinfurt
    Salm-Horstmar

Bentheim-Tecklenburg-Rheda
Isenburg-Büdingen in Wächtersbach
Isenburg-Büdingen in Meerholz
Solms-Rödelheim
Stolberg-Wernigerode
Stolberg-Stolberg
Stolberg-Rossla
Bentinck
Radziwill
Carolath-Beuthen
Lichnowski
Sagan
Hatzfeldt-Trachenberg
Biron von Curland
Blücher von Wahlstatt
Sulkowski
Lynar
Putbus
Salm-Reifferscheidt-Dyck
Pückler-Muskau
Sayn-Wittgenstein-Berleburg (Ludwigsburg special line)
Rheina-Wolbeck
Pless
Rohan
Hatzfeldt-Wildenburg
Bismarck

11. The Vice-President of the Prussian Ministry of State
12. Active Generals of Infantry and Cavalry
13. Ministers of the Royal Household and active Ministers of State
14. The first Presidents of both Houses of the Landtag
15. Retired Generals of Infantry and Cavalry gazetted as such
16. Retired Ministers of State who at their retirement from office were accorded ministerial rank
17. Retired Generals of Infantry and Cavalry not gazetted as such
18. Active Lieutenant-Generals
19. Privy Councillors with the title Excellency
20. Archbishops and Princely Bishops
21. Retired Lieutenant-Generals gazetted as such
22. Senior Court Officials with the title Excellency
23. Senior Court Officers in the Kingdom of Prussia
24. Retired Lieutenant-Generals not gazetted as such
25. Other persons with the title Excellency

26. The off-spring of the Princely and Count families listed under 10, provided they have been awarded the *Cordon* of a Prussian order
27. The Vice-Presidents of both Houses of the Landtag
28. The Ober-Präsidenten if they do not hold a higher personal rank
29. The active Major-Generals
30. The Councillors (First Class) and similarly ranked officials
31. The Bishops of both Confessions
32. The Senior Court Officials without the title Excellency
33. The retired Major-Generals
34. The Deputy Senior Court Officials
35. The Colonels
36. The Councillors (Second Class) and similarly ranked officials
37. The General-Superintendents provided they are ranked Councillor (Second Class)
38. The Chaplains-General of both Confessions
39. The Lord Mayor [Oberbürgermeister] of Berlin
40. The Cathedral Provosts and Deans of Seminaries
41. The Castle Governors (Schlosshauptleute)
42. The remaining Royal Court Officials and the Court Marshals of Their Royal Highnesses the Princes of the Royal House, headed by the Court Marshal of His Imperial and Royal Highness the Crown Prince
43. The Royal Chamberlains
44. The Flügel-Adjutanten of His Majesty the Kaiser and King
45. The incumbents of hereditary offices in the provinces
46. The Senior Court and Cathedral Preachers and Catholic clergy of the same rank
47. The Rectors of the Universities and the Permanent Secretaries of the Academy of Sciences, and the President and Director of the Academy of Arts
48. The Lieutenant-Colonels
49. The Councillors (Third Class)
50. The Territorial Directors (Landeshauptleute)
51. General Estates Directors and Principal Directors of Orders
52. The Canons
53. The Orders and Estates Directors
54. The Majors
55. The Councillors (Fourth Class)
56. The Regional Elders and Regional Councillors
57. The Gentlemen presented at Court
58. The Members of both Houses of the Landtag
59. The Captains of Infantry and Cavalry
60. The Gentlemen of the Bedchamber and Gentlemen of the Hunt

61. The First Lieutenants
62. Second Lieutenants

Married ladies who were *courfähig*, that is to say presentable at court, the list concluded, took their place according to the rank of their husbands.[108]

This Court Precedence Regulation was, with its obvious military character[109] and its sixty-two grades, unique in court history. Even the Austrian court, notorious for its suffocating ceremonial, was able to get along, like the Saxon court, with five grades, and the Bavarian court managed with only three. But however strange the business of court precedence may seem to us today, for the contemporaries concerned it was of the greatest importance. In her pseudonymous book *La Societé de Berlin*, published in Paris in 1884, Princess Katharina Radziwill wrote of the 'fearful commotion in the upper circles at Berlin' which came about because the new Court Precedence Regulation of 1878 laid down that the Knights of the Order of the Black Eagle ranked *above* the heads of the mediatised Princely and Imperial Count families.[110] More than twenty years later the word in well-informed political circles in Berlin was that Reich Chancellor von Bülow, himself newly elevated to the rank of prince, was opposing the nomination of the Hereditary Prince Ernst zu Hohenlohe-Langenburg to the post of Secretary of State in the Reich Colonial Office partly because Hohenlohe's wife – a Princess of Sachsen-Coburg and Gotha – would have taken precedence before Princess Marie von Bülow at court.[111] How difficult questions of precedence could be, even in All-Highest circles, can be seen from the note written by Philipp Eulenburg in October 1895 concerning an intrigue of Princess Charlotte Erbgrossherzogin zu Sachsen-Meiningen, the Kaiser's eldest sister:

> Charlotte Meiningen appears to have been intriguing with the King of Saxony against Friedrich Meiningen, whose wife is a Lippe-Biesterfeld (daughter of the Detmold Pretender). After the King had permitted Princess Friedrich to take part in a family dinner in Dresden as a person of royal birth, following which the Berlin court granted her a rank of precedence, King Albert suddenly declares that this dinner 'had not counted'. This of course puts Berlin in an embarrassing position. But Friedrich Meiningen will now do everything he can to induce the Biesterfeld Count to accept the throne of Detmold so that he will have a wife of royal birth.[112]

In his unpublished memoirs General von Plettenberg reminisces how as a young, very tall Guards officer he had often been obliged to perform as Vortänzer, that is as leader of the dance, at court balls, and that this had involved him in witnessing all kinds of arguments about precedence:

> Often differences of opinion arose between the court chamberlains on either side whether the leader of the dance should dance the cotillion with the oldest Princess Charlotte [Meiningen] or the higher ranked Princess Wilhelm [the later Empress]. Entertaining the latter was not an easy task; but I anyway felt obliged, against strict

court ceremonial, to lead the conversation. When I tried this again after an absence of many years in Bückeburg, it was deeply resented and I was badly treated for a long time.

Plettenberg later established with relief that the Chief of the Military Cabinet had succeeded in preventing his appointment as a Flügeladjutant at court. 'I was not cut out for the post', he admitted.[113]

The political significance of the arguments over precedence becomes clearer when we consider the middle and lower levels of the Court Precedence Regulation. At the height of the power struggle between the court and the highest state authorities in the 1890s, Reich Chancellor Prince Hohenlohe learned that the Kaiser, to mark his birthday, intended to elevate August Count zu Eulenburg, the Senior Marshal of the Court and Household and Senior Master of Ceremonies, and also Hermann von Lucanus, the Chief of the Civil Cabinet, to 'the rank of Minister of State'. Hohenlohe immediately convened the Prussian Ministry of State which unanimously took the view 'that "Minister of State" is an *office*, not a title or a rank'. After this resolution had been communicated to the Kaiser, General von Hahnke approached the Reich Chancellor with the request that the Kaiser should at least be allowed to confer 'the rank of *inactive* Ministers of State' on August Eulenburg and Lucanus, but Hohenlohe rejected this as well. Holstein claimed that if the plan had been carried out, 'Hohenlohe's régime would probably have collapsed under the weight of ridicule. Making a petty courtier into a Minister – in the whole history of Prussia, even in the period of absolutism, that has never happened.' The last word was not Holstein's but Kaiser Wilhelm's, however: in January 1897 August Eulenburg and Lucanus received the Order of the Black Eagle and thus advanced to the highest levels of court precedence.[114]

In the lower reaches of the order of precedence there was also continuous friction. All Members of the Reichstag were 'presentable at court', but not all were equally welcome there. After a particularly violent clash between the 'responsible government' and the Kaiser over the question of inviting some leaders of the Catholic Centre party to a court ball, the Foreign Secretary stated wearily that 'His Majesty can invite whoever he wants to court festivities'.[115] In actual practice the procedure for issuing invitations was a great deal more complicated. As Marschall explained to Philipp Eulenburg in February 1895, it had been the practice 'for years for requests for invitations to members of parliament to be given by ministers to court officials, who accepted them with gratitude'. In the case in question he had been at a lunch in the Hotel Bristol to which Krupp had invited a number of members of the Bundesrat and Reichstag, when Marshal of the Court Baron von Egloffstein had joined the company. The high-ranking Centre party deputy Prince Arenberg had suggested 'that a few influential Centre party members should be invited to the next court ball'. Marschall supported this suggestion with the remark that at the last great court ball he had 'seen various members of the Radical party . . . who are no use to us' politically. At Egloffstein's request Marschall wrote down on the back of a menu the names of the members of the Centre party who sat on the influential budget committee of the Reichstag. Marschall gave the list to Egloffstein with the suggestion that he 'find out whether and which of these gentlemen had left cards at court and to arrange invitations for the relevant ones for the next . . . court ball'.[116] Certainly neither the Foreign Secretary nor the Marshal of the Court could have imagined that the Kaiser would refuse to speak to that 'complete scoundrel' Ernst Lieber, the leader of the Centre party, at the ball, nor that Prince Heinrich would reject Marschall's suggestion that he might like to direct a few friendly words to Lieber with the statement that 'he should give the swine a kick up the a—'.[117]

Limitations of space prevent me from presenting here a full picture of the number and diversity of the court festivities and the ceremonial prescribed for them. The complications surrounding the various meals alone which the Kaiser had to attend can perhaps best be seen from a memorandum of 5 March 1889 drawn up jointly by the Principal Chamberlain Otto Count zu Stolberg-Wernigerode and the Minister of the Household von Wedell, for the attention of the young Wilhelm II. It dealt with the 'demarcation of responsibility between the Senior Master of Ceremonies and the Senior Marshal of the Court and Household in the matter of *placement* at meals taking place at the royal court', and reads:

During the lifetime of His Majesty Kaiser and King Wilhelm I this responsibility was so arranged that the Senior Marshal of the Court and Household was in charge of meals which took place in the Royal Palace [in Potsdam], while the Senior Master of Ceremonies was responsible for the organisation of meals held in the Royal Schloss [in Berlin]. This division rested on the principle that meals held in the Royal Palace would always have a more private character while those taking place in the Royal Schloss seemed certain to have a more official character as a result of the locality if for no other reason.

However, in the last years of His late lamented Majesty this principle was not rigidly adhered to, as meals of an undeniably official nature were held in the Palace, which served as His Majesty's residence. The detrimental effects which arose from the non-participation of the Senior Master of Ceremonies at such events led even then to the thought that the demarcation line for the co-responsibility of the Senior Master of Ceremonies should be drawn differently, and not on the basis of locality of such festivities. This seems all the more necessary now that Your Majesty has chosen as your All-Highest place of residence not a particular palace but the Royal Schloss itself.

The idea, which was sensible in itself, of involving the Senior Master of Ceremonies in all cases where the meal took place not in Your Majesty's private apartments but in the state rooms of the Royal Schloss, encountered many difficul-

ties in practice, and so we believe ourselves obliged to seek Your Majesty's permission to institute the rule outlined above, namely that the Senior Master of
Ceremonies should participate at all meals of a more or less official nature. This
seems justified by the official involvement of the Senior Master of Ceremonies with
matters of precedence and with all the many special factors which have to be taken
into account in the various cases. Such participation would have the best possible
chance of ensuring that proper forms had been followed.

Whether any particular meal is invested with an official character could be
indicated outwardly by which of the official persons attending occupies the middle
seat opposite Your Majesty, which at normal lunches is occupied by the Senior
Marshal of the Court and Household. It would be sensible to indicate the circumstances which would in general invest the meal with this character.

In this connection we would most humbly beg to suggest that the middle seat in
question should

1. at all the most significant gala meals prompted by family celebrations in the
royal house, to honour the presence of a prince of foreign sovereign houses provided
he has been invested with an honour, to honour the birthdays of friendly foreign
sovereigns etc., be occupied by the Principal Court Chamberlain, or alternatively by
the Principal Marshal or the Minister of the Royal Household,

2. at meals of a more political character, as for example at coronation and Order
celebrations, to honour parliamentary bodies, following the laying of foundation
stones or the unveiling of monuments, [be occupied] by the Reich Chancellor or
Minister-President respectively, or alternatively by his representative, and at
coronation and Order celebrations perhaps by the Chancellor of the Order of the
Black Eagle,

3. at meals of a military character [be occupied] by the War Minister or perhaps
a Field Marshal or Commanding General,

4. at meals prompted by considerations of foreign policy, for instance to honour
foreign sovereigns staying at the royal court, provided they have been invested with
an honour and are not in residence at the royal court purely in order to attend family
celebrations, or further to honour special ambassadors from foreign states, [be
occupied] by the Reich Chancellor in his capacity as Minister of Foreign Affairs,
or alternatively by the Secretary of State for Foreign Affairs,

5. at meals to honour the Knights of the Order of the Black Eagle [be occupied] by
the Chancellor of the Order.

These official meals should be supervised by the Senior Marshal of the Court and
Household together with the Senior Master of Ceremonies, and the latter should
have special responsibility for the *placement*. All that would remain outstanding is for
cases of difficulty in defining the character of a festivity to be resolved by a decision
by Your Majesty at a meeting with both court officials.[118]

For the larger festivities, too, which at other courts could be extremely
chaotic,[119] the Prusso-German court laid down the most detailed instructions. At the *Defilir-Cour*, the *salut du trône*, 'first all the ladies and then all
the gentlemen, singly according to their rank, are to parade before the
All-Highest and Highest personages who will be beneath the throne, and by
bowing give expression to their reverence for the same'.[120] This ceremony

was usually staged at the annual celebrations in January of the Coronation and Order Festival, at which the Knights of the Order of the Red Eagle, the Crown Order and the Order of the Royal House of Hohenzollern were presented. Much more impressive, however, was the *Defilir-Cour* which took place on the eve of a royal wedding: even during Wilhelm I's reign, over a thousand people took part in such *Spiel-Couren*, which accounts for the fact that they were regarded as 'one of the most difficult tasks the Senior Master of Ceremonies had to perform'.[121] Every person who was entitled to be present at the royal court and who wished to attend court festivities during the Berlin 'season', had to apply in writing for the first event, the so-called *Sprech-Cour*. At such Promenades 'the invited company, divided according to rank, take up position in different rooms . . . which Their Royal Majesties are pleased to visit in turn, greet the assembled company and talk to many of the individuals'.[122] Dress for all court Promenades was laid down as 'the most formal gala dress, which means for the ladies court dress (*robe de cour*) to which the retention of the barbel as headdress', as Count Stillfried argued in 1878, 'seems necessary'. The gentlemen 'appear at the Promenades similarly in the most formal gala dress, that is, always with white underclothing'.[123] Dress at court balls was similar: 'for the ladies ball gowns, for gentlemen gala dress, for officers court ball dress'.[124] Up to 2,000 people took part in such balls, and the number would have been higher if the space available in the Berlin Schloss had permitted it. The company attending the court ball were divided into two groups by the various Masters of Ceremonies, whereupon the higher-ranking group took up position in the White Hall, the remainder in the Portrait Gallery – again strictly in accordance with the rules of precedence. Even the dancing was carefully regulated: a Master of Ceremonies gave the signal for the start of the polonaise, at which a Flügeladjutant and one of the 'Ladies-in-Waiting' of the Empress, assisted by two guards officers who functioned as Vortänzer, led off the dance.[125] Care had to be taken that never more than three pairs joined in while the princes and princesses were dancing. The strictly hierarchical ceremonial which accompanied the final stages of a typical court ball was described by Count Stillfried in its full complexity in the following terms:

After dinner was announced some time after eleven o'clock, Their Royal Majesties moved towards the New Gallery adjoining the Elector's Apartments preceded by the pages, the Court, Senior Court and Principal Court Officials who remained standing in the Royal Chamber to form a guard of honour.

Following the All-Highest personages came the Heads of the Princely houses, all the Princely ladies, the ambassadors and their ladies, the Ministers and Ministers-Resident accredited to the royal court and their ladies, the General-Fieldmarshals, Active Generals of Infantry and Cavalry, Active Ministers, Knights of the Order of the Black Eagle plus all ladies with the rank of Excellency. These personages were awaited by the Senior Master of Ceremonies, His Majesty's Marshal of the Court and a Deputy Senior Master of Ceremonies in the Royal Chamber and conducted to the New Gallery.

The Chargés d'affaires and other members of the diplomatic corps, all gentlemen with the title Excellency not belonging to one of the above categories and members of Princely houses who were not heads of them, were conducted by a Deputy Master of Ceremonies to the Brunswick Hall, members of courts by a Master of Ceremonies to the first Brunswick chamber, ladies and gentlemen who had participated in the dance by a Master of Ceremonies and an aide des cérémonies to the Swiss Hall, while the remaining company, namely the ladies who had not participated in the dance and who did not have the rank of Excellency, were conducted by a Master of Ceremonies and an aide des cérémonies to the two Queen Elisabeth rooms, and the gentlemen who had not participated in the dance and did not have the title Excellency were conducted by an aide des cérémonies to the Gallery and the Great Hall of Queen Elisabeth, in which rooms these groups were served a buffet.

Towards the end of dinner, and in fact before the All-Highest and Highest personages had moved back to the White Hall, the ladies and gentlemen who had dined in the Swiss Hall were conducted back there by the relevant gentlemen.

The remaining sections of the company followed the procession of Their Majesties which, as before, entered through the arcades.

After the conclusion of the ball Their Majesties, preceded by the Principal Court, Senior Court and Court Officials, left the White Hall, this time through the door nearest to the throne.[126]

The future Chief of the General Staff Helmuth von Moltke remarked of a ball which took place in February 1905: 'The entry of the court into the White Hall always makes an extraordinary impression on me, the Kaiser always seems to bring something of the Middle Ages into the proceedings; ... it is as if the dead had risen up complete with pigtails and powder.'[127]

No less strict was the ceremonial at other court events: at the Feast of the High Order of the Black Eagle, for example, or at concerts, dramatic entertainments in the evening, at entrances and the lowering of flags, at the opening and closing of the Landtag or Reichstag, or the erection of public monuments.[128] No wonder that many members of the court, not least the old Kaiser Wilhelm I himself, looked forward especially to the Order Feasts, subscription balls and opera house balls which had 'a quite special character' because of the fact that at such events 'that part of Berlin society which did not belong to court society as such, was brought into a certain loose connection with the court'. Here 'aristocrats and commoners, officials and men of learning, people from the industrial and commercial professions, artists, writers, important figures of the theatre etc.' came into contact with 'court society in the narrower sense'.[129]

Kaiser Wilhelm II was himself entangled in a suffocating web of senseless court ceremonial, and matters were made worse by the feeling that he was 'constantly surrounded by a network of spying lackeys of the empress'.[130] In May 1910 he wrote (in English) to a young Englishwoman that he had at last been able to flee to Bad Homburg 'after a heavy three months at Berlin, full of tedious Court and Society obligations!' Berlin court society was in reality, he said, 'a Society that burns to be invited on every possible occasion, and laughs at you behind your back!'[131] Critical observers recognised very early on how ambivalent Wilhelm II felt in regard to court ceremonial. It was a peculiarity of the Kaiser that, while he loved great celebrations and pomp, he did not like to be hemmed in by considerations of etiquette, wrote Baden's Bundesrat Plenipotentiary, Arthur von Brauer, during the 1892 'season'.[132] Often Wilhelm behaved in accordance with his personal inclinations rather than with the rules of court ceremonial. Thus the parliamentarians at one dinner were 'very disappointed because H.M. almost completely ignored the forty-two participants, did not circulate and spoke with no-one except his neighbour at table and with a few other chosen people'. For similar reasons the members of the diplomatic corps were 'unpleasantly surprised' at a court ball:

The whole corps, gentlemen and ladies, were drawn up according to seniority because 'H.M. wished to circulate'. The company had to stand for more than an hour in rank and file until the court appeared. But H.M. only spoke a few words to the two ambassadors present and their wives while everyone else was completely ignored. The envoys of the non-German states were naturally unpleasantly surprised, and they gave vent to their feelings in language which was not always characterised by normal diplomatic reserve.[133]

Brauer's colleagues on the Bundesrat were 'somewhat upset' when Wilhelm struck out all their names from the guest list which had been laid before him for approval, requesting instead 'a more informal company'. Brauer considered the Kaiser's behaviour at a small court ball with a sit-down dinner to be typical:

The princely personages were scattered at a number of tables and received various diplomats and higher dignitaries allocated strictly according to rank ... Only H.M. the Kaiser's table did not observe this etiquette. H.M. had on his right and left hand side the pretty wife of the Rumanian envoy Madame Ghika and the beautiful Countess Arnim-Muskau (née Countess Bismarck-Bohlen) and besides these the wife of the well-known Polish deputy von Koszielski, Countess Asseburg, the major's wife, and the young Frau von Stägemann, whose husband is a Captain or Lieutenant, had been summoned. This aroused the displeasure of the ambassadors who said with some justification that at such a small court ball H.M. could easily have dispensed with *placement* according to etiquette *entirely*. But as etiquette was observed strictly at all other tables, the ambassadors' ladies had a right to expect to be summoned to the Kaiser's table.[134]

Wilhelm II frequently distanced himself from Berlin and Potsdam altogether. Soon he spent less than half the year in the midst of the court society proper; 'alternative courts' sprang up in other places which were more to his taste. After the end of the Berlin 'season' his journeyings took him in March to the Mediterranean, in the spring to Alsace, Wiesbaden and to Prökelwitz in East Prussia, in June to Kiel Week, in July on his North Sea cruise, in August to Cowes or Wilhelmshöhe, in October to East Prussia again, in November to Letzlingen, Liebenberg, Silesia and (from 1905) to Donaueschingen in the Black Forest. Just as this hectic annual round of visits was undertaken on a regular basis, so the company at each location was assembled according to a settled routine: here was the aesthetic Liebenberg circle, there the uniformed Flügeladjutanten; here Silesian magnates, there Anglo-American millionaires; here Prussian Junkers, there South German or Austrian high nobility; here the Commanding Generals, there the archaeologists.[135] Even the richest of his hosts secretly groaned at the cost of a visit by the Kaiser, though not all of them felt obliged, as did Franz Herbert Count von Thiele-Winckler, to provide 20,000 pheasants to be shot down by the monarch and his entourage.[136]

If Wilhelm II himself found the demands of court etiquette too burdensome, this was all the more true of those members of the Hohenzollern family who could derive few benefits from court life, and to whom the obligations and restrictions which came with their social position seemed by no means always a matter of course. Wilhelm, however, insisted on applying strictly to these members of the Hohenzollern family the numerous irksome rules laid down by the Hohenzollern house statutes.[137] When, for example, Prince Friedrich Wilhelm of Prussia asked permission of the Kaiser in 1907 to marry Countess Paula von Lehndorff, Wilhelm's abrupt reply read: 'He can marry her, but as I do not tolerate morganatic marriages he will have to surrender title and possessions. Wilhelm I.R.'[138] Not everyone was willing to make such a sacrifice for the sake of love (as was the Crown Princess of Saxony, who in 1902 ran off with her children's French tutor).[139] Prince Friedrich Wilhelm of Prussia surrendered not title and possessions but the Countess Lehndorff. In 1910 he married Agathe Princess von Ratibor und Corvey, Princess zu Hohenlohe-Waldenburg-Schillingsfürst, a lady of royal status, but even then only after her father had solemnly promised the Kaiser that 'the wedding would be conducted entirely in accordance with official Protestant usage and the offspring would be given a Protestant christening and would be brought up in accordance with Our religion'.[140] When in 1896 the empress's brother, who was becoming most impatient to marry, sought to wed the beautiful Johanna von Spitzemberg, the niece of the Württemberg Bundesrat Plenipotentiary Axel Baron von Varnbüler, both the Kaiser and the Empress were outraged. The latter, as Philipp Eulenburg put it in a letter to Varnbüler, 'would be overcome by a thirst for revenge if she were to be placed in a position in which she would have to address you and your wife more-or-less as Uncle and Aunt'.[141] And Wilhelm himself wrote no less dramatically:

Now, my dear Axel, I have had enough of this pretence and manoeuvring. The poor empress has already had sufficient trials and tribulations, but this business has really burdened her heart. You know that the empress has positively declared to the duke [her brother Ernst Günther] that, should he take your niece, all contact with him would cease and she would for the rest of her life never again be able to visit her home in Primkenau. The empress was so overcome by this thought . . . that she burst out in streams of bitter tears. I can no longer look upon the wretchedness and the misery, it must come to an end. Only yesterday I again made clear to the duke what a hopeless situation would be created for him, for the family and above all for his intended. She would not be recognised, could never appear with him at court and could never be seen in the family circle . . . I then said to the duke that, as head of one of the oldest and most respectable German princely houses, he had been prescribed obligations from heaven which forced him to remain within certain boundaries. These had already been relaxed to the extent that he could choose from among the old mediatised imperial families and the houses of the reigning counts and princes, but to go beyond this was completely out of the question.[142]

The Kaiser was determined that his brother-in-law should marry the daughter of Count Emil Görtz, another 'Liebenberger', who, as the reigning Reichsgraf of Schlitz, was of appropriate standing. In the end, however, Ernst Günther married the very young Princess Dorothea of Sachsen-Coburg and Gotha.

Alongside the question of birth, there was another matter which the Kaiser and the Kaiserin watched over carefully when it came to marriage in court society: the question of confession. When the Kaiser's aunt, Landgräfin Anna of Hessen, converted to the Catholic faith, Wilhelm II laid down that henceforth 'no-one from my house may have any contact with the renegade'.[143] When his sister Sophie, the Crown Princess of Greece, converted to the Orthodox faith in 1891, the Kaiser, despite violent protests from his mother and from the remainder of his English relations, ordered her 'to go into exile from the country for ever'. Later the punishment was reduced so that he 'did not wish to see her for three years', yet even this decision caused a huge amount of 'bad blood', not only in England but also, and even more so, 'in Russia and above all with the Tsar', as Arthur von Brauer reported to Karlsruhe.[144] Such clashes, which included the 'unforgivable'[145] conversion of the young Tsarina Alexandra (Princess Alix of Hessen-Darmstadt) and her sister Ella to the Orthodox faith, without doubt contributed to the growing hostility towards the Prusso-German court of Wilhelm II on the part of many of the most influential courts of Europe such as Russia, England, Denmark, Greece, the two Hessens and Coburg.

However fateful in its consequences was Wilhelm II's use of his prerogatives under the Hohenzollern house statute, we should not overlook the fact that his powers were in no way restricted to the private lives of members of the family alone. On the contrary, he was able to intervene in a similar fashion in the private sphere of each member of court society; indeed as late as 1903 distinguished lawyers advanced the view that all matters concerning the nobility were '*purely* matters of grace' and were subject to 'the decisions of the head of state' alone.[146] In innumerable ways, ranging from a few friendly words in a congratulatory telegram to the placing of a photograph on his desk in a hunting lodge,[147] Wilhelm II could activate the 'kingship mechanism' in order to manipulate the whole of court society including the Reich Chancellor, the officer corps and the senior ranks of the civil service.[148] Dietrich Count von Hülsen-Haeseler, for instance, later Chief of the Military Cabinet, had a long-standing relationship with the Royal Solo Dancer Wisotzky, who bore him a son. When in 1892 he wanted to marry Hildegard von Lucadou, the daughter of a wealthy general, he made sure that his sometime mistress married the retired Bavarian Lieutenant-Colonel Bischoff, who was prepared to take in the son as well, but who was without means. Accordingly Hülsen, via his brother Georg and Lucanus, sent a request to the Kaiser 'that His Majesty may be pleased to order – as in many similar cases, most recently concerning the Royal Court Actress Fräulein Clara Mayer – that the pension [of the dancer Wisotzky] should not be discontinued *after* the marriage', a request that was granted.[149] On the other hand Colonel Werner Count von Alvensleben-Neugattersleben, Governor of the Castle of Quedlinburg, had to trail around after the Kaiser for weeks on end in the hope of eliciting permission for his daughter to marry a Catholic. When this was finally granted, the Count wrote to the monarch full of gratitude and with the following assurance:

It will be a Protestant wedding, as befits the state church; a second, Catholic ceremony is being dispensed with, and should the marriage not prove to be childless, daughters will follow the mother's confession, sons however will adopt the religion of the father. I thought it right to concede this as they would carry the name Radowitz and not Alvensleben, and had it been otherwise I would certainly not have done so. I faced the alternative of losing my daughter, who has become nervous in the most extreme degree.[150]

Even the Kaiser's closest friend, Philipp Eulenburg, had the greatest difficulty in obtaining Wilhelm's consent to the marriage of his eldest son to a wealthy Austrian Catholic girl, Marie Freiin Mayr von Melnhof. Wilhelm, who initially asked 'whether the bride is an Israelite', then declared: 'The children are not to be brought up as Catholics, especially the sons, your princely house must remain Brandenburgish and Protestant, it would be best if Fräulein von Mh. were to become Protestant.'[151] In the end Eulenburg had to assure the Kaiser that his son's bride was 'basically of a Protestant character', that to the suggestion that 'any possible male offspring should be brought up as Protestants, and female as Catholics, she had replied that *all* children *must* be *Protestants*', and that the real reason for opposition to the marriage in court circles in Berlin should be sought in the 'envy and resentment' provoked by the bride's fortune 'among our *Prussian mothers* and their hangers-on'.[152]

Even before his accession Wilhelm had announced his intention to do 'battle against vice, high living, gambling, betting etc.', against 'all the doings of our so-called "good society"'.[153] This battle was not particularly successful, however. Soon after he came to the throne, hundreds of obscene anonymous letters began to circulate around the court, and although this went on for years the author was never discovered, even though (or perhaps precisely because?) the culprit must have been a member of the close circle surrounding Wilhelm and the empress.[154] A decade later the Wilhelmine court experienced its greatest scandal when Philipp Eulenburg and his 'Liebenberg round table' were publicly attacked on the grounds of their homosexuality and finally had to be banned from the court. In the course of the trial more and more members of court society and the court administration came under suspicion: Reich Chancellor Bernhard von Bülow and two of his brothers, a son of General Gustav von Kessel, the court officials Edgard von Wedel and Baron von und zu Egloffstein, General Kuno von Moltke, General Intendant Georg von Hülsen and the majority of the members of the 'Liebenberg Circle', the two Counts Hohenau, Count Johannes von Lynar, Prince Friedrich Heinrich of Prussia, Prince Aribert of Anhalt, Karl Eduard Duke of Sachsen-Coburg and Gotha, Grand Duke Ernst Ludwig of Hessen and many others.[155] Embarrassing questions were asked even about the Kaiser.[156] The German system of government, already inefficient, suffered an immediate collapse into 'complete disequilibrium at the top'. Nationalist circles inclined to the view that they must press either for an external war or else for the abdication of Wilhelm II. 'To clear ourselves of shame and ridicule', wrote Maximilian Harden in November 1908, 'we will *have* to go to war, soon, or face the sad necessity of making a change of imperial personnel on our own account, even if the strongest personal pressure had to be brought to bear'.[157] As Maurice Baumont has rightly remarked in his study of *L'Affaire Eulenburg*, 'la réalité pathologique des scandales Eulenburg doit prendre place parmi les causes complexes de la guerre mondiale'.[158]

If these sexual scandals can to some extent be explained in terms of the claustrophobia and boredom induced by court ritual, it is nonetheless impossible to overlook the fact that disputes of rank within court society also helped to stir up the scandals and to hurl them self-destructively into the public domain. In the anonymous letters scandal the initiated soon realised that the target of the most obscene of the letters was Countess

Charlotte Hohenau, who by birth was a mere von der Decken. The suspicion arose that the highly placed anonymous author might have been motivated by a craving for revenge against this intruder into the innermost circle of the court.[159] This motive is unmistakable in the court hostility directed at Philipp Eulenburg which led to his arrest and moral destruction.

At the opening of the hunt at Liebenberg in 1899, Wilhelm II revealed to his friend that he intended to raise him to the rank of Fürst (prince). His intention was to 'pierce the ring of high-born equals comprising the small number of Protestant princes'. For this reason Eulenburg asked in December 1899 'for the title Erlaucht and the closed crown' – 'naturally with the retention of the title of *count*' – for his descendants.

Because this would *materially* help to *ease* the question of high-born equals, which is Your Majesty's chief concern. Your Majesty cannot of course eliminate the distinction between higher and lower nobility established by the Vienna Memorandum. That would be fatal! But if Your Majesty were prepared to concede the title Erlaucht and the use of the closed crown to *houses of ancient lineage* (or indeed to single branches of these houses), then it would be possible to reckon with a gradual fusion of the new princely families with the present higher nobility. But *not* if only the head of the house becomes a prince and his family remain *simple* counts, like the Bismarcks, the Plesses, the Radolins and others. Examples of houses of ancient lineage are Eulenburg, Dohna, Knyphausen (but not, for instance, Arnim, Dönhoff).[160]

Eulenburg's friends nervously warned him against accepting the title of prince. Bülow and Varnbüler counselled: 'Tu es certain que ta nomination en question étonnera beaucoup et fera mauvais sang surtout en Prusse et parmi le parti conservateur',[161] and how right they were! The old Reich Chancellor Prince Chlodwig zu Hohenlohe-Schillingsfürst, who, as a relative of the Empress was addressed by the Kaiser as 'Uncle' and with the familiar Du, wrote in great anger to his son Alexander:

'Fürst' Philipp came to see me today. He made an extremely poor impression on me. I am surprised that I did not find him so antipathetic in the past as I do now. Mama, with her sharp, clear eye, got the correct measure of him years ago! What this man told me today for lies supersedes anything I've ever known! He explained to me dramatically how he had so resisted the princely title that the Kaiser had almost become cross with him, whereas I know for a fact that he begged for it. It is shocking that this prize scoundrel [*Erzlump*] should be the friend of H.M.[162]

Alexander Hohenlohe also mocked the 'newly baked princes'. In an unmistakable allusion to Eulenburg's homosexual tendencies he wrote to his father:

I have just read in the newspapers that Phil. E. is to be raised to the rank of prince . . . The assumption that Ph. Eul. is aiming to acquire the post of Statthalter of Alsace Lorraine seems *very* plausible to me. The [salary of] 200,000 marks he could make good use of, as we know, for all kinds of purposes. It's a matter of indifference to me as I certainly won't become Statthalter in the near future. And if he should treat me badly, I'll simply submit my resignation [as Bezirkspräsident in Colmar] and buy myself a hundred thousand acres of land in Siberia.[163]

The princely elevations of 1 January 1900 – besides Eulenburg three other counts were raised to the rank of prince by Wilhelm II on that day – provoked 'much shaking of heads' not only among the old princely families or the democrats but throughout society as a whole. But they were also seen as a sign of the times. Varnbüler's sister Baroness Hildegard von Spitzemberg noted in her diary on 5 January 1900:

The best criticism of the 'new princes' is the face that people make when they talk about the subject: a smile, a shrugging of shoulders, a few derisive remarks, especially with reference to Phili Eulenburg, the 'Count Troubadour', who has little money, few achievements to his credit and many children, and is not even the head of his house. Dohna was apparently very ambitious to acquire the dignity; so far as Hatzfeldt is concerned it's just another title; how Knyphausen views it I have no idea. Methinks that this kind of reward is hardly appropriate at the present time, where rank without money is more than ever ridiculous and a burden; but it corresponds to the Kaiser's taste for pomp to surround himself with princes and dukes, and as he has offended most of the old ones, he creates new ones with more pliable spines. If only he could at least give them some money or land to go with their names! The Reich Chancellor apparently said with a shake of the head: 'So many new princes! Soon I shall feel like calling myself simply Herr Hohenlohe!' . . . It is a lucky thing that Axel [Varnbüler] is not a Prussian; otherwise he too would in the near future have become a count rich in children and poor in means. It's strange: after '66 and '70 Bismarck became a prince, Roon and Moltke and a few others were made counts; since then, when there have truly been few successes to record, elevations in rank have increased in inverse proportion![164]

In many other respects as well the expansion of Wilhelmine court society, widely felt to be un-Prussian, was a noticeable feature of the time. If there were twenty officers in the Kaiser's military entourage in 1888, they had climbed to forty-four by 1914. The number of *Kammerherren* increased in the last twelve years of the Kaiser's reign from 252 to 283. Suddenly thirteen 'palace ladies' appear in the Court Calendar under the empress's household, a novelty introduced by Wilhelm II in 1904.[165] The long-serving Austrian ambassador in Berlin, Count Szögyény, reported in January 1898 that the size of the court was increasing year by year,[166] while the court reporter of the *Hamburger Nachrichten* described the number of guests attending a court ball in 1897 as 'colossal'.[167] Just before the opening of the 'season' in 1904 Baroness Spitzemberg remarked ironically: 'That six small and large balls are planned for the short carnival time is the best proof of how well the Kaiser is feeling . . . Knesebeck said that this type of social activity at court is definitely taking on the character of a persecution of the

Christians!'[168] At the turn of the century she observed, correctly, that 'the
Black Eagle has become a decidedly common little creature'.[169] During the
reign of Wilhelm II the number of incumbents in the Order rose from 81 to
120. 'How can one continue to speak of Prussian tradition?' asked Holstein
in despair when Lucanus received the Order of the Black Eagle. When the
younger Moltke was invested with this, the highest Order in Prussia, he
'was really rather ashamed'. His uncle, he wrote, had needed a victory in
war to attain such an honour; 'we epigoni achieve it with three days of
manoeuvres!!!'[170] Eulenburg's reaction, when he was invested with the
Order of the Black Eagle in 1906, was somewhat different: 'I was not able',
he wrote to the Kaiser, 'to express fully in the presence of the lunch guests at
Henkel's ... what my true feelings were when Your Majesty conferred on
me the highest Prussian Order, and I saw the brightness of your dear gaze,
from which streamed joy at being able to make me joyful!'[171] But it is
significant for the impending downfall of Eulenburg – the investiture of the
Order of the Black Eagle in effect gave the signal for his destruction – that
even the 'old countess', Agnes Pourtalès, who was a good friend of both
Kuno Moltke and Axel Varnbüler, could write about the investiture: '*Radowitz – Eulenburg*. One with the most complete justification, the other
with...? It is a pity that a proper sentiment should be so diminished in
value.'[172]

   Apart from the inflation in court positions and honours and the senseless-
ness of court ceremonial – Helmuth von Moltke spoke of 'this nonsense' and
'all this frippery' at a time when what was needed was 'to prepare seriously
and with bitter energy for war'[173] – it was the extravagance which provoked
a feeling of concern among most contemporaries and not least among the
members of court society themselves. A theatre critic mocked the fact that
the tobacco workers in a performance of *Carmen* at the Royal Opera House
strutted about dressed in real silk, while the gypsies in *Il Trovatore* did so in
velvet costumes.[174] Symbolic of this tendency was perhaps the bath-tub.
Where Wilhelm I had had a zinc bath-tub brought to the Schloss from the
Hotel de Russie once a week, for his grandson's special train a bathing
wagon was manufactured in the final year of the war out of copper seized
from private homes in Brussels.[175]

   Clearly, the 'monstrous' flowering of court culture in the Wilhelmine Reich,
which in other areas was modernising itself with such rapidity, presents a
fascinating field of research for psychologists and cultural anthropologists.
But structural and social historians, too, will hardly be able to avoid
reflecting on the function of the gigantic court complex under Kaiser
Wilhelm II. At least four questions immediately present themselves: what
role did the Kaiser and his court play in relation to his 'subjects'? What was

the function of the court from the point of view of the ruling elite? What significance was attached to the Prusso-German court in the representation of German power abroad? Finally, what was the political significance of the relationship between the court and the state in Wilhelmine Germany? A few brief remarks of a more general nature based on the empirical evidence outlined above may provide a provisional answer to these four questions.

Kaiser Wilhelm II set out to 'charismatise' the Hohenzollern monarchy. By his ubiquity, his innumerable speeches, parades, swearing in of recruits, 'nailing' of flags and unveiling of monuments, Wilhelm II wanted to turn the Imperial throne into the 'bulwark of the Reich idea', not least in order to take the wind out of the sails of the growing Bismarckian movement.[176] Even the most glowing royalists knew only too well, however, that this attempt to imbue the monarchy with charisma involved grave dangers for the latter, indeed that the attempt had about it an air of desperation. Bülow spoke of 'going under' if the attempt should fail,[177] and Philipp Eulenburg maintained in 1895: 'In these circumstances one can only come to the conclusion to be *for the Kaiser* sans phrase. If we do not work to ensure that *he* is regarded as the personification of Germany – even if the task is made difficult for us by his character traits! – then we shall lose *everything*.'[178]

Indeed, these efforts to 'charismatise' the monarchy quickly came up against obstacles of both an internal and an external kind. It is in the very nature of monarchy 'by the grace of God' that the first-born son of the king becomes king himself on his father's death, whether or not he measures up to the needs of the time, and few would now claim that Wilhelm II's character was what the young, powerful but uncertain Reich needed on the threshold to the twentieth century! As his reign began, the states of Europe were entering upon an 'age of boundless publicity' which, as Bülow recognised, could work either for or against the continued existence of monarchy.[179] The history of the last hundred years has shown that a monarchy in a modern state can only hope to survive if it restricts itself firmly to its purely representational functions and avoids making any political comment and exerting any influence. That Wilhelm II did precisely the opposite is a matter of embarrassing record. But even if he had been a monarch less inclined to making 'Hun speeches' and committing other *faux pas* which deeply offended the nation again and again,[180] even if Wilhelmine court society had been less prone to scandal, it is questionable whether it would have been possible to 'charismatise' the Prusso-German monarchy in the longer term. Would it have been possible, for instance, to integrate the industrial workers into state and society with pomp and ritual rather than with genuine political reform? Was not the dynastic cult propagated by the Kaiser – the cult of 'Wilhelm the Great', the 'Hero-Emperor' – the least appropriate method for winning over to the Hohenzollern monarchy the

Catholic third of the population or the Bismarckian or democratically orientated middle classes? What is certain is that, given the exposed position into which it thrust itself, each and every setback, whether at home or abroad, represented a direct threat to the very survival of the monarchy. And with it the whole of court society ran the risk of losing '*everything*', too.

The role of the court in relation to the ruling elite was that of integration and hierarchisation, but here too the limitations to which it was subject are quickly apparent. After all, the ultimate purpose of court life was to reinforce the vassal loyalty to the Hohenzollern monarch not just of the old Prussian nobility. The noble families in the provinces which were annexed to Prussia in 1815, 1866 and 1870, and also those of the non-Prussian federal states which had been absorbed into the Reich in 1871, had to be persuaded to regard the Imperial court in Berlin, rather than the royal court at Munich, Dresden or Stuttgart or the grand ducal court at Karlsruhe, Darmstadt or Schwerin (not to mention the Imperial court in Vienna or the Vatican) as the focus of their social aspirations and loyalties. On top of this, the industrial middle classes, whose wealth was constantly on the increase, and the mainly middle-class state bureaucracies,[181] would, so it was hoped, also be won over to the Hohenzollern monarchy by the glitter of court balls, the traditions of court etiquette, the conferment of honours, elevations to the nobility, appointments as suppliers to the royal court, congratulatory telegrams, invitations to the hunt and, not least, promotions to posts (for one's sons as well as for oneself) in the army, navy and bureaucracy. In 1903 the Kaiser declared his intention of establishing 'genuine relations' between the industrialists and 'his nobility'. In Kiel Week he had thrown them together 'like shot-gun pellets into a drum'. The look on the faces of 'his gentlemen' at this encounter with the industrial magnates had albeit been 'worth photographing', he declared.[182] We have seen how this integrationist function of the court all too frequently conflicted with the hierarchical principle embodied in the Court Ranking Regulation leading, for example, to the incessant squabbles about rank and to the resentment against 'intruders' and 'favourites'.

A further explanation for the flowering of court culture under Kaiser Wilhelm II is to be found in the endeavour to represent the enormous power of the German Weltreich to the outside world. Just as the British Empire was seen as the standard by which Germany's world power aspirations should be measured, so the court at Windsor was regarded as the authoritative example for Potsdam and Berlin to follow. It is interesting in this respect that Kaiser Wilhelm II could never free himself from a certain embarrassment when at Windsor; and also that he was always somewhat ashamed of the relative meagreness of the Potsdam court. 'It won't be like Windsor', he warned the British ambassador shortly before his uncle's state visit to Germany in 1908, 'but we shall do the best we can in any case.'[183] A comparison of the European courts on the eve of the First World War would now be a rewarding and revealing research topic for historians to explore.[184]

Finally, we need to clarify the political relevance of the foregoing study with some remarks about the relationship between the court and the state, between the 'monarchical principle' and the 'principle of state omnipotence'. For too long the problem of the 'personal rule' of Kaiser Wilhelm II has been seen as a dichotomy between the person of the monarch on the one hand, and the 'traditional oligarchies in conjunction with the anonymous forces of the authoritarian polycracy' on the other.[185] From such a standpoint it does indeed seem incredible that a single person – especially one who was psychologically 'not quite normal' – should have been able to put his stamp on German politics. But if the Prusso-German court is viewed in its totality, the decidedly inferior rank which with few exceptions was assigned by the Court Ranking Regulation to the representatives of the state and Reich bureaucracy, despite the fact that by virtue not only of their offices but also by birth, upbringing and marriage they all belonged to court society, is unmistakable. On the other hand Kaiser Wilhelm II – far from standing alone against the enclosed corps of officialdom – was served by more than two thousand court officials and servants, was surrounded by a vast, hierarchically structured court society, was in possession of unrestricted 'powers of command' in all military matters, and above all was in a position to corrupt and to force into a relationship of subservience the whole Reich and state civil service by means of his absolute control over appointments, honours and even marriage plans. A symbol of this is the fact that the German Reich Chancellor, Chlodwig Prince zu Hohenlohe-Schillingsfürst, the 'highest official' of the Reich, the Kaiser's 'prime adviser', was constitutionally authorised by the Reichstag to receive a salary of only 54,000 marks per annum. Secretly an extra 120,000 marks were passed to him each year from the funds of the crown.[186]

4   The 'kingship mechanism' in the Kaiserreich

For Walther Peter Fuchs   *il miglior fabbro*

To the two volumes of documents which have been available since 1927 on the role of Grand Duke Friedrich I of Baden in the unification of Germany[1] are now added four further volumes covering the period from the foundation of the Reich to the Grand Duke's death on 28 September 1907. These documents, superbly edited by Walther Peter Fuchs, not only extend the chronological range of the original edition; they also enlarge its theme.[2] This collection is without question one of the most important sources for the political and social history of the German Reich, containing as it does some 2,644 hitherto unknown documents on German politics as seen from the viewpoint of Baden, backed up with numerous parallel documents in the footnotes. The volumes emphasise the need for the publication of similarly detailed collections from the Baden archives (and indeed from those of the other federal states) for the years 1907–14, years for which – not entirely coincidentally – there is a relative paucity of source material. *One* Baden source – perhaps the most significant of them all – does not appear in the four volumes edited by Fuchs, however. Like many documents from the years immediately prior to the First World War, including some which survived the Second World War,[3] this source will be unavailable to historians for ever more. For when in November 1918 certain foreign newspapers demanded 'the publication of the letters of His Majesty the Kaiser' to his aunt, Grand Duchess Luise of Baden (she was the sister of Kaiser Friedrich III), the Senior Court Chamberlain of Baden, Richard von Chelius, decided on his own initiative 'to have all of the [Kaiser's] letters, and especially His Majesty's letters from the war years, transferred as quickly as possible from the castle to the Victoria boarding school'. The evacuation of the Grand Duchess's papers took place during the night of Saturday 30 November 1918. One week later the headmaster of the school, Dr von Engelbert, informed the Chamberlain 'that as a result of the sharpened mood and situation' in Karlsruhe he had no choice but 'to burn the whole collection of correspondence as quickly as possible'.[4] One can only guess at what was contained in the papers of the Grand Duchess Luise; Kaiser Wilhelm II's letters to her must have numbered around sixty, however, for that is the number of replies from the Grand Duchess housed in the Prussian Archive in Merseburg.[5]

The attitude which led to the *auto-da-fé* in the Victoria boarding school on 8 December 1918 and, more generally, to the destruction or at best the concealment from the Entente of documents which would have been unhelpful in the struggle to defend the honour of the fallen Kaiser and to counter the Allies' 'war guilt lie', prevailed not only in court and military circles but also in the German historical profession, and in the latter until some thirty years ago.[6] Since the great 'Fischer controversy' of the 1960s many taboos have been broken. Countless studies have cast light on the war aims of imperial Germany, the July crisis of 1914, the foreign policy, trade and tariff policy of the Wilhelmine Reich, its industrial and agrarian organisations and nationalist leagues, the labour movement, the army and navy and much else besides. One aspect alone continues to be excluded, and it is precisely the aspect which contemporaries in Germany and abroad considered to be the most decisive one – the personality, the political role and social significance of Kaiser Wilhelm II himself. Not a single professional German historian has written a scholarly biography of Wilhelm. Whereas in America and Britain an unbroken tradition of biography continues to concern itself, amongst others, with monarchs and other princely personages[7] and while in France the structure and socio-political function of the royal and imperial courts through to the court society of Napoleon III has been carefully examined,[8] in Germany, as Nicolaus Sombart has put it, historians write the history of the Kaiserreich without the Kaiser, that of Wilhelminism without Wilhelm.[9]

That the older orthodoxy, despite – or perhaps precisely because of – its preoccupation with the 'great Germans', should have neglected the last German Kaiser is both psychologically and politically understandable, even though this neglect has meant that it was not able to fulfil its obligation to research the past and to counter the well-oiled propaganda machine directed from Doorn.[10] After all, the promotion of the 'national cause' in the Weimar Republic would hardly have been assisted by memories of 'suprema lex regis voluntas' or 'sic volo, sic jubeo', of the 'lackeys and pygmies' or 'Hun' speeches, or of the Eulenburg-Moltke trials; and if one hoped for a revision of the Versailles Treaty it was certainly prudent to consign the letters of the Supreme War Lord to his aunt to the flames. This makes it all the more astonishing that the 'new orthodoxy' of 'critical social history', which established itself so quickly as soon as the credibility of the older orthodoxy had been shattered by the 'Fischer controversy', and which in many respects had the hallmarks of an allergic reaction to all of the values of the older generation of historians, should *de facto* have perpetuated the Kaiser taboo. Yet the 'new orthodoxy' also condemned as *Personalismus* any attempt to investigate the role of Kaiser Wilhelm II in the complex process of decision-making in Wilhelmine Germany.

The grounds for this remarkable attitude on the part of the 'new orthodoxy' towards the role of personalities in general and of Kaiser Wilhelm II in particular are not so obvious as are the motives of the older generation. They are in part to be sought in the otherwise praiseworthy attempt to explain the fatal *Sonderweg* of modern German history by constructing a comprehensive explanatory model. But no less an authority than Otto Pflanze, the editor of the *American Historical Review* and Bismarck's biographer, has criticised these historians for being led by their methods into an interpretation of the course of German history from 1806 to the Third Reich 'which is frequently determinist and thoroughly depersonalised', and that for some among them the models 'have ceased to be merely heuristic instruments but have themselves developed into fictitious historical reality'. Pflanze goes even further and points to the remarkable paradox that the key concepts of this school of historiography – concepts such as 'negative integration', *Sammlungspolitik*, 'Bonapartism' and 'social imperialism' – all possess a concealed 'biographical character' as they are derived from the methods of government supposedly adopted by Bismarck, who is thus treated even by his most savage critics as a genius.[11]

Both the (negative) fixation with Bismarck and the depersonalised approach of the new historiographical school become clear when we examine more closely the statements of its leading protagonist on our central theme, the political and social function of Kaiser Wilhelm II in his era. In his influential and controversial book *Das Deutsche Kaiserreich 1871–1918* Hans-Ulrich Wehler characterises Bismarck's system of government as 'a Bonapartist dictatorial régime bolstered by plebiscite' which was succeeded from 1890 onwards by a 'permanent state crisis' in which the 'authoritarian polycracy lacked coordination'. After Bismarck's dismissal by the young Kaiser (*nota bene!*), Wehler writes,

the Prussian-German power-pyramid lacked an apex. Both in real terms and in terms of atmosphere, a power-vacuum arose, which diverse personalities and forces tried to fill. Since neither they nor the parliament succeeded for any length of time in so doing, there arose in Germany, behind the façade of a grandiose [personal] régime, a permanent crisis of state which led to a polycracy of rival power-centres.

It is true, Wehler admits, that for a brief period after 1890 the young monarch did try to be both Kaiser and 'his own Chancellor' in an effort to establish his 'personal rule'.

But this did not come about in constitutional terms, nor did Wilhelm II succeed in bringing about a lasting transformation of constitutional reality, however much his advisory clique with their Byzantine word-play might have surrounded the decision-making process with the illusion of the Kaiser's powers to decide. Both from the point of view of personal capacity and of institutional necessity, ... the last Hohenzollern Kaiser was incapable of ruling the Reich monocratically. Even before the turn of the century he had lost this basically anachronistic game.

As the First World War was to reveal, Wehler argues, Wilhelm II was never more than a *Schattenkaiser* – a shadow Kaiser – without say or significance in German affairs. Wehler therefore arrives at the conclusion:

It was not Wilhelm II who impressed his stamp on Reich policy but the traditional oligarchies in conjunction with the anonymous forces of the authoritarian polycracy. Their power sufficed even without a semi-dictator [Bismarck], although with the help of a Bonapartist strategy, to defend the citadel of power – however fatal the consequences.[12]

Clearly, this cannot be the last word on so crucial an issue as that of the real distribution of power in the mightiest state in Europe in the quarter-century before the outbreak of the First World War. For Wehler's observations raise more questions than they answer. By what standards was the German Reich after Bismarck's fall in a state of 'permanent crisis'? Do we possess a notion of the 'normal' degree of chaos in a modern political system, and if we do, can it be applied to the remarkably 'unfinished' Wilhelmine Reich, which not only stood in the shadow of Bismarck but was bitterly attacked by him after his dismissal, and even beyond that *d'outre tombe*? Why were reformism and 'attentism' predominant in the Social Democratic movement if the crisis of state was so permanent and so profound, and why were so many of the Socialist leaders still monarchist in 1918? Is it really sufficient to explain this phenomenon as a product of the 'Bonapartist strategy' employed by the ruling elites? Why did the Catholic Centre party, south German particularism, the 'Austrian-clerical party' in Bavaria and the dynastic claims of the Wittelsbachs appear in the eyes of many contemporaries to be a greater danger to the survival of the Prusso-German Reich than Social Democracy? Who, exactly, were the 'anonymous forces of the authoritarian polycracy' who allegedly manipulated the entire restless nation of 60 million people with the aid of a Bonapartist strategy? How, and by whom, were they appointed? Who were the 'traditional oligarchies' and the 'pre-industrial elites', and by what mechanisms did they decide on the strategies to be adopted? Who ultimately arbitrated between the courses advocated by the 'rival power-centres'? (Or was the 'Bonapartist strategy' allegedly taken over from Bismarck so clear even after 1890, and the room for manoeuvre available to the elites so constricted by the great economic and social structures, that the strategy to be adopted in each single instance was more or less self-selecting?) Who belonged – and who did not belong – to the Kaiser's 'advisory clique' with their penchant for 'Byzantine word-play'? How did all these groups relate to each other, to the army and navy, and also to the so-called 'responsible government'? And what was the role of the Kaiser in the midst of these nameless and faceless forces and factors? By what criteria are we judging him when we assert that his grandiose personal rule was nothing but an 'illusion' and a 'façade', even though his contemporaries in the Reichstag and the press constantly complained about his power and his interventions? Why were men like Friedrich Naumann of the opinion in 1900 that there was 'no stronger force in present-day Germany than the Kaiser'?[13] Why did the English radical statesman Viscount Morley think Kaiser Wilhelm II 'the most important man in Europe',[14] and why did the English historian Sir John Wheeler-Bennett, who visited him in Doorn shortly before the outbreak of the Second World War, describe the ex-Kaiser as 'the man who dominated the political stage of Europe for thirty years'?[15] My aim in this chapter is to look for answers to these and other questions in the Baden documents edited by Walther Peter Fuchs. For surely the historian is obliged, now as ever, to adhere to the principle that theories and models are valid only as long as and only in so far as they are capable of explaining and interpreting the empirically ascertainable reality.

It is important to bear in mind, as was noted at the beginning of this chapter, that Fuchs's edition is thematically more broadly conceived than its title would suggest. It is only in small part concerned with the correspondence of Grand Duke Friedrich I of Baden: the letters from him and to him comprise less than 25 per cent of the last two volumes, with which we are primarily concerned. The correspondence between the Grand Duke and his imperial nephew represents only a tiny fraction of the whole – in total twenty letters from the Grand Duke to Wilhelm II and twenty-one letters from the Kaiser to his uncle by marriage are printed, and even here it should be noted that the majority of the letters from Wilhelm which are described as being 'in his own hand' were not composed by him personally but were merely formal courtesy letters copied by him from a draft prepared in the Ministry of the Household or the Civil Cabinet. The edition is therefore in no way an intimate exchange of private correspondence between monarchs which could justify the objection that the monarchical element might be overstated in the collection. On the contrary, the overwhelming majority of the material consists of the reports of the Baden envoys Brauer, Jagemann and Berckheim, whose informants in their turn were mainly the state secretaries of the Reich Offices, the Prussian ministers, higher officials of the central administration, fellow members of the Bundesrat and some of the party leaders in the Reichstag. The relationship of the Baden envoys to the imperial and royal court was – in so far as it existed at all – of a purely formal character. Indeed the intelligent Arthur von Brauer had the (no doubt justified) reputation in the Kaiser's eyes of being too 'Bismarckian' and too 'independent',[16] and Eugen von Jagemann had to be recalled after both the Kaiser and Chancellor von Bülow had complained with dramatic directness of the deficiencies in his social skills.[17] This observation on the character of these volumes is significant when we turn to the evidence contained in the individual documents.

We can state at the outset that the central theses of Hans-Ulrich Wehler and the so-called 'Bielefeld school' are scarcely supported by this abundant new evidence. We learn, for instance, that the *Sammlungspolitik* inaugurated by the Prussian Finance Minister Johannes von Miquel in 1897, which according to the doctrine of the 'primacy of domestic policy' must be seen as the key in explaining the Tirpitz battleship programme and the expansionist *Weltmachtpolitik*, 'found no resonance' among the public and was regarded even by the leaders of the National Liberal party as an 'artificial idea'.[18] The whole idea of Miquel's rallying call – his *Sammlungspolitik* – was 'extraordinarily unclear', and Jagemann was critical of the fact that 'despite many attempts ... it had not proved possible to persuade the Finance Minister to make a clear statement on its real meaning, especially in relation to the Centre party'.[19] The thesis that the agrarians were granted high grain import duties in return for their support of the 'dreadful' fleet is not only not mentioned in the hundreds of documents in this edition which touch on fleet-building on the one hand and tariffs on the other; it is directly contradicted by the fact, which is evident here as elsewhere, that the Reich leadership under Bülow, fully supported by Kaiser Wilhelm II, consistently and successfully pursued a 'middle-of-the-road' policy on customs duties in the face of agrarian demands.[20] In the light of these documents the question must be asked whether the Tirpitz battleship programme can be seen at all as a 'domestic crisis strategy'. At all events it hardly seems to have been successful as such, as Tirpitz himself complained in a letter to the Grand Duke of Baden in March 1903 that 'genuine enthusiasm among the people and therefore also among their parliamentary representatives is lacking for the vigorous development of our forces at sea'.[21]

If doubts already arise as to whether the model proposed by the 'new orthodoxy' can explain the constitutional peculiarities of the German Reich, they are further strengthened by an element in the Kaiserreich's constitutional reality which surfaces very clearly in this collection of documents but is barely recognised by Wehler and his school (and which indeed cannot be subsumed as a significant factor in their model). I refer to the Reich's federal structure, which was designed to take account of the special rights and sensitivities of the south German states in particular.

The establishment of a Baden Legation in Berlin and a Prussian one in

Karlsruhe is an indication in itself of the remarkably 'unfinished' character of the Reich's structure – it is as if the development towards a modern, unitary constitutional state had stopped at the half-way mark. But the federal system of the Kaiserreich went further: in 1894 Baden Legations were also opened in Munich and Stuttgart,[22] and a little later Russia even suggested that a Russian military attaché should be stationed in Bavaria.[23] These legations were not merely courtesy institutions but represented an important component of the political structure of the Reich, and they were a pointer to the fact – hardly touched upon in (arid) debates concerning the 'primacy' of domestic or of foreign policy respectively – that the Lesser German Reich, forged by war and diplomacy, in many respects continued to be governed by foreign policy methods even after its so-called unification. A related problem, frequently reported on by the Baden envoys, was the continued existence and indeed the constant growth of particularism, especially in Bavaria. The perceptive Baden envoy in Munich, Baron Ferdinand von Bodman, reported in December 1895 from the Bavarian capital that 'under the influence of the all-dominating court and of the Austrian-clerical party, all measures ... are directed at building up Bavaria as a *self-sufficient* ... state'. Above all in the two Bavarian army corps, according to Bodman, 'the Reich and its head, the Kaiser, are being eliminated to the furthest possible extent'. Count Anton Monts, the Prussian envoy in Munich, was convinced that 'a process of detachment [by Bavaria] from the Reich was taking place', Bodman reported.[24] Similarly, the astute Arthur von Brauer, who had served for many years under Bismarck, observed in May 1893 that Bavarian particularism was making enormous advances. He wrote to the Grand Duke: 'Under the influence of the Old-Bavarian party the monstrous idea is gaining more and more ground that south Germany should be placed under the special hegemony of Bavaria just as north Germany is under Prussia's.'[25] In 1898 the Grand Duke of Baden himself felt obliged to warn the Reich government against moving too close to the Catholic Centre party because the aim of this party was 'to destroy the present Reich in order to create a new federal constitution with a Catholic head'.[26] With each publication of documents from the post-Bismarckian era it becomes clearer how widespread and deeply rooted such fears about the dissolution of the Reich were in leading political circles. Whether they were based on a sober assessment of the objective circumstances or are ultimately explicable only in psychological terms, these anxiety complexes are of absolutely crucial importance in evaluating the political culture of Wilhelmine Germany.[27]

Moreover, it rapidly becomes clear from this collection of documents – as indeed it does from Philipp Eulenburg's correspondence,[28] from the 'secret papers' of Friedrich von Holstein[29] and other recent publications – that the

policies of the German Reich (as of every political system) were not determined by some 'anonymous forces' or 'oligarchies', but by men of flesh and
blood, with all their emotions and vanities. 'The *strongest* mainspring of all
action – and therefore also of politics – will always be personal passion',
observed Philipp Eulenburg in 1905 in a letter to Bülow.[30] A good example
from the present collection of this human element in politics is the attempt
by Bavaria to appoint Count Eduard von Montgelas as its envoy in Stuttgart
and Karlsruhe. In the summer of 1895 the elderly Prince Regent Luitpold
of Bavaria had gone to Vienna and while there was so entranced by the
'fascinating' Countess Maria Magdalene von Montgelas – a Russian born in
Lisbon – that he promised to appoint her husband as Bavaria's representative at the courts of Württemberg and Baden. On his return to Munich the
Prince Regent expressed his wish to see Montgelas appointed to these posts
so strongly that the 'responsible' head of the Bavarian government, Count
Crailsheim, could not resist him. Crailsheim's objection that while in
Vienna Count and Countess Montgelas had acted in a manner so hostile to
the Reich that they were no longer received by the German ambassador
there (Philipp Eulenburg) made as little impression on the Prince Regent as
did the observation of the horrified Stuttgart government that the count and
countess lived so far beyond their 'financial circumstances and salary' that
speculation abounded as to 'whether the means for this lifestyle flowed from
clerical funds or even from the lively intercourse' of the 'charming and
happy-go-lucky' countess with Archduke Ludwig Viktor and other highly
placed gentlemen. However curious it might seem to us today, there was in
fact for a time a real threat that 'Bavaria might break off diplomatic relations
with Stuttgart'! Only with the help of the influential Chief of Cabinet,
Baron Friedrich von Zoller, was the Bavarian Prime Minister finally able to
persuade the Prince Regent to send instead of Montgelas the 'somewhat
eccentric' Baron von der Pfordten as envoy to Stuttgart and Karlsruhe. But,
as Bodman reported to Karlsruhe, the 'tensions between the courts of
Munich and Stuttgart which were already present beforehand' were
naturally exacerbated by this incident.[31] If Bavarian politics in the Regency
era cannot be understood without taking into account the foibles of the
members of court society, this is all the more true of Berlin politics under
Kaiser Wilhelm II.

For Wehler's thesis that the Prusso-German power pyramid lacked an
apex after Bismarck's fall, and that Wilhelm II was no more than a 'shadow
Kaiser', is quickly undermined by the evidence of the Baden documents.
The politically initiated among the Kaiser's contemporaries – who were, we
must assume, in a better position to understand the Wilhelmine system of
government than we are today – were at any rate of a completely different
opinion. The employment protection conference of 1890, according to

Jagemann, 'sprang from the personal initiative of H.M. the Kaiser'.[32] The choice of the Krupp director Jencke to be Prussian Minister of Finance (in the event he turned the post down) was the 'product of the Kaiser's own initiative', reported Brauer.[33] The Kaiser's sensational speech of December 1890 outlining the future of Prussia's schools flowed, according to another of Brauer's reports, 'directly from H.M.'s own inspiration'.[34] The replacement of Count Kuno Rantzau, Bismarck's son-in-law, by Philipp Eulenburg as Prussian envoy in Munich could be traced back to 'H.M. the Kaiser's very own initiative'.[35] The controversial canal policy of the Prussian government was based 'on the special initiative of the Kaiser', wrote Jagemann in October 1898.[36] Such examples could be multiplied almost indefinitely. They point to the conclusion that in many if not in all cases, the Kaiser's power of decision-making did indeed play a central role. 'The decision on the question whether and what should happen ... lies entirely with H.M. the Kaiser himself', Jagemann stated in a report of April 1896.[37] According at any rate to the understanding of contemporaries, as reflected in the choice of words used by the Baden envoys, the Wilhelmine system of decision-making was not only federal, not only personalised, but also and above all monarchocentric. The Wilhelmine Kaiserreich was no rationalised, modern, constitutional and administrative state, governed in all important matters by a 'responsible' Reich Chancellor as leader of an anonymous bureaucracy operating in the interests of 'traditional oligarchies'. It was a league of monarchs with the 'sacred person of the Kaiser and King'[38] at its head. 'The strength of the Reich', as the Grand Duke of Baden formulated it in 1897, 'rests on a firm union of the federal states; but these must be so structured that no doubt can exist as to the validity of their monarchical basis'.[39] But this basis stood, as Bülow himself recognised, in direct contradiction to the 'principle of state omnipotence' which 'negated monarchy by the grace of God, undermined the monarchical principle and paved the way for a republic'.[40]

The debate on the role of Kaiser Wilhelm II in the decision-making process of the Wilhelmine Kaiserreich has got stuck on the issue of the applicability of the contemporary polemical catchphrase 'personal rule'. If the sometime democratic Reichstag deputy Erich Eyck, following in the footsteps of Eugen Richter, was still willing to give his political history of the Reich from 1890 to 1914 the overall title *Das persönliche Regiment Wilhelms II.*,[41] the constitutional historians Fritz Hartung and Ernst Rudolf Huber sought – at times with highly arcane jurisprudential arguments – to deny the very existence of a 'personal rule' of Kaiser Wilhelm II.[42] However, neither the absolutist delusions of Wilhelm II as invoked by Eyck, nor the obviously apologist attempts of Hartung and Huber to restrict the concept of 'personal rule' to its 'precise meaning in constitutional law' as a 'breach of the constitution "from above"',[43] can serve as a scholarly standard by which to measure the real power and influence exercised by Kaiser Wilhelm II. In order to avoid such misunderstanding, it would perhaps be advisable to replace the term 'personal rule' with the more neutral and flexible term 'kingship mechanism'. In any discussion of the political and social function of the Kaiser, it would at all events be useful to bear in mind the following five points:

1. Kaiser Wilhelm's participation in the formulation of German policies was not constant; different phases can be identified during the thirty years of his reign. The years 1888–90 were dominated by the conflict with the all-powerful Bismarck; the years 1890–7 should be seen as the transition from an 'improvised' to an 'institutionalised personal rule' (Huber); the Bülow era (1897–1908) represented in reality, just as he had promised in 1896, the era of 'personal rule in the good sense'. The extent to which the Kaiser's position was shattered by the Eulenburg–Moltke–Harden trials and the *Daily Telegraph* crisis of 1908 urgently needs to be ascertained by a detailed analysis of the relationship between court and Wilhelmstrasse in the first five years of Bethmann Hollweg's Chancellorship. That Wilhelm II was little more than a 'shadow Kaiser' during the First World War is not in dispute.

2. In the phase of 'personal rule in the good sense', the Kaiser's political initiative no longer bore the character of interference in the business of the official departments of state. On the contrary the key departments in the 'responsible government' were in the hands of men (Bülow, Tirpitz, Miquel, Podbielski) who had been appointed by the Kaiser precisely in order to carry out his intentions. In this system of 'institutionalised personal rule' interference by the Kaiser in the machinery of government was hardly necessary.

3. In elucidating the role played by Wilhelm II in the formulation of German policy it is not enough to enumerate the measures which he initiated. We must take account too of those which were *not* put into effect because it was known in advance that the Kaiser and his entourage would block them, and because each Reich Chancellor, Minister and Secretary of State knew only too well that a difference of opinion with the Kaiser could lead to an immediate loss of 'All-Highest confidence' and with that to the termination of one's career. This blocking mechanism by the actual or indeed perhaps only assumed opposition of the Kaiser to measures deemed essential or desirable could perhaps be termed 'negative personal rule'.

4. The 'polycratic chaos' of the rival centres of power, much emphasised by some present-day historians, was not an indication of the impossibility of the Kaiser's exercising a role of central importance; it was, on the contrary, the consequence of a system of government constructed on the principle of

'All-Highest confidence'.[44] The separation of the civil and military spheres was supposed to guarantee the monarch's ultimate power of decision-making and to secure his absolute power of command in military matters. Even within the army and navy the system of direct access to the monarch was extended further and further under Wilhelm II, with fatal organisational consequences. Over and above this it must be remembered that not a single appointment to an official position, and no political measure, could be undertaken without the express consent of the Kaiser. Each statesman and official, each army and naval officer, each political grouping within the ruling elite, each member of court society, all were condemned to try to enlist the favour of the 'All-Highest Person'. Whoever enjoyed the Kaiser's support could assert himself against his rivals and indeed often against his own superiors.[45] It is precisely this attempt by the contending groups and individuals to win the ruler's confidence and with it his support that the sociologist Norbert Elias has called the 'kingship mechanism'.[46]

5. In the development of his position and in exercising his monarchical powers, the Kaiser was by no means acting alone. He had at his disposal not only a considerable administrative apparatus (the Ministry of the Household, the Civil, Military and Naval Cabinets), but he was also surrounded by friends and by men who revered him – the General Adjutants and Flügeladjutanten, the Liebenberg circle around Philipp Eulenburg, Messrs Krupp, Stumm, Henckel, etc. – who were ready with their advice as each question arose. As this circle of friends was selected purely on the basis of the monarch's inclinations, it can be said to have represented the institutionalisation of the Kaiser's personality. As Isabel Hull has convincingly demonstrated in her study of the Kaiser's entourage, here too 'personalities' and 'structures' are inextricably interlinked.[47]

We can now elaborate on these points by turning to the Baden documents. First, let us ask the simple question: which German policy measures in the Wilhelmine epoch can be traced back unambiguously to the Kaiser's initiative? One example would be the Lex Heinze against prostitution, which was announced by Imperial Decree in the official *Reichsanzeiger* in October 1891;[48] another, Wilhelm's school speech of December 1890, to which reference has already been made, which decisively changed the entire direction of Prussian education policy;[49] a third, the great Army Bill, which he simply 'commanded' the War Minister to prepare through a Flügeladjutant on the third anniversary of his accession to the throne, and which, after many painful crises and convulsions, became law after the Reichstag dissolution of 1893;[50] or finally the trade treaties and customs tariffs, which, both in the early 1890s[51] and again a decade later, were accomplished basically because the Kaiser, with remarkable consistency, stuck to a moderate middle-of-the-road policy in the face of the vociferous demands of the East

Elbian landed nobility. The monarch's position on this issue had 'clearly been completely consistent and unchanging throughout', Jagemann reported in March 1902, adding that even the agrarians now had to recognise 'that because of H.M.'s declaration of his will no further concessions could be gained for agriculture'.[52] The three best examples of policies inaugurated by the Kaiser, however, are the social and socialist policies, the gigantic fleet-building programme and the Prussian canal policy.

Reference has already been made to the fact that the international conference on workers' protection in 1890 as well as the whole social welfare policy pursued by Baron von Berlepsch 'sprang from the personal initiative of H.M. the Kaiser'.[53] It was only logical, therefore, that Berlepsch had to submit his resignation in 1896 when he recognised that the Ministry of State, 'and with it of course the highest will of the Kaiser', was no longer behind his reformist programme.[54] As early as December 1891 the Kaiser had 'provoked panic in all timid souls' when he made a forceful speech against social democracy at a swearing-in ceremony of new recruits. Arthur von Brauer reported to Karlsruhe that this speech was in no way the product of 'overhasty oratory' but 'the expression of the Kaiser's innermost conviction'. 'Given the character of H.M.', he wrote, it was 'psychologically explicable' that disappointment over the political effects of the social welfare policy he had initiated 'should have brought about a complete reversal of attitude'. Brauer expressed the fear that the Kaiser had now 'come to the conclusion that ... the problem of the workers could only be solved ... by force'.[55] With a consistency which contrasts so sharply with the widely held view of him as an impulsive and unpredictable monarch, amenable to all influences and therefore not to be taken seriously, the Kaiser henceforth pursued a series of anti-socialist projects which, while they could and did encounter opposition in the Reichstag, were *not* repudiated by the so-called 'responsible government'. Following the assassination of the French President Sadi Carnot in the summer of 1894, for example, 'H.M. ... gave the Chancellor the command' to draw up measures 'aimed at the anarchist-social-democratic movement'.[56] The 'government' had long ago ceased to regard the placing of suggestions before the Kaiser as its task; *it* was the body which received the Kaiser's 'commands'. Jagemann reported in October 1894 that Raschdau regarded it as certain that the anti-revolutionary 'speech made by H.M. the Kaiser in Königsberg also contained a legislative initiative' and the only question was whether, alongside 'a general penalty for attacks against the foundations of the state (religion, monarchy, marriage, property) a new offence of engaging in strikes and boycotts should also ... be created'.[57] Four years after the failure in the Reichstag of the 'Anti-Revolution Bill' which emerged from the Kaiser's initiative, the monarch in a speech in Bad Oeynhausen announced a sharp law for the protection of those willing to work: anyone found guilty of intimidating 'blacklegs' would be punished with hard labour. The Ministry of State complied with the Kaiser's command but had throughout the whole time that the bill was being drafted the fear that 'the Kaiser would not approve the resolutions so far decided on because they did not go far enough'.[58] The ministers' fear was perfectly justified, for on his journey to Palestine the Kaiser sharpened in his own hand the punishments provided in practically every clause of the draft bill prepared by the Ministry of State.[59] The Secretary of State for the Interior was not even able to delay the introduction of the so-called Hard Labour Bill: he received the abrupt 'command from H.M. ... to introduce the bill' into the Reichstag.[60] Whatever historians of the right or left might later say, in 1899 Count Posadowsky was certainly not of the opinion that Wilhelm II was a mere 'shadow Kaiser'.

If the Anti-Revolution Bill and the Hard Labour Bill failed in the end because of Reichstag opposition, things were different in the case of the fleet policy similarly initiated by the Kaiser, even if Admiral von Hollmann, the Secretary of State in the Reich Navy Office, was forced to admit in February 1896 'that there are not as many as ten people in the Reichstag in favour of great future fleet plans'.[61] The driving force behind the great fleet plan was demonstrably neither the elderly Reich Chancellor Prince Hohenlohe nor the Navy Secretary von Hollmann, but Kaiser Wilhelm II and his Chief of Cabinet Admiral Gustav Baron von Senden-Bibran. As early as June 1896 the Baden envoy was able to report to Karlsruhe that a great fleet plan had been drawn up which set out a programme of ship construction through to the year 1908. 'The pressing factor in this question', as Jagemann explained, 'is the Naval Cabinet, which reinforces H.M.'s inclinations.'[62] The Foreign Secretary had already complained in February 1895 that the Kaiser had 'nothing but the navy in his head'.[63] Jagemann reported that Wilhelm, at the conclusion of a two-hour lecture delivered without notes, had emphasised 'as a perspective for the future the need to acquire further armoured ships' because it was on such ships that 'the outcome of naval battles depended'.[64] The introduction of the first Navy Bill in October 1897 seemed to many members of the 'responsible government' to be 'tactically inopportune'; the Bill was put before the Reichstag nevertheless because 'in this matter H.M. the Kaiser has already ... made up his mind' and was unwilling to brook further discussion.[65]

If, on the evidence of these reports, the conclusion seems inescapable that Kaiser Wilhelm II was the originator and co-author of the 'Tirpitz Plan', this is even more the case in relation to the second Navy Bill of 1900. 'H.M. the Kaiser regards the significant strengthening of the naval armed forces as a necessity', the Reich Chancellor informed the Allied German Governments on 6 November 1899,[66] and this was no empty diplomatic rhetoric. The timing of the introduction of the Bill was not the only issue settled by an imperial 'command'; all the details of this momentous step were similarly determined by the Kaiser. Immediately before his departure for Britain in November 1899, Kaiser Wilhelm II gave

> Admiral Tirpitz the command that the Navy Bill should not be introduced in the Reichstag and that generally all discussions on the expansion of the naval plan must be avoided until after his return from England. The Kaiser intends to be close by during the debates on this matter so that he can intervene with his directives at any time.[67]

As a third example of the evidently rather one-sided relationship between the Kaiser and the 'responsible government', the Baden reports offer the events surrounding the failure of the Prussian Canal Bill in the Prussian Landtag at the turn of the century. After the rejection of the Bill the ministers, according to Eugen von Jagemann, were saying quite openly that

> they did not know what was going to happen with regard either to personnel changes or the question of a dissolution. Everything depends in effect solely on the decision of H.M., and it is all the more difficult to predict what that will be as it is precisely the personal element within the Kaiser's sensibility ... which is to the fore at the moment.[68]

Everyone in the Wilhelmstrasse was therefore 'very curious to know what decisions, if any, the Kaiser would announce to his Ministry of State on his return here from Rominten'.[69]

Anyone studying these documents without prejudice cannot but arrive at the conclusion that Kaiser Wilhelm II, far from being a mere 'shadow Kaiser' when compared to the 'traditional oligarchies' and the 'anonymous forces of the authoritarian polycracy', was in possession of a degree of power after ten years of his reign which made him appear in the eyes of all informed observers as his own Reich Chancellor. Even Maximilian Harden, whom no-one could accuse of being a member of the Kaiser's 'Byzantine court clique', wrote in *Die Zukunft* in 1902: 'The Kaiser is his own Reich Chancellor. All the important political decisions of the past twelve years have been made by him.'[70] The Reich Chancellor, the Secretaries of State of the Reich Offices and the Prussian ministers had in effect sunk to the level of the monarch's lackeys, who simply accepted and as far as possible sought to put into effect 'the decisions normally already arrived at by H.M.' the Kaiser.[71] As Jagemann informed his predecessor von Brauer on 8 November 1899, the position of the ministers 'had completely altered in comparison with earlier times': 'These days the principle of influential, responsible advisers with their own ideas has retreated far into the background; instead we have executive organs of a higher will, who put into effect decisions which are sometimes reached independently of the advice tendered, and sometimes even contrary to that advice.' Jagemann observed that the ministers had in fact become executive royal secretaries rather than constitutional advisers to the monarch and he regarded it as indicative of the times that Wilhelm II had even abolished the right of ministers to submit their resignation. The Kaiser, Jagemann explained, had recently written on a minister's request to be allowed to resign that 'he wished that in future such requests should not be initiated' by the minister in question; 'he himself would announce when the time for such a step had arrived!'[72] In the light of so many and unambiguous declarations by contemporaries, it is incomprehensible that no fewer than three North American historians have recently come to the conclusion that the struggle for power between the Kaiser and the administrative bureaucracy resulted in 1897 in a clear victory for the latter.[73] The reverse was the case: the 'personal rule' of Kaiser Wilhelm II had become 'institutionalised'.

In the whole history of the German Reich, no Reich Chancellor was so carefully chosen nor so extensively prepared for office as Bernhard von Bülow. Proposed repeatedly by Philipp Eulenburg since 1893,[74] accepted by the Kaiser's military entourage as future Chancellor since early 1894,[75] Bülow was to be a different kind of Chancellor from his three predecessors. He was convinced that Caprivi and Hohenlohe had made the mistake of thinking of themselves as representing the *'gouvernement'*, and to a certain extent even parliament, against the Kaiser. With his own appointment, he promised, everything would be different. In a letter to Eulenburg of 23 July 1896 he declared that he would regard himself 'as the executive tool of His Majesty, so to speak his political Chief of Staff. With me, personal rule – in the good sense – would really begin.'[76]

No-one recognised more clearly than Bülow that the machinery of German government could only be driven on the basis of 'All-Highest confidence'. He had seen how Reich Chancellor von Caprivi had been able to settle 'all awkward questions, and even those which were unwelcome to H.M.'[77] *for as long as* he retained the Kaiser's confidence. But as soon as that confidence was shattered over the School Bill crisis in the spring of 1892, with the result that he lost 'his leading position with the Kaiser', Caprivi had found himself 'facing many opponents, including some at court'. At that time Brauer had reported to Karlsruhe with prophetic insight: 'It seems to be the fate of all leading statesmen in Prussia that they rapidly encounter enemies at court who force them to adopt a defensive posture upwards as well as downwards.'[78]

At first Prince Hohenlohe – 'Uncle Chlodwig' as Wilhelm called him – had also enjoyed the Kaiser's confidence. Hohenlohe, too, was determined not to make Caprivi's mistake of disrupting that vital relationship by 'sudden, resolute opposition', but to nurture it 'by sympathy, hard work and care'.[79] But the Köller crisis of November/December 1895, in which Hohenlohe felt compelled to act as the spokesman of the Prussian Ministry of State and to oppose Wilhelm II's wishes, was enough to destroy the relationship of trust between Kaiser and Chancellor. 'The Reich Chancellor's position is no longer what it was', wrote Marschall von Bieberstein in his diary after a conversation with the Kaiser's ex-tutor Dr Hinzpeter in January 1896.[80]

Bülow's promise of July 1896 that he would be nothing more than the Kaiser's 'executive tool' was not, of course, to be taken entirely literally. Needless to say he calculated that he would be able, by a constant stream of flattery, to gain or retain the confidence of the All-Highest in order to realise his own plans (in so far as he had any). Soon after he took over the Foreign Office in the autumn of 1897, he wrote that the cultivation of his personal relations with the Kaiser had to form the focus of his entire political activity because 'if I don't maintain constant (verbal and written) contact with His Majesty, the *status quo*, which was welded together with such difficulty, will fall apart at the seams'.[81] Precisely because he recognised so clearly the central importance of the Kaiser's confidence for his position as Reich Chancellor, it was unthinkable for Bülow to damage this relationship of trust by making an unwelcome suggestion. He once wrote to Holstein, in terms which betrayed the nature of his entire system: 'I cannot consider it useful to make suggestions to His Majesty the Kaiser which have no prospect of actual success and only make him annoyed with me.'[82] To put it another way, Bülow's 'personal rule in the good sense' amounted to what I have suggested we call 'negative personal rule'.

By assiduously cultivating his relations with Wilhelm II, Bülow was able to enjoy the monarch's special trust for a longer period than any other Chancellor. With the Kaiser's support behind him he was then able to control the complicated Prusso-German system of government with more authority than had been possible since Bismarck's fall. After the ministerial crisis of May 1901 Jagemann reported: 'Under the present Kaiser no Chancellor has been able to construct his ministry on his own terms to the same extent.'[83] The absolute dependence of Bülow's position on the Kaiser's personal confidence, however, was something which every informed observer clearly recognised. When the Chancellor revealed one of the Kaiser's marginal comments in the Reichstag, Jagemann feared that the moment of truth had already arrived. And although an immediate crisis was avoided, he nonetheless remained concerned. 'The main question albeit remains', he wrote, 'whether H.M. the Kaiser has not been annoyed by this, and whether this could flare up again at some point in the future.'[84] Only when, even later, no act of revenge on the Kaiser's part followed, did

Jagemann feel justified in assuming that 'the Chancellor's position . . . must be extraordinarily strong . . . at the All-Highest level'.[85] And when Bülow on one occasion even dared to publish one of Wilhelm's telegrams 'without first having sought All-Highest permission', Brauer too came to the conclusion: 'The Chancellor feels secure in his master's confidence.'[86]

By its very nature, however, this system of flattery based on the principle of 'All-Highest confidence' and on the avoidance of all difficult or disputed questions had sooner or later to result in catastrophe. By 1905/6 at the latest, with the fiasco over the Björkö treaty, the Morocco crisis, the colonial debates and Bülow's fainting fit in the Reichstag, sufficient ingredients for a massive explosion had been assembled. It almost occurred in November 1906, when Wilhelm II twice in one week *commanded* the Prussian Minister of Agriculture, General Viktor von Podbielski, who had been picked by the Kaiser personally, to stay in office – even though he had become so unacceptable to parliament that Bülow and the whole Prussian Ministry of State had to insist on Podbielski's resignation – so creating a situation that was exactly parallel to the Köller crisis of 1895. As Jagemann's successor Count Siegmund von Berckheim reported, the experienced Bavarian envoy, Count Lerchenfeld, was offering the prognosis that Bülow would indeed succeed in pushing through Podbielski's resignation, 'but this would be a Pyrrhic victory from which he would not benefit for very long because the relationship between the Kaiser and the Chancellor is at the moment very tense'.[87]

It was no coincidence, then, but a development springing naturally from the system itself, that at this very moment rumours began circulating in many places – not only and not at the outset in Harden's *Zukunft* – about the backstairs influence of the 'Liebenberg round table' led by Philipp Eulenburg. And if Bülow temporarily succeeded by means of the Reichstag dissolution and the formation of the 'Bülow Block' in 'strengthening his position anew at the All-Highest level'[88] – and simultaneously in breaking the neck of his best friend, Eulenburg, as well as that of his closest adviser on internal policy, Posadowsky – the 'disequilibrium at the top' (Harden) was now complete, and the national outcry against the Kaiser's 'personal rule' which manifested itself in the *Daily Telegraph* crisis was nothing but the logical and overdue outcome of the Bülow system. It was just as logical, however, that Bülow's days as Reich Chancellor were numbered the moment he was compelled in that crisis of November 1908 to come off the fence, thereby forfeiting for good the 'All-Highest confidence'.

Bülow's dependence on the support of the 'All-Highest' master was anything but exceptional. The whole government of the Reich and Prussia, all the higher civil service, indeed in the last analysis the entire *classe politique* of Wilhelmine Germany, were suffused with the desire to win or retain the favour of the 'All-Highest Person'. The 'kingship mechanism' was – as the Baden documents show – widespread to an astonishing and disturbing degree.

Not long after Bismarck's fall from power Brauer felt compelled to report a worrying spinelessness amongst ministers, officials and officers in relation to the Kaiser. Even in their 'intimate private conversations' the officials of the Wilhelmstrasse were more and more muted, he said, because 'everyone knows that H.M. . . . is very sensitive to the slightest critical remark which his officials or other persons of higher society might allow themselves to pass'.[89] Brauer reserved his sharpest condemnation for the Byzantinism of the army officers who constantly said what their Supreme Warlord wanted to hear. On the question of the length of military service, which dominated the politics of the early 1890s, the army leaders knew what one '*wished*' to hear 'on high', as Brauer wrote to Karlsruhe, 'and you can imagine how the reports then sound'.[90] The Baden representative in Berlin was soon observing that 'whoever has a sense of caution or has to have consideration for others . . . hardly [dares] to speak any more about the Army Bill, at any rate other than in terms of praise', since the Kaiser regarded 'every contradiction almost as a malicious act'.[91] At the New Year reception for the Commanding Generals in January 1893, Kaiser Wilhelm II 'stressed very sharply that he would not tolerate any divergent opinion . . . from his Generals'. 'The effect was marked', Brauer recorded. 'I spoke to several [Generals] who clearly did not dare to voice any criticism of the Bill.'[92] Brauer even reproached General von Loë with having spoken to the Kaiser about the Army Bill in terms which were in direct contradiction to his own innermost convictions. The Baden diplomat who had learnt his trade in the service of Bismarck then asked in despair: 'On whom can the Kaiser still rely if such highly placed military people simply tell him what he wants to hear? The number of men who still have the courage of their own convictions is getting smaller and smaller.'[93]

Brauer thought it absolutely typical that General Adolf von Bülow should first enquire of his relative, the Chief of the Military Cabinet General Wilhelm von Hahnke, 'whether one could yet risk saying something in favour of the Courts Martial Regulations'. Hahnke gave Adolf Bülow the nod 'that it would not now be dangerous, because H.M. has already decided to make this concession'. Brauer observed on this episode that 'Herr von Bülow . . . would certainly never have expressed himself in the way he did unless he had received hints to this effect from Hahnke, who was in a position to know'.[94] In the autumn of 1897 the Grand Duke of Baden personally tried to talk Admiral Tirpitz, who had only just been appointed and still stood high in the Kaiser's esteem, into taking a position on this awkward question which threatened to damage the grandiose fleet plans.

After consultation with the Reich Chancellor and the Chief of the Naval Cabinet, however, Tirpitz turned down the Grand Duke's request on grounds which anticipated Bernhard von Bülow's in 1899 almost word for word: 'I would be worsening my position in relation to H.M. for a subsidiary aim without any hope of success.'[95] We see that 'negative personal rule' was not confined to the Kaiser–Chancellor relationship.

How firmly the Kaiser, by operating the 'kingship mechanism', had the whole apparatus of civil and military power in his hands can be seen from the ease with which he was able to persuade ministers, secretaries of state, generals or governors to remain in office by a simple gesture of friendship or favour, or alternatively to drive them to resign by deliberately injuring their feelings. The notion that it was the duty of a public servant to fight for a policy he considered correct was completely lost. A smile, a handshake, a greetings telegram or the conferment of an honour was quite sufficient to reverse a threatened resignation. Heinrich von Boetticher withdrew his letter of resignation in 1892 when Wilhelm II rejected it 'in the most flattering manner'.[96] After the fall of Reich Chancellor von Caprivi, his deputy von Boetticher declared: 'He himself was not entirely sure whether the Kaiser placed any value on his remaining in office, but it seemed to him that it would appear disloyal to depart in the middle of a change' of Chancellors.[97]

When the Prussian Minister of Finance and Vice-President of the Ministry of State, Johannes von Miquel, 'announced his intention to resign' after a violent clash with the Kaiser, the latter, who at this time 'did not want to break with him', sent him 'his best wishes on New Year's night ... which had a calming effect'.[98] Injuring people's feelings was also a tactic deliberately employed by the Kaiser as part of the Wilhelmine system of government. General Paul von Leszczynski, who had distinguished himself in the Franco-Prussian war, submitted his resignation because 'H.M. had greeted the General ... only very curtly and frostily', and had conducted a conversation with the Mayor of Cuxhaven 'without further acknowledging the General by speaking to him'.[99] Adolf Baron Marschall von Bieberstein, the Badenese Secretary of State in the Berlin Foreign Office, tolerated the Kaiser's offensiveness longer than most. 'What does it matter to me if one day I am cut and the next I am flooded with charm', he once mused, seemingly above such 'comedy'.[100] In the end, however, he too had to recognise that 'without H.M.'s confidence [he] would not be able to stay' in office.[101] In February 1897 all informed observers recognised that Marschall had lost the 'All-Highest confidence' and would consequently soon have to resign. As Jagemann wrote in his report of 1 February 1897: 'Neither when authorising [Marschall's] leave, nor during his sick leave, nor on his return, has H.M. given the slightest sign of gracious sympathy, which seems unusual in view of the abundant demonstrations of kindness made to those who are in highest favour.'[102]

The most common cause of the loss of the Kaiser's trust was without doubt the qualities of honesty and independence of spirit, which were consistently interpreted by the monarch as malice and personal insult. Bismarck, Waldersee, Caprivi, the Prussian War Minister General Walter Bronsart von Schellendorf – all were relieved of their duties for such reasons. Even Bronsart's successor, Heinrich von Gossler, who initially had to promise that he wished only to be 'his Kaiser's general' and who, according to Tirpitz, rapidly 'sank to the level where he was merely implementing [Military] Cabinet orders',[103] had to pack his bags and go because he had 'behaved in a more independent manner towards H.M. than was deemed acceptable'.[104] The Baden documents also illuminate the way in which, alongside these more political reasons, purely personal factors played a significant role in the Kaiser's decisions. The recall of Eugen von Jagemann from Berlin in the Spring of 1903, for instance, was caused not least 'by H.M. the Kaiser's dislike of the envoy's pushiness and talkativeness', as the German Chancellor told the Prussian envoy in Karlsruhe.[105] The 'incredibly ruthless' retirement of Count Arthur von Posadowsky after fourteen years as head of a Reich Office was linked in part with the fact, as Berckheim reported, 'that the Kaiser had never particularly liked Count Posadowsky personally' and that, 'more especially', the 'strange, loud and always intrusive' character of Countess Elise von Posadowsky 'had never been congenial to H.M.'[106]

Whoever enjoyed the Kaiser's confidence had political power and social advantages, whether or not he occupied a government position. Four years before Theobald von Bethmann Hollweg was appointed Reich Chancellor, Berckheim could report to Karlsruhe that Bethmann 'was in great favour with H.M. the Kaiser', with the result that he had been 'granted permission to give direct advice to the monarch, frequently on matters not directly relevant to his ministerial responsibilities'.[107] The industrialist Carl Baron von Stumm-Halberg was able, thanks to his close relationship to Kaiser Wilhelm II, to play a major role in formulating the anti-socialist policies of the 1890s, even though he occupied no official post. When Stumm once dared to contradict the Kaiser, however, the 'Stumm era' was over. 'From that time onwards', Jagemann reported, 'H.M. avoided all except purely formal intercourse with Baron von Stumm.'[108] Holstein once warned Philipp Eulenburg that the Kaiser could not select his ministers 'as one chooses a mistress',[109] and yet he came very close to doing just that in the ministerial crisis of May 1901. Jagemann reported on a dinner at which Wilhelm and his '*Bülowchen*' visited various rooms 'in which could be found ministerial candidates *en cachette*, separated off from each other for individual interview'.[110]

Even in the conduct of his representative duties the Kaiser not infrequently allowed himself to be governed by his own personal likes and dislikes. At a dinner organised by Boetticher for parliamentarians in 1892, the Kaiser ignored the forty-two guests 'almost completely' and only conversed with the persons sitting next to him.[111] A court ball arranged for the diplomatic corps went off in a similar fashion: the representatives of various German and foreign courts stood for one whole hour strictly according to seniority until Wilhelm appeared with his retinue, and even then the Kaiser 'spoke a very few words only with the two ambassadors who were present and their wives, while everyone else was totally ignored'.[112] Caprivi's attempt to get the Kaiser acquainted with some of the Prussian envoys at the courts of the middle German states failed 'because the talkative Postmaster General . . . was able to captivate H.M. with his somewhat risqué jokes', so that the diplomats were scarcely able to have a word with him and 'were in turn hardly taken notice of by H.M.'[113] When the Saxon envoy Count Hohenthal invited the spokesmen on the Bundesrat to a meal with the Kaiser, Wilhelm II struck all the names from the guest list and called for 'a more informal company'. Brauer commented ruefully that his Saxon colleague 'should have known H.M. well enough to realise that the representatives of all the federal states . . . would not in the eyes of the Kaiser be particularly welcome guests at table'. The Baden representative thought it characteristic of Wilhelm II that he should surround himself at a court ball with five beautiful young ladies (including the wife of a mere captain or lieutenant), while the other princely personages, diplomats and dignitaries were forced to take up positions strictly according to rank. 'It is a peculiarity of H.M.', Brauer observed in a report of 6 March 1892, 'that while he loves great celebrations and the pomp that goes with them, he does not like to allow himself to be confined by considerations of etiquette.'[114]

The Baden documents demonstrate with great clarity that, above the economic and social structures but also above the administrative bureaucracy with the Reich Chancellor and Prussian Minister-President at its head, there existed a further structure, namely court society, without which the whole system cannot be understood. Originating in the age of absolutism and persisting in its essentials almost unchanged into the second decade of our own century, this court society now appears alien to our eyes.[115] But only those who recognise in the Court Precedence Regulation the inner structure and value system of this court society, only those who comprehend the social radiation and the integrationist function of the court, which found expression, for example, in promotions in the army, navy and civil service, in the award of Orders and elevation to noble rank, in patronage for trade and artistic endeavours, in the marriage merry-go-round associated with the court balls, will be able to understand the relationship between this old courtly world and the modern 'principle of state omnipotence' with its republican implications. The central focus of court society, however, – of this there can be no doubt – was the 'All-Highest Person' and the entourage with which he chose to surround himself.[116]

The conclusion is compelling: Kaiser Wilhelm II's personality, and the character of the small circle of friends in whom he reposed a genuine and constant trust, were of decisive significance for the course of Wilhelmine politics. But with this realisation we find ourselves in a world which could not be further removed from the 'anonymous forces of the authoritarian polycracy'. It is a world which simply cannot be comprehended without a knowledge of the most intimate relationships; a world in which a mediatised imperial Count could allow himself to be led before the Kaiser as a poodle 'with a marked rectal opening';[117] in which the Chief of the Military Cabinet could dance before the Kaiser in a tutu and a feather hat; in which obscene letters which might even have been written by a member of the royal family circulated for years without anyone being able to identify the author;[118] in which a Hanoverian without much property or education could attain a princely title and the Governorship of Alsace-Lorraine not least because, while he was adjutant, he had performed certain delicate services for the future Kaiser;[119] in which, in the midst of the great government reshuffle of 1897, one of the greatest fears of court officials was that a police commissioner might attest in a law court that the Kaiser had an illegitimate daughter in Alsace.[120] In this edition of Baden documents such questions are admittedly touched on very discreetly, if at all. Only after the appearance of several newspaper articles, for instance, did the Baden envoys in Berlin and Munich, Berckheim and Bodman, feel obliged in November 1906 to report back to Karlsruhe what all informed observers had known about for years, namely that Kaiser Wilhelm II's closest friends were homosexual.[121]

Grand Duke Friedrich I of Baden did not belong to this trusted circle of intimates. His frequently invoked influence over his nephew by marriage is revealed by this edition – one is tempted to say 'unfortunately' – to have been slighter than generally assumed. In the School Bill crisis and over the question of two-year military service, he restrained himself from expressing his strong views. Whenever his advice was apparently heeded, it was only because Wilhelm – under the influence of others – had already decided to adopt the course in question, as with Bismarck's dismissal or Hohenlohe's appointment, the reconciliation with Bismarck or the adoption of the great battlefleet plan. In questions, however, where the Kaiser was of a different opinion – over public access to Courts Martial, for instance, or the Hard Labour Bill – the well-considered advice of his always thoughtful uncle was politely but firmly rejected. Not even in a personnel question closest to the heart of the Grand Duke and the Grand Duchess Luise – the appointment of their elder son and heir to be Commander of the 14th Army Corps in the Baden capital – was the elderly uncle able to get his way. 'The blow is more painful for the Grand Duke and myself than I can say', exclaimed the Grand Duchess,[122] and the Grand Duke personally told Reich Chancellor von Bülow that the rejection of his request meant that the evening of his life had been 'turned into joyless drudgery'.[123] News of the Grand Duke's death reached Wilhelm while he was hunting at Rominten. His reaction was emotive and at the same time full of impatience to get on with more pressing matters. On 5 October 1907 he telegraphed to his close friend Max Egon Prince zu Fürstenberg, whose ancestral home was at Donaueschingen, at the source of the Danube in southern Baden:

Am deeply saddened by the passing away of my splendid dear uncle, the Nestor among German princes, the shepherd of our national ideals and feelings. May God console my Aunt, heavily bowed down with grief! Under these circumstances and also because of national mourning, I have – with a very heavy heart – given up [the hunt at] Donaueschingen! – My score here 18 stags, 6 with full antlers. Wonderful sunny weather. Good hunting and greetings to Irma. Wilhelm I.R.[124]

With the death of this 'wonderful man'[125] one more voice of reason within court society was silenced, and this precisely at a time when the military entourage was gaining unfettered influence over the Kaiser by virtue of the destruction of the 'Liebenberg circle'. Whether, had he lived longer, Grand Duke Friedrich I of Baden would have wished and would have been able to give a different direction to the fatal course of German politics in the years 1907–14 must however remain very questionable.

Shortly after Bismarck's dismissal Arthur von Brauer expressed the wish that the Grand Duke should keep his influence on the young Kaiser in reserve in case it should ever come to a matter of life and death for the Reich:

For the succesful development of conditions here in Germany, I know of nothing which even remotely approaches in importance the continuation of the influence which Y[our] R[oyal] H[ighness] thank goodness has with H.M.! In the face of the many disagreeable phenomena of the present day, the hopes of wide sections of the German population are pinned on the fact that in difficult times when peace or the Reich's future may be threatened, H.M. will be able to rely on the well-tried advice of the Federal Prince who alone survives of the decisive founders of German unity. This hope for the future must be preserved for the German nation.[126]

Some years later, after Wilhelm II had spoken of Bismarck and Moltke as 'lackeys and pygmies', Baron von Bodman reported from Munich that the Prussian envoy there, Count Monts, thought it out of the question that the Kaiser's excitability 'was other than psychological in origin'. Monts predicted, he said, that 'the Kaiser would go the same way as King Friedrich

Wilhelm IV of Prussia'.[127] At the same time Bodman reported a conversation between the Munich newspaper editor, Dr Jolly, and Bismarck in Friedrichsruh in which Bismarck 'declared Wilhelm II to be mentally disturbed'. As early as 1888 Bismarck had become convinced that the young Kaiser 'suffered from a condition inherited from his English and Russian ancestors'. But Bismarck warned: 'His [Wilhelm's] removal from among the generals surrounding him will not be as easy as the removal of King Ludwig II of Bavaria.'[128] Only a few weeks later the Reichstag deputies received a pseudonymous pamphlet in which the Kaiser's mental illness was claimed to be a proven fact and which called for the establishment of a regency.[129] In 1897, and again three years later, soon after Bülow assumed office as Reich Chancellor, rumours circulated and were taken seriously in political circles in Berlin, of a plan by the Federal Princes – which meant in the first instance the Grand Duke of Baden – in combination with the Reichstag to declare Kaiser Wilhelm II to be unfit to rule.[130] Neither then nor after the great political crisis of 1908, however, was anything serious done to check the Kaiser's power and to place control of the 'kingship mechanism' in more reliable hands. Kaiserdom had become too much the focus of the Wilhelmine apparatus of power, and was too deeply anchored in the psychic structure of the German 'national soul', for its removal to be a practical possibility.[131] 'The German people do not want a shadow Kaiser', cried Bülow in the Reichstag in 1903, 'the German people want a Kaiser made of flesh and blood.'[132]

Administrer, c'est gouverner; gouverner, c'est régner: tout se réduit là.
Mirabeau to Louis XVI, 3 July 1790

In the last two or three decades of the nineteenth century, the scope of governmental activity began to increase at an unprecedented rate in the industrialised countries of Europe and North America. As it did so, as governments came to intervene more and more in the day-to-day lives of individuals, demands for a thorough reform of recruitment methods in the higher branches of the civil service grew more insistent. In Britain, France and the United States, patronage had to make way for recruitment by competition, for it was intolerable that the affairs of a modern industrialised society should be in the hands of people who might barely be able to read or write.[1] In Prussia-Germany the problem was the very reverse. Ever since the days of Frederick William I, Prussia had recruited talented commoners to the bureaucracy. Frederick the Great had set up a commission to test aspirants to public office, and candidates were expected to have a university education and to pass two or even three examinations. The Prussian *Allgemeines Landrecht* of 1794 laid down that 'no-one must receive a post who is not sufficiently qualified and has not given proof of his ability. Whoever has achieved office through bribery or other impermissible means must be dismissed forthwith.' In the Government Instruction of 23 October 1817 the Prussian departments of state were directed to 'act always with strict checks and impartiality in the matter of appointments, looking first and foremost to loyalty, industriousness and skill rather than length of service'. 'Public offices are open to all those who have the talent thereto', read clause 4 of the Prussian Constitution of 1850, 'provided they fulfil the conditions laid down by the law.' By the time Bismarck united Germany and transferred the Prussian tradition to the Reich administration, candidates had to study jurisprudence for three years at university, undergo a four-year training period in the law courts, and pass two stiff civil service examinations before qualifying for the higher grade of the civil service.

It is therefore not surprising that the machinery of administration in the parliamentary systems of western Europe was frequently seen in Germany as corrupt and incompetent. 'Only flagrant ignorance', wrote Treitschke, 'could explain any attempt to compare the German civil service with that of France which consists in the overwhelming majority of subalterns, *employés*, and thus constitutes a herd with no will of its own.' The British civil service consisted of a 'system of nepotism, of patronage' which offends 'our innermost being, the most sacred concepts of justice of the Germans'.[2] The judgment on Britain by the conservative *Grenzboten* of 1881 was much the same: 'From beginning to end ... hardly a trace of patriotic spirit and striving, almost nowhere an idealistic aim, everywhere naked, cold egoism, in every respect patronage, cliqueyness, nepotism, protection of the worst sort, humbug and hypocrisy of the most hateful kind, the pursuit of material gain.'[3] In his *Erinnerungen*, published in 1919, Admiral von Tirpitz expressed his opposition to parliamentarism in Germany, but at the same time he added that the German people would only be truly lost 'if it were to lose the incorruptibility of the old state administration. The corrupt German is worse than the corrupt Italian or Frenchman who at least never betrays his own country.'[4] Psychologically speaking, then, Gustav von Schmoller was not entirely wrong when he replied to the question 'Would parliamentarism be right for Prussia or Germany?' with the answer: 'In those states which have for the most part been created by hard-working Royal houses down to the present day, such as Prussia and Austria, and where at the same time a large body of honest professional civil servants mainly governs and administers, the preconditions for parliamentary government are lacking most of all.'[5] If it was the parliamentary system of government in the west which in many ways obstructed the development of a competent bureaucracy, so it can also conversely be said that it was not least the much admired Prusso-German bureaucracy which stood in the way of parliamentarisation.

It is now widely accepted that the appropriate state structure for a modern pluralistic society is the combination of a government accountable to a legislative body representative of the people together with an efficient professional administration. If one asks the question why Germany's path to this synthesis was so much more crisis-ridden than Britain's, one answer is to be sought in the retention and stabilisation of a pre-industrial state and social order in a time of rapid industrialisation. For the character of German society was fast changing. When the Reich was founded in 1871, two-thirds of its population lived and worked in the countryside; by 1914 two-thirds lived in the towns. The peasants who went to work in the factories became politically conscious, joined the trade unions, and voted in large numbers for the Social Democratic Party, which by 1890 had become the largest single party when measured in terms of the popular vote; in 1912 it received no less than one-third of the votes cast. Other sections of the community were also organising with a view to participating in politics. The Conservatives adopted 'demagogy' at the Tivoli conference in 1892. The Agrarian League, founded in 1893, soon had a membership of some 200,000.[6] The Navy League, founded with Krupp's support in 1898, had a million members by 1906. There were nearly 5,000 ex-servicemen's clubs in 1889 with a combined membership of over 400,000. Nine years later there were 19,626 such associations with a total membership of 1,613,962.[7] At the same time the state was playing an ever-increasing part in the life of every citizen. The amount of money spent by the Reich Office of the Interior jumped from 8 million marks per annum in 1890 to 108 million in 1914. The length of railway owned and administered by the Prussian state rose from under 5,000 kilometres in 1878 to over 25,000 in 1890, and over 37,000 in 1910. It was only natural that people should question whether a bureaucracy composed almost entirely of lawyers was capable of fulfilling the multifarious needs of a highly industrialised society. Above all, however, it appeared doubtful whether men who possessed 'the qualities of a useful official, but no breath of statesmanlike talent', should occupy the highest positions in the state as a result of 'administrative advancement or fortuitous court acquaintance'.[8]

The problem with the Prussian and German higher civil service, then, was not insufficient education, but, if not an excess of education, then education of the wrong kind. The first breach in the old system of recruitment came, after mounting public pressure, in 1879. By a law of that year, implemented in Prussia in 1883, those graduates in jurisprudence who aspired to a post in the higher civil service had to spend only two (instead of four) years practising at a law court; the rest of the four-year probationary period was to be spent gaining experience in one of the provincial administrative bodies (Oberpräsidium, Regierungspräsidium or in the Landratsamt). Candidates could then sit the second civil service examination and, if successful, enter one of the Reich or Prussian central departments on a provisional basis until a permanent post fell vacant.[9] This reform, however, did little to satisfy the critics inside or outside the executive. Bismarck, who is supposed once to have remarked that a dozen civil servants should be shot every three years to keep the others on their toes, talked shortly before his dismissal of further reforms to turn the bureaucrats into 'educated Europeans'.[10] In 1895 Johannes von Miquel, the dynamic Prussian Finance Minister who had earlier been a banker and a brilliant National Liberal parliamentarian, complained of 'hair-raising gaps' in the education of most civil servants. He proposed reducing the training period in the law courts to one year, and raising that in the provincial administration to three. He also demanded that at university candidates should be required to study the social sciences, economics and administrative law in addition to theoretical law. Miquel was opposed by Reich Chancellor Prince Chlodwig zu Hohenlohe-Schillingsfürst, who denied that a legal education encouraged narrow-mindedness and pointed to himself and his colleagues as living proof of his view. He went so far as to claim that the pre-1879 system was ideal, as it ensured greater mobility between the bureaucracy and the entire legal profession, and thus enabled the civil service to recruit its members from a wider range.[11] A committee set up under the chairmanship of the Under-Secretary in the Prussian Ministry of the Interior recommended only minor changes to the existing system. At university, there should be compulsory lectures on administrative law, economics and fiscal policy, and students should be given the opportunity to attend seminars on practical problems in the vacations. In line with Miquel's proposals, the committee recommended the reduction of the period spent in the law courts to one year. The remaining three years were to be spent in the provincial administration, including at least three months with an urban council. Another report, completed in 1900, proposed more radical changes. The university course should be extended from six to seven semesters, only three of which would be concerned with jurisprudence and the rest with more practical subjects. In addition, a Civil Service Academy should be set up at which all aspirants to the higher bureaucracy would have to spend at least one year. To broaden the outlook of civil servants already in office, lectures and seminars should be arranged on economics and other subjects. Finally the report strongly recommended greater flexibility in recruitment, and above all the appointment of able men from the universities, from agriculture and from industry.[12] The bill introduced in 1902, which eventually passed into law in 1906, was more in line with the recommendations of the first committee than with those of the second. The university course was left at three years, though some knowledge of economics and political science now became a requirement. The training period, too, was left at its former length of four years, but the time spent at a law court was now reduced to one year (and in some cases only nine months), while that in the administration was extended to three years. This system survived into the period of the Weimar Republic, when further piecemeal changes were made.

The civil servants who administered the most dynamic society in Europe were thus trained lawyers with little or no practical experience of the world. As Herman Finer put it: 'The training of future officials and their selection had in process of time ceased to keep pace with the demands of the modern State. Law had become divorced from its origin and its purpose, and a narrow and pedantic formalism had invaded a field in which pre-eminently the truth of real life is essential.'[13] Young men entering the administrative branch of the German civil service were already approaching thirty years of age – five or six years older than their British counterparts.[14] The general narrowness of vision which the system produced was further encouraged by the fact that about a quarter of the men appointed to public office had taken a doctorate in jurisprudence.[15] But especially in the technical departments there was a desperate need for men 'who were not exhausted by many years of legal studies and out of touch with practical needs'.[16] Yet the number of those appointed to the central Prussian and Reich departments without a training in law was insignificant. Dr Hugo Thiel of the Prussian Ministry of Agriculture had begun life as a farmer, had taken a doctorate of philology at Bonn university, and had then become a lecturer in Agriculture and National Economy at the Darmstadt and Munich Polytechnics. In 1879, at the age of forty, he became a Vortragender Rat at the Ministry. Professor Post, a chemist at Göttingen university until 1891, became increasingly interested in questions of public health and was called into the Prussian Ministry of Trade by the progressive Minister, Freiherr Hans Hermann von Berlepsch. There was considerable resistance within the bureaucracy itself to such outside appointments, as Hohenlohe discovered when he tried to appoint a Bavarian university professor to the secretariat of the Prussian Ministry of State:

Whoever has not been a Prussian Landrat, a Prussian Regierungsrat, etc., for the required number of years cannot enter this sanctuary . . . If the Reich Chancellor and even His Majesty fail in the attempt to appoint an able and decent man to the Prussian bureaucracy, then I must concede defeat and record with dismay that the bureaucracy is more powerful than the Kaiser and the Chancellor.[17]

Rules for entry into the consular and diplomatic services were less rigid. The 1867 Law on Federal Consulates laid down that apart from the normal civil service examinations there should be another method of entry designed 'to attract good men from other professions into the consular service'. A special examination could be taken by men who had not qualified in the normal way. An official handbook published in 1896 pointed out that in the consular service 'practical experience is more important than in any other branch of the Reich service', since its function was 'to encourage trade, commerce and shipping abroad'. It advised aspirants to learn Turkish, Arabic and other oriental languages in addition to the European languages which were an entrance requirement. In the final examination, jurisprudence carried little weight. Candidates had to demonstrate their knowledge of history 'with special reference to Germany', and of the geography of 'the main countries and peoples of the earth, their forms of government, population, produce, trade, industry, financial position and colonies'. A good grounding in economics, with a knowledge of the development of the discipline since Adam Smith, was also essential.[18] Similarly, a degree in jurisprudence was not a requirement for entry into the diplomatic corps. A memorandum of 1908 on recruitment to the foreign service said only that 'a sound education' was necessary; those who did not have a degree would be required to spend five instead of four years on probation, and to attend lectures on history, economics, international law, finance and commerce. In the final examination there were papers in English and French, and some of the essays written in the examination room had to be written in these two languages. The oral examination in history and geography was likewise conducted in French and English. The main requirement, however, was 'the possession of qualities essential in diplomacy', and the Chancellor was entirely free to decide what these qualities were, and who did or did not possess them.[19]

Noble birth was almost essential for service in the embassies: the only envoys of bourgeois origin in the 1890s were those in Peru, Venezuela, Colombia and Siam. In 1914 the German foreign service consisted of eight princes, twenty-nine counts, twenty barons, fifty-four untitled nobles and only eleven commoners.[20] Prince Alexander von Hohenlohe, who was noted for his liberal opinions, justified the predominance of the aristocracy in the diplomatic corps on the grounds that noblemen were acquainted with the outside world to a greater degree than commoners. It was certainly true that young aristocrats who aspired to serve in the diplomatic corps were often more widely travelled than their middle-class rivals. Most of them, further-more, had foreign wives: in 1891 only one of Germany's ambassadors – Prince Reuss in Vienna – was married to a German (she was a Princess of Saxony-Weimar), and the proportion among the younger diplomats was similar.[21] Those commoners who entered the service were mainly the sons of great industrialists or rich traders, many of whom had in fact acquired a title through their wealth and influence. Membership of one of the 'feudal' student corps – especially the *Borussen* in Bonn, the *Saxo-Borussen* in Heidelberg and the *Sachsen* in Göttingen – was as important a precondition of entry into the diplomatic service as having a commission in one of the Guards regiments. The consular service, on the other hand, was almost wholly middle class, though even here it was useful to have studied at the right university, joined the right student corps, and to have a sizeable income.[22]

When in 1887, after having passed the first law examination, the Hereditary Count Siegfried von Castell-Rüdenhausen expressed the wish to enter the Reich consular service, he provoked a certain degree of astonishment not just because this career was unusual for a mediatised prince, but above all because his father, who had seven sons and three daughters, was not in a position to support the Hereditary Count by more than 2,000 marks. Philipp Eulenburg, who supported his cause with

Herbert von Bismarck, noted: 'If you wish to do something for the young gentleman, this will prove possible despite his position as Hereditary Count, despite the fact that it is the consular service and despite the 2,000 marks.' But the Foreign Secretary replied: 'Concerning your Hereditary Count from Rüdenhausen, it seems to me that from the pecuniary point of view, the position is far too meagre; if only he had two thousand taler! But marks! We look for support being provided on that scale for Chancellery servants. Still, his application will be examined at the relevant time in the usual conscientious way.'[23]

The stiffness of the entrance requirements for all departments other than the Foreign Office might lead one to suppose that talent was the only criterion. This was far from being the case. In contrast to the British system, the Prussian (and therefore also the Reich) system of recruitment was not one of *open* competition. The government made frequent use of its right to refuse to appoint qualified candidates for political or other reasons. Conservatives might have liked to recall Hegel's words that the Prussian system guaranteed 'to every citizen the chance of joining the universal estate' of civil servants,[24] but in practice all women and more than half of the male population were excluded for reasons which had nothing to do with their ability.

Only with regard to regional origin was an attempt made to achieve a kind of proportional representation in public appointments. An elaborate system operated to ensure that each of the larger states in the Reich received a number of places in the Reich bureaucracy in keeping with its size. Hohenlohe once insisted on the appointment of a Saxon to a vacancy in the Reich Treasury Office because 'the number of Saxons in the higher Reich civil service is disproportionately small'.[25] Caprivi refused to appoint a Hanoverian as Secretary of the Reich Justice Office as there were already two Hanoverians on the committee drafting the *Bürgerliches Gesetzbuch* (the Civil Code).[26] When Huber left the Reich Office of the Interior in 1895, care was taken to put another Württemberger in his place. Similarly, when Count Maximilian von Berchem, a Bavarian, was dismissed as Under-Secretary of the Foreign Office, another Bavarian, Freiherr Wolfram von Rotenhan, replaced him. In the Reichsgericht, the Supreme Court at Leipzig, all posts were allocated on a quota basis, and when Prussia tried to secure for herself one of the posts reserved for Württemberg, the non-Prussian states prevented the change in the Bundesrat.[27]

Nothing reveals more clearly the fragility of the Second Reich than this constant preoccupation with the rights of the states. It was perhaps understandable that most Bavarians should have 'displayed some estrangement' when Count Berchem decided to enter the Foreign Office in 1871. That such resentment should still be smouldering a quarter of a century later was most disconcerting, and gave rise to strong fears that the Reich would disintegrate if put to the test.[28] Yet the Badenese Adolf Freiherr Marschall von Bieberstein could at first turn down the Foreign Secretaryship in 1890 because he feared that the Prussian civil servants in Berlin would be offended by the appointment of a young non-Prussian.[29] And Adolf Buchenberger, the Baden Finance Minister, refused to become Secretary of the Reich Treasury Office on the grounds that he detested the Prussian landowners and would in turn be disliked as a south German with a middle-class name.[30]

In 1888 Eulenburg wrote to Herbert von Bismarck recommending Baron Seefried von Buttenheim for the Reich diplomatic service, and he added:

He is Protestant, wealthy, good-looking and one of the nicest young gentlemen of Munich. He has plenty of professional training. I am not in a position to judge the extent to which these diplomatic wishes of young Bavarians should in general be treated. I for my part favour *Prussia*. Brothers in the Reich service from the other states are still a kind of double-edged sword. It will be different in a few generations. But against that I should certainly like to emphasise that youths who have been turned away and who then throw themselves into the arms of the Foreign Ministry here [in Munich], constitute a disaffected element ... who may create some problems for us in the future.[31]

Those non-Prussians who were appointed were carefully vetted for signs of particularism. Chancellor von Caprivi, when considering a Bavarian, Hanauer, for the Reich Justice Office in 1892, was only won over when assured of the man's credentials in the following terms: 'He is politically *gut deutsch*, stands firmly in support of Kaiser and Reich and is free of all particularist leanings. Indeed, if he has such leanings at all, they are more of the black-and-white [i.e. Prussian] than the blue-and-white [Bavarian] variety. For during his nearly twenty years of service in Berlin he has grown close to Prussia.'[32]

Such screening did little to remove the mutual hostility and suspicion in Berlin. When the south German Prince Chlodwig zu Hohenlohe-Schillingsfürst was made Chancellor in 1894, a south German baroness living in Berlin predicted an outcry among the Prussians: 'A Bavarian Catholic as Chancellor and Prussian Minister-President, a Protestant Bavarian (Rotenhan) in the Foreign Office, a Badener as Secretary of the latter, and a Württemberger as Statthalter [of Alsace-Lorraine] – that will cause a pretty outburst among the dyed-in-the-wool Prussians.'[33] After four years in office, Hohenlohe was still struck by the vast gulf between him and 'the Prussian Excellencies': 'South German liberalism is helpless against the Junkers. They are too numerous, too powerful, and they have the throne and the army on their side ... My task here is to keep Prussia attached to the Reich. For all these gentlemen despise the Reich and would sooner be rid of it today rather than tomorrow, Miquel included.'[34]

In sharp contrast to the desire of the government to allocate a fair share of the Reich posts to non-Prussian citizens was its attitude towards Catholics and Jews. Almost one-third of Germany's population was Catholic, yet Catholics were virtually excluded from holding high office in either the Reich or the Prussian bureaucracy. One Catholic publicist, collecting statistics in 1899 on the 'parity' question, as it was called, established 'that the proportion of Catholics employed in public office falls as the importance of the post increases, so that hardly any Catholics are to be found in the highest positions'.[35] Another calculated (not entirely accurately) that out of a total of ninety Chancellors, Reich Secretaries and Prussian ministers to hold office in the period 1888–1914, only seven were Catholics.[36] Of the men appointed in the 1890s, the Chancellor Hohenlohe, the Secretaries of Justice Hanauer and Nieberding, and the Prussian Minister of Justice Schönstedt were Catholic, but Hohenlohe had stood on the liberal side in the *Kulturkampf* and Schönstedt had married a Protestant and allowed his children to be brought up in the Lutheran faith.

In the body of the bureaucracy the situation was if anything worse. At the end of the century, there were four directors, twenty-five Vortragende Räte and twenty Hilfsarbeiter in the Foreign Office; of these, two Vortragende Räte and three Hilfsarbeiter were members of the Roman Church. In the other Reich Offices I could discover only two Catholics – Seckendorff in the Justice Office and Wackerzapp in the Railway Office – though there may have been one or two others. In recommending Seckendorff as head of the Prussian Ministry of State secretariat in 1899, Hohenlohe wrote of his 'unconditional reliability', and added: 'The fact that he is a Catholic does not affect this judgment, as he is a declared opponent of the [Catholic] Centre party.' In the Prussian bureaucracy the most notorious department in this respect was the Ministry of the Interior, where the only Catholic was a messenger boy. One Minister, Hans Freiherr von Hammerstein, was so anxious to appoint members of his student corps *Vandalia* that people spoke of the invasion of Berlin by the Vandals. In the Finance Ministry there was only one Catholic, Vagedes, 'of whose loyalty and reliability there are no doubts whatever'.[37] In the Ministry for Ecclesiastical Affairs and Education, in whose activities the Catholics were more than usually interested, there were two Catholic civil servants, Ludwig Renvers and Adolph Förster. The latter, whose 'loyalty to the state is beyond question', would have been made a director in 1899 if he had been a Protestant. In 1902, when his promotion became inescapable, an elaborate reshuffle was executed to avoid putting him in charge of the schools department.[38] The only ministry in which some degree of parity was achieved was that of Agriculture, where the under-secretary and four of the Vortragende Räte were Catholics. There was some talk in the early 1890s of appointing a member of the Centre party as Minister of Agriculture, but the idea was soon shelved. Not until 1911 was Klemens von Schorlemer-Lieser, one of the very few Catholic Oberprä-sidenten, made Prussian Minister of Agriculture.

If Catholics were the least educated sector of the German population, the best qualified on average were the Jews. For every 100,000 males of each denomination in Prussia, thirty-three Catholics, fifty-eight Protestants and 519 Jews became university students.[39] Though they made up less than 1 per cent of the population, Jews should have had far more than that percentage of public offices if recruitment had been based on the merit system alone, and if the law of 1869 which guaranteed that appointments would be made irrespective of religious denomination had not been a dead letter. In practice it was almost as difficult for an unbaptised Jew to enter the higher civil service as to become an army officer. Bülow appointed the last of the German Rothschilds to a minor diplomatic post after he had failed to enter the army, and he incurred the hostility of the otherwise liberal Holstein for so doing.[40] When the banker Bernhard Dernburg was appointed head of the Reich Colonial Office, Holstein strongly advised Bülow against appointing 'more non-professional civil servants, especially Semites', because it would undermine public confidence in the bureaucracy. In 1908 Holstein noted that 'Dernburg has remained the only wedge.'[41] Baptised Jews could enter both the army and the higher bureaucracy, including the Foreign Office. As Alexander Hohenlohe observed on this subject in his memoirs: 'If the father or grandfather had allowed himself to be baptised ... and if the son had refurbished the tarnished glory of some noble family with his inherited wealth by marrying one of the daughters, then people were prepared to disregard his race so long as this was not all too obvious in his facial features.'[42]

Nevertheless, even the Christian of Jewish origin was seldom allowed to forget that origin. Dr Paul Kayser, the tutor of Bismarck's sons and Director of the Colonial Department of the Foreign Office, came under vicious attack from anti-semites like Ahlwardt. In 1891 he wrote to an uncle with some bitterness: 'I take all this trouble only to get insulted and to prepare a comfortable place for my Aryan successor.'[43] Heinrich Friedberg, the brilliant Minister of Justice of the later Bismarck era, was depressed after the accession of Wilhelm II because 'he knows that the Kaiser does not protect Semites'.[44] Dr Karl Julius von Bitter, once a civil servant in the Prussian Ministry of the Interior and then Regierungspräsident in Silesia, was turned down as the Minister of the Interior in 1895 because of 'his still somewhat Semitic tendencies'. Most ministers and the Kaiser were willing to accept him in 1896 as Minister of Trade, but Hohenlohe prevented his appointment because he was 'an ambitious Jew' (*ein jüdischer Streber*).[45] Even men whose Jewish ancestry was rumoured to be remote were regarded with some suspicion. Ludwig von Schelling, the arch-Conservative Prussian Justice Minister, was referred to by Holstein as a *Semitenmischling*. Count Berchem, a Catholic whose mother was Jewish, was said by Holstein to excel in economic questions but to be 'inclined to flaunt his Catholic tendencies so as to obscure the fact of his Jewish blood'.[46] Philipp Eulenburg once suggested that it would be to Prussia's advantage if Berchem became Bavarian Minister-President, as his Jewish blood would make him totally unacceptable in court circles in Vienna. In 1892, when Hanauer (another Bavarian Catholic) was being considered for the Reich Justice Office, an ex-Secretary of that office assured the Chancellor that Hanauer was not a Jew: 'His external appearance and name admittedly indicate a Jewish origin. However, that must lie a long way back, for the family is said to be a well-known Catholic one and Hanauer's wife is of noble birth.'[47]

Social Democrats and even the sons of known Social Democrats were excluded from the bureaucracy automatically. In view of the long training period and the expensive education necessary for entry into the higher civil service, there was in any case little opportunity for factory workers and others without private means to become contenders for a place. In 1889, when Wilhelm II suggested lowering the 'far too onerous entry requirements for high schools', Hohenlohe protested on the grounds that it was imperative to obstruct the creation of an 'educated proletariat'.[48] Most of the internal memoranda on entrance to the civil service stressed that throughout the four-year probationary period there must be neither payment of any kind (not even expenses) nor a promise of eventual appointment. To embark on a public career without adequate financial support was foolhardy. Kirschner, the head of the Bundesrat secretariat (a post in the middle grade), got as far as the *Referendar* stage before being forced by lack of means to abandon the attempt to enter the higher grade.[49] The civil servant's salary was not commensurate with his social obligations. A Vortragender Rat generally earned under 10,000 marks, a director 15,000 and a state secretary 24,000. The Chancellor himself received only 54,000 marks, which was less than half the amount earned by an ambassador. It was even expected of a Chancellery servant, as we have seen, that he should augment his salary from private means. As Maximilian Harden reports, Bismarck added 120,000 marks per annum to his salary and a further 30,000 marks to that of his son.[50] Caprivi was able to manage on his salary because he was a bachelor; but Prince Hohenlohe only accepted the Chancellorship on condition that his salary would be secretly increased by approximately 120,000 marks, and this in turn was supposed to have made him more compliant in the face of the Kaiser's attempts to intervene in political decisions.[51] Bülow requested a similar increase in his salary. The cost of living for civil servants one rung down could also create severe anxieties:

The husband has in the meantime taken up a career. He is Vortragender Rat in a Ministry ... The question of clothes for the daughter worries the mother, because at the moment the money does not stretch to that. Naturally the daughter takes second place to the son and he – needs plenty. It's not the boy's fault, he was always cheerful and hardworking! But of course he had to join a student corps, and there it's not possible for him to be outshone by the other young people ... In reality we led an illusory existence: social obligations devoured far more than our income. We had to live in accordance with our social position, and social position meant over-expenditure.[52]

If capable men were nonetheless attracted to a career in the bureaucracy, this was because of the prestige which holding high office conferred. After the army officer no-one was more respected in Wilhelmine Germany than the higher civil servant. To the educated middle classes a career in the bureaucracy could bring rank, decorations, perhaps ennoblement, and in exceptional cases political power. Friedrich Karl Hermann Lucanus, to name but one example, was born in 1831 in Halberstadt, the son of a pharmacist. (Years later, when he had long been a political figure and a man of great influence, he was still referred to in the aristocratic circles of the Foreign Office as the 'apothecary'.[53]) At the age of twenty he began his legal studies in Heidelberg, twice he was punished for 'disturbing the peace during the night and participation in a tumult', and he subsequently went to Berlin where in 1854 he sat his examinations. He was excused military service on the grounds of 'chest and general physical weakness', and in 1856 he passed his Referendar examination. Thereafter he was employed in the law courts of his home town. After his Assessor examination in 1859 he became an assistant in the office of the Prussian Minister for Ecclesiastical Affairs and Education, but only in 1871 was he promoted to Vortragender Rat. With this appointment his comet-like rise began. In 1878 he became director of the religious department of the Education Ministry, three years later he was Under-Secretary of State. In 1884 he received an honorary degree of medicine from the University of Halle and an honorary degree of law from the University of Göttingen. In 1886 he was awarded the title Exzellenz, and three years later he was, despite his marriage to the daughter of a minor official, ennobled by Kaiser Friedrich III. In the same year he managed to rise to a position of political influence, namely Chief of the Kaiser's Civil Cabinet. In 1897 he received the Order of the Black Eagle. His financial position no doubt improved when a little later he was appointed canon of Merseburg.[54] Had Lucanus remained a professional civil servant, his very modest social origins would have attracted little attention. At court, however, he possessed rarity value. Eulenburg supported his appointment as a minister on the grounds that Lucanus would create few problems in order not to damage his own position. 'If this subaltern being becomes a minister', he wrote to Holstein, 'he will attempt above all to secure his position . . . He will be less willing than anyone else to risk his ministerial salary.'[55]

Social advancement for one's family was another important motive for joining the civil service, as is demonstrated by the case of Dr Friedrich Schulz, the Chief of the tiny Reich Railway Office from 1887 until his retirement in 1910. Throughout this whole period he expressly sought a rise in salary, a rise in status for his office, the award of the title Exzellenz and, when approaching retirement, elevation to the nobility. He sought the latter, which was granted only after a detailed examination of his family and his wife's background as well as of his financial circumstances, 'in consideration of my three sons, two of whom work in the domestic Prussian administration'.[56]

Otto Braunbehrens, Under-Secretary of State in the Prussian Ministry of the Interior from 1890 until 1900, was another official who was ennobled on his retirement. He was better off than Lucanus and Schulz. His father and his uncle owned landed estates, and he himself married the daughter of an estate owner. His brother and his three sisters were 'all in possession of reasonable wealth' and his own fortune was estimated at 350,000 marks. His daughter married an officer, and his four sons had the prospect of successful careers. The first worked in the administration and married the daughter of a Pomeranian estate owner; the second held a doctorate in law and worked in the Dortmund high court, and he was married to the daughter of the Ruhr industrialist Springmann; the third was an officer and married to Baroness von Fricks; and the fourth was trained as a professional banker in Berlin with a view to taking on the family business in due course.[57] Upward social mobility was naturally greatest where, as in the case of the Wilmowski family, both father and son held high office in the bureaucracy. The family, which had moved from Silesia to Brandenburg in the seventeenth century, was relatively undistinguished (there was only one estate) until Karl von Wilmowski became Chief of the Civil Cabinet in 1870. On retiring in 1888 he received the title of baron for himself and his heirs. His son Kurt served in the Franco-Prussian war, passed the second civil service examination in 1876, and, after some years in the provincial administration, became a Vortragender Rat in the Prussian Ministry of Agriculture. In 1894, on Bennigsen's suggestion, he became head of Hohenlohe's Reich Chancellery. Soon after the Chancellor's retirement he was made Oberpräsident first of Schleswig-Holstein and then of his native province of Prussian Saxony. He ended his career as leader of the Conservatives in the Prussian House of Lords, and his son Tilo married Barbara Krupp herself.[58]

There were, of course, some who were not satisfied with prestige. Ludwig Raschdau, a member of the Foreign Office, married a rich Jewish widow some twenty years his senior. 'My salary', he explained afterwards, 'enabled me to live comfortably enough, and I was even able to save a little. But with my marriage my financial position became what most people would describe as brilliant ... I was now able to develop my naturally independent character to the full. From now on I really was a completely free man.'[59] Others jumped from the bureaucracy into industry and back again. Karl Jacobi became Under-Secretary in the Prussian Ministry of Trade in 1879. Two years later he gave up that post to become chairman of the Prussian Land Credit Bank. In 1886 he returned to the Ministry of Trade. A few months later Bismarck made him Secretary of the Reich Treasury. After a further two years he left the bureaucracy for good, returned to the Land Credit Bank, and also joined the board of the Disconto-Gesellschaft and the Norddeutsche Bank. Similarly, General Budde, Chief of the railways department of the General Staff, left this post to become a director of a big armaments firm and several other concerns because this would 'guarantee him an income of 150,000 marks'.[60] He returned to the public service two years later as Prussian Minister of Public Works.

Stock exchange speculation was frowned upon but not disallowed.[61] Freiherr von Broich, born on a large estate near Aachen, became first a Landrat and then a Hilfsarbeiter in the secretariat of the Prussian Ministry of State. He inherited 600,000 marks and began to found a series of companies designed to 'initiate and develop economic and moral progress as well as healthy social reforms' and thereby to protect 'civil servants, officers and landowners from the clutches of usurers'. When the first such venture ran into difficulties, Broich unsuccessfully asked for backing from the Society of German Aristocrats (Deutsche Adelsgenossenschaft) and the Prussian Ministry of the Interior. He invested his entire wealth in the Pioneer Company, which had similar aims, and was by 1897 in debt to the tune of 32,000 marks. Hohenlohe repaid some of this debt from the funds at the Crown's disposal. By this time, Broich's superiors were showing signs of unease. When he asked for permission to join the board of the newly founded German Land Bank – one of the ministers described it as 'a capitalist undertaking masquerading as an enterprise beneficial to the whole community' – the Government refused on principle. In 1898 Broich asked Ludwig Brefeld, the Minister of Public Works, to help him out of his difficulties by recommending him to the Bleichröder Bank. The minister refused to do this but did write a letter expressing complete faith in Broich and the Pioneer Company. Broich thereupon resigned from the civil service to devote himself to speculation. In 1900 the Ministers discovered that he was using Brefeld's letter to borrow huge sums of money from disreputable moneylenders, and promising to use his influence with the Government to secure honours for them in return. Some of the ministers wanted to institute legal proceedings, but the majority felt this would create too much of a scandal. Brefeld's letter was retrieved, and Broich was forced to retire from the Pioneer Company by its board of directors.[62]

The landowning aristocracy showed little interest in a career in the central bureaucracy. Apart from the diplomatic service, they were mainly attracted to the Prussian provincial administration. Qualifications for entry into this branch of the bureaucracy were very much lower: candidates had to reside in the locality for at least one year, and to have spent at least four years as a Referendar or as an elected official. The discrepancy between the salary and the obligations which went with a post in the field was far greater than in Berlin. A Landrat would receive about 6,000 marks a year, but would be expected to entertain some 200 guests and to pay the salary of a dozen or so assistants. It was in any case Government policy to appoint the highest possible number of conservative aristocrats to these posts.[63] In 1891 62 per cent of the Landräte were of noble birth. Of the appointments made in the years 1888–1901, 62 per cent of the Oberpräsidenten, 73 per cent of the Regierungspräsidenten and 83 per cent of the Police Directors were noble.[64] Twenty years later the situation had not changed. All but one of the 12 Oberpräsidenten were aristocratic, as were 23 of the 37 Regierungspräsidenten and 268 of the 481 Landräte. Entirely different was the position of the nobility in the Berlin offices. Of the 126 Vortragende Räte and directors who worked in the Reich Offices (excluding the Foreign Office) in the period 1867–90, only 14 were noble.[65] Of the 86 higher civil servants in the same offices in February 1895, no more than 12 were of noble birth, and the percentage of nobles working in the Prussian Ministries was less than 13.[66] A considerable gulf separated the officials in Berlin from those in the provinces. 'How is it possible for us to pursue liberal policies', one Secretary of State for the Interior asked. 'For twenty-five years no Landrat, no Regierungsrat nor Regierungspräsident, hardly any Oberpräsident, no head of department, hardly the head of a local council in East Elbia, has been appointed to office who was not conservative to the marrow. We find ourselves in an iron net of conservative administrators.'[67] The Bavarian envoy reported in 1903 that a Chancellor who wished to work with a Liberal majority in the Reichstag would have to begin by re-staffing the entire Prussian provincial administration, since the Landräte and Regierungspräsidenten would refuse to carry out a policy to which they were fundamentally opposed.[68]

Unless they were members of the Bundesrat (this included the ministers and secretaries of state, and the under-secretaries of certain departments), all civil servants had a constitutional right to seek election to parliament, and in the early years of the Reich many of them did so. In the first Reichstag there were thirty-five civil servants in the National Liberal party alone, and in the second no fewer than fifty-one. From the end of the 1870s, the number of parliamentary civil servants began to fall. There were seventeen in the 1890 Reichstag, twelve in the 1893 Reichstag, seven in the 1898 Reichstag and only one in the 1903 Reichstag. The number sitting in the Prussan House of Deputies was higher until 1899.[69] Virtually all these parliamentary civil servants were members of the Prussian provincial administration. No more than two central civil servants sat in the Reichstag at any one time. Brauchitsch and Bitter, both of the Prussian Ministry of the Interior, were Reichstag members in the late 1880s. In the 1890 Reichstag, the only central civil servant was Baron von Gamp, a Vortragender Rat of the Ministry of Trade. He was joined in 1893 by Bernstorff of Ecclesiastical Affairs; both were members of the Free Conservative party. With the growth of mass politics in the 1890s, the presence of civil servants in the parliaments became an embarrassment to the Government. Many civil servants had been disciplined during the Prussian constitutional conflict of the 1860s, and Bismarck had had to issue a stern warning in 1882 to the effect that civil servants in and out of parliament must toe the official line, but it was in the post-Bismarck decade that the question caused the greatest trouble. In 1891 Caprivi failed to persuade the Prussian ministers that public servants should be made to give up their parliamentary seats before accepting a position in the *central* departments. He did instruct the secretaries of state to tell future recruits to the Reich Offices that they were being appointed on condition that 'they renounce the right to accept a seat in any parliament for as long as they remain in one of the central offices'.[70]

In December 1893, during a Reichstag debate on a trade treaty, von Colmar, the Regierungspräsident of Lüneburg, voted against the Government, and Gamp of the Ministry of Trade shouted insulting remarks throughout the Chancellor's speech. Caprivi afterwards complained that Gamp was becoming 'the leader of the opposition to the trade treaties in the Free Conservative party'. He demanded Gamp's dismissal, but Gamp remained at his post until October 1895, and took up a seat in the Prussian House in addition to that in the Reichstag. A wealthy industrialist who had bought a *Rittergut* and a noble title, Gamp refused to accept a pension on retirement and instead set up a 'Bismarck Fund' for the benefit of needy civil servants. With Gamp's retirement the problem caused by the central civil servant in parliament was at an end.[71]

The opposition of the provincial officials was more widespread and more difficult to deal with. Count Stolberg, the Oberpräsident of East Prussia, was dismissed in 1895 for coming out in support of the Agrarian League during an election campaign. In the following year the Regierungspräsident of Frankfurt-on-the-Oder was one of the signatories of a petition demanding the abolition of the civil marriage ceremony. At last the Prussian ministers decided to issue a decree forbidding all public servants to criticise the Government. One minister who had come under attack in the House of Deputies maintained that unless such behaviour were stopped, 'civil servants would actually become the leaders of the opposition'. The ministers were coming round to the view that provincial officials must be discouraged from accepting seats in the parliaments. Shortly before the 1898 elections, they decided 'that Oberpräsidenten and Regierungspräsidenten should on principle refuse to seek election to the Reichstag and the Landtag'. One state secretary complained that Tiedemann, the Regierungspräsident of Bromberg who also sat in the Prussian Lower House, hardly did any work at all. He resided in Berlin throughout the parliamentary session and then spent several weeks on holiday before going to his office for a brief two months. The long-awaited showdown came in August 1899, when the Government's Canal Bill fell because some twenty-six of the thirty-seven provincial civil servants who were members of the Prussian House of Deputies voted against it. Miquel now admitted that the provincial officials 'have for a long time been putting the interests of their localities before the general welfare of the State, and have for the most part furthered the aims of the Agrarians'. He estimated that almost seven-eighths of the Landräte were opposed to the Government's policy. On the Kaiser's orders, those officials who had voted against the Canal Bill were dismissed from their posts; all civil servants were told to leave the Agrarian League. A considerable number of the 'rebels' of 1899 were reinstated within a year, and some were even appointed to the central departments, but in each case reinstatement was conditional on relinquishing his seat in parliament.[72] Henceforth all civil servants were strongly discouraged from seeking election.

The exclusion of officials from parliament was an unavoidable consequence of the advent of mass politics, yet in the long run it made the Government less capable of dealing with that very trend. If it had long been the practice for 'energetic officials who have ministerial potential to put themselves forward for election for a limited period in their early years precisely in order to gain parliamentary experience', this link between Government and parliament was now abandoned rather abruptly. A large number of ministers, state secretaries and other high officials (for example Tiedemann and Wehrenpfennig) of Bismarck's day had been eminent members of the Reichstag or the Prussian House of Deputies. Bismarck himself had of course made his mark as a parliamentarian, as had Prince Hohenlohe, and even Bethmann Hollweg, the first Reich Chancellor with a background in the home civil service, had a brief spell in the 1890 Reichstag as a Free Conservative deputy. In Bismarck's last Cabinet there were some, like Gossler and Lucius, who had been President and Vice-President of the

Reichstag before receiving appointment to the Government. Bismarck's son Herbert was a member of the Reichstag from 1884 until his appointment as Foreign Secretary, and then again from 1893 until his death. Maltzahn, the head of the Reich Treasury, owned six large estates in Pomerania. After a brief period as Landrat he retired to devote himself to farming and politics: he sat as a Conservative in the Reichstag from 1871 until his appointment in 1888. Of the men prominent in the 1890s, a large number had gained some parliamentary experience. Johannes Miquel had been leader of the National Liberals before his appointment as Prussian Finance Minister in 1890. Theodor von Möller, the new Minister of Trade in 1901, was not only a National Liberal deputy in both Berlin parliaments but also a leading member of the Central Association of German Industrialists. General Viktor von Podbielski, who became Postmaster-General in 1897 and Prussian Minister of Agriculture in 1901, was a great landowner with extensive commercial interests and a vociferous Reichstag member up to his appointment.[73]

Several other men had gained their parliamentary experience while holding office in the provincial administration. It was partly for this reason that increasingly it was the provincial civil servants rather than the central bureaucrats who rose to become Ministers. The practice of appointing men from the provinces to ministerial office was virtually unknown before 1871. In the period 1871–90 only four Oberpräsidenten became Prussian Ministers. Yet in the 1890s, half of all ministerial appointments went to Oberpräsidenten or Regierungspräsidenten.[74] Diplomats, army officers and some parliamentary leaders were also appointed, but the number of central civil servants was small by comparison. Robert Bosse became Under-Secretary in the Reich Office of the Interior, then Secretary of the Reich Justice Office and finally Prussian Minister for Ecclesiastical Affairs and Education; Ludwig Brefeld was promoted from Under-Secretary in the Prussian Ministry of Public Works to Minister of Trade. In the Reich the only men to rise from the central bureaucracy were the three Secretaries of Justice Bosse, Hanauer and Nieberding. After the turn of the century, when both central and provincial officials were excluded from parliament, the reservoir of civil servants with parliamentary experience began to shrink rapidly, and this undoubtedly aggravated the growing constitutional crisis in the Empire.

In 1890 Holstein could still boast that since the Prussian-German Government was composed entirely of civil servants, 'it is more comfortable for the monarch and more efficient technically than a parliamentary Cabinet. It is one of the Chancellor's greatest achievements to have isolated the Cabinet from parliamentary majorities and made it independent of them.'[75] Before the century's end men like Holstein had come close to appreciating the serious defects in the Bismarckian constitution. The 'comfortable' ministers lost the power struggle with the court in the years 1894–97 because, being loyal servants of the Crown, they could not countenance wholehearted resistance to the monarch. On the other hand, in an effort to keep abreast of the times, ministers were being recruited not from the 'technically efficient' bureaucrats in the central departments, but from the aristocrats and landowners of the provincial administration whose educational qualifications often left much to be desired[76] and whose 'isolation from parliamentary majorities' was purely notional. Because of its artificiality and fragility, the Second Reich was incapable of organic growth. Its civil service, though highly trained, had to be recruited from that diminishing section of the population which was regarded as *staatserhaltend*, state-sustaining; Catholics and Jews, Radicals and Socialists were almost wholly excluded. The myth had to be upheld that Germany was governed not by politicians but by professional civil servants who stood above party, yet increasingly after Bismarck's dismissal *political* skill came to be recognised as essential at the ministerial level. The number of men in Germany who were both civil servants and able politicians was exceedingly small, and declined still further after the exclusion of civil servants from parliament at the turn of the century. 'It is frightening to see', wrote Alexander Hohenlohe when a ministry fell vacant in 1899, 'how few suitable people there are for such a post.'[77] The higher civil service had nothing comparable to set against the elemental lust for power exhibited after Bismarck's fall by Kaiser Wilhelm II and his court.

6   The splendour and impotence of the German diplomatic service

'Mistakes in internal administration can be rectified by a change of minister. Financial errors can normally be put right within a few months, economic errors within a few years. Even defeats on the battlefield can be compensated for, if usually only after decades. But gross, flagrant errors in the field of foreign policy can often *never* be made good.'[1] With these words of warning Bernhard von Bülow, then German ambassador in Rome and soon to become Foreign Secretary and Reich Chancellor, anticipated as early as 1895 the catastrophic course of German history in the first half of the twentieth century, thereby touching on a question which will always preoccupy historians of the German nation-state: why was the German diplomatic corps unwilling or unable to guide the promising political, economic and cultural rise of Prussia-Germany as a Great Power along a peaceful trajectory; why did it participate, actively or passively, in the self-destruction of Germany – and the self-destruction of Europe – in two European civil wars?

No serious historian will wish to challenge the view that the second of these wars was deliberately unleashed by Germany. The only question here is whether the traditional ruling elites – in this instance the diplomatic corps – collaborated willingly in this second attempt to establish German hegemony over Europe, or whether instead they overlooked certain 'excesses' of the National Socialist régime and allowed themselves to be 'shot dead' for Hitler.[2] The part played by Germany in the causation of the First World War is of course much more controversial. But even if we assume for the moment that Germany's role in July 1914 was of a similar order to that of the other Great Powers involved, the German diplomatic corps of the Wilhelmine epoch cannot escape censure for failing to prevent this war by warning in good time of its hopelessness. It is a difficult thing for me to say, but German diplomacy could also be open to censure on the grounds that, if war really was unavoidable, it should have created a more favourable starting-position, one more likely to produce a swift victory, and thus have averted the death of millions of human beings and unspeakable political catastrophes. If war really is, as Clausewitz says, the continuation of politics by other means, one can even ask the question why German diplomacy was not able, by diplomatic achievement, to create for the German Reich a position in the world commensurate with its internal dynamism, thus rendering unnecessary the recourse to the old Prussian recipe of war.

This mixture of delusion and failure in the German diplomatic corps has been interpreted by historians in two ways. Some analyse prosopographically the inner structure of the German Foreign Office, the Auswärtiges Amt, and the diplomatic corps and stress its narrow and – despite the reform attempts of the Weimar period[3] – increasingly anachronistic social composition. This leads on to the second perception, namely that the diplomatic corps – whether due to internal dissension or servility towards the rulers of the day – was not in a position to determine to any significant degree the foreign policy direction of the German state.

In this brief survey I shall explore these two basic questions – the inner composition of the German foreign service, and its powerlessness in terms of the formation of foreign policy in the years 1871–1945. If I place special emphasis on the first fifty years of this fateful period, this is primarily because the continuity of the social and administrative structure of the diplomatic service as well as the ideological conceptions and behaviour patterns of its members, even across the caesurae of 1918, 1933 and 1938/9, is very clear. Like other historians, those concerning themselves with German diplomacy also reach the conclusion that the foundations for later catastrophes were laid in the Kaiserreich.

Formally speaking, recruitment into the diplomatic service of the Reich was undertaken in line with the bourgeois principle of talent and achievement. Generally speaking, a candidate had to have completed a degree course in jurisprudence. He became a Referendar and then an Assessor before presenting himself for the great diplomatic examination. No less than a third of the diplomats in the Reich bore the title 'Dr.jur.' In practice, however, the principle of the *carrière ouverte aux talents* was undermined by two further criteria. First, a substantial private income was necessary – until 1908 this was a formal requirement, thereafter simply a practical necessity. In 1880 a candidate for entry into the service had to be able to demonstrate a private income of 6000 marks per annum. In 1900 this had climbed to 10,000 marks, and from 1912 onwards one had to have a minimum of 15,000 marks per annum.[4] Looking back, Prince Philipp zu Eulenburg held the proverbial parsimony of the Prussian state responsible for the poor quality of German diplomacy which he regarded as one of the causes of the First World War.[5] Eulenburg was thereby overlooking the fact that other states, which were supposed to have had better diplomats, had similar regulations. In Britain prior to 1919, for instance, proof of a private income of the equivalent of 8,000 marks for members of the diplomatic service (which, unlike in Germany, was completely separate from the Foreign Office) was required.[6] Nevertheless, it remains the case that in Germany only the sons of richer families were considered for recruitment into the diplomatic service, not least because both the long period as a student and the three-year service as 'Hilfsarbeiter' were unpaid until the Schüler reforms of the period 1918–20. It is also hardly surprising that diplomats tended to marry richer women. The marriages of Kühlmann and Schubert are often cited in this respect, but Dirksen, Monts, Raschdau, Flotow, Tschirschky, Wedel, Stumm, Renthe-Fink, Bergen, Schnitzler and Keller – to name but a few – also made a so-called 'good match'.[7]

This system would have led to a plutocratic diplomatic corps had it not been so to speak redressed by a second principle: the principle of aristocracy. No statistical information about the diplomatic corps in the Kaiserreich is so striking as the share of nobles. Of the 548 diplomats in service in the period 1871–1914, no fewer than 377, i.e. 69 per cent, were noble. The percentage of nobles was higher if we count only the foreign missions and not the Auswärtiges Amt itself. The ambassadors of imperial Germany were noble to a man. The most important department in the Auswärtiges Amt was the Political Department IA, which in the period from 1871 to 1914 was 61 per cent noble. It is true that there was a constant increase in the share of middle-class members of the diplomatic service in this period and beyond it. But during the period of the Kaiserreich such commoners were deployed almost exclusively either in the less important departments of the Auswärtiges Amt, namely in the Trade, Legal or Colonial Departments, or else in the Consular Service. If middle-class people entered the diplomatic missions abroad at all, then during the Wilhelmine period they were on the whole sent to South America or the Middle or Far East, areas which were important commercially but where aristocrats were unwilling to serve.

Of central importance for the history of the German diplomatic corps is the question of continuity in the personnel structure after the collapse of the Kaiserreich. The research of Kurt Doss and Peter Krüger has convincingly demonstrated that a measure of reorientation along middle-class lines did occur following the 'Schüler reforms' of 1918–20 (above all through the recruitment of 'outsiders'), a process which was *partially* reversed under Schubert's organisational streamlining in the period 1923 to 1930. However, the extent of this development remains difficult to estimate. According to Krüger's calculations, of the 160 diplomats of the Weimar Republic whom he investigated, only 62 were of noble origin, though the ratio among the 'influential top officials' was decidedly higher. But it is important to note that the statistical information presented by Lamar Cecil for the Kaiserreich on the one hand and Peter Krüger for the Weimar Republic on the other is not completely commensurable. Cecil records data on the whole of the foreign service including Vortragende Räte in the Wilhelmstrasse and Legation and Embassy Secretaries in the missions; but he excludes the consular service which was overwhelmingly middle-class and strictly separated from the diplomatic career during the imperial period. Krüger's statistics, by contrast, are restricted to the leading officials of the Auswärtiges Amt and to the ambassadors and ministers; but on the other hand he includes the Consuls-General (First Class). This is entirely logical in view of Schüler's amalgamation of the diplomatic with the consular service, but it does make direct comparisons difficult.[8] It is particularly regrettable that the personnel files for the German foreign service in the Third Reich remain inaccessible to historians, with the result that exact statistics for this period are still unavailable. Hans-Adolf Jacobsen has nevertheless been able to establish that the diplomatic corps of the Nazi period largely comprised men from the nobility and from the families of officers and higher officials, and that despite the threat of radical National Socialism with which they were faced they continued to be a homogeneous and 'extremely exclusive community of the like-minded' with 'a strongly conservative cast of mind'.[9] A significant degree of continuity thus prevailed in the social composition of the diplomatic service across the caesurae of 1918 and 1933. An indication of the Foreign Office mentality even in an era of revolutionary upheaval can perhaps be seen in the fact that it was less important to Secretary of State Dr Edgar Haniel von Haimhausen at the height of the Schüler reform whether his candidate for the post of ambassador in Rome was 'particularly prepossessing' or indeed had shot his wife's lover; what was important above all other considerations was that he was a 'reliable man with superb social skills and ... a not inconsiderable income'.[10]

The exclusive *esprit de corps* of the German diplomatic service was also promoted by a degree of confessional discrimination. Until 1945 the ratio of Catholics among the diplomats was significantly lower than the national ratio. This situation can only partially be explained by the fact that until 1918 the German middle states maintained their own diplomatic service. What was perhaps more important was that the majority of south German aristocratic families loathed the idea of state service under the detested Hohenzollerns and that until the turn of the century they saw the real focus of their social aspirations in the Hofburg in Vienna rather than in Potsdam and Berlin. Whoever reads the extensive private correspondence of German diplomats of the imperial period[11] will be astounded at the almost pathological fear of so-called 'Ultramontanism' which prevailed among even the highest and apparently most open-minded diplomats and statesmen in

Berlin. There was a widespread conviction that any softness towards 'Ultra-montanism' would have as a logical consequence the disintegration of the Reich. Catholics could therefore only be recruited into the service of the Reich if they had taken a firm and unequivocal stand against Rome and against the Centre party. It is a remarkable fact that this discrimination was continued even after 1918, with the result that in the Weimar Republic, as Krüger shows, only 15 to 20 per cent of German diplomats were of the Catholic confession.[12] And in the Third Reich itself, as Herr von Keller informed a conference in Büdingen in April 1982, of the 611 diplomats, consuls and other officials of the Foreign Office, only 118 (19 per cent) were Catholics.

That there were so few Jews in the German foreign service is remarkable not in terms of confessional parity, as only about 1 per cent of the total population was of the Jewish faith, but in view of their achievements and also their affluence. In the diplomatic corps during the whole of the Wilhelmine Reich there were only three non-converted Jews: Rudolf Lindau, Wilhelm Cahn and, in a subordinate position, Albert von Goldschmidt-Rothschild. Among converted Jews were the Vortragende Rat in the Trade Department, Max von Philippsborn, and the two heads of the Colonial Department (later Reich Colonial Office) Paul Kayser and Bern-hard Dernburg. Those who were reputed to be partly Jewish included: Limburg-Stirum, Thielmann, Berchem, Mühlberg and Lynar.[13] Analogous information should now be collected from the time of the Weimar Republic – and even more for the Third Reich – to complete this data.

The recruitment policy of the diplomatic service was of an unexpectedly generous character only in relation to the regional origins of those appointed. When it is remembered that around two-thirds of the population of the Reich were Prussian subjects, the fact that only a half of the diplomats of that time came from Prussia is certainly worth noting, especially as the personnel of the Prussian Legations at other German courts, but not those of the Bavaria, Württemberg, Saxony, Baden, the Grand Duchy of Hessen and the Hanseatic cities, were included in this figure. It seems doubtful that the real reason for this is to be sought in the agrarian crisis which allegedly hit the East Elbian nobility harder than other owners of landed estates.[14] It is more likely that here too political considerations – above all Bismarck's attempt to strengthen loyalty to the Reich by drawing in non-Prussian noble families – predominated. It is at any rate a matter of record that both Reich Chancellor Prince Chlodwig zu Hohenlohe-Schillingsfürst and his succes-sor Bernhard von Bülow were convinced that the East Elbian *Krautjunker* was too poor, too provincial and too ill-educated to appear as anything other than a figure of fun on the polished surface of the diplomatic stage.[15] Whatever the reasons, the representatives of the East Elbian landed gentry were in a minority as early as the turn of the century, not only among ambassadors and ministers but among the Vortragende Räte within the Auswärtiges Amt itself,[16] and in the Weimar Republic, too, Prussians cannot be said to have been treated preferentially.[17]

In summary, it can be said that the German diplomatic corps before 1945 (and beyond) was characterised above all by its social exclusivity. The ambassadors and ministers as well as the members of the all-powerful Political Department IA of the Auswärtiges Amt (abolished by Schüler after the First World War but significantly reinstituted in 1936) were at least until 1918 predominantly noble, wealthy and Lutheran and were therefore, even if not particularly Prussian, certainly comparable in terms of social origins with Berlin court society as a whole,[18] with the Guards officers[19] and the Oberpräsidenten, Regierungspräsidenten and Landräte of the Prussian provincial administration.[20] In contrast the consular service, as well as the Legal, Trade and Colonial Departments of the Auswärtiges Amt were – like the rest of the higher civil service in Berlin (for instance, the Prussian Finance Ministry or the Reich Office of the Interior) and also the naval officer corps[21] – almost exclusively middle-class in composition. Even after the integration of the consular service with the diplomatic corps at the beginning of the Weimar Republic the German foreign service remained, as Friedrich Payer said, 'a closed organism within the government' over which hovered 'a spirit of exclusivity'.[22]

This conclusion now needs to be placed in the context of an international comparison. If we look first across the Rhine to France, we are struck by the fact that the proportion of nobles in the French diplomatic corps, which until Mac-Mahon's unsuccessful *coup d'état* of 1877 had amounted to 89 per cent, had dwindled to a mere 7 per cent in the decade before the outbreak of the First World War.[23] This statistic does indeed seem to support the view that Germany was following a *Sonderweg*, a 'separate path', setting it apart from the rest of Europe.[24] But if we compare the German diplomatic corps not with that of republican France, but with the British foreign service – ignoring for the moment the highly aristocratic diplomatic representatives of Austria-Hungary and Russia – we arrive at an entirely different picture. In the Britain which the reformers Stresemann, Kühlmann, Brockdorff-Rantzau, Müller-Franken, Köster and Schüler in many respects held up as an example for Germany to follow, 67 per cent of the members of the diplomatic service before 1914 had been to *one school* (Eton). As late as 1930 a minister could proudly declare in the House of Commons that of the 110 newly recruited trainee diplomats, five had *not* gone to public school. In Britain, too, the diplomatic corps was criticised as 'a system of outdoor relief for the sons of the nobility'. There, too, efforts were made either to bring about fundamental reforms in the diplomatic service or else to hand over some of its responsibilities to other, more modern authorities, and yet it was only in 1943 that the consular service was united with the diplomatic corps.[25] All British diplomats without exception had to be of the Anglican faith; for an unconverted Jew such as Rothschild it was still not possible in the middle of the nineteenth century to take up his seat in the House of Commons. Seen in this perspective, it was not German but French diplomacy which was taking a 'separate path' in a Europe which until 1918 was predominantly monarchist.

The diplomatic service originated, and until the end of the nineteenth century had a certain legitimacy, as the extension and institutionalisation of the international monarchical system, as the amplification of the correspondence which monarchs conducted amongst themselves. In order to maintain this intercourse, it was not necessary to be particularly virtuous (consider the scandalous lifestyle of Chlodwig Hohenlohe in Paris, of Hatzfeldt in London or of the unmarried General von Werder in St Petersburg[26]), nor was exceptional ability a precondition. Bismarck is supposed to have said that the entrance examination for diplomats should be so regulated that he could choose whomever he wanted, whether that person was gifted or not.[27] Of primary importance was high birth in itself. No fewer than thirty-seven of the German ambassadors during the Second Reich were mediatised princes or the sons of morganatic royal marriages. In the great embassies of Europe – in London, Vienna, St Petersburg, Rome, Madrid and Constantinople, but in Paris, too – only an aristocrat of one of the highest-born families could play the role in court society which his position as ambassador demanded. He had to invite the right people and be invited by them in return in order to represent the interests of his country with dignity – and also in order to collect the secret information which he required for his reports. His wife, too, had to be acceptable at court and preferably possess money, charm and intelligence. In St Petersburg the charming Countess Alvensleben was often able to achieve more than her husband. Prince Radolin, who had a Talleyrand as mother-in-law, had as good a standing in certain circles in Paris as Bülow, whose mother-in-law was Donna Laura Minghetti, had in Rome. Conversely, the appointment of Count Wolkenstein as Austro-Hungarian Ambassador in Berlin was feared there on the grounds that his wife was the widow of the former Minister of the Royal Household at the Prussian Court, Count Schleinitz, and therefore knew a dangerous amount about the secret life of Berlin society.[28] The descendant of a Hessian leather manufacturer like Wilhelm (from 1885: von) Schoen, of a sparkling wine manufacturer like Mumm (from 1903 Baron Mumm von Schwarzenstein) or of a prosperous Bavarian sheep breeder like Speck von Sternburg could achieve little in the great European embassies of the old Europe. There a Prince Reuss, a Fürst Hohenlohe or Stolberg or

Lichnowsky, a Count Münster or Hatzfeldt was needed. With this observation we come to the second part of our investigation, the inner and outer limitations of the German diplomatic corps.

The diplomatic corps was without doubt the leading group within the German civil service. Judged not only by its splendid social standing, but also by the political talents of its leading representatives, which are amply attested to by their extensive correspondence with one another,[29] the Auswärtiges Amt and the Chiefs of Mission might have been expected to claim the right to determine the course of foreign policy. Indeed in times of a power vacuum (as after Bismarck's fall or the collapse of 1918), in times of extreme danger (as in the years preceding the outbreak of the First World War or during the Hitler régime), the diplomatic corps might even have been tempted to assume political power in order to avert catastrophe. Instead it was content to accept the role of a subordinate executive body. Why?

A number of reasons have already become apparent: the miniscule reservoir of talent from which the diplomatic corps was recruited; the incompetence (and even the vulnerability to blackmail) of some of the most important ambassadors (Münster, Werder, Eulenburg, etc.); the lack of co-operation between the Auswärtiges Amt at the centre and its representatives abroad; the arrogant spirit of exclusivity which, as the Luxburg case exemplified,[30] made it difficult for some German diplomats to grasp the world of the twentieth century with its economic pressures and mass politics; the rise of rival state institutions and party organisations which sought to fill the gaps left by the traditional diplomatic corps. But here I wish to draw attention to three predominant themes which recent research has illuminated very clearly. They can be characterised most succinctly as obedience, intrigue and the bid for 'world power'.

First a few remarks on the subject of *obedience*. Diplomacy is not foreign policy. A diplomat is merely, as a cynical Englishman once said, 'a man hired by his country to lie for it abroad'. His Foreign Office certainly tells him *how* he should 'lie', but this is rarely determined by the diplomat himself. The officials of the central Foreign Office are themselves subject to the 'structural power' of that institution, and only under the most favourable circumstances can individuals like Friedrich von Holstein, Carl von Schubert or – to name a non-German example – Lord Vansittart, play a significant role in the shaping of foreign policy. Equally, the degree of control which a Secretary of State or Foreign Minister can exert over his subordinates will vary from case to case; nor is every Reich Chancellor, President or Prime Minister equally interested in matters of foreign policy. These general points must of course be fully borne in mind when we speak of the obedience of the diplomatic corps. If this question is nevertheless posed in a particularly acute form in the case of the German diplomatic corps, then this is because, firstly, the obedience necessary for state service degenerated first under Bismarck and then under Kaiser Wilhelm II to obsequiousness, and because, secondly, under the criminal régime of Adolf Hitler, this obsequiousness had not only serious political but also grave moral consequences.

That Prince Bismarck would not tolerate the slightest degree of contradiction from his colleagues and subordinates is generally well known. Not only did he appoint his son Herbert as Secretary of State in the Foreign Office at the age of thirty-six; he also monitored the correspondence – and indeed the private lives in general – of the Empress Augusta, the Crown Princess Victoria and other members of the extended royal family.[31] It was not only his lackeys in the Auswärtiges Amt – people like Busch, Bucher and Aegidi – who were blindly devoted to him; even some who bore very old titles of nobility were content to do his will. The British Ambassador Knaplund wrote of Count Paul Hatzfeldt, for instance, that he was 'a shrewd, cautious man without convictions, who does what he is told intelligently and diligently, and that is what Bismarck likes in his agents'.[32]

In the course of the decade after Bismarck's fall this servility was reorientated towards Kaiser Wilhelm II and it intensified to such a degree that critical contemporaries labelled it 'Byzantinism'. A Hessian Reichsgraf allowed himself to be led before the Kaiser dressed as a poodle;[33] the Chief of the Military Cabinet danced for the Kaiser dressed in a ballet-dancer's tutu.[34] Within the diplomatic corps two ambassadors, Eulenburg and Bülow, set themselves the task, despite the urgent warnings of Holstein and Marschall in the Auswärtiges Amt, of making the 'personal rule' of the Kaiser into a reality. Bülow promised that as Reich Chancellor he would simply be the Kaiser's 'executive tool', no more than his 'political chief of staff'.[35] Even those who prefer to see in such protestations – the authenticity of Bülow's letter is not in dispute – little more than a cynical manipulation by Bülow of a 'not quite normal' monarch[36] and his devoted favourite will not be able to deny that they represented a disturbing 'degeneration' (Krüger) of the political culture of the diplomatic service which in many ways anticipated its conduct during the Third Reich, as expounded by Hans-Adolf Jacobsen. Not only Hitler but Wilhelm II before him expressed drastic views on the diplomatic corps. The Kaiser once remarked that the diplomats 'had so filled their pants that the entire Wilhelmstrasse stinks of — '.[37] Already under Wilhelm II there were among the German diplomats those who were boundless admirers of his genius, leading officials who despite certain inner reservations were nonetheless always willing to carry out 'their King's commands', but also people like Holstein who, out of concern for the future of their Fatherland, from time to time stood on the very edge of high treason. But just as in the Third Reich, so all these people in the Wilhelmine system were dependent on the favour of and access to the head of state,[38] while even in matters of foreign and armaments policy the monarch all too often accepted the advice of his Flügeladjutanten, Chiefs of Cabinet and favourites and ignored that proffered by his 'responsible advisers'. Not infrequently, as in the case of Lichnowsky, Wilhelm II even appointed ambassadors directly *against* the advice of the Reich Chancellor and the Auswärtiges Amt.[39] 'The Foreign Office?', he once asked. 'Why? I am the Foreign Office!'[40]

This brings us to my second theme: the *culture of intrigue* in the German diplomatic corps. If there ever was a chance in the period 1871–1945 for the Auswärtiges Amt to rise to the position of being the real 'governing elite', then that chance came in the decade after Bismarck's dismissal. It was squandered by intrigues within the diplomatic service itself. No doubt intrigue is a part of the very essence of politics, and this is one of the features which distinguish politics from mere administration, so that it might be possible to interpret the greater propensity towards intrigue in the Auswärtiges Amt as a natural consequence of its efforts to transform itself from an administrative body into a centre of power. We should also not overlook the fact that group-formation is typical of all diplomatic services. Peter Krüger has convincingly shown how the close co-operation of Stresemann, Maltzan and Schubert in the Auswärtiges Amt laid the foundations for the Locarno policy. Even so, the Auswärtiges Amt of the 1890s presents a unique picture of conflict. Eulenburg saw the Wilhelmstrasse as a veritable 'witches' kitchen'. Under a Chancellor-General (Caprivi) who understood nothing of foreign policy, and a Foreign Secretary (Marschall) whom Bismarck called 'ministre étranger aux affaires' the imperial German diplomatic corps intrigued against the 'Bismarck fronde', against the army (which was establishing a dangerous independence, not least in matters of foreign policy and espionage, by the creation of the system of military attachés), against the Prussian Ministers (who despite this title were for the most part nothing other than worthy civil servants), against the governments and the envoys of the German middle states, against the Kaiser's Secret Cabinets and against other influential elements at court. Above all, however, the diplomats intrigued against each other. The Auswärtiges Amt itself intrigued against the ambassadors, ministers and secretaries both within the Reich's boundaries and abroad. The ambassadors with Bismarckian affiliations – Radowitz, Stumm, Rantzau, Schweinitz, Reuss – were dismissed and replaced by Holstein's people. The 'grey eminence' of the Wilhelmstrasse did not shrink from telling some of them what they should report, thus confirming the despairing words of a Russian ambassador that one had to bring to bear more diplomatic skills when dealing with one's own government than with foreign ones.[41] But also within the Auswärtiges Amt itself intrigue was common. The famous poems which appeared in *Kladderadatsch* attacking Holstein, Kiderlen-Wächter, Philipp Eulenburg and the 'fourth man', Axel Varnbüler, were in fact nothing more than the 'flight into the open' of an 'outsider group' (Raschdau and Bothmer) within the Foreign Office in opposition to a genuinely dominant clique.[42] Finally, the diplomats abroad also intrigued against each other. From May 1894 onwards, Bülow in Rome and Eulenburg in Vienna employed a private code for their secret correspondence with one another.[43] They secretly passed on to each other the letters they received from the Auswärtiges Amt. To the Eulenburg-Bülow clique belonged Lichnowsky, Philipp Eulenburg's influential cousins August and Botho Eulenburg, and Axel Varnbüler and Kuno Moltke. Together they worked from 1893 onwards to undermine the influence of the Holstein group and under Bülow's leadership to build up the 'personal rule' of Kaiser Wilhelm II. In 1897 they achieved their aim. The diplomatic corps's chance of filling the power vacuum created by Bismarck's fall had vanished.

Even if one is unwilling to acknowledge the existence of 'personal rule' – however it is defined – after 1897, the fact is nevertheless indisputable that the legal *fiction* of 'personal rule' by the monarch was sufficient in itself before 1918 to prevent the formation of a Reich cabinet or of some other body in which the foreign policy situation of the Reich could have been discussed in depth. Lord Palmerston once said: 'We have no eternal allies and we have no eternal enemies; we have eternal interests.' But who in the Second Reich decided how Germany's 'eternal interests' in the ever more threatening world situation should be defended? Who ensured that the armaments policies on land and at sea matched each other and suited the foreign policy pursued by the Reich Chancellor in conjunction with the Foreign Office? 'That's priceless!' – cried the Austrian Foreign Minister Count Berchtold in despair during the July crisis of 1914 – 'Who governs: Moltke or Bethmann . . .?'

But would German foreign policy have been fundamentally different if the Auswärtiges Amt had had a greater share in its formulation? The question cannot be answered in this hypothetical form. What is certain is that by the turn of the century wide circles of German society were gripped by *dreams of 'world power'*, and that the diplomatic corps, whose professional duty it was to assess Germany's international position realistically, with very few exceptions shared the widespread illusions about her strength and potential. Fritz Fischer's findings, which thirty years ago were so controversial, have in the intervening years been largely accepted by international scholarship and, except for a few nuances, even by his former

German adversaries.[44] Fischer's views were so controversial partly because they placed Hitler's expansionist aims in a quite different perspective. Not only could Wilhelmine *Weltmachtpolitik* and Tirpitz's battlefleet programme be seen as a first attempt to acquire for Germany the status of a 'world power' – by means of a world war if need be; even the revisionist policy of the Weimar Republic could be interpreted as merely a transitional phase to Hitler's later, second attempt. Jacobsen has shown how in the early phases of the National Socialist dictatorship, the traditional diplomatic corps, 'in ignorance of the true aims of the Nazi leadership', was able to approve of the new course in foreign policy without suffering pangs of conscience. Only one among the diplomats and officials of the Auswärtiges Amt seems to have seen clearly in advance the 'qualitative change' of German foreign policy under Hitler, and submitted his resignation on grounds of conscience: the ambassador in Washington, Friedrich Wilhelm von Prittwitz und Gaffron. Even the Reich Foreign Minister Constantin Baron von Neurath, with all his abhorrence of certain 'excesses' perpetrated by the régime, developed into 'an unmistakeable admirer of Hitler and the National Socialist idea', while his successor Joachim von Ribbentrop was possessed by an almost pathological devotion to Hitler.[45] Among the secretaries of state in the Foreign Office too, attitudes towards the Nazi régime were, if certainly not unanimous, on the other hand not so very different. Bülow and Weizsäcker had their reservations but were not oppositional; Mackensen and Steengracht were enthusiastic supporters. With this example set by their superiors, it is not surprising that by 1941 76 per cent of the diplomatic corps had become party members, nor that so many had risen to high positions in the SS.[46] One is nevertheless shocked by the fact uncovered by Christopher Browning and Hans-Jürgen Döscher that Under-Secretary of State Martin Luther and his 'young guard' were involved in the deportation of the Jews to Auschwitz.[47] Such dedication went beyond the call of duty.

One might say in conclusion that the German diplomatic corps was no worse than other elite groups. Perhaps the problem is that, in view of its social splendour and its political potential, in view of its exclusivity and the claims to leadership which it based thereon, it should have been better.

7 Dress rehearsal in December: military decision-making in Germany on the eve of the First World War

For Fritz Fischer

Few documents on the history of imperial Germany have caused as much of a stir – but also as much racking of brains – amongst historians[1] as the entry for 8 December 1912 in the diary of the Chief of the Kaiser's Naval Cabinet, Admiral Georg Alexander von Müller.[2] It reads:

Sunday. Ordered to see His Maj. at the Schloss at 11 a.m. with Tirpitz, Heeringen (Vice Admiral) and General von Moltke. H.M. speaks to a telegraphic report from the Ambassador in London, Prince Lichnowsky, concerning the political situation. Haldane, speaking for Grey, has told Lichnowsky that England, if we attacked France, would unconditionally spring to France's aid, for England could not allow the balance of power in Europe to be disturbed. H.M. greeted this information as a desirable clarification of the situation for the benefit of those who had felt sure of England as a result of the recent friendliness of the press.

H.M. envisaged the following:

Austria must deal energetically with the foreign Slavs (the Serbs), otherwise she will lose control of the Slavs in the Austro-Hungarian monarchy. If Russia supports the Serbs, which she evidently does (Sasonoff's declaration that Russia will immediately move into Galicia if Austria moves into Serbia) then war would be unavoidable for us too. We could hope, however, to have Bulgaria and Rumania and also Albania, and perhaps also Turkey on our side. An offer of alliance by Bulgaria has already been sent to Turkey. We have exerted great pressure on the Turks. Recently H.M. has also pressed the Crown Prince of Rumania, who was passing through on his way back from Brussels, to come to an understanding with Bulgaria. If these powers join Austria then we shall be free to fight the war with full fury against France. The fleet must naturally prepare itself for the war against England. The possibility mentioned by the Chief of the Admiralty Staff in his last audience of a war with Russia alone cannot now, after Haldane's statement, be taken into account. Therefore immediate submarine warfare against English troop transports in the Scheldt or by Dunkirk, mine warfare in the Thames. To Tirpitz: speedy build-up of U-boats, etc. Recommendation of a conference of all naval authorities concerned.

General von Moltke: 'I believe a war is unavoidable and the sooner the better.[3] But we ought to do more through the press to prepare the popularity of a war against Russia, as suggested in the Kaiser's discussion.'

H.M. supported this and told the State Secretary [Tirpitz] to use his press contacts, too, to work in this direction. T[irpitz] made the observation that the navy would prefer to see the postponement of the great fight for one and a half years. Moltke says the navy would not be ready even then and the army would get into an increasingly unfavourable position, for the enemies were arming more strongly than we, as we were very short of money.

That was the end of the conference. The result amounted to almost 0.

The Chief of the Great General Staff says: War the sooner the better, but he does not draw the logical conclusion from this, which is to present Russia or France or both with an ultimatum which would unleash the war with right on our side.

In the afternoon I wrote to the Reich Chancellor about the influencing of the press.

There are certainly profound and complicated reasons for the confusion surrounding this document. A major cause of the trouble was that the Müller diaries were originally published in a deliberately distorted and mutilated form, in which the last sentences of the entry for 8 December 1912 were simply omitted.[4] The impression was thereby created that Müller himself was withdrawing half of the message of his diary record by dismissing the result of the conference in an apparent conclusion as 'almost zero'. Müller's disappointment that the Chief of the General Staff, Helmuth von Moltke, had not insisted on presenting an ultimatum to Russia or France (or both) which would have 'unleashed war with right on our side', therefore remained unknown, as did the fact that Reich Chancellor von Bethmann Hollweg was personally informed by Müller on the same day of the 'discussion of the military-political situation' that had taken place and received from him the 'All-Highest command to enlighten the people by means of the press what great national interests were at stake for Germany, too, in a war arising from the Austro-Serbian conflict'.[5] Years elapsed before the confusion produced by the falsified publication of the diary could be cleared up. However, an accurate version of the complete diary entry has been publicly available from 1977 at the latest, and as the handwritten original of the diary is stored in the Bundesarchiv-Militärarchiv in Freiburg and can be examined there by scholars, there is now no room for doubt about the authenticity of this key document.

In the meantime, further reports on the 'military-political conference' of 8 December 1912 have come to light which – even if at second hand – fully confirm what the Chief of the Naval Cabinet had written in his diary and in certain respects even amplify it. Thus the Saxon Military Plenipotentiary in Berlin, Major-General Freiherr Leuckart von Weissdorf, wrote to the Saxon Minister of War Freiherr von Hausen on 12 December 1912:

I have heard in the *strictest confidence* from a reliable source that last Sunday H.M. the Kaiser had a frank discussion in Potsdam [*sic*] with the Chief of the General Staff of the Army and the State Secretary of the Reich Navy Office. His Excellency von Moltke wants war, because he believes that it would not now be welcome to France, as is shown by the fact of her intervention in support of a peaceful solution to the situation. His Excellency von Tirpitz on the other hand would prefer it if it came in one year's time, when the Canal and the harbour for submarines in Heligoland would be ready. On this occasion H.M. the Kaiser is said to have declared on the basis of secret information that England, if war should break out in Europe, would stick unconditionally to the Entente and stand on France's and Russia's side. And this despite the continuing friendly assurances of England and the declaration of intimate relations between Germany and England made by the Reich Chancellor![6]

Three days later the Bavarian Military Plenipotentiary in Berlin, General von Wenninger, reported to his superior, the Bavarian Minister of War, Freiherr Kress von Kressenstein:

In my last report I held out the prospect of an oral briefing for Your Excellency. But as His Excellency von Lerchenfeld has just informed me that he has made a report on the same matter today to His Excellency von Hertling, I think it is necessary that I also submit a brief report to Your Excellency. Whereas the Reich Chancellor, in his official statements and through his press, expresses his confident hope in peace, the Kaiser himself is in an openly war-like mood.

A week ago today H.M. summoned Moltke, Tirpitz and Müller (Bethmann, Heeringen and Kiderlen were not invited!) and informed them in a most agitated state that he had heard from Lichnowsky that Haldane had come to tell him, probably on Grey's orders, that England would stand on the side of Germany's enemies, whether Germany attacked or was herself attacked. (Echo of the Chancellor's speech!) England could not look on while France was thrown completely to the ground and a power arose on the Continent which possessed absolute hegemony in Europe.

Moltke wanted to launch an immediate attack; there had not been a more favourable opportunity since the formation of the Triple Alliance. Tirpitz demanded a postponement for one year, until the Canal and the U-boat harbour on Heligoland were finished. The Kaiser agreed to a postponement only reluctantly. He told the War Minister the following day only that he should prepare a new large Army Bill immediately. Tirpitz received the same order for the Fleet. The War Minister likewise demanded the postponement of the introduction of the Bill until the autumn because the entire structure of the Army, instructors, barracks etc., could not digest yet more big increases; all troop exercising areas were overfilled, the armaments industry could not keep pace. The War Minister told me this himself and he authorised me to tell Your Excellency that he would request first and foremost a repeated and substantial rise in the numbers comprising companies, squadrons and battalions so that they would never again face the situation they do now, with 47 men to a company with the immediate prospect of war.

The Kaiser instructed the General Staff and the Admiralty Staff to work out an invasion of England in grand style.

Meanwhile his diplomats are to seek allies everywhere, Rumania (already partly secured), Bulgaria, Turkey, etc.

Your Excellency will see that the picture behind the scenes is very different from that on the official stage.[7]

Finally, a diary entry by the then Naval Captain Albert Hopman, a close confidant of Admiral von Tirpitz, has also been published. It confirms everything which appears in Müller's record but contains the further interesting claim that besides Moltke, Tirpitz, Müller and the Chief of the Admiralty Staff, Vice-Admiral August von Heeringen, the latter's brother, the Prussian Minister of War General Josias von Heeringen, and the Chief of the Military Cabinet, Moritz Freiherr von Lyncker, were present at the conference in the Berlin Schloss. On 9 December Hopman noted:

Schultz has told me that a conference took place yesterday morning at H.M.'s, at which the State Secretary of the R[eich] N[avy] O[ffice], the War Minister, the Chief of the Admiralty Staff, the Chief of the General Staff and the two Cabinet Chiefs took part. Afterwards Tirpitz told me that the matter under discussion had been the following. Lichnowsky had reported that Haldane had come to see him and indicated after all sorts of rhetorical embellishments etc. that if it were to come to a general European war, England would stand on France's side, since it could not tolerate that any particular power should have a distinct superiority on the Continent. H.M. therefore regards the situation as being very serious, particularly as Sassonow is supposed to have said that Russia would let loose if Austria should attack Serbia. H.M. sees in Austria's demands the vital interests of the Habsburg Monarchy which it can under no circumstances give up and which we must support. Doesn't believe that Serbia will eat humble pie. The Chief of the General Staff sees war as unavoidable and says the sooner the better. Tirpitz contradicted him and said that it was in the interests of the Navy to postpone war if possible for another 1–2 years. The Army, too, could do much before then to improve the exploitation of our population surplus. Rumania stands firm by Austria, and Bulgaria too is leaning towards the Triple Alliance. I myself do not *yet* believe in the inevitability of war, and believe, on the contrary, that it will not come to that. Haldane's declaration is a counter-move against the Chancellor's speech and is a bluff, a method used constantly by all governments these days.

The English City is doing everything possible to avoid war, in which it can only lose, at least for the next few years; the same is true of High Finance in all the other countries. The whole story has lasted too long already for it to develop into a general world conflagration. But who knows. 8 o'clock in the evening, went to dinner at Tirpitz's house, at which the Kaiser had said that he would be present. Those invited were Admirals von Müller, von Heeringen. The Admirals of the R[eich] N[avy] O[ffice] and 4 gentlemen from the Central Department. H.M. was in a very good mood. I heard nothing of any significance of his conversation.'[8]

The evidence on the secret 'military-political conference' of 8 December 1912 must therefore be described as unusually abundant. If historians nevertheless encounter difficulties in interpreting this meeting, that is primarily because the 'war council' – as Bethmann Hollweg angrily described it on 20 December 1912[9] – cannot be separated from the emotive controversy on the immediate causes of the First World War which overshadows it. With few exceptions, even those historians who see German policy in the July crisis of 1914 as the main cause of the outbreak of the world war are reluctant to accept that this policy was formulated a year and a half earlier by the Kaiser and 'his faithful followers in the army and navy' meeting in a hastily convened 'war council'. Historians of all shades of opinion have thus placed themselves in the unusual position of arguing to a certain extent against the sources. For them, the evidence on the 'war council' of 8 December 1912 is too sharp, too exact, 'too good to be true'. One almost has the feeling that the evidence would be easier to accept if the timing and the method envisaged for the unleashing of war – by means of an Austrian–Serbian conflict after the completion of the widening and deepening of the Kiel canal in July 1914, exactly one and a half years after the conference of December 1912 – had conformed less precisely to the actual course of events!

The wider question of the historical significance of the 'war council', and in particular of the relationship between the deliberations of 8 December 1912 and German policy in the July crisis of 1914, must therefore remain open until further new sources, such as for instance the missing pre-war diaries of Bethmann's confidant Kurt Riezler (which were allegedly destroyed in Munich as late as the mid-1960s[10]), permit a less ambiguous conclusion. If we nevertheless regard an assessment of the pre-history and history of the 'war council' as worthwhile, this is because no other event is capable of illuminating so clearly the military-political decision-making process in the Kaiserreich on the eve of the First World War. Even if there was no direct causal connection between 8 December 1912 and German policy in the July crisis of 1914, the men who in December 1912 stood on the threshold of a world war were (with the exception of the Heeringen brothers and Foreign Secretary Alfred von Kiderlen-Wächter, who died suddenly at the end of December 1912) the same as those who, after the assassination in Sarajevo, were prepared to risk the 'leap into the dark'. Such an investigation reveals in frightening clarity their political relationships with one another, the extent of their influence in the confused power-structure of the Bismarckian Kaiserreich in its final phase, their mentality following the domestic and foreign catastrophes of the Bülow years, the second Morocco crisis of 1911 and the disastrous Reichstag elections of January 1912. It reveals how Kaiser Wilhelm II remained the focus of the military-political decision-making process even if now, more unstable and lacking the counter-balance of Eulenburg and his Liebenberg circle, he was more vulnerable than ever to manipulation by the generals and his military entourage; how Reich Chancellor von Bethmann Hollweg and the Foreign Office under Kiderlen, though they had from the outset adopted a forceful stance in the first Balkan war which had broken out in October 1912, were nevertheless excluded from the 'war council' because, as mere civilians, they were responsible only for 'purely political' questions and not 'military-political' matters – even though the issue under discussion was whether (or rather when) to start a war! Above all, our investigation demonstrates how mistaken it would be to seek to understand the mechanism of decision-making in the final phase of the Wilhelmine Reich – and therefore in the July crisis of 1914 itself – without acknowledging that the decisive power in such matters had long ago slipped away from the Reich Chancellor and the Foreign Office and was exercised instead largely by the Supreme War Lord in conjunction 'with his faithful followers in the army and navy'.

Surprisingly, Kaiser Wilhelm II at first adopted a far more peaceful attitude than the Reich Chancellor or the Wilhelmstrasse when the first Balkan war broke out in mid-October 1912. Suddenly he stood, as his Chief of Naval Cabinet von Müller noted on 19 October, 'on the side of the Balkan states' and he regarded their declaration of war against Turkey as an 'historical necessity (*Völkerwanderung* in reverse)'. The Turks deserved to be 'flung out of Europe' as they had dethroned 'my friend the Sultan' and 'repaid all the services we had rendered by going over to the English'.[11] Even after the sudden collapse of the Turkish army on 22–24 October, the Kaiser's attitude did not change. On 1 November he put this defeat down to 'the undermining [*Zersetzung*] of the morale of Turkish soldiers by the Young Turks'; on 5 November he repeated his view of the Eastern Question, which Müller described as 'non-intervention at any price'.[12] Two days later Wilhelm II received a lengthy letter from the recently appointed ambassador in London, Prince Lichnowsky, which contributed significantly to the strengthening of his peaceful position. It was greatly to be welcomed, wrote Lichnowsky, that Germany had not made common cause with Turkey. It would equally be regrettable if Germany were to lend her support 'to the imagined needs of Vienna in Albania or Old-Serbia'. The spirit of the Triple Alliance guaranteed only the continued existence of present boundaries, and it would therefore be 'incomprehensible' if Germany were to run 'even the faintest risk of becoming involved in a war' on account of the expansion of Serbia.[13] Entirely consistent with the import of this letter, the Kaiser telegraphed to Kiderlen on 7 November: 'I see absolutely no danger for Austria's existence or even prestige in a Serbian harbour on the Adriatic.' It would be disturbing if Vienna were to resist the Serbian wish because 'Russia would immediately support Serbia.' The assertion of special wishes on the part of Austria '*with all the consequences that would then follow (war etc.)*' was solely 'a matter for *Austria and not for its alliance partner*'. Germany could not 'expose herself to the danger of entanglement in war' over the issue of Durazzo or Albania; he, Kaiser Wilhelm, could 'not accept the responsibility for that either before my people or my conscience'.[14] On 8 November, the Kaiser studied war maps and telegrams concerning the Balkan war during a two-hour rail journey to Letzlingen, and then and later in the evening he delivered lectures to those accompanying him 'justifying our "désintéressement" in the Balkans'.[15] On 9 November, the monarch telegraphed to Kiderlen: 'Have spoken in detail to the Reich Chancellor along the lines of my instruction to you and have emphasised that *under no circumstances* will I *march against Paris and Moscow* on account of Albania and Durazzo.'[16] It was only on the evening of the 9 November that the Reich Chancellor, who had 'cleverly not put in an appearance in the restaurant car' on the journey to Letzlingen,[17] was half able to change the Kaiser's mind and thus re-establish the 'right basis' for his foreign policy.[18]

In Letzlingen Bethmann asked for Admiral von Müller's opinion on the question 'whether Germany should uphold its alliance obligation towards Austria even if Austria should provoke a war by its demand (that Serbia must not annex Albania nor get a harbour on the Adriatic)'. Müller's answer to this fateful question shows not only that he and Bethmann – unlike Lichnowsky and at this point in time Wilhelm II – were fully prepared to risk a European war over the Austrian-Serbian conflict, but also the conviction on the part of the Chief of the Naval Cabinet that the German people would only support such a war if Russia first put herself in the wrong. Müller answered the Chancellor's question as follows:

If we now inform Austria, as the Kaiser wishes, that we would not recognise a war begun by Austria over Albania as a casus foederis, we would lose all credit. The German people would be furious and the Triple Alliance finished. On the other hand we must take care that Austria's demands on Serbia remain so moderate as to make their rejection or the intervention of Russia appear injurious to Austria's honour and so make our intervention on Austria's behalf comprehensible to the German people.

Bethmann Hollweg, who according to Müller had 'from the first adopted a vigorous stand', agreed with the Cabinet Chief. 'Then during the course of the day he spoke to H.M. along these lines and he thinks he has convinced H.M. that it would be impossible to drop Austria.'[19]

On his return from Letzlingen, Kaiser Wilhelm discussed German–Austrian relations with Kiderlen in the Berlin Schloss. From his own handwritten resumé of this discussion, it is clear that while he had taken up Müller's suggestion, he was still far from willing to support a hard-line Viennese policy which might lead to a world war. He criticised the 'abrupt, dictatorial tone' which Austria had adopted towards Serbia. He realised that Austria and Russia could quarrel so seriously with each other over the issue of Serbian aspirations

that it could come to an armed conflict. Then the casus foederis arises for Germany, since Vienna will be attacked by Petersburg – in accordance with the treaty. The latter lays down mobilisation and a war on 2 fronts for Germany, i.e. in order to be able to march on Moscow, Paris will first have to be captured. Paris will undoubtedly be supported by London. Germany will therefore have to enter a struggle for existence with 3 Great Powers in which *everything* will be at stake and which could end in Germany's destruction. All this could follow just because Austria does not want the Serbs in Albania or Durazzo.

Such an Austrian aim could not serve Germany as a justification for a 'war of annihilation'. There was therefore 'no possibility of finding a slogan which would inflame the German Nation in a war fought on such grounds'. No-one would be able to bear the responsibility of 'risking the very existence of Germany for such a cause'. It would in any case be quite wrong to place the German army and people at the disposal of the whims of another state, the Kaiser argued. 'The casus foederis will, it is true, arise if Austria is attacked. But only if Austria has *not provoked* Russia into attacking.' The policy conducted by Vienna must 'avoid this at all costs' and come forward with suggestions for mediation. Should the Russians thwart such mediation proposals approved by the other Powers, then 'the *Russians* would be putting themselves in the wrong vis-à-vis Austria ... and thus, as the provoking party which would not leave Austria in peace, they would provide our government with a good slogan for mobilisation if it should come to war!'[20]

During the next few days the Kaiser's attitude, here still somewhat hesitant, began to harden. On 11 November he left Potsdam again to take part in a hunt in Silesia. He spent the period 17–20 November with Tirpitz and other senior naval officers in Kiel.[21] On his return he claimed on the basis of the European and above all the English press to be able to detect a change in public opinion in Austria's favour. As Austria was now generally regarded as the 'provoked party', he wrote, 'the position which I wanted has been reached'. If the Russians should order hostile measures, Germany would have to support Austria. 'Should Russian counter-measures or remonstrations follow which force Kaiser Franz Josef to launch a war, then He will have right on His side, and I am prepared – as I already explained to the Chancellor in Letzlingen – to execute the casus foederis to the fullest extent with all the consequences.'[22]

On the following day, the Austrian Chief of the General Staff von Schemua and Archduke Franz Ferdinand, the heir presumptive to the Habsburg throne, arrived in Berlin. Both Wilhelm II and Moltke assured them that Austria-Hungary 'could fully count on Germany's support in all circumstances'.[23] Austria must show the Powers and especially England clearly that it could not tolerate an Adriatic harbour or corridor to the sea for Serbia. As soon as Austria's prestige demanded it, it should move forcefully against Serbia. Germany would support its alliance partner 'in all circumstances', even if this should result in a world war 'with the three Entente Powers'.[24] That afternoon the Kaiser's special train once again left Berlin, this time for the hunt at Springe, with a company of important political figures. Present at the hunt were Kaiser Wilhelm II, Archduke Franz Ferdinand, the latter's Senior Court Master of Ceremonies Baron von Rumerskirch, the Austrian Military Attaché Baron von Bienerth, Reich Chancellor von Bethmann Hollweg, Chief of the General Staff von Moltke, Grand Admiral von Tirpitz, the three Chiefs of Cabinet, the Court officials August Eulenburg and Max Lyncker, Colonel-General von Kessel and the Princes Dohna, Münster and Solms. Müller noted that the presence of the Austrians, the Reich Chancellor and the Chief of General Staff gave to the hunting party 'a strongly political stamp' and that the mood was 'really very grave'.[25]

The Kaiser's disposition, which dated from Letzlingen and even more decisively from 21 November, to support Austria against Serbia even if this should lead to a major war, was fully shared by his so-called 'responsible advisers'. On 19 November Foreign Secretary von Kiderlen-Wächter wrote to the German Ambassador in St Petersburg: 'I hope that somehow or other we can still avoid a European war ... At some point, of course, patience must get exhausted – otherwise not only the Austrians but we too will be accused of weakness.'[26] On his return from Springe, Admiral von Müller noted on 26 November that Kiderlen had a 'very calm assessment of the situation, which is decidedly more advantageous to us than in 1909 at the time of Austria's annexation of Bosnia' because 'today both Italy and England are on our side'. Bethmann, according to Müller, also appraised the situation 'very calmly'.[27] Both the Secretary of State and the Reich Chancellor gave public expression to this confident appraisal in their speeches before the Bundesrat Committee for Foreign Affairs and in the Reichstag. Kiderlen declared on 28 November: 'If Austria is forced, for whatever reason, to fight for its position as a Great Power, then we must stand by her side.'[28] Bethmann Hollweg spoke in a very similar vein in the Reichstag on 2 December, saying that if the Austrians in asserting their interests should unexpectedly be attacked by Russia, 'then we would fight for the maintenance of our own position in Europe, in defence of our own future and security. I am firmly convinced that in this policy we will have all the people behind us.'[29] Wilhelm II must have had this speech in mind when he told Müller on 14 December that now the Chancellor, too, had grown accustomed to the idea of war.[30]

Significantly, it was Bethmann Hollweg who repeatedly raised the question of the need for a new Army Bill.[31] In a memorandum of 25 November 1912 the General Staff, under Ludendorff's domination, now also demanded that the German army should be strengthened to an extent which 'alone will guarantee ultimate success in the next war'. The Germans must once again become the 'nation in arms into which great men in great times made us'.[32] Moltke and Ludendorff sought to sweeten this prospect of an expansion of the army, which they realised amounted to 'military-political and therefore also an internal-political revolution',[33] for the reluctant Conservative War Minister by pointing out that 'it was clear from a statement made by the Reich Chancellor that he was inclined to introduce an army bill in the spring'. Germany's military-political situation was at present favourable because Russia was not ready, France was still deeply engaged in Morocco and was threatened by the fact that Italy had joined forces with Austria and Germany. But in two to three years Germany would have to be strong enough 'to be able to rely on its own strength'.[34] On 2 December 1912, with Bethmann's express approval, the War Minister Josias von Heeringen ordered the preparation of an army bill in broad outline.[35] In their assessment of the situation on the Continent and in the implications for German policy which they drew from it, the Kaiser and the Chancellor, the military men and the Wilhelmstrasse therefore seem to have been broadly in agreement. The situation with regard to Britain was quite different, although here too the illusion was universally shared until 8 December 1912 that if a Continental war were to break out in the Balkans, Britain would remain neutral at least at the outset.

On his return from Kiel on 21 November, the Kaiser had noted that 'a European war is possible and for us perhaps a war for our very existence against 3 Great Powers'.[36] The ambassadors in Paris and London had now to establish 'clearly and beyond question' and report directly to him 'whether Paris under such circumstances would unconditionally side immediately with Russia, and which side England would be on'.[37] Lichnowsky answered the Kaiser's question in a detailed private letter of 23 November. Sir Edward Grey, he wrote, was clearly determined to 'render the political relationship between us as close as possible'. He wished, in the company of the overwhelming majority of British politicians, 'to live with us in peace and friendship without, however, thereby abandoning his relationship with France and Russia'. The idea that there could be a general war over northern Albania seemed as 'absurd' to Grey as it did to Lichnowsky himself. To the crucial question of Britain's position in the event of such a war, however, the new ambassador was still unable to provide an unambiguous answer. He wrote:

Whether in the event of a general war – which we also cannot impose on the German nation for the sake of Serbs and Albanians – the [British] Government would intervene, is a difficult question to answer. In the last resort, it will probably depend on what secret agreements exist between the Entente Powers. My impression here is that England would not decide on a forward move if there were any chance at all of her staying out of the conflict.[38]

Kaiser Wilhelm II evidently only read this letter on his return from Donaueschingen on 3 December. He stood, as Müller recorded in his diary, 'very much under the impression of the rather surprising English rapprochement with Germany', though at the same time he was determined 'no longer to be fooled by words but to await actions'.[39] Immediately after his return from Baden on 3 December, Wilhelm II received the Chief of Admiralty Staff August von Heeringen in order to discuss with him the various operational plans which had been worked out by the Admiralty Staff after the great naval manoeuvres of the autumn. In the memorandum 'Concerning the conduct of war against Russia and France in the case of a wait-and-see attitude or neutrality on the part of England', Heeringen expressed the hope that Germany 'at least at the beginning, and perhaps for the whole duration of the war, would have only Russia and France as enemies'. In this case Germany's 'undisputed dominance' of the Baltic Sea would have to be secured by a 'pre-planned, carefully prepared surprise attack immediately after the declaration of war'; in the west, on the other hand, because of the probably still 'uncertain' attitude of England, restraint would have to be exercised. The German battleships must not be put at risk in secondary undertakings against France but kept in readiness for a great battle on the high seas. The 'large ships that cannot pass through the Kaiser Wilhelm [i.e. Kiel] Canal' must for this reason be stationed in the North Sea in order that they are constantly available should England decide to come to the aid of its Entente partners after all.[40] In his 'Draft of Operational Orders for a War against England', the Vice-Admiral set out the reasons why Germany should avoid a large-scale attack on the distant English coast, but why on the other hand 'offensive mine warfare against the enemy coasts' should be undertaken from the start of the war onwards.[41] In a third memorandum, on attacking English troop transports, Heeringen argued in favour of conducting such operations 'primarily by means of U-boat operations and by contaminating the lines of approach to the embarkation and disembarkation harbours'.[42] All three operational plans were approved by the Kaiser on 3 December. He would refer to them directly at the 'war council' five days later.

On 5 December Kaiser Wilhelm II left Berlin once again, this time accompanied only by his close entourage,[43] in order to take part in the hunt at Bückeburg as a guest of Prince Georg zu Schaumburg-Lippe. He returned on the evening of 7 December and on the following morning found awaiting him Lichnowsky's Report of 3 December 1912, which provided the immediate stimulus for the convening of the 'war council'.

Concerned over Bethmann's Reichstag speech of 2 December, the Lord Chancellor Lord Haldane called on the German ambassador in order to clarify Britain's position in the event of a Continental war, as defined in the recent correspondence between Grey and Cambon.[44] Haldane repeatedly stressed that London was 'unconditionally' in favour of peace, but warned that if the conflict between Austria and Serbia should lead to a Continental war, it was improbable that Great Britain would be able to remain 'a silent observer'. As always, Haldane stressed, British foreign policy was rooted in the belief that the balance of power between the two alliance groups had to be maintained. 'England would therefore in no circumstances be able to tolerate a subjugation of the French', as she would afterwards be faced with 'a unified Continental group under the leadership of one single Power'.[45] On the following day, 4 December, Lichnowsky discussed this crucial issue directly with Sir Edward Grey. The Foreign Secretary expressed his astonishment that the German Chancellor had referred in his recent Reichstag speech to the 'possibility at this early stage of a war between the Continental alliance groups'. Grey asked Lichnowsky if this speech should be interpreted to mean that Germany 'intended to guarantee to support Austria-Hungary in all eventualities and in whatever steps she believed she should take in pursuance of her interests, in other words to issue her as it were with a blank cheque'. In a tone that was 'unmistakable', Grey warned the German ambassador that the 'consequences' of such a policy would be 'incalculable'. It was 'an absolutely vital interest' for Great Britain 'to prevent this country (France) from being completely subjugated by us'. Britain 'would therefore feel absolutely obliged to come to the support of the French if, as expected, we were to defeat them'.[46] Two days later in Sandringham King George V surprised Prince Heinrich, the Kaiser's brother, by declaring: 'If there is a European war, then England, France and Russia [will stand] against us and the Triple Alliance!'[47] Germany must know, the King wrote to Grey, 'that we would not allow either of our friends to be crippled'.[48]

When, early on 8 December 1912, Kaiser Wilhelm II read Lichnowsky's Report on his conversation with Haldane, he covered it with the most violent marginal comments. In a characteristic attack of anger, he declared the English principle of the 'balance of power' to be an 'idiocy' which would make England 'eternally into our enemy'. The principle of the balance of power was nothing more than an attempt by that 'nation of shopkeepers' to prevent other Powers from defending their interests with the sword. Above all the Kaiser was disappointed that in the unavoidable 'final struggle [Endkampf] between the Slavs and the Teutons', the 'Anglo-Saxons will be on the side of the Slavs and Gauls'.[49] Wilhelm II had already threatened at the end of September 1912 that if England refused to comply with Germany's wishes, then 'we shall be able to take our mobilisation plans out of the drawer, for then everything will be clear'.[50] Now, on 8 December, he greeted Haldane's statement to Lichnowsky on Britain's position in the event of a European war as 'a desirable clarification, which from now on must form the basis of our policy'; all 'veils of uncertainty' had been torn asunder. In the coming 'struggle for existence [Existenzkampf]' between the

'Teutons' and the 'Slavs supported by the Latins (Gauls)', the Kaiser thundered, England – motivated by 'envy and hatred of Germany' and by her 'fear that we are becoming too strong' – would stand on the side of the Slavs and Gauls.[51]

On that Sunday morning, as we have seen, Kaiser Wilhelm II summoned his Chief of General Staff von Moltke and the three Admirals von Tirpitz, von Heeringen and von Müller (and possibly also the Chief of the Military Cabinet Moritz von Lyncker) to the Schloss and informed them that in a future war of the Triple Alliance against France and Russia, England would stand at the side of her Entente partners. This news, which had just arrived from Lichnowsky, was, he declared, a 'desirable clarification of the situation'. Austria should now deal energetically with the Serbs, since she would otherwise lose control of the Slavs within the Danube Monarchy. Should Russia support the Serbs, 'which she evidently does', then 'war would be unavoidable for us too'. But Austria could count on the military support of Bulgaria, Rumania, Albania and perhaps Turkey as well, and Germany would then be free to 'fight the war with full fury against France'. The fleet would have to prepare for a war against England, since 'the possibility . . . of a war with Russia alone' must now be discounted. 'Therefore immediate submarine warfare against English troop transports in the Scheldt or by Dunkirk' and 'mine warfare in the Thames'. These statements by the Kaiser were enthusiastically supported by the Chief of the Great General Staff. He too considered 'that war was unavoidable, and the sooner the better', though he did argue that first 'we ought to do more through the press to prepare the popularity of a war against Russia'. Grand Admiral von Tirpitz, on the other hand, objected that 'the navy would like to see the postponement of the great fight for one and a half years' – until the completion of the widening of the Kiel Canal in the summer of 1914![52]

The Kaiser's excitement over the declarations of Haldane and Grey persisted for at least a week. On 9 December he wrote to the heir to the Austrian throne, Archduke Franz Ferdinand, that Haldane's statement had been 'typically English'. 'Full of poison and hatred and envy of the good development of our mutual alliance and our two countries.' Britain's 'balance of power' policy had been revealed 'in all its naked shamelessness' as the 'playing off of the Great Powers against each other to England's advantage'. 'This has come as no surprise to me', the monarch added, 'and the necessary precautions will be taken.'[53] Three days later, Wilhelm wrote to his brother Heinrich that Haldane's statement to the effect that England 'could *not tolerate* our becoming the strongest Power on the Continent and that the latter should be united under our leadership!!!' amounted to a moral declaration of war on Germany. At least the clarification of the situation had made Germany's 'preparatory measures' easier to undertake.[54] The Kaiser also wrote to the Prussian Envoy in Karlsruhe, von Eisendecher, on 12 December that Haldane had declared 'in unscrupulous, raw and typically English terms ... that if Germany were to become involved in a war with Russia-France – in support of Austria – England would not only not remain neutral, but would immediately come to France's aid'; according to Haldane, England could 'not tolerate Germany's becoming the predominant Power on the Continent and that the latter should unite under its leadership!!' In terms of military preparations, England would from now on count as Germany's enemy. Marschall's mission, like that of Lichnowsky, had been 'to secure England's neutrality towards us, at all events in the case of a conflict with Russia-France', but that had now finally failed.[55]

On the following day, Kaiser Wilhelm II visited the Bavarian envoy in Berlin, Count Lerchenfeld, and told him too that Haldane had explained to Lichnowsky that England 'could not permit Germany to subjugate France, after which there would be only one Power on the Continent which would then exercise an absolute hegemony'. The 'Germanic English', the outraged Kaiser exclaimed, would therefore 'fight with the French and Russians against their own racial comrades'. To the long-serving representative of Bavaria, the 'salient point' in his detailed and agitated conversation with the Kaiser was the realisation that 'soon everything might be at stake for Germany'.[56] When on 14 December Theodor Schiemann spoke to the Kaiser in Potsdam, he also observed that Wilhelm saw in Haldane's statement –'that in the event of a general war, England would be compelled to stand on France's side in order to prevent Germany from becoming all-powerful' – a threat to which he must respond with a new Navy Bill.[57]

The veteran Swiss ambassador in Berlin, Alfred de Claparède, was not a little surprised when, after having lunch with the Kaiser on 10 December, Wilhelm launched into a 'grave and agitated' tirade on the situation in the Balkans and in Europe as a whole. The war of the Balkan states against Turkey was, the monarch exclaimed, 'not a religious war but purely a racial war, the war of Slavdom against Germandom'. Russia clearly intended 'to unite all Slavs, not merely those in the Balkans, but the Slavs of other States, in particular of Austria-Hungary, so weakening Austria militarily through the loss of so-and-so many million Slavs'. Austria was fully aware of the danger, however, 'as are we in Germany too, and we will not leave Austria in the lurch: if diplomacy fails, we shall have to fight this racial war'. Only a few days earlier, the Kaiser told Claparède, he had learnt that Lord Haldane had announced to Lichnowsky 'that England would never tolerate Germany's taking a predominant position over her neighbours in Central Europe. Is this not an impertinent statement which should really have been answered by a breaking off of diplomatic relations?', the Kaiser demanded indignantly. 'Is it not incredible ... that these Anglo-Saxons with whom we are related by common ancestry, religion and civilisatory striving, now wish to allow themselves to be used as the tools of the Slavs', Wilhelm demanded. The Kaiser then declared that Austria and Germany would have to prevent the creation of a strong Serbian state. The vital interests of both empires required that they must not be 'encircled by a Slav ring'. Again he stated emphatically: 'If this question ... cannot be solved by diplomacy, then it will have to be decided by armed force. The solution can be postponed', declared the Kaiser, echoing the discussion in the 'war council' of two days earlier. 'But the question will arise again in 1 or 2 years'. The Kaiser then repeated: 'The racial struggle cannot be avoided, – perhaps it will not take place now, but it will probably take place in one or two years.'[58] On 15 December the Kaiser told Albert Ballin in undiminished excitement that a 'racial struggle [Rassenkampf]' between the 'Teutons [Germanen]' and the 'insolent Slavs' could not be avoided because at stake was the future of the Habsburg Monarchy and 'the very existence of our Fatherland'. But Haldane had now declared that England could not tolerate 'a subjugation of France by ourselves'. It could not allow 'us to achieve a predominant position on the Continent under which the Continent could then be united'.[59]

Is it possible that we are mistaken in assuming that these agitated exclamations of the Kaiser in the period 8–15 December 1912 reveal his innermost intentions of making the German Reich 'the strongest Power' with 'absolute hegemony' over the European Continent? It seems to have been axiomatic for him that such a breakthrough to predominance in Europe could only be achieved by means of a war against France and Russia. Instead of being warned off this course of action by Haldane's 'honest and well-meaning attempt ... to urge caution upon us',[60] however, the Kaiser's determination not to wait too much longer but to unleash a world war before Austria-Hungary became worthless as an ally because it had been 'undermined by the Slavs' appears only to have hardened. Indeed, at the 'war council' of 8 December 1912, he together with the Chief of General Staff von Moltke argued for an 'immediate attack' and accepted the 'postponement of the great fight for one and a half years' demanded by Tirpitz only 'reluctantly'. Müller too recorded his disappointment at the postponement of the war in his diary, as we saw at the beginning. He wrote: 'That was the end of the conference. The result amounted to almost 0. The Chief of the Great General Staff says: War the sooner the better, but he does not draw the logical conclusion from this, which is to present Russia or France or both with an ultimatum which would unleash the war with right on our side.'[61]

These discussions as to the merits of triggering a war at once or alternatively after the completion of the widening of the Kiel Canal in the summer of 1914, remained anything but secret. Captain Hopman learned all the salient details of the 'secret' conference as early as the following morning – through Schultz, his masseur! The numerous letters Wilhelm II sent, the agitated discussions he held with German and foreign diplomats, in themselves ensured a wider audience. As Bethmann Hollweg complained to Eisendecher on 20 December, the Kaiser had 'told God and the whole world about Haldane's conversation, fantastically embellished'.[62] Soon the Military Plenipotentiaries of Bavaria and Saxony, who were in daily contact with the Prussian War Minister von Heeringen (whose brother had taken part in the 'war council'), were able to report that Moltke had argued for an immediate war, while Tirpitz 'would prefer it if it came in one year's time, when the Canal and the harbour for submarines in Heligoland would be ready'.[63] The Bavarian General von Wenninger reported more fully still on the 'war council' after he learned that Count Lerchenfeld had already written to the Bavarian Minister-President Count Hertling on the subject. The Kaiser, Wenninger stated in his report of 15 December, was 'in an openly war-like mood'. At a conference held a week before, Moltke had spoken out in favour of an 'immediate attack', as 'there had not been a more favourable opportunity since the formation of the Triple Alliance'. Tirpitz on the other hand had 'demanded a postponement for one year, until the [Kiel] Canal and the U-boat harbour on Heligoland were finished'. The Kaiser, Wenninger continued, 'agreed to a postponement only reluctantly'. He ordered new Army and Navy Bills to be introduced immediately, a plan for the 'invasion of England in grand style' to be worked out, and new alliance partners to be sought.[64] After Lerchenfeld's and Wenninger's Reports, it is not surprising that the new Prince Regent of Bavaria, the future King Ludwig III, should ask Bethmann in consternation what lay behind the news that the Kaiser was pressing for war and planning an invasion of England.[65]

Within the officer corps, too, the conviction was widespread that a great war would soon begin. On 14 December Admiral von Müller had to inform the Kaiser of the 'numerous withdrawals from bank accounts and the deposition in gold in the safety-vaults of the banks of the sums thus withdrawn, as well as the sending of bank deposits abroad (Zürich)'. Wilhelm II was already aware of this and observed that 'many high-ranking officers were also involved'.[66]

How did the so-called 'responsible government' react to the decisions taken by the Kaiser and his 'faithful followers in the army and navy' at the so-called 'war council'? Does the fact advanced by Mommsen, Turner and Baumgart that neither Bethmann Hollweg nor Kiderlen-Wächter took part in the deliberations of 8 December suffice to deny that 'military-political conference' the status of a decision-making meeting? Is it, as Hölzle maintains, a 'misunderstanding of the political leadership of the Kaiserreich' to believe that the basic direction of the foreign and armaments policy of the Prusso-German military monarchy was in the final analysis laid down not in the Wilhelmstrasse 76 or 77, but by the Kaiser in the Berlin Schloss or in the New Palace in Potsdam, following discussion with his top-ranking generals and admirals? After the catastrophic collapse of the authority of the 'responsible government' in favour of the monarch and his court in the decade after Bismarck's fall, and after the fiasco of Bülow's tentative efforts to reassert the Reich Chancellor's authority in the years 1906–9, did Theobald von Bethmann Hollweg really possess the power (assuming for the moment that he had the will) to 'put the Kaiser in his place' and to 'nullify' the decisions taken at the 'war council'?[67] These are all questions which now urgently require clarification through further research. A detailed examination of Bethmann's reaction to the 'war council' suggests, however, that he was far better and much sooner informed than some historians have assumed, and that with the single exception of the new Navy Bill demanded by the Kaiser, Bethmann accepted and carried out (either personally or through the appropriate administrative department) every decision made at that military-political meeting.

It is simply not correct, as Wolfgang J. Mommsen has claimed, that the Chancellor was only informed a week later of the 'war council', and even then semi-officially; it is also not correct, as Mommsen again asserts, that 'there is not the slightest evidence to support the argument that William II's excited order to prepare the country for war by means of an official press campaign was followed up by deeds'.[68] Immediately after the 'war council', Admiral von Müller officially informed the Chancellor in writing that 'a conference on the military-political situation [took place] today in the Royal Schloss', in accordance with which the Kaiser was now ordering Bethmann Hollweg 'to enlighten the people through the press of the great national interests, which would be at stake also for Germany, if a war were to break out over the Austro-Serbian conflict. The people must not be in a position of asking themselves only at the outbreak of a great European war, what are the interests that Germany would be fighting for.' The Chief of the Naval Cabinet hinted that further decisions had been taken in the course of the meeting: he was, he said, only informing the Reich Chancellor of the command regarding the new press policy because this was 'a purely political measure'.[69] It was obviously the admiral's view that the 'military-political' discussions and decisions of the 'war council' were not the business of the civilian Reich leadership.

Bethmann Hollweg and Kiderlen-Wächter carried out the Kaiser's instruction without further ado and to the latter's complete satisfaction.

Kurt Riezler himself wrote an article with the title *For the sake of Durazzo?* which was published as early as 9 December in the *Deutsche Tageszeitung* and which the monarch, still in his agitated state, approved as 'very good'.[70] On 10 December the Reich Chancellor sent this 'article on Germany's interest in the event of an Austro-Russian war' to the Kaiser, stating expressly that it had been 'prepared at this end in accordance with Your Majesty's Most Gracious instruction conveyed to me by Admiral von Müller'.[71] On Wednesday, 11 December 1912, Foreign Secretary Alfred von Kiderlen-Wächter had an audience with the Kaiser on the subject of the new press policy, following which he informed Müller that 'the matter . . . would be pursued further in the press'.[72] In the light of such clear evidence it is surely impossible to continue to maintain that 'the responsible statesmen as well as the Wilhelmstrasse' were left 'completely in the dark' about the new orientation of official press policy.[73]

This is not of course to say that the articles authored in the Foreign Office conformed in all respects to the ideas of Moltke and Ludendorff in the Great General Staff. As the Austrian Military Attaché, Baron Karl von Bienerth, was able to report after a conversation 'with several gentlemen' of the General Staff:

It seems a striking fact that the real cause of the present difficulties in the Balkans is not discussed in the press here at all; instead the talk is always of the favourable course of negotiations and of an improvement in the situation. Only one or two newspapers, mainly conservative ones, touch on the real theme of the Greater Slav question. There is therefore a justified fear that the disappointment and dismay would then be all the greater if the German Reich were to be forced to intervene. There is regret that the press does not receive better information or alternatively is always instructed to write in the above sense in order to provide artificial support for stock market levels. The Press Bureau of the Foreign Office is held to blame, but it receives its instructions mostly from the Reich Chancellor himself. The General Staff is striving to improve the situation, which is assured if war does come but which should as far as possible be brought about at the present moment.[74]

An even deeper gulf lay between Bethmann Hollweg and the Reich Navy Office, which was also, according to the Kaiser's instructions in the 'war council', to mount 'a vigorous press campaign'.[75] Müller's communication to the Reich Chancellor of 8 December was originally supposed to be sent in duplicate to Grand Admiral von Tirpitz as well; but on 9 December Müller noted on the draft of his letter that he had 'settled the matter orally' with Tirpitz.[76]

On 14 December 1912, the Director of the Political Department of the Foreign Office, Wilhelm von Stumm, complained of the growing 'propaganda of the navy'.[77] A typical example of this press campaign, which was directed by the Reich Navy Office and executed by the Pan-German

League, and which stressed the interrelationship between naval and Continental policy, was the article by Professor Martin Spahn entitled 'Austria's Affair is our Affair' in *Der Tag* on 15 December 1912.[78] The Chancellor, Spahn noted in the article, had declared in the Reichstag on 2 December that Germany would stand by Austria in the Balkan troubles. However, there was a legitimate concern over how widely the grave issues involved were understood by the nation at large. It was true, Spahn wrote, that Kaiser Wilhelm II had, soon after his accession, put an end to the 'mistaken presupposition' that the Lesser German Reich was satiated:

The German Reich under his [Wilhelm II's] leadership has broken out of the confines of Prussian foreign policy. That is the Kaiser's contribution and one which lifts him high above all his German contemporaries in significance for the nation. But the nation has still not placed itself sufficiently strongly behind the Kaiser ... And this situation will not really change until it is made clear to the nation again that in terms of foreign policy the entire region from the North Sea to the Adriatic must be regarded now as ever as a single entity to be covered by us jointly with Austria.

The Greater German movement, as opposed to the Lesser German school of thought, had always had such extensive national aims in view. According to Spahn it knew that

Germany's only serious rival was England; for the contest with England, everything that was amenable to German influence had to be brought together – from Hamburg to Triest. But equally, everything had to be brought together for the moment that Turkey collapsed, so that the standstill in the movement of German influence and German culture along the Danube in a downstream direction, far from being perpetuated by the others, should rather be at last remedied.

England's sudden endeavour in the present crisis to stay on friendly terms with Germany should bring home to the German people 'how closely Austrian Eastern policy and German North Sea policy are intertwined', Spahn said. The present world crisis should clarify the fact that 'Austria's position in the Adriatic and our position in the North Sea are mutually dependent'. The question whether Germany would ever acquire land for settlement in Asia Minor 'appears at the present time to be wholly subordinate to the one great issue, namely that now and in the future, and with full determination and might, Austria and the German Reich together will defend Hamburg and Bremen in the Adriatic, Triest in the North Sea'. Spahn's article seemed to the Reich Chancellor to be indicative of the way in which 'His Majesty is now being worked on'. The numerous submissions from local Pan-German associations were also in Bethmann's view inspired by the navy. For instance, after a meeting in Wanne-Eickel on 12 December 1912 at which the retired Admiral Breusing had spoken on the subject of 'The World War and the German Fleet', those present had passed a resolution demanding Army and Navy Bills so that the Reich 'would be able to match the threatening onslaught of the combined armed forces of France, England and Russia'.[79]

These growing signs of a substantial campaign in favour of new military bills persuaded Bethmann Hollweg on 14 December to inquire directly of the Chief of the Kaiser's Headquarters, Colonel-General Hans von Plessen, as to the Kaiser's intentions. He learned from Plessen that Wilhelm II had in fact ordered not only an official press campaign to enlighten public opinion on Germany's vital interests in an Austro-Russian war, but also both a new Army Bill and a new Navy Bill.[80] As late as 17 December, the Chancellor was forced to confess to Kiderlen-Wächter that he still did not know 'precisely what instructions H.M. had issued concerning the preparation of military bills'. The only thing that was certain was that 'immediately after he had received Lichnowsky's report on his discussion with Haldane, H.M. had telegraphed to General von Moltke as well as to some gentleman of the navy (probably Tirpitz and Heeringen) summoning them to him', and that he had said to them: 'Now mount a vigorous press campaign.' The Reich Chancellor was determined to put a stop to the press campaign in support of new military bills.[81]

Immediately after confronting Plessen on 14 December, Bethmann asked the Prussian War Minister Josias von Heeringen and Admiral von Tirpitz to come to see him and explained to them that, having heard their plans for new bills, he 'at first sight regarded such projects as completely impractical but did not wish for the present to take a view as to their contents'. He did, however, have to insist 'that they did not bind themselves behind my back even vis-à-vis His Majesty, that not even the slightest news of any possible preparatory work being undertaken in their departments must be allowed to reach the ears of the public, and that I could not tolerate under any circumstances any kind of press campaign in support of the projects'.[82] However, both Heeringen and Tirpitz denied being connected in any way with the rumours concerning military bills.[83]

On 17 December, shortly before his departure for Munich for the funeral of Prince Regent Luitpold, the Chancellor asked for an urgent meeting with Kiderlen to discuss the modalities 'by which I could submit a protest to H.M. against the Navy Bill'.[84] The outcome of this urgent discussion was a lengthy coded telegram to the Kaiser in which Bethmann insisted on secrecy with regard to the military bills at least for the time being. 'It is certain that a war with Russia will also mean for us a war with France', he wrote. 'On the other hand there are numerous indications that it is at least doubtful whether England would intervene if Russia and France were to appear to be directly responsible for *provoking*' hostilities. Seizing on a statement of Lichnowsky's of 9 December,[85] the Chancellor expressed the hope that

England would intervene 'on behalf of a subjugated France' only in retrospect and even then only diplomatically. In any case Germany would have such a chance 'if *we* avoid all provocation'. For this reason it was imperative that 'no German plans for army and navy increases should become known' at this time, for that could 'easily be exploited against us as a provocation'. The Kaiser should therefore instruct the naval and military authorities to keep absolutely secret any preparatory work that might be being undertaken on future military bills. Bethmann described the 'agitation' which had already begun in support of a new Navy Bill was 'truly dangerous'. He hoped that the Kaiser would instruct Tirpitz accordingly. After his return from Munich, the Reich Chancellor would request an audience in order to brief the Kaiser 'on the totality of these questions on which the whole of our future policy depends'.[86]

Wilhelm II agreed only reluctantly to the Chancellor's urgent request that the two great military bills should for the time being be kept secret. He declared that his agreement to do so would above all not change anything in the demands themselves for army and navy increases 'which will be made later' and which he was 'absolutely determined to have'. The Kaiser also stated that he did not doubt 'for a moment' that England would intervene immediately in a Continental war. Russia and France would certainly ensure 'with the help of the mutually bribed press' that they did not appear to have provoked the war. Bethmann, he said, in any case placed far too much emphasis on the question of provocation, for 'such a provocation can *always be constructed* by reasonably skilful diplomacy and by a skilfully guided press (candidacy for the Spanish throne, for example, [in] 1870) and must always be kept to hand!' The Kaiser also emphatically rejected Bethmann's argument that England would only intervene after the subjugation of France by the German army. 'Haldane has expressly declared that the possibility of subjugation would not be tolerated, which makes an *immediate* intervention on Engl[an]d's part an absolute certainty; but not in *retrospect*!'. Despite all this, Wilhelm ordered his three Chiefs of Cabinet 'immediately', 'this very day' and 'in person' to inform the Prussian War Minister, the Reich Navy Office and the General and Admiralty Staff of the contents of the Chancellor's telegram.[87] To his considerable relief, Bethmann could concur with the Chief of the Civil Cabinet von Valentini that the 'immediate purpose' of his telegram – that 'His Majesty should not discuss the military bills with the Federal Princes' – had been accomplished.[88] To his consternation, the Reich Chancellor was nonetheless forced to acknowledge that the new Prince Regent of Bavaria (the later King Ludwig III) was better informed on the deliberations of the 'war council' of 8 December, thanks to the reports of Lerchenfeld and Wenninger, than he himself, the 'responsible' leader of German policy! In the last few weeks, the

Prince Regent told him, 'the view was widespread that H.M. was pressing for war'. Prince Ludwig 'moreover expressed the fear that H.M. was planning an invasion of England'. He had learned 'from an entirely reliable military source' – Wenninger – 'that H.M. had ordered a military plan for the invasion of England to be worked out'. Bethmann protested most vigorously that 'any aggressive intentions towards England were completely alien not only to our policy but also to the Kaiser personally', without however being able to make much impression either on the Prince Regent or on the Bavarian War Ministry.[89]

It was now that Bethmann complained bitterly to Karl von Eisendecher, whom he would have preferred to send to London as ambassador instead of Lichnowsky,[90] that the Kaiser had in a state of dreadful excitement and behind the back of Kiderlen and himself 'held a war council with his faithful followers in the army and navy', had 'ordered the preparation of an Army *and a Navy* Bill and trumpeted this and the Haldane conversation, fantastically embellished, to God and the world'. Bethmann here hinted that he would agree to a major new Army Bill, but only on condition that the fleet plans were deferred. The Navy Bill of the previous year had already served to strengthen England's ties with France, he explained. 'If H.M. in combination with Tirpitz wishes to make that bond wholly unbreakable, he will succeed in doing so without difficulty with the help of a new Fleet Bill.' England had acted with complete loyalty in the Balkan crisis, and had in particular exercised a moderating influence on Russia. England, the German Chancellor wrote, did 'not desire a continental war for the clear reason that it would itself become involved in such a war but did not wish to fight'.[91]

After receiving this letter together with Kiderlen's of 19 December[92] enclosing a copy of Lichnowsky's report of 3 December, the far-sighted old Eisendecher also began to exert a calming influence on the Kaiser, and in particular to speak out against a new Navy Bill. Haldane's statement, he said, had been 'honest and well-intentioned'. England needed peace and would try to avoid any situation in which she would be obliged to fulfil her military commitments to her Entente partners. He, Eisendecher, could therefore not share the Kaiser's view that Germany should now undertake special measures against England. On the contrary, 'sooner or later the two great Germanic nations of Europe would have to stand shoulder to shoulder in the face of the world situation if Slavdom, the Yankees and ultimately the yellow race were not to gain the upper hand. The time would certainly come for the whole of western Europe to unite with Germany and England at the head.' If one nonetheless thought, as obviously the Kaiser did, that 'the great conflagration and military conflict with the Britons was unavoidable', and that 'the present moment was a propitious time for it', then a new Navy

Bill was 'probably the most suitable method for bringing that conflict about'. Nobody would hold it against Germany if she filled in the gaps in the original fleet plan 'and especially if it should undertake all necessary replenishments in the army', but he could only regard new large demands for the fleet as justified 'if we wanted war'.[93]

These arguments, reinforced perhaps by Lichnowsky's presence in Berlin,[94] helped to calm the Kaiser somewhat. Prince Heinrich wrote in his diary on 31 December 1912: 'W[ilhelm] spoke to me about relationship with England, about G[eorge] and takes a calm view of the situation'.[95] The Kaiser's New Year address to the Commanding Generals also turned out to be, as Müller noted, 'amply peaceable'.[96] On the question of the Navy Bill, on the other hand, the monarch was not yet willing to give way. On 4 January 1913 he ordered Tirpitz to submit to him at his next audience on 11 January 'proposals on an increase in the construction tempo of large ships' as the time had come to implement the three-ship construction cycle. The Reichstag, in the Kaiser's view, was unlikely to make trouble on this issue. Tirpitz should however, before his audience, come to an agreement with the Reich Chancellor and the War Minister on armaments requirements in general.[97] Müller was also ordered to inform Bethmann 'that H.M. at last expects to receive next Saturday proposals on a possible Navy Bill (stabilisation of the three-ship construction cycle)'.[98]

But the Reich Chancellor had now finally decided to oppose the planned Navy Bill in earnest. At midday on 5 January he called Müller and told him that he would introduce in the Reichstag supplementary requests for 300–400 million marks for the army, but that a Navy Bill in addition to this was 'out of the question'. When Bethmann asked for Müller's support in dealing with the Kaiser, Müller told the Chancellor that he appreciated the latter's point of view but that, as a naval officer, he strongly desired an increase in naval armaments.[99] Later that same day, Bethmann had his long-awaited audience with the Kaiser. He informed the monarch of his intention to introduce a large Army Bill, news which the latter received 'with very joyous surprise'. The Chancellor then explained that on the other hand 'in view of the more trusting relationship which was now developing with England, a Navy Bill could not be introduced. The stabilisation of the three-ship construction cycle, though justified in itself, would have to be postponed for 1 year.' On the following morning the Kaiser called together his three Chiefs of Cabinet, Valentini, Lyncker and Müller, and told them that he had 'made this concession' to Bethmann. Müller was given the task of writing to Tirpitz immediately.[100] Shortly afterwards the State Secretary of the Reich Navy Office visited Müller and spoke 'very arrogantly and disparagingly about the Kaiser's "about-face".'[101]

If the great Army Bill of 1913 was thus the most important immediate outcome of the 'war council' of 8 December 1912, there were at the same time a string of smaller military-political measures introduced whose symptomatic importance should not be ignored. Wilhelm II's repeated assertion that Haldane's declaration had made it easier for Germany to undertake certain 'preparatory measures', and that from now on England would count as an enemy in relation to these preparations, also corresponds to the actual course of German policy. From the beginning of December 1912 a 'Standing Committee on Mobilisation Matters' met in the Reich Office of the Interior. The Bavarian Military Plenipotentiary learned on 24 December 1912 that representatives of the Prussian War Ministry, of the General Staff and of the Reich Navy Office were taking part in the Committee's deliberations, and that an important theme being discussed was how to deal with the labour movement in the event of war. At the heart of the Committee's discussions, however, was 'the question of the feeding of the population in case of war'. The alarming prospect which had suddenly arisen of Germany's being excluded from seaborne trade had, according to Wenninger, led for the first time to consideration of the question 'how, in view of the fact that Germany is dependent for the most important of all its raw materials, grain, on the import of an annual surplus of 6½ million tons, the feeding of people and livestock can be assured in the event of a war between the Triple Alliance and the Triple Entente'.[102]

As the Minutes of the 'Economic Committee' meeting of 26 May 1914 show, this question was never adequately answered.[103] The situation was different with regard to the feeding of the army. At the beginning of December 1912, the army's provisions offices were instructed to expedite the purchase of hay and oats until all storerooms were full. The army administration even rented extra warehouses and stores for the fodder. 'The process', Wenninger reported, was undertaken 'inconspicuously and gradually' so as to avoid price increases; when these nevertheless occurred at the end of December, Wenninger feared that the Prussian army administration would be attacked in the Reichstag for poor judgment of the movement of prices. At the same time 'an experiment' was undertaken to establish whether large-scale shipments of oats and rye could be secretly made through an agent in Antwerp. Following this experiment, Wenninger was able to report that Berlin was now satisfied 'that even in case of mobilisation and war it would be possible to obtain deliveries up the Rhine from the same source by using cover addresses'. Smaller orders were placed with German firms in Danzig, Königsberg and Flensburg. Here too the intention was 'to develop the possibility of keeping open overseas sources for the feeding of the army in case supplies were cut off by England'.[104]

Even the supply of tinned food to the troops was secretly tested and overhauled. Under the pretext that a 'new method of preparation' was to be introduced, the use of tinned food in troop rations was temporarily suspended; the point of this measure was to accumulate the highest possible quantity of tinned food. At the beginning of December 1912 the state-owned canning factories in Mainz and Spandau were temporarily enlarged by the employment of about one hundred extra workers. This measure too led to embarrassment by the end of December: 'The maximum quantity of stock which can be accumulated from regular means will be reached by the end of January instead of, as is usual, the end of March', and consequently it would be necessary to lay men off in winter unless Austria bought up the tinned food at cost price. The real purpose of this exercise was of course, as Wenninger realised, 'to test the production capacity' of the state-owned canning factories in case of mobilisation.[105]

The precision with which war preparations were also being handled by the civilian authorities can be seen from the Foreign Office file entitled 'German Army Matters, Measures in the Event of War'.[106] Following a suggestion from Kiderlen on 24 December 1912, Tirpitz entered into negotiations with the Reich Treasury Office on the 'safeguarding of cash requirements' for the Far East cruiser squadron 'in the event of mobilisation'. It soon emerged that the existing system, whereby the German consuls in Tientsin and Manila were supposed to acquire the large sums necessary through a chequing arrangement with the German-Asiatic or the Hongkong Bank, was unsatisfactory for a number of reasons. The German-Asiatic Bank was unwilling to pay interest on sums deposited for such purposes, with the result, as the Reich Treasury Office observed, that this was 'a system which ... involves a serious loss to the Reich'; and the Hongkong and Shanghai Banking Corporation was a 'purely British' enterprise which would almost certainly refuse to honour the cheques of the German Consulate in the event of a mobilisation against England. The first problem was solved by depositing with the German administration in Tsingtau 'the money needed in China for the first four weeks after the outbreak of war'. (This was decided after it became clear that it would be too costly to construct a fire- and burglar-proof safe in the basement of the Consulate-General in Shanghai.) And on 1 December 1913 Consul Zitelmann was able to report, not without satisfaction, that he had used the unfriendly attitude of the new director of the Hongkong Bank in Manila as a 'welcome opportunity' to transfer all German state funds 'inconspicuously from the Hongkong Bank to the Bank of the Philippine Islands', which was in the hands of Spaniards and Americans and therefore 'free of all British influence'. This step was expressly approved by the Foreign Office on 28 February 1914 after consultation with Helfferich.

Such manipulations on the money markets did not go unremarked by the astute British financial experts. Above all the deliberate accumulation of gold in Berlin since the end of 1912 gave rise to much racking of brains in the City of London, especially as it was all too obvious that this could be done only by accepting considerable losses. In his survey of the world's money markets in January 1914, the Director of the London City and Midland Bank, Sir Edward Holden, expressed his astonishment at German finance policy. 'The German character, I think, calls for great admiration', he said. 'Whenever the Germans make up their minds to do a thing, they do it, no matter what the cost may be.' Holden had in mind the declaration of the President of the Reichsbank, Havenstein, at the beginning of 1913, in which he announced his intention 'to increase the general stock of Gold in the Bank at least 20 millions sterling'. Despite widespread scepticism whether, under prevailing conditions, this target could be reached, Holden demonstrated at the beginning of 1914 that the Reichsbank had indeed raised its gold reserves by £20 million since the end of 1912, i.e. by 50 per cent.[107] He also showed very clearly, however, that this accumulation had not proceeded 'in accordance with economic law'. The Reichsbank had not only employed a variety of methods to prevent the export of gold from Germany; it had also bought gold abroad at a loss.

Here we have another example of German determination. The President of the Reichsbank made up his mind to increase the Bank's stock of Gold, and he has done it even though it has been at a loss ... Taking into account the Gold imported from this and other countries, amounting to about 12 millions sterling, together with 8 millions taken by the Bank from circulation by the issue of additional Notes, we arrive at the total increase of 20 millions in the stock of Gold as desired by the President and this is exclusive of what has been transferred to the War Chest, which would appear to be about £3,800,000.

Sir Edward Holden provided no direct explanation of this (for him) incomprehensible monetary policy. But it was perhaps not pure coincidence that he concluded his remarks on Germany with the prediction that the Reichsbank would suspend cash payments 'should Germany again become involved in war'.

Within the German army, too, steps were taken in December 1912 which might point to the conclusion that the unleashing of a great war had been decided on, not immediately but in the foreseeable future. As early as 12 December the Reich Chancellor and the War Minister jointly decided to allow Christmas leave for officers and men to go ahead and for the usual duration.[108] At the same time the army command arrived at the decision that while the current war academy courses 'should not be terminated prematurely, for the new ones a shorter length was to be laid down from the beginning'.[109] This shortening of the war academy courses from nine to seven months was admittedly, as the Prussian War Minister stated, 'not intended as a preparation for war', but it did amount, in Wenninger's words, to 'a kind of Krümper system' with the aim 'of filling up more quickly the many posts which are at present vacant'.[110] In the Military Cabinet on 14 December, Wenninger asked what was behind the rumour that the army was 'holding back retirements because of the danger of war'. This was 'most emphatically denied', he reported, and 'on the contrary it was stated that the opportunity offered by the current war mood would be used on a large scale to persuade the "weak links" – i.e. those higher officers who would not be capable of matching up to their positions of leadership in war, – to retire *beforehand*.'[111]

Some of these measures, and most especially the gigantic Army Bill of 1913, bore the character of a time bomb, as Dieter Groh has shown.[112] The massive army increases of 1913, which 'overstretched the entire framework of the army', admittedly made it impossible to unleash war while the reorganisation was taking place, but they made the implementation of the Schlieffen Plan within a certain timescale almost a necessity. (It is highly significant that the 'Great Eastern Campaign Plan' for a war against Russia alone was abandoned by the General Staff in April 1913[113].) For on the one hand it could be foreseen that both Russia and France would follow Germany by introducing their own army increases and that then, after transitional difficulties had been overcome, the Entente Powers would achieve a military superiority which would again negate the Schlieffen Plan's chances of succeeding. On the other hand yet another strengthening of the German army was impossible because, as Groh argues and as is shown by the most recent research, 'the Wilhelmine Reich was not in a position, for reasons of domestic politics, to arm any further'.[114] It is true that Groh and some other historians still speak of a 'defensive readiness for preventive war' on Germany's part which, they claim, was transformed into a concrete readiness to go to war only after the assassination at Sarajevo – even if as a 'systematic and logical consequence' of the decisions of December 1912.[115] Against this we must ask whether, in the light of the thought patterns and decision-making processes which we have reconstructed here for the last three months of 1912, it is not more credible to assume that the men who ruled in Berlin – not just the Chief of General Staff von Moltke and his generals, for whom this can hardly be disputed, but also Kaiser Wilhelm II and Reich Chancellor von Bethmann Hollweg – acted in full awareness of the very serious longer-term consequences which the decisions they took in December 1912 were bound to have.

At the very time when Kaiser Wilhelm II was holding his now so controversial 'war council' with his 'faithful followers in the army and navy', the Reich Chancellor had a meeting with Field Marshal Colmar von der Goltz on the latter's return from Turkey. Their conversation ran as follows:

BETHMANN: We can get any military demand we make approved [by the Reichstag].

GOLTZ: Well in that case let us make our demands.

BETHMANN: Yes, but if we make such large demands, we must have the firm intention of striking soon.

GOLTZ: Yes of course, then we would be pursuing a proper policy!

BETHMANN: But even Bismarck avoided a preventive war in the year [18]75.

GOLTZ: That's right! He could do that after fighting 3 preventive wars for the benefit of the Fatherland![116]

8   Kaiser Wilhelm II and German anti-semitism

In 1894, when Kaiser Wilhelm II had been on the throne for only six years and Bismarck in angry retirement for four, when Adolf Hitler was not yet old enough to go to school, an obscene broadsheet costing 30 Pfennigs appeared on the streets of Berlin which, seen from the vantage point of the present day, poses the question of continuity in modern German history about as starkly as it is possible to pose it. Entitled 'In the 20th Century', an ornate cartoon (fig. 2) pictures the German capital in the year 1950. It projects two scenarios: *either* the Germans have defeated the Jewish menace, *or* the Jews have taken over Berlin.

In the latter case, Rothschild rules over Germany, the anti-semites – Böckel, Foerster, Dühring, Schönerer, Stoecker, etc. – are in prison and Ahlwardt is being beheaded. The German people is enslaved in a socialist 'German Workers' Colony' run for the benefit of Jewish profiteers. Opposite the colony, beyond the statue commemorating the Liberal parliamentarian Heinrich Rickert, we see the flourishing stock exchange, the Jewish National Theatre and the Jewish National Museum, whereas the Christian Church is being closed down. Germans are being expelled from their own country, their 'fresh' young children sold along with geese for Jewish kitchens. Everywhere, Jewish 'world supremacy temples' in the form of kiosks are being erected to mark their domination over the 'German slave-nation'.

An altogether different world reveals itself as we raise our eyes to the higher section of the picture. In 1950, Kaiser Wilhelm the Third and his empress have just come to the throne. German artisans and peasants march happily through the streets shouting 'Heil!' and 'Gott mit uns!'; German athletes compete in German Games; the people stream into the *Deutsches Volks-Haus* to celebrate the glories of Beethoven, Mozart, Goethe and Schiller; German children listen once more to German fairy tales. The Church is back at the centre of society; a statue depicts St George slaying the Jewish dragon. The canonical laws discriminating against Jews have been reinstated, the synagogue has been closed and the Rabbi has committed suicide. The last Jew is being expelled from the country – 'Juden raus!', proclaims the policeman's banner. Many are in the *Zuchthaus*, all are forced, before being led away with ropes around their necks, to return their 'stolen goods' to the Church for redistribution to the German poor. And in the high street, to the sound of trumpets and clarinets, to the smell of incense, with the burghers of Berlin looking gleefully on, Jews are being publicly hanged.

In the accompanying text the author prophesies that Germany would, come what may, 'conduct the struggle against Juda in deadly earnest', although in typical Germanic fashion, he declares, 'a cruel streak of humour will not be entirely absent'. But it would be in the Jewish interest for the 'solution [*Lösung*]' to be found soon, and to be directed from above by a royal hand, since otherwise the German people might be seized by an 'ecstasy' under which the Jews would suffer an even more painful fate. The pamphlet appeals to Kaiser Wilhelm II to undertake 'this most arduous struggle of the soul'. But it warns: 'If the Jewish Question is not solved by Wilhelm II, then it will be solved under Wilhelm III.'

As a ghostly prefiguration of the holocaust to come, this *Dreigroschen-pamphlet* of 1894 is breathtaking and, along with the other cartoons in the *Politischer Bilderbogen* series, deserves close study by historians of German anti-semitism.[1] But the pamphlet, with its linking of extreme anti-semitism to the Hohenzollern monarchy, and specifically to Kaiser Wilhelm II, raises the question of continuity in German history in a more general way. What had led the pornographic pamphleteer to imagine that Kaiser Wilhelm II might 'solve' the 'Jewish Question', and what had occasioned the defiance and disappointment apparent just beneath the surface in this cartoon? What *was* Wilhelm's relationship with the anti-semitism that was so pervasive in Germany before, during and after his long reign? Could it even be that the last German Kaiser, in this respect as in some others, was a sort of precursor of Adolf Hitler, the missing link, so to speak, between the 'Blood and Iron Chancellor' and the Führer? If Wilhelm II proved to be an anti-semite, it would have the effect of bringing extreme anti-semitism out of the gutter into the imperial palace from which he dominated German politics for thirty years; the specifically German roots of Hitlerian anti-semitism would come more clearly into focus and the idea of continuity in German history would be substantially strengthened.

The notion of the Kaiser as an anti-semite is novel, historically highly controversial, politically inopportune and emotionally disturbing.[2] In the 1960s, when Fritz Fischer succeeded in demonstrating the high degree of continuity that existed between Germany's aims in the First World War and those pursued by Hitler in the Second, some historians were at pains to break the continuity chain again by insisting that Hitler's anti-semitism was unique, and his Third Reich consequently 'qualitatively' different from anything that had gone before: in this perverse way, the holocaust was

Figure 2 Max Bewer's 1894 cartoon 'In the 20th Century', showing h

...ightmare vision of Berlin in 1950. Source: *Politischer Bilderbogen* no. 14.

actually used as an alibi for the German nation. More recently, one or two historians have argued that the Nazi holocaust is inexplicable, having no historical antecedents and being comparable only to the Pol Pot régime in Cambodia. One German historian, Ernst Nolte, virtually caused riots on the streets by claiming that Nazi holocaust anti-semitism had no roots in German history, but was merely a response to the 'earlier and more fundamental [*ursprünglicher*]' Asiatic barbarism of Stalin![3] Even in more mainstream circles of the historical profession, there would appear to be little understanding of the extent and nature of Kaiser Wilhelm's anti-semitism. Influential historians have argued that, since the Kaiser numbered Jews like Ballin and Rathenau among his friends, he could not have been anti-semitic. They seem unimpressed by (or perhaps simply unaware of) the fact that, on several occasions, Wilhelm stated that he did not regard Ballin as a Jew, and that he reviled Rathenau as a 'mean, deceiving, rascally traitor' whose murder in 1922 'served him right'.[4] When confronted with new evidence of the Kaiser's anti-semitic expectorations in his exile years, they profess themselves shocked but claim that these statements were the result only of personal bitterness: before the abdication, they say, no such anti-semitic expressions are to be found, with the possible exception of one or two remarks made by Wilhelm before his accession to the throne, when he was very young and under the influence of Waldersee.[5]

Until very recently, then, the overwhelming consensus on this not unimportant issue was that Kaiser Wilhelm II was not an anti-semite. Unlike Ahlwardt and the other German anti-semites of that day, Wilhelm does not even merit an entry in the *Encyclopaedia Judaica*. Only three or four historians or literary scholars, Hartmut Zelinsky, Lamar Cecil, Willibald Gutsche and myself, have uncovered and published evidence to the contrary. This new evidence, however, is overpowering in both quantity and quality. It clearly shows that anti-semitism was a central element in the *Weltanschauung* of the last German Kaiser, and would therefore seem to necessitate a major revision in our assessment of his 'place' in German history.

Before I review the evidence, it might help to establish an interpretative framework by drawing some distinctions between the various kinds or degrees of anti-semitism to be found in Germany, either in practice or in the form of demands, in the seventy-five years between unification in 1871 and the *Götterdämmerung* of 1945. There is, first, the *anti-semitism of the salon*, consisting of personal prejudice and collective but still informal discrimination against Jews. This was the type of anti-semitism with which the Jewish minority – 1 per cent of the population of the Reich – was faced in the imperial period. Second, there is the exclusion *by law* of Jews from certain public positions and the withdrawal from them, again *by law*, of their civil rights. Legal discrimination of this kind was not institutionalised until 1935, though demands for such legislation are much older, as we shall see. Third, there is *pogrom anti-semitism* of the type prevalent in both Tsarist and Soviet Russia; there was no such mob brutality against Jews in Germany between Bismarckian unification and Hitler's rise to power. Fourth, we have the *anti-semitism of expulsion*, the call for the 'solution' of the 'Jewish problem' by expelling all Jews from the land; this, as we know, became terrible reality in the years after 1933, but demands for such policies can be heard in Germany more than fifty years earlier. Finally, there is the ultimate horror, the *anti-semitism of extermination*, the anti-semitism of the holocaust. In examining the anti-semitism of Kaiser Wilhelm II, we shall need to be mindful of these five different types of anti-semitism. The baneful truth, however, is that at one time or another in the course of his long life he subscribed to all five.

There *was* a period in Wilhelm's life when he was not an anti-semite. At the Gymnasium in Kassel, when he was in his mid-teens, his closest friend was 'a young jew called Sommer', as Wilhelm himself proudly wrote in English to his mother. Wilhelm insisted that Siegfried Sommer hang up his cap next to his own, and that they share each other's *Butterbrod*. On one occasion the Prince put his arm round his friend's waist 'as one might around a pretty girl's'; on another he even asked Sommer whether he might accompany him to the temple. Sommer was top of the class and, with a little help from Wilhelm, rose to become a judge. He happens also to have been the grandfather of that master historian of Tudor England, Sir Geoffrey Elton.

Though Wilhelm became an enthusiastic member of the aristocratic student fraternity Corps Borussia at the University of Bonn in 1877, no anti-semitic statements are on record from that period.[6] What is on record from his student days is Wilhelm's wish that he could drain all the 'damned' English blood from his veins![7] The bitter conflict with his parents, to which this curious wish alludes, is the most fundamental fact in the mental and psychological development of the future Kaiser. It lies at the heart of the virulent anti-semitism which he internalised in the 1880s, at the height of the first wave of anti-semitism to sweep German society since unification.

Only three years after the Reichsgründung and the emancipation of the half million Jews that lived in the new Reich, the Great Crash of 1873 and the beginnings of the 'Great Depression' shook the faith of millions in the values of capitalism, free enterprise and progressive Left Liberalism with which the Jewish minority, by virtue of its unique occupational structure, was closely identified. As the cartoon demonstrates (see fig. 2), in the new Germany of burgeoning cities, rapid industrialisation, mass circulation newspapers and mass politics, those in traditional occupations, high and

Figure 3 The Hohenzollern monarchy as the bastion against Jewish influence. Bewer's cartoon of 1891. Source: *Politischer Bilderbogen* no. 28.

low, felt threatened by this modern world and longed for the security of the old monarchic 'Christian state'. The Hohenzollern military monarchy was looked up to as a bastion against the rising tide of modernity, symbolised by the Jews (see fig. 3). Distinctly Manichaean Christian images and thought structures survived even where Christianity was formally rejected. Pamphleteers and agitators had little difficulty in demonising the Jews, in claiming that 'the Devil himself is a Jew'.[8] By 1890, the new-fangled word 'Aryan' was in common usage in anti-semitic circles as a synonym for earlier code-words for 'non-Jew' such as 'Christian' or 'Christian-German'. In one cartoon of 1901, the Jewish Satan is seen slaying the foolishly tolerant Aryan, destroying Christianity and Monarchy and taking over the European continent (see fig. 4).[9]

If the Jews were synonymous with modernity and specifically with the Left Liberal Progressive Party at home, commercialised, industrialised, parliamentary England (and by extension republican France and America) played the same role abroad. In the minds of German anti-semites there was an almost complete identification of the Jewish and the English menace to

Figure 4 The Jewish Satan slays the Aryan and takes over the world. Bewer's cartoon 'Der Weltboxer' of 1901. Source: *Politischer Bilderbogen* no. 33.

traditional Christian-German (or Aryan) values. The 'nation of shop-keepers', also represented as Satan, was the 'vampire of the Continent', keeping the European nations at each others' throat in order to profit from the dissension.[10] We shall see that, towards the end of his life, Wilhelm II conflated these twin dangers to 'Germandom' by coining the term 'Juda-England'.

One of the more depressing truths about this first wave of German anti-semitism is the extent to which it was led not by guttersnipes such as Ahlwardt, Glagau, Böckel, Foerster, Henrici and their ilk, but by university professors such as Treitschke and court clergymen such as Stoecker. Another is the degree to which, even at this early stage, the anti-semitism of these learned agitators was unequivocally racial. Adolf Stoecker, who founded his 'Christian-Social Workers' Party' in 1879, proclaimed in the Prussian House of Deputies that the Jews were 'leeches' and 'parasites', 'an alien drop in our blood'. The struggle against them was a struggle of 'race against race', for the Jews were not part of the German nation but 'a nation unto themselves', linked to all other Jews in the world to form 'one mass of exploiters'. The 'war' against the Jews was a fight for the very existence of the German nation, cried Stoecker in 1882. 'We offer the Jews a fight until complete victory and we will not rest until they have been thrown down from the high pedestal on which they have placed themselves here in Berlin into the dust where they belong.' Berlin must be a Hohenzollern city, not a Jewish city, he declared.[11] As the Left Liberal parliamentarian Eugen Richter explained in November 1880, there was something 'particularly perfidious' in this anti-Jewish movement, since what it nourished was 'racial hatred, that is to say something that the individual cannot alter and which can therefore only end either in his being clubbed to death or his expulsion over the border'.[12]

The significance of Stoecker's movement for the political and cultural development of Germany can, as Werner Jochmann has pointed out, hardly be overestimated.[13] In 1881, a quarter of a million people signed a petition demanding the prohibition of Jewish immigration into Germany, the exclusion of Jews from public office, their removal from all teaching posts in public schools and the reduction of their numbers at universities.[14] As Norbert Kampe's excellent study has shown, the many thousands of university students who signed this mass petition were destined to move into positions of great influence in the state bureaucracy, army, diplomatic corps and the medical, legal and teaching professions at all levels.[15] Most alarming of all was the support the movement received from the Prussian officer corps and the imperial court.

Just about the only ray of light on this dark stage was the extraordinarily courageous stand taken by Wilhelm's parents, the German Crown Prince – who was an enthusiastic freemason – and his English wife, Queen Victoria's eldest daughter. Wilhelm's mother regarded 'Treitschke and his supporters as lunatics of the most dangerous sort'.[16] She suggested that Stoecker, Kögel, Puttkamer, Kleist-Retzow and the other anti-semites might like to found a lunatic asylum in Berlin with themselves as inmates.[17] She was ashamed that men like Treitschke and Stoecker 'behave *so hatefully* towards people of a different faith and another race who have become an integral part (and by no means the worst) of our nation!'[18] In early 1880, Wilhelm's father attended in the full uniform of a Prussian Field Marshal the service at the Berlin synagogue in a deliberate demonstration against Treitschke's 'disgraceful' attacks on the Jews. A few days later he publicly condemned the anti-semitic movement as a 'shameful blot on our time', thereby reassuring many Jewish families who had been preparing to leave Berlin in terror. 'We are ashamed of the *Judenhetze* which has broken all bounds of decency in Berlin but which seems to flourish under the protection of the Court clerics', he wrote. On the eve of the first debate on the 'Jewish question' in the Prussian parliament, the Crown Prince and Crown Princess caused an uproar by attending a concert in the synagogue at Wiesbaden 'to demonstrate as clearly as we can what our convictions are'.[19] And in 1881 the Crown Prince made another speech in Berlin in support of the 'poor ill-treated Jews', as Queen Victoria recorded with warm approval.[20] One is forcefully reminded of the heroic stand taken by the Danish monarchy against German anti-Jewish policies during the Second World War. But in reactionary and 'chauvinistic' circles in Germany in the 1880s these public demonstrations only fuelled the growing conviction that the Crown Prince and his liberal English wife were an alien, un-German force that must not be allowed to accede to the throne.

From 1879, when Wilhelm re-joined his Potsdam Guards Regiment, his parents looked on with trepidation as their eldest son became more and more 'ver-Potsdammt'; they feared that, given his 'lack of depth and spirit, the superficial, banal, petty opinions of the First Regiment of Guards will be pure poison for his mind'. 'I am afraid that he is turning into the archetypal Potsdam Lieutenant with that evil admixture of a very loud mouth and the chauvinist's hatred and ignorance of all things foreign', his mother wrote in 1879.[21] By the middle of 1880, she was complaining to her mother: 'Willy is *chauvinistic* and *ultra* Prussian to a degree & with a violence wh[ich] is often very painful to me.'[22]

In 1883, Crown Prince Rudolf of Austria noted with disgust that Wilhelm was a 'dyed-in-the-wool Junker and reactionary' who spoke of parliament invariably as 'this pig-sty [*Saubude*]' and of the members of the opposition as 'those *Hundekerle* who deserve to be whipped'. Rudolf was appalled by Wilhelm's intention of having the Liberal parliamentarian Eugen Richter beaten up by six NCOs.[23] In his letters from this period, Wilhelm referred to the progressive Freisinnige Partei as 'die Blödsinnigen'; its leader Forckenbeck he called Ferckelbock.[24] He declared that, as Kaiser, he would eliminate Jewish influence in the German press.[25] In 1887, Wilhelm told two Austrian call-girls that in Austria 'the entire state was rotten' and about to collapse, its German provinces falling 'like ripe fruit' to Prussia, which alone was healthy and strong. Wilhelm likened Crown Prince Rudolf to his own father as being a spineless, characterless popularity-seeker totally under Jewish influence.[26] As Colonel of the Hussars, Wilhelm mounted a crusade against the high society Union Club with the express aim, he said, of creating an 'old-Prussian, genuinely Christian-German officer corps'. His real objection to the Club, as his friend and mentor Waldersee noted in his diary, was that it numbered among its members 'people, including Jews, with whom an officer could not associate'.[27]

In 1885, Adolf Stoecker was found guilty in a libel case brought by a Jewish newspaper editor. The publicity surrounding the case had been highly damaging to the Court, and Kaiser Wilhelm I, though himself an anti-semite, decided that Stoecker must forfeit his position as Court Chaplain. Stoecker pleaded in vain that his enemies were 'at the same time the enemies of Christendom and Monarchy': if he fell, 'atheists and democrats' would triumph and the 'Christian-monarchic revival' of Berlin would be jeopardised. The emperor persisted in demanding Stoecker's resignation – until, that is, the preacher was 'saved by Prince Wilhelm'.[28]

On 5 August 1885, Wilhelm wrote a letter to the old Kaiser, praising Stoecker as the Hohenzollern monarchy's most powerful pillar and bravest warrior against the 'ghastly and infamous slanders' of the 'damned' Jewish press and the Jewish law courts. 'You will have read and heard', the Prince wrote,

of the wholly irresponsible and reprehensible way in which the entire *Judenthum* of the Reich, with the support of its damned press, has fallen upon poor Stöcker and covered him with insults, slanders and defamation and finally forced him into a monstrous legal case ... Now, after the judgment of the court, which is unfortunately far too much under Jewish control, a veritable storm of indignation and anger has broken out in all levels of the nation ... One cannot believe that, in our time, such a heap of vileness, lies and wickedness can be brought together in one place. From all sides, from far and near, I am receiving letters with the question 'Does the Kaiser know what is going on? Does he realise what the score is? How the Jews – and behind them the Socialists and the Progressives – are trying everything to get Stöcker sacked?' One even says the Jews have tried to secure friends in Court circles in order to work on you against Stöcker! ... Stöcker is ... the most powerful pillar, the bravest, most fearless fighter for Your Monarchy and Your Throne among the people! ... He has personally and alone won over *60,000 workers* for you and your power from the Jewish Progressives and Social Democrats! in Berlin! ... O dear Grosspapa, it is disgusting to observe how in our Christian-German, good Prussian land the *Judenthum*, twisting and corrupting everything, has the cheek to attack such men and in the most shameless, insolent way to seek their downfall.[29]

It is not difficult to discern in this letter the influence of Wilhelm's *Ersatzvater* Count Waldersee. To read the original, unexpurgated diaries of this warmongering, pietistic general is to cross the border into the realm of abnormal psychology. Waldersee seems to have suffered from some form of paranoid megalomania. He believed in a world conspiracy of the 'entirety' of international Jewry in league with all democratic forces at home and the majority of foreign Powers abroad to destroy the heroic-aristocratic warrior monarchy of Prussia. 'We have far too many enemies' he declared in 1885, 'the French, the Slavs, *above all the Catholics*, and then the entire little rabble of the dispossessed, with their supporters.'[30] 'Everywhere the masses are on the move, everywhere there is rebellion against authority, the negation of all religion and the generation of hatred and envy against those with wealth. We are probably facing major catastrophes.'[31] 'The ghost of socialism is beginning to show a very earnest face', he warned in 1886.[32] Equally dangerous was the Catholic Centre Party, which in Waldersee's words consisted of 'hypocritical blackguards without a

Fatherland, intent on the collapse of Germany and the destruction of Prussia'.[33]

Surrounding the Reich were countries in which parliamentarism had either already established itself, such as England, France and Italy, or countries whose internal affairs were so rotten that they would not be able to withstand the pressure from below much longer, such as Russia, Austria-Hungary and Turkey. Only the Reich in the middle had the strength and the will to save the old order. The German Reich stood firm still, Waldersee declared in 1886, providing the 'mainstay for the whole of Europe; [but] if we become weak, the entire old world will fall apart'. He was convinced that Germany must fight some great apocalyptic battle against the modern world, a war against the future. The struggle at home and the struggle abroad were one and the same, two battlefronts in the same war. For if Liberal parliamentarism were to establish itself in the Reich, what would be the point of foreign conquest? The enemy would have won!

The gravest threat therefore came from the *laissez-faire*, parliamentary ideals of the Progressive Party, with which both the Crown Prince and the Jewish community were identified. Permitting such ideals to establish themselves in Germany would be tantamount to capitulating to the enemy without a fight; it would be the end of the Christian-German monarchy, the end of the privileged position of the aristocracy and the end of the exclusion of the Prussian Army from State control. Waldersee would stop at nothing to prevent such a capitulation. He urged that universal manhood suffrage be abolished, that Germany should take out France, Russia or even Austria-Hungary in a lightning first strike. He plotted to separate the English Crown Princess from her weak husband and to have her expelled in disgrace from the country; he even plotted an Army coup to replace Kaiser Friedrich III with his son Wilhelm on the German throne.

But the most dangerous foes of all, in Waldersee's mind, were the Jews. In his correspondence with the young heir to the throne, he identified as the Prince's enemies

all the Progressive people with their supporters, the entire *Judenschaft* [and] most foreign countries, that is to say, taken together formidable foes ... In view of the colossal influence which the Jews [*die Judenschaft*] wield by virtue of their wealth, through which they have secured the services of Christians in influential positions, even though they themselves are few in number, they are by far the most dangerous of our enemies.[34]

Only days after receiving these lines in November 1887, Wilhelm created an international outcry by addressing a meeting in support of Stoecker's 'Christian-Social' Inner Mission at Waldersee's house. Anti-semites were jubilant; almost everyone else was aghast. Herbert Bismarck shook his head in disbelief when Wilhelm, with shining eyes, described Stoecker as a 'second Luther'. Herbert was 'stormed' by influential Court officials urging him to beg his father to 'keep Prince Wilhelm away from the Stoeckerite path'.[35] Wilhelm and Waldersee of course attributed the whole fuss to the Jews and the people in their pocket. As Waldersee noted, 'the entire row in the press comes from the Jews', whose 'attacks are aimed less at Stoecker than at the Prince'.[36] 'Too many people are under the influence of the Jews', he noted as the protests mounted. The Jews were afraid of Prince Wilhelm, Waldersee wrote, as indeed were 'all our enemies – the French, the Russians, the Progressives and the Social Democrats'.[37]

In 1888, when his father lay dying of throat cancer, Wilhelm came close to believing that there was an Anglo-Jewish plot, led by his mother, to take over Germany. In letters to his intimate friend Philipp Eulenburg he described the doctors in attendance on his father as '*Judenlümmel*', 'dogs', 'scoundrels' and '*Satansknochen*' filled with 'racial hatred' and 'anti-Germanism to the very edge of the grave'.[38] He would never be able to forget, he wrote, that 'the family shield had been besmirched and the Reich brought to the edge of destruction by an English princess who is my mother'.[39] In time he came to believe not only that Jewish and English doctors had killed his father, but also that an English doctor had been responsible for crippling his left arm.

When Wilhelm acceded to the throne in 1888, anti-semites from Paris to Vienna crowed: 'All those who are truly Christian-German are devoted with their entire soul to Kaiser Wilhelm II and cheer him along the paths that he has chosen to go.' Wilhelm was 'the hope, the future, the shining star of the German people', cried the Austrian anti-semite von Schönerer. The Germans had only one hope of salvation from the Jewish yoke, he declared, and that hope was Kaiser Wilhelm II.[40] The cartoon of 1894 (fig. 2) was part of this jubilation, though it also sounded a note of disappointment and defiance. For Wilhelm, having dismissed Bismarck – the Iron Chancellor's use of Bleichroeder, his banker, as intermediary to the Catholic Centre Party had been the last straw – appointed the relatively Liberal General von Caprivi to the Chancellorship. It was in opposition to Caprivi's progressive policies that the Conservative party in 1892 adopted anti-semitism as an integral part of its official programme. Wilhelm's anti-semitic convictions had not, however, disappeared, they had only gone underground, to surface again as his reign careered erratically towards the abyss.

By the mid-1890s, Kaiser Wilhelm II had adopted a thoroughgoing racism as a central element of his *Weltanschauung* and lost no chance of proclaiming the need for a pure and exclusive Germanic race. In 1895 he declared the North Sea to be a 'purely Germanic sea' whose partition between 'Britons' and 'Slavs' he would not tolerate.[41] The excruciating ballad 'Der Sang an Ägir' which he composed in 1895 was steeped in Nordic

Figure 5 Kaiser Wilhelm II's 1895 drawing 'Nations of Europe,
Protect your holiest Goods!', warning against the 'yellow peril'.

mythology. He regularly spoke of the French as 'Gauls' and 'Latins', of the
English as 'Anglo-Saxons' and of the Russians as 'Slavs'. He warned
repeatedly of the 'Pan-Slav Peril'.[42] As the realisation dawned on him that
in the coming racial 'Endkampf' of the Teutons against the Slavs and Gauls,
Britain would side against Germany, the Kaiser was overwhelmed with
incredulity and indignation: How could the 'Germanic English', he asked in
bewilderment, side with the Russians and French against their racial *Stam-
mesgenossen*?![43]

From now to the end of his life, he became obsessed with what he called
the 'yellow peril' (fig. 5). His painting *Völker Europas, wahrt eure heiligsten
Güter!*, sketched in 1895, shows the nations of Europe as pre-historic
warrior-goddesses being led by the Archangel Michael against the 'yellow
peril' (represented by a buddha) in the east.[44] In 1900, he ordered German
troops on their way to China to behave like Huns, showing no mercy and
taking no prisoners.[45] With the outbreak of the Russo-Japanese War
Wilhelm predicted that the Japanese would soon be parading through the
streets of Moscow and Poznan.[46] In 1907 he announced that in the coming
conflict between Japan and America, England would have to side with the
latter since this was 'a question of Race, not of Politics, only *Yellow* versus
White'. The British newspapers, he noted with satisfaction, had 'for the first

time used the term of "Yellow Peril" *from my picture*, which is coming true'. Wilhelm informed the Tsar that a German agent had 'counted 10,000 Japanese men in the plantations in South Mexico, all in Military Jackets with brass buttons'. This secret Japanese army, he claimed, was intending to seize the Panama Canal. The Japanese, he said, were 'going in for the whole of Asia, carefully preparing their blows and against the *white Race in general*! Remember my picture, it's coming true!'[47] Graciously he offered to send the Prussian Army to protect the Californian coast in the event of a war between the United States and Japan.[48]

Inevitably with such a world-view, Wilhelm's visceral anti-semitism of the 1880s resurfaced, albeit somewhat uncertainly, at the turn of the century. From time to time he sought the company of intelligent, successful Jewish bankers and businessmen such as Ballin, Rathenau, Warburg, Simon and Carl Fürstenberg whose intellectual horizons were more extensive than those he encountered at court.[49] In 1898, referring presumably to the Dreyfus case, he even spoke in horror of 'the hydra of the crudest, most ghastly anti-semitism' which everywhere was raising 'its horrible head'.[50] But the ambivalence of his attitude in the period is best captured in the curious episode of his meeting with Theodor Herzl. In an extraordinary letter to the Grand Duke of Baden, Wilhelm wrote in 1898 that he had always been interested in the 'basic idea' of a Jewish state in Palestine. Now he was 'convinced that the settlement of the Holy Land by the wealthy and hard-working nation of Israel would soon bring to the former unsuspected prosperity' – a blessing which could spread to produce a significant economic revival in Asia Minor. That in turn would restore the financial fortunes of Turkey, and so the sick man of Europe would be sick no more.

In addition, the energy, creativity and efficiency of the tribe of Sem would be diverted to worthier goals than the sucking dry [*Aussaugen*] of the Christians, and many an oppositional Semite now supporting the Social Democrats would go off to the East, where there is more rewarding work to be done ... Now I realise [the Kaiser explained] that nine-tenths of all Germans would recoil in horror if they were to discover that I sympathised with the Zionists or would even, as I intend to do if asked, place them under my protection.

But he, Wilhelm, had his defence ready: 'Our dear God knows even better than we do that the Jews killed Our Saviour, and he has punished them accordingly. But neither the anti-semites nor others, myself included, have been asked or empowered by Him to bully these people after our own fashion *in majorem Dei Gloriam*!' One must remember the Christian exhortation to love one's enemies, the Kaiser exclaimed. And besides, 'from an earthly, realistic political standpoint it should not be forgotten that, considering the immense and extremely dangerous power which international Jewish capital represents, it would after all be of huge advantage to

Germany if the world of the Hebrews looked up to it in gratitude?!'[51] The Sultan's unexpected objection put a quick end to Wilhelm's plan for a German Protectorate of a Jewish state in Palestine; the Kaiser (literally) took the road to Damascus and there proclaimed himself Protector of 300 million Mohammedans instead.

On his return from Palestine, in a speech to his beloved Brandenburgers, he described how, standing on the Mount of Olives, he had looked upon the spot 'where the most powerful struggle that has ever been fought on earth, the struggle for the redemption of mankind, was fought out by the One', and how this had inspired him, Wilhelm, to swear anew an oath of allegiance to God to leave nothing undone 'to unite My Volk' and to eliminate (*beseitigen*) those elements making for discord and dissent. His God-given task was to ensure that the German oak tree, *die deutsche Reichseiche*, continued to flourish. 'The journey to the Promised Land and the Holy Places will help me to protect this tree' and 'to search out and destroy [*auszurotten*] the beasts that seek to gnaw at its roots.'[52] This was, as we shall see, an image which was to recur.

In 1901, through Eulenburg's good offices, Kaiser Wilhelm met that 'Evangelist of Race' Houston Stewart Chamberlain, who was destined to have a more lasting influence on him than Theodor Herzl.[53] In Chamberlain, Wilhelm found the philosopher who had put into words his own innermost thoughts. 'God sent your book to the German people, just as he sent you personally to me, that is my unshakeably firm conviction', he averred. The Kaiser recognised in Chamberlain his 'comrade-in-arms and ally in the struggle for Teutons against Rome, Jerusalem etc.', for the '*Urarisch-Germanische* that lay deeply buried and dormant within me' and was now fighting its way to the surface.[54] To Chamberlain Wilhelm wrote in 1902: 'May you save our German Volk, our *Germanentum*, for God has sent you as our helper!'[55] In his letters to Wilhelm, Chamberlain demanded the creation of a 'racially aware, ... centrally organised Germany with a clear sense of purpose', a Germany which would 'rule the world'.[56]

From around the turn of the century, under Chamberlain's influence, and unnerved by the rising tide of democracy and socialism at home and Germany's increasingly exposed position internationally, Wilhelm II gave voice ever more openly to anti-semitic convictions. Susan Townley records a conversation in which the Kaiser described the Jews as the 'curse' of his country. 'They keep my people poor and in their clutches', he complained. 'In every small village in Germany sits a dirty Jew, like a spider drawing the people into the web of usury. He lends money to the small farmers on the security of their land and so gradually acquires control of everything. The Jews are the parasites of my empire. The Jewish question is one of the great problems I have to deal with, and yet nothing can be done to cope with it!'[57]

On his visit to England in 1907 he 'declaimed vehemently against the Jews', telling Sir Edward Grey: 'There are far too many of them in my country. They want stamping out.' At the same time he boasted, wavering uncertainly between pogrom anti-semitism and extermination anti-semitism, that there would be a 'Jew-baiting' in Germany if he, the Kaiser, did not keep his people in check.[58] Even at a personal level, Wilhelm made no secret of his strong anti-Jewish prejudice, saying in disgust to his American dentist that if he walked through the Tiergarten he would 'have to greet all the fat Jewesses in the park!'[59] (It is when I read passages like this that I think to myself: if the All-Highest had been any more high-minded, he would have struck the top of his head on the underside of a *Stammtisch*!)

To Nicholas Butler, the President of Columbia University, Wilhelm explained that the revolutionary threat in Europe came from international Jewry. 'If you take a Russian Jew and bring him to Berlin to learn theoretical anarchy and then send him to Paris to learn practical vice, he becomes a dough out of which no nation can bake a digestible bread. There were 19,000 such persons who went from Germany to Paris last year', the Kaiser believed.[60] The 'leaders of the Revolt' in Russia in 1905 were Jews, naturally. They worked hand in glove with 'their kinsmen in France who have the whole Press under their nefarious influence', Wilhelm declared in a letter to the Tsar.[61]

Wilhelm's anti-semitism reached new heights of intensity in 1908, in the wake of the two greatest domestic crises of his reign – the trial of his best friend Philipp Eulenburg for homosexuality, and the *Daily Telegraph* crisis. His intimate circle of friends had been suddenly broken up by 'Jewish cheek, slander and lies', he complained to Chamberlain.[62] Maximilian Harden, Eulenburg's tormentor, was in the Kaiser's words a 'loathsome, dirty Jewish fiend';[63] a 'poisonous toad out of the slime of hell, a disgraceful stain on our Volk'.[64] The journalists attacking him in the press were a *Schweinepack, Saubengels*, he railed during the *Daily Telegraph* crisis, which was entirely the work of the 'lying press of European pan-Jewry' and the 'Jewish press carnival'.[65] Early in 1909 he warned darkly of the fate in store for the Jews when the Germans finally 'awoke' from their long sleep. To his friend Max Egon Fürst zu Fürstenberg he wrote: 'The Golden International has our Fatherland in its grip and plays ball with our holiest possessions through the press which it controls! One is gradually turning into a convinced anti-semite. If the German *Volk* ever wakes from the torpor of the hypnosis induced by the Jewish press and becomes seeing, we could be in for a nice surprise!'[66]

However, there was still a major gap between Wilhelm's opinions and what he felt could be done in terms of practical policy. Not long before the outbreak of war, as Hartmut Pogge has shown, he found himself having to ward off demands for radical restrictions on German Jews made by ex-Generals and other radicals in the Pan-German League and strongly supported by his own son. The young Crown Prince sent his father a copy of the anti-semitic brochure *Wenn ich der Kaiser wär'*, by the Pan German leader Heinrich Class, which called for the exclusion of Jews from the civil service, the Army and teaching positions, and a removal of their right to vote. Wilhelm's reply to the Crown Prince was actually drafted by the head of the Civil Cabinet, Rudolf von Valentini, a close political ally of Chancellor von Bethmann Hollweg. Valentini pointed out that, if the Jews left or were expelled from Germany, the German economy would be set back some hundred years. Not only that, but Germany would, with such a step, leave the ranks of the civilised nations of the world. He did concede, however, that Jewish influence on German culture had become too predominant and that measures were needed to thrust it back.[67]

Not surprisingly, Wilhelm's brutality in general and anti-semitism in particular, like that of Chamberlain and many others, grew more intense still with the outbreak of war. In September 1914, after the German victory at Tannenberg, the Kaiser proposed that the 90,000 Russian prisoners of war be driven onto a barren spit of land in the Baltic and kept there till they died of thirst and hunger: it was left to one of his generals to point out that that would be 'genocide'.[68] In conversations with the American ambassador, he made it clear that 'mere democracies like France and the United States' could never take part in a peace conference, since 'war was a royal sport, to be indulged in by hereditary monarchs and concluded at their will'. He said that 'he knew Germany was right, because God was on their side'. Woodrow Wilson's special envoy Colonel House, when he heard of these conversations, asked whether the Kaiser was 'crazy'.[69] Chamberlain for his part extolled the German Kaiser as an 'Aryan soldier-king' and as a Siegfried who had taken up the 'struggle against the corroding poison of Jewry'.[70] He proclaimed that the war was a 'life-or-death struggle ... between two human ideals: the German and the un-German'. Germany must therefore, 'for the next hundred years and more', pursue the strengthening of all things German and the 'determined extermination of the un-German [*die entschlossene Ausrottung des Undeutschen*]'. The 'pure, Germanic force' had to be protected from the 'disgusting worm', '*dem eklen Wurm*'.[71] The central concern of the 'struggle' was 'salvation from the claws of the un-German and anti-German', he declared in 1915, and went on, quoting almost directly from the most offensive passages in Wagner's *Das Judentum in der Musik* (1850): 'Against this devil's brood [*Teufelsgezücht*] stands Germany as God's champion: Siegfried against the worm'.[72]

By 1917, Chamberlain unambiguously identified the Jews (and with them now the United States of America) as Germany's chief enemy. In his letters to Kaiser Wilhelm, he argued that England and Germany had been destined by 'the bonds of blood' to be friends and allies; if they had pursued the 'high mission of Germandom' together, they could effortlessly have dominated the world. But it was not to be, for

England is completely in the hands of the Jews and the Americans. That is why no-one will understand this war unless he is quite clear that, at its most fundamental level, this is the war of the *Judentum* and the *Amerikanertum*, which is closely related to it, for the domination of the world – a war against Christendom, against spirituality [*Geistesbildung*], against moral strength, against pure art, against every Ideal life-philosophy, and in favour of a world consisting only of finance, factory and commerce – in short, an unbridled plutocracy.

'The Jew and the Yankee are the driving forces' behind the war, he declared. This was a war of 'modern mechanical "Civilisation" against the archaic, holy, eternally reborn "Kultur" of the chosen races of mankind.'[73] Wilhelm shared these sentiments without reserve. In January 1917 he wrote to Chamberlain: 'The war is a struggle between 2 *Weltanschauungen*: the Teutonic-German for morality, right, loyalty and faith, genuine humanity, truth and real freedom, against the Anglo-Saxon [*Weltanschauung*], the worship of mammon, the power of money, pleasure, landhunger, lies, betrayal, deceit and [. . .] treacherous assassination! These two *Weltanschauungen* cannot be "reconciled" or "tolerate" one another, one must be *victorious*, the other *go under*!' Lloyd George and Briand were, Wilhelm believed, 'under the spell of Satan [*dem Satan verfallen*]', but they had unwittingly succeeded in turning the war into a German 'crusade' – 'a crusade against *evil* – Satan – in the world, prosecuted by us as *tools* of the Lord, [. . .] We *warriors of God* [*Gottesstreiter*] will fight until the band of robbers in the service of mammon [*Mammonsdienende Räuberpack*] and the *foes of the Kingdom of God* lie in the dust!, whose coming into the world would be rendered completely impossible by the Anglo-Saxon *Weltanschauung*, but which will be assisted by our victory! God wants this struggle, we are his tools, He will direct it, we need not worry about the outcome, we will suffer, fight and be victorious under His Sign! Then we shall have *the* peace, the *German* peace, *God's* peace, in which the entire liberated world will breathe a sigh of relief!'[74] Just a few months later, on 24 August 1917, the Kaiser, kindling a fire for the devil, invited that anti-semitic 'horror' Max Bewer, whose obnoxious cartoons we examined in the first part of this essay, to take lunch with him along with 'our Wotan', Hindenburg, and the 'Siegfried of our time', Ludendorff.[75]

After his flight to Holland on 9 November 1918 (and perhaps stung by assertions that he was Jewish himself![76]), the Kaiser thirsted for revenge. He demanded that the Army recall him as 'dictator' or 'Führer'; on another occasion he demanded that Ludendorff take over military power and Helfferich civilian control pending his own return. When Hitler's and Ludendorff's beer-hall putsch failed on the fifth anniversary of his, Wilhelm's, fall from power, he declared that their failure showed that he alone was capable of restoring order at home.[77] He warned that on his restoration 'blood must flow, much blood, [the blood] of the officers and civil servants, especially of the aristocracy, of all those who have deserted me'.[78] He had heated discussions with his entourage about whether the enemy at home or the enemy abroad should be dealt with first, declaring (as he had in 1905) that he intended to draw the sword 'first against the Sozis and then against the French'.[79]

In the isolation of exile, Wilhelm evolved the most bizarre and harebrained conspiracy theories according to which the Jesuits, the Freemasons and the Jews were plotting together to take over the world.[80] After visiting the Kaiser in Doorn in 1921, an ex-Minister of Education captured the atmosphere well when he noted that Wilhelm had a 'profound abhorrence for the Jews', and in particular for the Jewish press. 'He was convinced that the World War had been started by the Jewish masonic lodges in France, England and Italy and handed me literature of the most questionable kind on this topic.' Wilhelm also handed his visitor a silver brooch in the shape of a swastika with the words: 'Now you have been admitted into the order of the decent people', adding that his wife had also worn such a brooch.[81]

In the mid-1920s, Wilhelm called for the formation of a 'Christian International' to launch the 'Kampf' against the 'Verjudung' of Germany; after the 'purification' of the Fatherland, the struggle would have to be continued against 'das Judentum' in the whole world.[82] He demanded that the Bible be re-written to eliminate most of the Old Testament, so leaving only genuinely Christian elements, which he claimed were Zoroastrian and therefore 'Aryan' in origin and 'not Semitic-Jewish' at all. 'Let us free ourselves from the *Judentum* with its Jawe!', he cried in one of his last letters to Chamberlain.[83] And just as the Jews were not 'our religious forebears', so of course Jesus was 'not a Jew', but a Galilean, a man, he liked to believe, 'of exceptional beauty, tall and slim, with a noble face inspiring respect and love; his hair blond shading into chestnut brown, his arms and hands noble and exquisitely formed'.[84]

Wilhelm's earlier racism now went completely haywire. In an article he wrote in 1928 for the American *Century Magazine* on 'the Sex of Nations', he declared the French to be a feminine race with an inbred love of parliamentary government, whereas the Germans were racially masculine, biologically in need of leadership because they were at home only in primitive, 'purely vertical masculine, monarchical' structures which were the 'opposite of parliamentarism'.[85] In 1923, after hearing a lecture by the anthropologist Frobenius, the Kaiser had an almost religious revelation. Suddenly he realised, he said, that the French and the English were not whites at all but blacks. The future mission of the German people was now clear to him: 'We shall be the leaders of the Orient against the Occident! I shall have to change my picture "Völker Europas". For we belong on the other side!' The Germans were not part of the West, but the 'face of the East against the West'; the main thing was that England, France and America should 'go under'.[86] The 'negroid nation of the French' were traitors to their own Continent, the Kaiser declared in his letters to his American friend George Sylvester Viereck.[87] He was appalled to learn, he wrote, that the English had 'allready begun to follow the French example and allow the Niggerboys to march shoulder to shoulder with the Lords son and the squiresboy in the Boy-Scout companies', for to him this was the 'beginning of treason to their Race formerly only executed by the French Negroids!'[88]

There was no doubt in Wilhelm's mind that the Jews, too, were of African negroid origin, only disguised for the moment, as he wrote in an essay of 1925 entitled 'The Jew Today', as Bolsheviks. Bolshevism, he declared, was but 'the outstretched arm' of international Jewry, out to destroy every government in the world.[89] The 'Moscow Jews' controlled the yellow and black races and therefore presented a grave danger to the white races of Europe and America, he warned.[90] Far from being terrified by Stalin's consolidation of power in the Soviet Union, Wilhelm was overjoyed, for he interpreted this as a famous victory over the 'Jewish-Bolshevik' leaders who had seized power in 1917. Now that Stalin was in control, he said in October 1926, the 'national Soviet Republic of the Russian worker' could be established.[91]

In the bitterness of exile Kaiser Wilhelm II made the final dreadful leap to the anti-semitism of extermination. 'The Hebrew race', he wrote in English to an American friend,

are my most inveterate enemies at home and abroad; they remain what they are and always were: the forgers of lies and the masterminds governing unrest, revolution, upheaval by spreading infamy with the help of their poisoned, caustic, satyrical [sic] spirit. If the world once wakes up it should mete out to them the punishment in store for them, which they deserve.[92]

On 2 December 1919, he wrote *manu proprio* to General August von Mackensen, referring to his own abdication:

The deepest, most disgusting shame ever perpetrated by a people in history, the Germans have done onto themselves. Egged on and misled by the tribe of Juda whom they hated, who were guests among them! That was their thanks! Let no German ever forget this, nor rest until these parasites have been destroyed and exterminated [*vertilgt und ausgerottet*] from German soil! This poisonous mushroom on the German oak-tree![93]

He called for a 'regular international all-worlds pogrom à la Russe' as 'the best cure'.[94] 'Jews and Mosquitoes' were 'a nuisance that humanity must get rid of in some way or other', he proclaimed, and added, again in his own hand: 'I believe the best would be gas!'[95]

It seems difficult to come to any other conclusion than that from the age of twenty to the age of eighty, Kaiser Wilhelm II, who ruled over Germany for thirty crucial years between Bismarck and Hitler, was a staunch anti-semite, and that his anti-semitism formed a central element of his outlook on the world. The fact that, in November 1938, he privately expressed disgust at the 'gangsterism' of the *Kristallnacht* cannot outweigh the mass of evidence now available on his deeply held anti-Jewish attitudes, especially when it is remembered that even Himmler was outraged by the mindless violence of that dark night.[96] Wilhelm II was a racist, an ideological autocrat and reactionary, the sworn enemy of Liberalism, Democracy, Catholicism and Socialism and of all foreign Powers that seemed to lend support to these forces, so limiting his own power at home and the expansion of German power in the world. With his forced abdication in November 1918, the last German Kaiser embraced world conspiracy theories of the bizarrest kind and, in what seems like a logical extension of his earlier anti-semitism, called for the extermination of the Jews.

Wilhelm died in June 1941, just three weeks before Hitler's attack on the Soviet Union, which surely he would have welcomed as warmly as he had exulted over the Führer's victories in Poland, Scandinavia, Holland, Belgium and France. In 1940, the Kaiser looked on in wonder as Hitler put into effect the goals for which he, Wilhelm, had striven in his own reign. This war was, he cried,

a succession of miracles! The old Prussian spirit of Frd. Rex, of Clausewitz, Blücher, York, Gneisenau etc. has again manifested itself, as in 1870–71 . . . The brilliant leading Generals in this war came from *My* school, they fought under my command in the [First] Worlds War as lieutenants, captains or young majors. Educated by Schlieffen they put the plans he had worked out under me into practice along the same lines as we did in 1914.[97]

By this stage in his long life, the Jews and England were so conjoined in his mind that he frequently hyphenated 'Juda-England' into one word. In a recently discovered series of letters written in his last year at Doorn, he declared Germany to be the land of monarchy and therefore of Christ; England the land of Liberalism and therefore of Satan and Antichrist. Germany's real enemy was not the British people but the English ruling classes, who were 'Freemasons thoroughly infected [*durchseucht*] by Juda.' 'The British people must be *liberated* from the *Antichrist Juda*', he wrote in 1940. 'We must drive [*vertreiben*] Juda out of England just as he has been chased [*verjagd*] out of the Continent.' It was the Jews and Freemasons who had twice – in 1914 and again in 1939 – unleashed a war of *Vernichtung* against Germany with the aim of establishing an international Jewish empire held together by British and American gold. But then 'God intervened and *smashed* their plan!' 'Juda's plan has been smashed to pieces and they themselves swept [*weggefegt*] out of the European Continent!' Now the Continent was 'consolidating and closing itself off from British influences after the elimination [*Entledigung*] of the British and the Jews!' The result would be a 'U.S. of Europe!', he cried in triumph.[98] To his sister he wrote in jubilation: 'The hand of God is creating a new World & working miracles. . . . We are becoming the *U.S. of Europe* under German leadership, a united European Continent, nobody ever hoped to see.' And he added, with undisguised satisfaction: 'The Jews [are] beeing [*sic*] thrust out of their nefarious positions in all countries, whom they have driven to hostility for centuries.'[99]

Even at the last, in Europe's darkest hour, Kaiser Wilhelm II showed no hint of compassion, no sign of common human decency. Far from rising to the world-historical moral responsibilities of the 'Christian' monarch he so passionately claimed to be, he surveyed the death and destruction all around him and exulted. He gazed upon the greatest evil and declared it to be the work of God.

Notes

INTRODUCTION

1 J. Daniel Chamier, *Fabulous Monster* (London 1934). This effusive apologia for the Kaiser was in fact written by Barbara Chamier, a British officer's daughter born in India in 1885. It was translated into German two years later by Dora von Beseler, the daughter of a Prussian Minister of Justice under Kaiser Wilhelm II who had been a member of the Prussian House of Lords and a Knight of the High Order of the Black Eagle. See J. Daniel Chamier, *Ein Fabeltier unserer Zeit. Glanz und Tragödie Kaiser Wilhelms II.* (Zürich, Leipzig and Vienna 1936). The German translation was sent to the exiled Kaiser in Doorn for his approval prior to publication. Geheimes Staatsarchiv Berlin, Rep. 192 Nl. Beseler Nr. 20. The book was an immense success in Hitler's Germany, going through at least eight reprintings before the war and selling over 60,000 copies in the first two years. After Germany's defeat it was revised and printed under the new title *Als Deutschland mächtig schien. Die Ära Wilhelms II.* (Berlin 1954). Recently, to mark the centenary of Wilhelm's accession to the throne, the book was published again, once more with a new title and a very fulsome preface by Prince Louis Ferdinand of Prussia. See J. Daniel Chamier, *Wilhelm II. Der deutsche Kaiser* (Berlin 1989).

2 Martin Doerry, *Übergangsmenschen. Die Mentalität der Wilhelminer und die Krise des Kaiserreichs*, 2 vols. (Weinheim and Munich 1986).

3 Friedrich von Holstein to Philipp Graf zu Eulenburg, 27 November 1894, in John C.G. Röhl (ed.), *Philipp Eulenburgs Politische Korrespondenz*, 3 vols., (hereafter *Eulenburgs Korrespondenz*) (Boppard-am-Rhein 1976–83), II, no. 1052.

4 See chapter 4.

5 Otto von Bismarck, *Die gesammelten Werke*, 15 vols. (Berlin 1923–35), XII, pp. 324ff.

6 Bülow to Eulenburg, 23 July 1896, cited in John C. G. Röhl, *Germany without Bismarck. The Crisis of Government in the Second Reich 1890–1900* (London 1967), p. 194.

7 See below Chapter 1, p. 14 and especially chapter 8.

8 Volker R. Berghahn, *Der Tirpitz-Plan. Genesis und Verfall einer innerpolitischen Krisenstrategie unter Wilhelm II* (Düsseldorf 1971); Paul M. Kennedy, 'Tirpitz, England and the second Navy Law of 1900: a strategical critique', *Militärgeschichtliche Mitteilungen* 2 (1970); Paul M. Kennedy, 'Maritime Strategieprobleme der deutsch-englischen Flottenrivalität', in H. Schottelius and Wilhelm

213

Deist (eds.), *Marine und Marinepolitik im kaiserlichen Deutschland 1897–1914* (Düsseldorf 1972).

9 See below, chapter 7.

10 Holstein to Kiderlen, May 1897. Cited in Röhl, *Germany without Bismarck*, p. 222. See also ibid., pp. 234 and 240. See also Holstein to Eulenburg, 20 April 1897, *Eulenburgs Korrespondenz*, no. 1316.

1 KAISER WILHELM II: A SUITABLE CASE FOR TREATMENT?

1 Graf Hans von Pfeil (?) to Professor Jakob von Uexküll, 25 August 1914. Incomplete letter in the possession of Professor Thure von Uexküll, Freiburg im Breisgau.

2 This point is well made in Nicolaus Sombart, 'Der letzte Kaiser war so wie die Deutschen waren', in *Frankfurter Allgemeine Zeitung*, 27 January 1979.

3 Laurence Wilson, *The Incredible Kaiser. A Portrait of William II* (London 1963); J. Daniel Chamier, *Fabulous Monster* (London, 1934).

4 Karl Alexander von Müller, 'An Preussen!' in *Süddeutsche Monatshefte*, special number, September 1914, pp. 826ff.

5 The opinion of the British statesman Viscount Morley, cited in Jonathan Steinberg, 'Kaiser Wilhelm II and the British', in John C.G. Röhl and Nicolaus Sombart (eds.), *Kaiser Wilhelm II: New Interpretations* (Cambridge 1982), p. 127.

6 Friedrich Naumann, *Demokratie und Kaisertum* (Berlin 1900, 3rd edn 1904), pp. 167ff.

7 Maximilian Harden, *Die Zukunft*, no. 40 (1902), p. 340.

8 Friedrich Meinecke, speech of 14 June 1913, cited in Elisabeth Fehrenbach, *Wandlungen des deutschen Kaisergedankens 1871–1918* (Munich and Vienna 1969), p. 91.

9 See Walter Goetz, 'Kaiser Wilhelm II. und die deutsche Geschichtsschreibung', *Historische Zeitschrift* 179 (1955), pp. 21f.

10 Bernhard von Bülow to Philipp Eulenburg, 15 February 1898. A facsimile of the handwritten original is reproduced in Friedrich Thimme (ed.), *Front wider Bülow* (Munich 1931), p. 8. The whole letter is printed in John C. G. Röhl, *Philipp Eulenburgs Politische Korrespondenz*, 3 vols. (Boppard-am-Rhein 1976–83) (hereafter *Eulenburgs Korrespondenz*), no. 1362.

11 Bülow to Eulenburg, 6 November 1896, ibid., no. 1271.

12 Robert Graf von Zedlitz-Trützschler, *Zwölf Jahre am deutschen Kaiserhof* (2nd edn, Stuttgart, Berlin and Leipzig 1924), p. 201.

13 Eulenburg to Bülow, 21 July 1899 in *Eulenburgs Korrespondenz*, no. 1399.

14 Sigurd von Ilsemann, *Der Kaiser in Holland*, 2 vols. (Munich 1967–8), II, p. 160, diary entry for 11 February 1931.

15 Isabel V. Hull, *The Entourage of Kaiser Wilhelm II 1888–1918* (Cambridge 1982), pp. 21f.

16 Ludwig Quidde, *Caligula, Eine Studie über römischen Cäsarenwahnsinn* (Leipzig 1894); Docteur Cabanès, *Folie d'Empereur. Une Dynastie de dégénérés. Guillaume II jugé par la science* (Paris n.d.).

17 Walter Görlitz (ed.), *Der Kaiser ... Aufzeichnungen des Chefs des Marinekabinetts*

Admiral Georg Alexander von Müller über die Aera Wilhelms II. (Göttingen 1965), p. 109.

18 Zedlitz, *Zwölf Jahre*, p. 68.

19 Holstein to Eulenburg, 3 March 1897, in *Eulenburgs Korrespondenz*, no. 1300.

20 Prince Wilhelm to Bismarck, 14 January 1888, printed in Bismarck, *Erinnerung und Gedanke* in *Die Gesammelten Werke*, xv (Berlin 1932), p. 470. Kaiser Wilhelm's speech before the provincial Landtag of Brandenburg on 5 March 1890, printed in Johannes Penzler, *Die Reden Kaiser Wilhelms II. in den Jahren 1888–1895* (Leipzig n.d.), pp. 95ff.

21 Kaiser Wilhelm II, speech given in Düsseldorf on 4 May 1891. Penzler, *Reden Kaiser Wilhelms II*, pp. 176ff.

22 Bernhard Fürst von Bülow, *Denkwürdigkeiten*, 4 vols. (Berlin 1930–1), i, p. 316.

23 Kaiser Wilhelm II to Lady Mary Montagu, 8 January 1910. The Kaiser's letters to Mary Montagu were generously placed at my disposal by Dr Walter Schwarz of Zürich.

24 John C.G. Röhl, *Zwei deutsche Fürsten zur Kriegsschuldfrage. Lichnowsky und Eulenburg und der Ausbruch des I. Weltkriegs* (Düsseldorf 1971), p. 16.

25 Diary entry by Admiral von Müller of 25 June 1915, printed in Walter Görlitz (ed.), *Regierte der Kaiser? Kriegstagebücher, Aufzeichnungen und Briefe des Chefs des Marine-Kabinetts Admiral Georg Alexander von Müller 1914–1918* (Göttingen 1959), p. 111.

26 Eulenburg to Bülow, 26 July 1903, in *Eulenburgs Korrespondenz*, no. 1498.

27 Ilsemann, diary entry for 7 July 1927, only partially reproduced in Ilsemann, *Der Kaiser in Holland*, ii, p. 62.

28 Ilsemann, *Der Kaiser in Holland*, i, p. 287.

29 Kaiser Wilhelm II to a pastor, March 1930, copy in BA-MA Freiburg N 39/263; see also Kaiser Wilhelm II to H.S. Chamberlain, 3 June 1923 in Chamberlain, *Briefe 1882–1924* (Munich 1928), ii, p. 273. See also below, p. 209.

30 Eulenburg's note of 27 July 1900 printed in Johannes Haller, *Aus dem Leben des Fürsten Philipp zu Eulenburg-Hertefeld* (Berlin 1924), p. 257.

31 Kaiser Wilhelm II to Bülow, telegram, 19 June 1900, *Die grosse Politik der europäischen Kabinette* (Berlin 1922–7), xvi, no. 4527; see also Bülow, *Denkwürdigkeiten*, i, pp. 358–61.

32 Quoted from the original version which appeared correctly in the *Weser-Zeitung* and in the *Wilhelmshavener Tageblatt*. Important in this context is Bernd Sösemann, 'Die sog. Hunnenrede Wilhelms II. Textkritische und interpretatorische Bemerkungen zur Ansprache des Kaisers vom 27. Juli 1900 in Bremerhaven', *Historische Zeitschrift* 222 (1976), pp. 342–58.

33 Admiral von Müller, diary entries for 14 October and 4 September 1914, BA-MA Freiburg, omitted by Görlitz, *Regierte der Kaiser?*, pp. 65 and 52f. See also Hull, *Entourage*, p. 267.

34 Eulenburg to Bülow, 21 July 1899, in *Eulenburgs Korrespondenz*, no. 1399.

35 Zedlitz, *Zwölf Jahre*, p. 75.

36 Eulenburg to Bülow, 9 August 1903, in Röhl, *Eulenburgs Korrespondenz*, p. 2098; see also ibid., p. 2095. Wilhelm II had already expressed these opinions in 1889; see Chlodwig Fürst zu Hohenlohe-Schillingsfürst, *Denkwürdigkeiten*, 2 vols. (Stuttgart and Leipzig 1907), ii, p. 459.

37 Kaiser Wilhelm II to Generalfeldmarschall August von Mackensen, 2 December 1919, BA-MA Freiburg, Mackensen papers.

38 Ilsemann's diary entry for 22 August 1934, omitted from the printed version.

39 Eulenburg to Bülow, 6 October 1901, in *Eulenburgs Korrespondenz*, no. 1458.

40 Walter Bussmann (ed.), *Staatssekretär Graf Herbert von Bismarck. Aus seiner politischen Privatkorrespondenz* (Göttingen 1964), pp. 378 and 388.

41 *Eulenburgs Korrespondenz*, I, p. 225.

42 Ibid., I, no. 111 and no. 153. See also Prince Wilhelm to Herbert von Bismarck, 23 March 1887, cited in Brigitte Hamann, *Rudolf, Kronprinz und Rebell* (Vienna and Munich 1978), pp. 328f.

43 Crown Prince Wilhelm to Eulenburg, 12 April 1888, in *Eulenburgs Korrespondenz*, no. 169.

44 Ibid., p. 225.

45 Hohenlohe, *Denkwürdigkeiten*, II, p. 464. Michael Balfour, *The Kaiser and his Times* (London 1964, paperback edition 1975), p. 139.

46 Rudolf Vierhaus (ed.), *Das Tagebuch der Baronin Spitzemberg geb. Freiin von Varnbüler. Aufzeichnungen aus der Hofgesellschaft des Hohenzollernreiches* (Göttingen 1960), entries for 12 and 16 January 1910, p. 517.

47 Zedlitz, diary entry for 24 March 1904, *Zwölf Jahre*, pp. 68f.

48 Ibid., diary entry for 2 March 1905, p. 118.

49 See the photograph of the Kaiser sitting on the Duke's stomach in Röhl and Sombart, *Kaiser Wilhelm II*, p. 34.

50 Ernst Jäckh (ed.), *Kiderlen-Wächter, der Staatsmann und der Mensch*, 2 vols. (Berlin 1924), I, p. 124.

51 Eulenburg to Bülow, 26 July 1903, in *Eulenburgs Korrespondenz*, no. 1498. See also Bülow, *Denkwürdigkeiten*, I, p. 456.

52 Eulenburg to Bülow, 29 July 1903, in *Eulenburgs Korrespondenz*, II, p. 2095.

53 Admiral von Müller, diary entry for 6 July 1911, printed in John C.G. Röhl, *Deutschland ohne Bismarck* (Tübingen 1969), p. 32; see also Görlitz, *Der Kaiser*, p. 172.

54 Jäckh, *Kiderlen-Wächter*, I, pp. 133 and 143.

55 Fürst Philipp zu Eulenburg, *Mit dem Kaiser als Staatsmann und Freund auf Nordlandsreisen*, 2 vols. (Dresden 1931), I, p. 107.

56 Jäckh, *Kiderlen-Wächter*, I, p. 95.

57 Georg von Hülsen to Emil Graf Görtz, 17 October 1892, printed in *Eulenburgs Korrespondenz*, II, p. 953.

58 Zedlitz, *Zwölf Jahre*, pp. 216ff.

59 Walther Rathenau, *Der Kaiser. Eine Betrachtung* (Berlin 1919), pp. 27f.

60 See for example the memoirs of the War Minister, Karl von Einem, *Erinnerungen eines Soldaten, 1853–1933* (Leipzig 1933), p. 126. Also Hamann, *Rudolf*, pp. 362, 384, 400, 406.

61 Balfour, *The Kaiser and his Times* (paperback edition 1975), pp. 87f.

62 Hamann, *Rudolf*, pp. 335ff and pp. 400ff.

63 Peter Broucek, 'Kronprinz Rudolf und k. und k. Oberstleutnant im Generalstab Steininger', in *Mitteilungen des österreichischen Staatsarchivs* 26 (1973), pp. 446f.

64 Hamann, *Rudolf*, pp. 401f and pp. 428f.

65 This case is now fully documented in John C. G. Röhl, *Wilhelm II. Die Jugend des Kaisers 1859–1888* (Munich 1993), pp. 464–8.

66 'Prinz Wilhelms grosses Spiel mit Politik und Liebe', *Quick*, 45 (10 November 1956). See W.E. Elisabeth geschiedene Gräfin von Wedel-Bérard, *Meine Beziehungen zu S.M. Kaiser Wilhelm II.* (Zürich 1900); Wedel-Bérard, *Aus den Katakomben!!! Historische Liebes-Aventüren meiner Vorfahren* (Zürich 1901); Felix Lützkendorf, *Die schöne Gräfin Wedel. Roman einer Liebe in Preussen* (Munich 1964).

67 Eulenburg to Bülow, 20 July 1899, in *Eulenburgs Korrespondenz*, no. 1399.

68 Prince Wilhelm to Marie Gräfin Dönhoff, 20 February 1879, cited in Hull, *Entourage*, p. 20; see also the report on a court ball in the year 1882 in Alson J. Smith, *In Preussen keine Pompadour. Wilhelm II. und die Gräfin Waldersee* (Stuttgart 1965), pp. 76ff.

69 Kaiser Wilhelm II to Lady Mary Montagu, 25 November 1912. This letter was kindly made available to me by Dr Walter Schwarz of Zürich.

70 Kaiser Wilhelm II to Lady Mary Montagu, 10 October 1910, Zürich.

71 Steininger to Crown Prince Rudolf, 19 April 1887, as quoted in Oskar Freiherr von Mitis, *Das Leben des Kronprinzen Rudolf* (2nd edn, Vienna 1971), p. 324. See also Bismarck's comment to the same effect in his *Erinnerung und Gedanke* in *Gesammelte Werke*, XV, p. 545.

72 Prince Wilhelm to Marie Gräfin Dönhoff, 11 December 1878, cited in Hull, *Entourage*, p. 20.

73 Philipp Graf zu Eulenburg, 'Drei Freunde' (unpublished typescript in the possession of the Eulenburg family), I, part 3, pp. 165f; see Hull, *Entourage*, p. 20.

74 Görlitz, *Der Kaiser*, p. 35.

75 Bismarck, *Erinnerung und Gedanke* in *Gesammelte Werke*, XV, pp. 541f.

76 Eulenburg to Bülow, 10 July 1899, in *Eulenburgs Korrespondenz*, no. 1396.

77 See below, chapter 2.

78 Harden to Holstein, 15 November 1908, printed in Norman Rich and M. H. Fisher (eds.), *The Holstein Papers. The Memoirs, Diaries and Correspondence of Friedrich von Holstein 1837–1909*, 4 vols. (Cambridge 1955–63, German edition Göttingen, Berlin, Frankfurt 1956–63), IV, no. 1151; Harden to Holstein, 16 September 1908, cited in Hull, *Entourage*, p. 141; Harden to Rathenau, 8 May 1908, printed in Hans Dieter Hellige and Ernst Schulin (eds.), *Walther Rathenau-Gesamtausgabe*, VI, *Briefwechsel Walther Rathenau-Maximilian Harden* (Munich and Heidelberg 1981), no. 222. See also Eulenburg to Crown Prince Wilhelm, May 1888, in *Eulenburgs Korrespondenz*, no. 176.

79 Hull, *Entourage*, pp. 20f. See below, pp. 61ff.

80 See Rathenau, *Der Kaiser*, pp. 27f.

81 Expert testimony of Privatdozent Dr Heinrich Walb, Bonn, 12 August 1879, Zentrales Staatsarchiv Merseburg, Brand.-Preuss. Hausarchiv Rep. 53 K I no. 3.

82 Sir Schomberg McDonnell to King George V, 26 October 1914, recalling a conversation he had had with Sir John Erichsen in the spring of 1888, Royal Archives Geo. V. M.688A. See also Herbert Bismarck to his father, 11 December 1887, in Walter Bussmann, *Herbert von Bismarck*, p. 489.

83 Holstein to Karl von Lindenau, 29 July 1896, *The Holstein Papers*, III, no. 573.

84 M. Gosselin to Lord Salisbury, 29 November 1895, Hatfield House, Salisbury

Papers 3M/A 120/18. I am grateful to Professor Paul Kennedy for drawing this important source to my attention.

85 Lamar Cecil, 'History as Family Chronicle: Kaiser Wilhelm II and the Dynastic Roots of the Anglo-German Antagonism' in Röhl and Sombart, *Kaiser Wilhelm II*, pp. 101f. See note 82, above.

86 Cited in Richard Hough, *Louis and Victoria. The Family History of the Mountbattens* (London 1975, 2nd edn 1984), p. 243. Hough is mistaken in naming Churchill as the author of this letter, which was from Asquith to the King.

87 Lord Esher, diary entry for 27 September 1908, cited in Jonathan Steinberg, 'The Kaiser and the British', in Röhl and Sombart, *Kaiser Wilhelm II*, p. 121.

88 D. Sommers, *Haldane of Cloan. His Life and Times, 1856–1928* (London 1960), p. 203.

89 Agent's report from Paris of 22 March 1892, printed in *Eulenburgs Korrespondenz*, II, pp. 839f.

90 Holstein to Eulenburg, 1 April 1892, ibid., II, no. 638.

91 Cited in Hull, *Entourage*, p. 16.

92 Holstein to Eulenburg, 17 February 1895, in *Eulenburgs Korrespondenz*, no. 1089.

93 Karl Alexander von Müller (ed.), *Chlodwig Fürst zu Hohenlohe-Schillingsfürst, Denkwürdigkeiten der Reichskanzlerzeit* (Stuttgart and Berlin 1931), p. 151.

94 Holstein to Bülow, 24 March 1897 and 2 April 1897, BA Koblenz, Bülow Papers.

95 Bülow, *Denkwürdigkeiten*, I, pp. 179 and 140.

96 See the letters from Monts to Bülow, ibid., pp. 40ff.

97 Monts to Eulenburg, 20/21 March 1897, in *Eulenburgs Korrespondenz*, no. 1309.

98 Freiherr Ferdinand von Bodman, Report from Munich, 7 March 1897, printed in Walther Peter Fuchs (ed.), *Grossherzog Friedrich I. von Baden und die Reichspolitik 1871–1907*, 4 vols. (Stuttgart 1968–80), III, no. 1657.

99 Bülow to Eulenburg, 22 November 1900, in *Eulenburgs Korrespondenz*, no. 1439.

100 John C. G. Röhl, *Kaiser Wilhelm II. 'Eine Studie über Cäsarenwahnsinn'* (Munich 1989), p. 28.

101 See Bülow's notes on a conversation with Eulenburg on 7 April 1897 and Eulenburg to Bülow, 24 April 1897, *Eulenburgs Korrespondenz*, nos. 1312 and 1317.

102 Eulenburg to Bülow, 15 July 1900, ibid., no. 1419.

103 Eulenburg to Bülow, 21 July and 9 August 1903, ibid., nos. 1497 and 1499.

104 Zedlitz, *Zwölf Jahre*, pp. 173f.

105 Admiral von Müller, diary entry for 6 September 1918, cited in Hull, *Entourage*, p. 266. See also Görlitz, *Regierte der Kaiser?*, p. 410.

106 Eulenburg's 'Political Testament' of 16 June 1913, in *Eulenburgs Korrespondenz*, no. 1558.

107 Dr Paul Tesdorpf to Bethmann Hollweg, 24 April 1916, sent on 3 December 1916, printed in P. Tesdorpf, *Die Krankheit Wilhelms II.* (Munich 1919); Dr Julius Michelsohns expresses a similar view in the *Neue Hamburger Zeitung*, 30 November 1918 (evening edition); see also Hermann Lutz, *Wilhelm II. periodisch geisteskrank! Ein Charakterbild des wahren Kaisers* (Leipzig 1919); Adolf A. Friedländer, *Wilhelm II. Eine politisch-psychologische Studie* (Halle 1919); Franz

Kleinschrod, *Die Geisteskrankheit Wilhelms II.* (Wörrishofen 1919); H. Wilm, *Wilhelm II. als Krüppel und Psychopath. Abrechnung mit der Entente und dem Monarchismus* (Berlin 1920); Ernst Müller, *Kaiser Wilhelm II., eine historische und psychiatrische Studie* (Gotha 1927).

108 Professor Johannes Haller to Eulenburg, 18 February 1919, BA Koblenz, Haller Papers.

109 Professor Eduard Martin's report on the birth of Wilhelm, 9 February 1859, Geheimes Staatsarchiv Berlin-Dahlem; copy in Royal Archives, Windsor.

110 These matters are now dealt with in considerable detail in the first two chapters of Röhl, *Wilhelm II. Die Jugend des Kaisers.*

111 Sigmund Freud, *New Introductory Lectures on Psycho-analysis* (Penguin edn, Harmondsworth, Middlesex 1979), pp. 97f.

112 Albert Hopman, diary entry for 6 October 1918, printed in Winfried Baumgart (ed.), *Von Brest-Litowsk zur deutschen November-Revolution. Aus den Tagebüchern, Briefen und Aufzeichnungen von Alfons Paquet, Wilhelm Groener und Albert Hopman, März bis November 1918* (Göttingen 1971), p. 615.

2 PHILIPP EULENBURG, THE KAISER'S BEST FRIEND

1 See Hartmut Pogge von Strandmann (ed.), *Walther Rathenau, Tagebuch 1907–1922* (Düsseldorf 1967), p. 281.

2 John C. G. Röhl, *Germany without Bismarck, The Crisis of Government in the Second Reich 1890–1900* (London 1967) pp. 251ff. See also Elisabeth Fehrenbach, *Wandlungen des deutschen Kaisergedankens, 1871–1918* (Munich and Vienna 1969); Dirk Stegmann, *Die Erben Bismarcks. Parteien und Verbände in der Spätphase des Wilhelminischen Deutschlands: Sammlungspolitik 1897–1918* (Cologne and Berlin 1970). Of seminal importance for the earlier era, Hans-Ulrich Wehler, *Bismarck und der Imperialismus* (Cologne and Berlin 1969); Michael Stürmer, *Regierung und Reichstag im Bismarckstaat 1871–1880: Cäsarismus oder Parlamentarismus* (Düsseldorf 1974).

3 Of fundamental importance: Volker R. Berghahn, *Der Tirpitz-Plan. Genesis und Verfall einer innenpolitischen Krisenstrategie unter Wilhelm II.* (Düsseldorf 1971); Berghahn, *Germany and the Approach of War in 1914* (London 1973); Berghahn, *Rüstung und Machtpolitik. Zur Anatomie des 'kalten Krieges' vor 1914* (Düsseldorf 1973); Peter-Christian Witt, *Die Finanzpolitik des Deutschen Reiches von 1903 bis 1913. Eine Studie zur Innenpolitik des Wilhelminischen Deutschland* (Lübeck and Hamburg 1970).

4 See in particular the brilliant study of Max Weber's political thought by Wolfgang J. Mommsen, *Max Weber und die deutsche Politik, 1890–1918* (Tübingen 1959).

5 Karl Mannheim, 'The Problem of Generations' (1927), printed in Paul Kecskemeti (ed.), *Karl Mannheim, Essays on the Sociology of Knowledge* (London 1952), pp. 276–320.

6 Some sixty letters from Bismarck to the Prussian Minister of the Interior Count Friedrich Albrecht zu Eulenburg are in the possession of the Eulenburg family. See John C. G. Röhl, 'Kriegsgefahr und Gasteiner Konvention. Bismarck, Eulenburg und die Vertagung des preussisch-österreichischen Krieges im Sommer 1865' in Imanuel Geiss and Bernd-Jürgen Wendt (eds.), *Deutschland in*

der Weltpolitik des 19. und 20. Jahrhunderts. Festschrift für Fritz Fischer (Düsseldorf 1974), pp. 89–103.

7 Bismarck's celebrated 'Dictation of Bad Kissingen' of 1877 is printed in *Die grosse Politik der europäischen Kabinette* (Berlin 1922–7), II, no. 294, pp. 153f.

8 See Mommsen, *Weber und die deutsche Politik*, pp. 78ff.

9 Reinhold Conrad Muschler, *Philipp zu Eulenburg* (Leipzig 1930), p. 35.

10 Philipp Eulenburg, 'Psychologische Untersuchungen', (MS.), written in 1915. Staatsarchiv Potsdam, Eulenburg Papers, no. 642, copy in Haus Hertefeld, cited in Muschler, *Eulenburg*, p. 75.

11 Eulenburg's letters to his parents 'aus dem Orient' are located in Staatsarchiv Potsdam, Eulenburg Papers, nos. 689–90; see also Philipp Eulenburg, *Das Ende Königs Ludwigs II. und andere Erlebnisse* (Leipzig 1934), pp. 131ff.

12 Rudolf Vierhaus (ed.), *Das Tagebuch der Baronin Spitzemberg geb. Freiin von Varnbüler. Aufzeichnungen aus der Hofgesellschaft des Hohenzollernreiches* (Göttingen 1960).

13 Axel Varnbüler, 'Memoiren' (unpublished typescript), p. 95, Schloss Hemmingen. See John C. G. Röhl, *Philipp Eulenburgs Politische Korrespondenz*, 3 vols. (Boppard-am-Rhein 1976–83) (hereafter *Eulenburgs Korrespondenz*), no. 15.

14 An essay by Eulenburg with the title 'Konstantin von Dziembowski, d. 7. Mai 1885; eine Erinnerung' is located in Staatsarchiv Potsdam, Eulenburg Papers, no. 591; see also *Fünf Jahre der Freundschaft in Briefen von Fritz von Fahrenheid-Beynuhnen und Philipp Graf zu Eulenburg-Hertefeld*, published by Eulenburg himself, pp. 89 and pp. 93ff. See also Maximilian Harden, *Prozesse* (Berlin 1913), pp. 188f.

15 See below p. 57.

16 Alfred Bülow and Karl Dörnberg had been to the same school; see *Eulenburgs Korrespondenz*, no. 17, note 6.

17 See ibid., no. 23.

18 The correspondence between Herbert Bismarck and Philipp Eulenburg on this subject was published in March 1923, see *Deutsche Rundschau*, 49 (1923), no. 6; Eulenburg, *Aus 50 Jahren. Erinnerungen, Tagebücher und Briefe aus dem Nachlass des Fürsten Philipp zu Eulenburg-Hertefeld*, ed. Johannes Haller (Berlin 1923), pp. 81ff. See also Walter Bussmann (ed.), *Graf Herbert von Bismarck. Aus seiner politischen Privatkorrespondenz* (Göttingen 1964), pp. 17ff.

19 See *Eulenburgs Korrespondenz*, no. 54.

20 See ibid., no. 137.

21 See below, p. 54.

22 Eulenburg, who in the late 1880s was repeatedly mentioned as a possible General Intendant of the Royal Theatre in Berlin, made a number of attempts to persuade the Kaiser to become patron of the Bayreuth Festival, because he considered that this would 'strengthen national awareness' which 'the German needs more than other nationalities'. See *Eulenburgs Korrespondenz*, no. 147.

23 Ibid., no. 66.

24 Ibid., no. 164.

25 Ibid., no. 41, note 4.

26 Eulenburg, diary entry for 19 March 1890, cited in Röhl, *Germany without Bismarck*, p. 30.

27 *Eulenburgs Korrespondenz*, no. 197.

28 Philipp Eulenburg, 'Aus der Art. Eine märkische Geschichte', *Nord und Süd*, 28, no. 8 (February 1884), pp. 147–70; see also *Eulenburgs Korrespondenz*, no. 50.
29 Staatsarchiv Potsdam, Eulenburg Papers, no. 505, cited in Muschler, *Eulenburg*, p. 35.
30 Eulenburg, 'Leid', cited ibid., p. 36.
31 Bussmann, *Herbert von Bismarck*, pp. 524–6. See also Bismarck's critical remarks on Eulenburg, repeated by Maximilian Harden in Harden, *Prozesse*, pp. 169ff.
32 Eulenburg, 'Deutsche Politik', August 1892 in *Eulenburgs Korrespondenz*, II, pp. 931–6, quoted in Röhl, *Germany without Bismarck*, p. 81. See also Eulenburg's essay on Archduke Franz Ferdinand, 'Umsonst' in Eulenburg, *Erlebnisse an deutschen und fremden Höfen* (Leipzig 1934), pp. 268–311.
33 Eulenburg to Kaiser Wilhelm II, 25 October 1889, *Eulenburgs Korrespondenz*, no. 231.
34 Eulenburg, 'Deutsche Politik'; Philipp Eulenburg to Botho Eulenburg, 14 April 1892, *Eulenburgs Korrespondenz*, no. 643; see also Haller, *Eulenburg*, p. 69.
35 Eulenburg to Bernhard von Bülow, 8 June 1896, *Eulenburgs Korrespondenz*, no. 1233.
36 Philipp Eulenburg to Botho Eulenburg, 14 April 1892, in ibid., no. 643; see also John C. G. Röhl, 'The Disintegration of the Kartell and the Politics of Bismarck's Fall from Power, 1887–1890', *The Historical Journal* 9 (1966), p. 89.
37 Quoted in Muschler, *Eulenburg*, p. 129.
38 Very informative on the co-operation between Eulenburg and Kraus: Christoph Weber, *Quellen und Studien zur Kurie und zur vatikanischen Politik unter Leo XIII*. (Tübingen 1973), pp. 442ff, 461f, 465f, 525ff.
39 Of fundamental importance: Norman Rich, *Friedrich von Holstein. Politics and Diplomacy in the Era of Bismarck and Wilhelm II*, 2 vols. (Cambridge 1965), pp. 229ff *et passim*. Cf. John C. G. Röhl, 'Friedrich von Holstein', *The Historical Journal*, 9 (1966), pp. 379–88.
40 See *Eulenburgs Korrespondenz*, nos. 71–4 and also Philipp Fürst zu Eulenburg-Hertefeld, *Das Ende König Ludwigs II. und andere Erlebnisse* (Leipzig 1934), pp. 114ff.
41 Heinrich Otto Meisner (ed.), *Aus den Briefen des Generalfeldmarschalls Alfred Grafen von Waldersee*, 3 vols. (Stuttgart 1928), I, pp. 302f. See Röhl, *Germany without Bismarck*, p. 46. Also John C. G. Röhl, 'Staatsstreichplan oder Staatsstreichbereitschaft? Bismarcks Politik in der Entlassungskrise', *Historische Zeitschrift*, 203 (1966), 610–24; Martin Reuss, 'Bismarck's Dismissal and the Holstein Circle', *European Studies Review*, no. 5 (1975), 31–46.
42 *Eulenburgs Korrespondenz*, no. 345.
43 Ibid., no. 349.
44 Ibid., nos. 347 and 348.
45 Adolf Freiherr Marschall von Bieberstein, diary entry for 29 January 1890, cited Röhl, *Germany without Bismarck*, p. 59.
46 See *Eulenburgs Korrespondenz*, no. 359, note 2 and also no. 373, note 4.
47 Detailed account in ibid., no. 368, note 5.
48 See Röhl, *Germany without Bismarck*, pp. 69f.
49 Ibid., pp. 60f, 63, 77f; *Eulenburgs Korrespondenz*, nos. 486 and 493.
50 See Helmuth Rogge, *Friedrich von Holstein: Lebensbekenntnis in Briefen an eine Frau* (Berlin 1932), pp. 155ff.

51 Report of the Baden envoy in Berlin, Arthur von Brauer, of 26 February 1891, Generallandesarchiv Karlsruhe, 49/8.
52 Holstein to Eulenburg, 18 February 1892, *Eulenburgs Korrespondenz*, no. 590.
53 Eulenburg to the Kaiser, 21 January and 10 March 1892, ibid., II, p. 747, note and no. 604; see also Haller, *Eulenburg*, pp. 66f; Röhl, *Germany without Bismarck*, pp. 78–84.
54 Kiderlen-Wächter to Eulenburg, 11 January 1893, *Eulenburgs Korrespondenz*, no. 761.
55 Anton Graf Monts to Bernhard von Bülow, 20 October 1894, BA Koblenz, Bülow Papers 106. Quoted in Röhl, *Germany without Bismarck*, p. 108.
56 Marschall, diary entry for 8 February 1894.
57 Monts to Bülow, 12 October 1894, see note 55 above. See also Helmuth Rogge, 'Die Kladderadatschaffäre. Ein Beitrag zur inneren Geschichte des Wilhelminischen Reichs', *Historische Zeitschrift* 195 (1962), especially pp. 122ff.
58 See *Eulenburgs Korrespondenz*, nos. 374, 397, 398 and 402, note 3.
59 Eulenburg to Varnbüler, 19 April 1893, ibid., no. 796.
60 A detailed though not entirely objective account is given in Carl Graf von Wedel, *Zwischen Kaiser und Kanzler* (Leipzig 1943), pp. 203ff. See *Eulenburgs Korrespondenz*, nos. 450, 465 and 466.
61 Eulenburg to Varnbüler, 19 April 1893, ibid., no. 796.
62 Eulenburg to the Kaiser, 27 August 1893, ibid., no. 819.
63 Kuno Moltke to Varnbüler, 4 October 1893, ibid., no. 829.
64 Rudolf Vierhaus (ed.), *Das Tagebuch der Baronin Spitzemberg* (Göttingen 1960), pp. 314ff. See Spitzemberg's critical judgment of the 'Eulenburg clan', ibid., pp. 268f; also Wedel, *Zwischen Kaiser und Kanzler*, pp. 203ff.
65 Varnbüler, 'Memoiren', pp. 440ff. Lichnowsky only became responsible for personnel matters in the Foreign Office in 1899, but this was under Bülow as Foreign Secretary.
66 Holstein to Eulenburg, 7 December 1893, *Eulenburgs Korrespondenz*, no. 859. See also Chlodwig Fürst zu Hohenlohe Schillingsfürst, *Denkwürdigkeiten*, 2 vols. (Stuttgart and Berlin 1907), II, p. 507; F. von Holstein, *Die Geheimen Papiere Friedrich von Holsteins*, 4 vols. (Göttingen, Berlin, Frankfurt 1956–63), III, no. 391; Bülow, *Denkwürdigkeiten*, IV, pp. 650f.
67 Caprivi to Bülow, 8 and 18 March 1894, BA Koblenz, Bülow Papers, 69. See also Röhl, *Germany without Bismarck*, pp. 106f.
68 The story of Eulenburg's appointment as ambassador to Vienna is fully documented in the second volume of *Eulenburgs Korrespondenz*.
69 Bülow to Eulenburg, 13 October 1892, ibid., no. 713.
70 Eulenburg to Holstein, 11 January 1893, ibid., no. 760.
71 See Eulenburg, *Das Ende König Ludwigs*, pp. 212–45.
72 Princess Reuss to Eulenburg, 26 October 1893; Eulenburg to Holstein, 29 June 1893, *Eulenburgs Korrespondenz*, nos. 832 and 809.
73 *Grosse Politik*, IX, no. 2138, pp. 105–9.
74 See for instance Eulenburg's letters of 8 April and 12 May 1892, *Eulenburgs Korrespondenz*, nos. 642 and 652.
75 See below, pp. 64–9.
76 Bülow to Eulenburg, 1 January 1894, *Eulenburgs Korrespondenz*, no. 878.
77 Cited in Johannes Haller, 'Bülow und Eulenburg' in Friedrich Thimme (ed.),

Front wider Bülow, Staatsmänner, Diplomaten und Forscher zu seinen Denkwürdig-keiten (Munich 1931), pp. 43f; see below, note 155.

78 Cited in F. Hellwig, *Carl Freiherr von Stumm-Halberg* (Heidelberg and Saar-brücken 1936), p. 516; see also Elisabeth Fehrenbach, *Wandlungen des deutschen Kaisergedankens*; Peter Domann, *Sozialdemokratie und Kaisertum unter Wilhelm II.* (Wiesbaden 1974); Peter Leibenguth, 'Modernisierungskrisis des Kaiser-reichs an der Schwelle zum wilhelminischen Imperialismus', unpublished disser-tation, University of Cologne 1975.

79 Bülow to Eulenburg, 6 April and 9 July 1892, *Eulenburgs Korrespondenz*, nos. 641 and 687, quoted in Röhl, *Germany without Bismarck*, p. 103.

80 Kaiser Wilhelm II to Eulenburg, 25 December 1895; Eulenburg to Kaiser Wilhelm II, 20 January 1896, cited Röhl, *Germany without Bismarck*, pp. 158ff.

81 Bülow to Eulenburg, 23 July 1896, *Eulenburgs Korrespondenz*, no. 1245, cited in Röhl, *Germany without Bismarck*, p. 194.

82 Karl Alexander von Müller (ed.), *Fürst Chlodwig zu Hohenlohe-Schillingsfürst: Denkwürdigkeiten der Reichskanzlerzeit* (Stuttgart and Berlin 1931), pp. 340f.

83 Holstein to Eulenburg, 4 December 1894 and 17 February 1895, *Eulenburgs Korrespondenz*, no. 1089. See also Haller, *Eulenburg*, p. 173; Rich, *Friedrich von Holstein*, II, pp. 484ff.

84 Holstein to Eulenburg, 27 November 1894, *Eulenburgs Korrespondenz*, no. 1052. Quoted in Röhl, *Germany without Bismarck*, p. 127.

85 Holstein to Eulenburg, 9 February 1896, printed in Haller, *Eulenburg*, pp. 193f; see also Holstein, *Geheime Papiere*, III, no. 528.

86 Holstein to Eulenburg, 21 December 1895, Holstein, *Geheime Papiere*, III, no. 515.

87 Eulenburg to Holstein, 2 December 1894, printed in full in Haller, *Eulenburg*, pp. 170–2; see also Rich, *Holstein*, pp. 487f.

88 Cited in Röhl, *Germany without Bismarck*, pp. 171–5.

89 Eulenburg to Bülow, 8 June 1896, *Eulenburgs Korrespondenz*, no. 1233, quoted in Röhl, *Germany without Bismarck*, pp. 190ff.

90 Eulenburg's memorandum of 20 March 1894, which is located in the Bran-denburg-Preussisches Hausarchiv, Zentrales Staatsarchiv, Merseburg, is printed in *Eulenburgs Korrespondenz*, no. 933. See Röhl, *Germany without Bismarck*, pp. 109f.

91 Caprivi to his brother, 23 October 1894, cited Heinrich Otto Meisner, 'Der Reichskanzler Caprivi', *Zeitschrift für die gesamte Staatswissenschaft* 3 (1955), p. 730.

92 Eulenburg to Kaiser Wilhelm II, 30 August 1894, *Eulenburgs Korrespondenz*, no. 989.

93 See Röhl, *Germany without Bismarck*, p. 114.

94 Grossherzog Friedrich von Baden to Eulenburg, 25 September 1894, *Eulenburgs Korrespondenz*, no. 998; Haller, *Eulenburg*, pp. 154 and 158.

95 Eulenburg to Kaiser Wilhelm II, 18 February 1895, *Eulenburgs Korrespondenz*, no. 1091. On the Marschall crisis, see Röhl, *Germany without Bismarck*, pp. 132–6.

96 Eulenburg to Bülow, 6 December 1895; Kaiser Wilhelm II to Eulenburg, 25 December 1895, *Eulenburgs Korrespondenz*, nos. 1169 and 1178.

97 Eulenburg to Bülow, 13 March 1896, ibid., no. 1198; see also Röhl, *Germany without Bismarck*, pp. 178–82.

98 Bogdan von Hutten-Czapski, *Sechzig Jahre Politik und Gesellschaft*, 2 vols. (Berlin 1936), I, pp. 289f.

99 Eulenburg to Bülow, 7 July 1896, *Eulenburgs Korrespondenz*, no. 1237. Röhl, *Germany without Bismarck*, pp. 192f.

100 The plan is printed in Röhl, *Germany without Bismarck*, pp. 196ff.

101 Shortly after his appointment Hohenlohe had accepted a secret – and highly unconstitutional – annual payment of 120,000 marks from Crown funds, in addition to his salary as Chancellor. See Röhl, *Germany without Bismarck*, pp. 175ff.

102 Hohenlohe, *Denkwürdigkeiten der Reichskanzlerzeit*, pp. 342–44.

103 Eulenburg, 'Notes on the year 1898' cited in Röhl, *Germany without Bismarck*, p. 245.

104 Bülow to Eulenburg, 26 December 1897, cited in Haller, 'Bülow und Eulenburg', *Front wider Bülow*, pp. 44f; see also the facsimile letter from Bülow to Eulenburg of 15 February 1898, printed ibid., pp. 8ff.

105 See below, p. 65. The poems 'Der Narr und das Meer' (1902) and 'Der Narr und die Berge' (1903) were nonetheless written at this time.

106 Reply of the Prussian Ministry of Justice to an enquiry from the Foreign Office of 5 June 1942, cited in Holstein, *Geheime Papiere*, IV, p. 478.

107 See Harden, *Prozesse*, pp. 268–71, p. 280.

108 Rogge, *Holstein und Harden*, p. 290; see also Eulenburg's piece 'Mein Freund Jan', Staatsarchiv Potsdam, Eulenburg Papers, 623.

109 Eulenburg's article appeared in *Bayreuther Blätter* in 1886 and was reprinted at the instigation of Ludwig Schemann as a separate publication under the title 'Eine Erinnerung an Graf Arthur Gobineau' in 1906.

110 Eulenburg to Hans von Wolzogen, 14 December 1884 and 6 February 1885, Wolzogen Papers, Richard-Wagner-Gedenkstätte, Bayreuth. In a letter to Farenheid Eulenburg expressed himself in a similar vein with regard to his correspondence with Gobineau; see *Eulenburgs Korrespondenz*, no. 19, note 1; see also Harden (ed.), *Die Zukunft*, 22 June 1907, p. 420.

111 This question is discussed in detail in *Eulenburgs Korrespondenz*, I, pp. 69f.

112 See ibid., nos. 19 and 22.

113 Philipp Eulenburg, *Fünf Jahre der Freundschaft in Briefen von Fritz von Farenheid-Beynuhnen und Philipp Graf zu Eulenburg-Hertefeld* (Liebenberg 1897). See Harden, *Prozesse*, pp. 186ff.

114 Maurice Baumont, *L'Affaire Eulenburg et les Origines de la Guerre Mondiale* (Paris 1933), pp. 199f; a second corrected edition appeared in 1973; see also Holstein, *Geheime Papiere*, IV, no. 1020.

115 Philipp Eulenburg, 'Aufzeichnungen des Fürsten Philipp zu Eulenburg-Hertefeld' (unpublished manuscript), I, part 1, p. 80. Elsewhere in the 'Aufzeichnungen' Eulenburg states: 'Original letters which Moltke and I exchanged never need to fear the light of day. Even those which contained references to the Kaiser', ibid., p. 92. The letters were destroyed nonetheless.

116 Eulenburg to Nathaniel Rothschild, 17 September 1904 (handwritten draft), Staatsarchiv Potsdam, Eulenburg Papers 615; *Eulenburgs Korrespondenz*, no. 1500.

117 Holstein, *Geheime Papiere*, IV, no. 1085; Harden, *Prozesse*, p. 206.

118 Philipp Eulenburg, Promemoria of 1900, Staatsarchiv Potsdam, Eulenburg Papers. It is disturbing to note that shortly after Friedrich Eulenburg's disgrace

his wife Klara married General Count Wartensleben, the president of the Court Martial!

119 Varnbüler, 'Memoiren', p. 73.
120 Cited in *Eulenburgs Korrespondenz*, no. 18, note 3.
121 Kuno Moltke to Axel Varnbüler, 31 March 1891, Schloss Hemmingen. It is unclear whether the name 'Philine' was intended to be a reference to the actress in Goethe's *Wilhelm Meister*. Bülow (*Denkwürdigkeiten*, IV, p. 487) thinks the nickname was coined by Dörnberg.
122 *Eulenburgs Korrespondenz*, nos. 498 and 505.
123 Sigmund Freud himself drew attention to the bisexuality or homosexuality of Dostoevsky; see Freud, 'Dostojewski und die Vatertötung' in *Gesammelte Schriften*, XII, pp. 7ff; *Gesammelte Werke*, XIV, pp. 399ff. Freud's notions were used by the American literary critic Simon O. Lesser especially in relation to Prince Myschkin in the novel *The Idiot*. See S.O. Lesser, 'Saint and Sinner – Dostoevsky's *Idiot*', in *Modern Fiction Studies*, 4 (1958), pp. 211–24; S.O. Lesser, 'The Role of Unconscious Understanding in Flaubert and Dostoevsky', *Daedalus* (1963), pp. 363–81.
124 Holstein, *Geheime Papiere*, IV, no. 1078.
125 Axel Varnbüler to Kuno Moltke, 15 April 1898, *Eulenburgs Korrespondenz*, no. 1366. Wilhelm II was referred to in other letters too by Varnbüler as 'das Liebchen' ('the darling'); see Varnbüler to Moltke, 7 May and 4 June 1898, ibid., no. 1373; see also Holstein, *Geheime Papiere*, IV, no. 1004; Rich, *Friedrich von Holstein*, p. 381.
126 Freiherr von Soden to Axel Varnbüler, 25 November 1907, Schloss Hemmingen. The Kaiser had travelled to Essen for the burial of Krupp on 26 November 1902 and had given two speeches in praise of him.
127 Holstein, *Geheime Papiere*, IV, no. 973.
128 Varnbüler's memorandum on the affair of honour between Holstein and Eulenburg of May 1906, with a secret addendum by Varnbüler, printed in *Eulenburgs Korrespondenz*, no. 1515. The copy of the memorandum placed in the files of the Foreign Office was removed, presumably by Holstein; see Holstein, *Geheime Papiere*, IV, no. 975.
129 Varnbüler, 'Memoiren', pp. 480–2.
130 For further details, see Harden, *Prozesse*, pp. 207–59.
131 Varnbüler to Laemmel, 22 April 1908, *Eulenburgs Korrespondenz*, no. 1539.
132 Varnbüler to Laemmel, 23 April 1908 (telegram); Laemmel to Varnbüler, 24 April 1908, *Eulenburgs Korrespondenz* III, p. 2070, note 10.
133 Prince Friedrich-Wend zu Eulenburg-Hertefeld to Kaiser Wilhelm II, 10 September 1927, Staatsarchiv Marburg, Schwerin Papers, P 26.
134 See *Eulenburgs Korrespondenz*, no. 17, note 6.
135 Ibid., no. 3, note 2.
136 Axel Varnbüler to Kuno Moltke, 24 October 1912, ibid., no. 1556.
137 See the pioneering work of Alfred C. Kinsey, *Sexual Behaviour in the Human Male* (Philadelphia and London 1948), chapter 21, especially pp. 636–59.
138 See above, pp. 56f. See also Monts, *Erinnerungen und Gedanken* (Berlin 1932), p. 183.
139 Axel Varnbüler to Kuno Moltke, 10 August 1888, *Eulenburgs Korrespondenz*, no. 191.

140 See above pp. 57f.
141 Emil Kraepelin, *Psychiatrie* (Leipzig 1893), pp. 646–92. Harden quotes extensively from Kraepelin in the chapter on Eulenburg in his book *Prozesse* (pp. 199–202); details of Harden's idiosyncratic picture of the 'Kinaedeninternationale' – the gay international – and of the 'different dominating ideas' which homosexuals are supposed to have, are on pp. 241–50 of *Prozesse*. On Kraepelin in general, see K. Kolle, *Kraepelin und Freud* (1957).
142 The question of Eulenburg's inability to stand trial has always been a subject of controversy. See for instance the reaction of the Kaiser, cited below, p. 63. As early as 7 June 1908, Eulenburg's youngest son Karl wrote to his mother that it was a good thing 'that the doctors have so much authority that they can intervene if necessary'. Staatsarchiv Potsdam, Eulenburg Papers 895.
143 See Rogge, *Holstein und Harden*, p. 465; Harden, *Prozesse*, pp. 415f. Even after the exchange of declarations between Moltke and Harden on 19 March 1909, the 'peace' was disturbed on numerous occasions. On 3 April 1909 Harden wrote to Albert Ballin, who had, together with Otto Hammann, negotiated the settlement, that people were still trying to bring the Moltke trial to a conclusion favourable to Moltke and Eulenburg. Advisers such as these 'simply forget that they thereby force me to produce without scruple all evidence, letters and witnesses and to give the matter a scope which for years, at the greatest sacrifice, I have done my best to avoid'. Harden to Ballin, 3 April 1909, Zentrales Staatsarchiv Potsdam, Hammann Papers 2. In a letter of 5 April 1909, Harden wrote to Ballin: 'However much I may wish for a quiet resolution (Moltke wishes it even more): a conclusion which in some way sanitises the Eulenburgers would enable the many affiliates of the same calibre, who are *still* up there, to feel all too secure.' Ibid. On 23 April 1909 Hammann reported to Ballin that Harden was complaining bitterly that Moltke was not sticking to the agreement. 'Moltke expressly denied on oath ... when questioned by the presiding judge, any form of homosexual inclination or activity. Harden now intends to produce evidence for Moltke's homosexuality, though in what case is still uncertain, possibly once again, as in the Eulenburg case, in a new trial in which Moltke would not be involved.' Hammann to Ballin, 23 April 1909, Zentrales Staatsarchiv Potsdam, Hammann Papers 2. The 40,000 marks were handed over to Harden by Ballin on 11 June 1909; Ballin received the same sum back from the Reich Chancellery on the following day. Rogge, *Holstein und Harden*, p. 465.
144 Harden to Holstein, 28 February 1907, Holstein, *Geheime Papiere*, IV, no. 1012.
145 Bussmann, *Herbert von Bismarck*, no. 366, pp. 523f.
146 Ibid., no. 367, p. 525.
147 Eulenburg to Kaiser Wilhelm II, 11 September 1888, *Eulenburgs Korrespondenz*, no. 196.
148 Axel Varnbüler to Kuno Moltke, November 1890, ibid., no. 442.
149 See above, pp. 55f.
150 Axel Varnbüler to Kuno Moltke, 4 June 1898, *Eulenburgs Korrespondenz*, no. 1373.
151 See Sergei J. Witte, *Erinnerungen* (Berlin 1923), p. 280; Alexei S. Suworin, *Das Geheimtagebuch* (Berlin 1925), p. 50.
152 Eulenburg to Axel Varnbüler, 13 May 1906, *Eulenburgs Korrespondenz*, no. 1518; see also Maximilian Harden, 'Dies irae' in *Die Zukunft*, 29 November 1906, p. 291.

153 Kaiser Wilhelm II to Bülow, 18 July 1908, cited in Rogge, *Holstein und Harden*, p. 314. The Kaiser later became convinced, on the other hand, that Eulenburg was 'absolutely innocent' and the victim of a judicial murder perpetrated by 'Holstein, Harden and international Jewry' which represented the 'preliminary first step' in the revolution against the Hohenzollern monarchy. Kaiser Wilhelm II to Prince Fritz-Wend zu Eulenburg-Hertefeld, 8 September 1927, Staatsarchiv Marburg, Schwerin Papers P 26.

154 In a letter of February 1907 to Holstein, Harden named: two Barons Fürstenberg, one Baron von Kurland, Egloffstein, Edgard Wedel, 'a young Limburg-Stirum', Johannes Count von Lynar, Prince Friedrich Heinrich von Preussen. Holstein, *Geheime Papiere*, IV, no. 1012. On 5 May 1908 Harden also named the Grand Duke of Hessen, the Duke of Coburg, the Duke of Anhalt, Prince Aribert von Anhalt, Knesebeck, Stülpnagel and a son of General Gustav von Kessel. Harden to Holstein, 5 May 1908, Foreign and Commonwealth Office Library, London, Holstein Papers, E 348794. Eulenburg counted his cousin Kessel as one of his 'worst enemies'. Eulenburg to Varnbüler, 31 May 1918, Schloss Hemmingen. After a confrontation between General von Kessel and Harden the young Kessel resigned from the army in May 1908 and travelled to India. See Rogge, *Holstein und Harden*, p. 288.

155 Bülow's letters to Eulenburg leave no doubt that he knew from the outset about Eulenburg's inclinations. Whether he genuinely sympathised with Eulenburg, or cynically manipulated him must remain an open question. See Haller, 'Bülow und Eulenburg', pp. 43ff; Rogge, *Holstein und Harden*, pp. 209, 211. See also above, pp. 45f. In 1931 the writer Joachim von Kürenberg, whose real name was Reichel and who was a nephew of Bülow, approached Haller with 'proof' of Bülow's homosexuality. Haller did not pursue this lead after he had established from the police that Kürenberg had been convicted for deception. BA Koblenz, Haller Papers 20. A brother of the Reich Chancellor, Flügeladjutant Karl Ulrich von Bülow, came under suspicion of homosexuality in July 1908. See Holstein, *Geheime Papiere*, IV, no. 1105; Rogge, *Holstein und Harden*, pp. 308–10; see also Monts, *Erinnerungen und Gedanken*, p. 513. Another brother, Alfred, belonged to the so-called Liebenberg round table from the beginning. See also the fascinating new evidence on Bülow's personal assistants Scheefer and Seeband in Katharine Anne Lerman, *The Chancellor as Courtier. Bernhard von Bülow and the Governance of Germany, 1900–1909* (Cambridge 1990), pp. 198ff.

156 Holstein, *Geheime Papiere*, IV, no. 1151.

157 *Eulenburgs Korrespondenz*, no. 176. On the joint journey through Bavaria undertaken at the end of August 1886 by Prince Wilhelm and Eulenburg, see also ibid., no. 88.

158 Varnbüler, 'Memoiren', p. 107.

159 Ibid., p. 109.

160 Ibid., pp. 107, 109. Karl Eulenburg to his mother, 7 June 1908, Staatsarchiv Potsdam, Eulenburg Papers 895. On 5 May 1908, Philipp Eulenburg wrote to his eldest son: 'But Jaroljmek's behaviour is *very suspicious*. Wronker has established (how I do not know) that *at the time of the Munich affair*, he was not in Florence but probably in *Munich*.' P. Eulenburg to Fritz-Wend Eulenburg, 5 May 1908, Staatsarchiv Potsdam, Eulenburg Papers 560; see also Holstein, *Geheime Papiere*, IV, no. 1008 and no. 1019.

161 Adine Countess Schwerin to Ebo Count Schwerin, August 1912, Staatsarchiv Marburg, Schwerin Papers P 21, Packet 6. See also P. Eulenburg to his daughter Adine, 27 September 1919, ibid.

162 Varnbüler, 'Memoiren', pp. 119f.

163 Ibid., p. 585. The deep involvement of the Moltkes with Rudolf Steiner and the anthroposophy movement has recently been revealed by a most unusual publication. After Moltke's death in June 1916 the Chief of General Staff continued to 'communicate' regularly with Steiner, who wrote down the deceased General's thoughts and smuggled them over the border to Moltke's widow! These 'post-mortem communications' have now been published in Thomas Meyer (ed.), *Helmuth von Moltke 1848–1916. Dokumente zu seinem Leben und Wirken*, 2 vols. (Basel 1993), II, pp. 119–299.

164 Varnbüler, 'Memoiren', p. 107.

165 Eulenburg's first biographer Johannes Haller insists on the somewhat forced distinction between spiritism and spiritualism. See Haller, *Eulenburg*, pp. 28ff.

166 Countess Mathilde Stubenberg, memorandum of January 1915, Staatsarchiv Potsdam, Eulenburg Papers 786.

167 Eulenburg to Nathaniel Rothschild, 17 September 1904, *Eulenburgs Korrespondenz*, no. 1500. Varnbüler and Bülow expressed similar opinions. See above, pp. 45f and p. 58.

168 Ibid., no. 604, note 5; see Rogge, *Friedrich von Holstein*, pp. 163f.

169 Kuno Moltke to Axel Varnbüler, 5 May 1891, Schloss Hemmingen. See *Eulenburgs Korrespondenz*, no. 505.

170 Ibid., no. 492.

171 Axel Varnbüler to Kuno Moltke, 10 August 1888, ibid., no. 191.

172 Eulenburg to his mother, 25 March 1888, ibid., no. 164. See also no. 492.

173 Kuno Count Rantzau to Herbert Count von Bismarck, November 1888, Schlossarchiv Friedrichsruh. See *Eulenburgs Korrespondenz*, no. 202, note 2.

174 Cited in Eulenburg to Varnbüler, 18 December 1893, ibid., no. 865.

175 Eulenburg to Bülow, 24 July 1901 and 18 February 1902, printed in Haller, *Eulenburg*, pp. 29–31. See also Haller, 'Bülow und Eulenburg', p. 29.

176 *Eulenburgs Korrespondenz*, no. 120 including appendix. Cf. the completely distorted version of this letter printed in Haller, *Eulenburg*, p. 29.

177 Eulenburg to Crown Prince Wilhelm, 27 March 1888, *Eulenburgs Korrespondenz*, no. 165.

178 See ibid., no. 207, note 2.

179 Eulenburg to Kaiser Wilhelm II, 15 October 1888, ibid., no. 199.

180 Eulenburg to his sister, 23 February 1889, ibid., no. 212. Eulenburg expressed himself in a similar vein in a letter to Bülow of 18 February 1902. Haller, *Eulenburg*, p. 30f.

181 Eulenburg to Bernhard Forsboom, 17 June 1889, *Eulenburgs Korrespondenz*, no. 223.

182 Ibid., no. 207, note 2.

183 Waldersee, *Denkwürdigkeiten*, II, p. 222. Cf. Haller, *Eulenburg*, p. 29, note 1.

184 Berghahn, *Rüstung und Machtpolitik*, pp. 87ff.

185 Zedlitz-Trützschler, *Zwölf Jahre*, pp. 160f.

186 See note 143 above.

187 Kaiser Wilhelm II to Prince Fritz-Wend zu Eulenburg-Hertefeld, 8 September 1927, Staatsarchiv Marburg, Schwerin Papers P 26.

3 THE KAISER'S COURT

1 See Nicolaus Sombart, 'The Kaiser in his Epoch: Some Reflexions on Wilhelmine Society, Sexuality and Culture' in John C. G. Röhl and Nicolaus Sombart (eds.), *Kaiser Wilhelm II. New Interpretations* (Cambridge 1982), p. 287.

2 Herzogin Viktoria Luise, *Im Glanz der Krone. Erinnerungen* (Munich 1967). Typical of the historiography of the court during the Wilhelmine epoch is the three-volume work of the house archivist Dr Georg Schuster, *Geschichte des Preussischen Hofes* (Berlin 1913).

3 Otto-Ernst Schüddekopf, *Herrliche Kaiserzeit. Deutschland 1871–1914*. With an introduction by Hans Joachim Schoeps (Frankfurt, Berlin and Vienna 1973).

4 Thus the Social Democrat Adolph Hoffmann in the Prussian House of Deputies on 7 June 1910. *Verhandlungen des Hauses der Abgeordneten*, 21. Legisl. III. Session 1910, p. 6649.

5 See Bernd Faulenbach, *Die Ideologie des deutschen Weges. Die deutsche Geschichte in der Historiographie zwischen Kaiserreich und Nationalsozialismus* (Munich 1980).

6 See for example Wolfgang J. Mommsen, 'Die latente Krise des Deutschen Reiches 1909–1914' in Leo Just (ed.), *Handbuch der Deutschen Geschichte*, IV, section I (Frankfurt 1973); Konrad H. Jarausch, *The Enigmatic Chancellor. Bethmann Hollweg and the Hubris of Imperial Germany* (New Haven and London 1973).

7 See for example the influential works of Hans-Ulrich Wehler, especially *Bismarck und der Imperialismus* (Cologne 1969); *Das deutsche Kaiserreich 1971–1918* (Göttingen 1973); and *Geschichte als Historische Sozialwissenschaft* (Frankfurt 1973).

8 For example, Graham Parry, *The Golden Age Restor'd. The Culture of the Stuart Court 1603–1647* (Manchester 1981); Philip Mansel, *The Court of France 1789–1830* (Cambridge 1988).

9 Norbert Elias, *Über den Prozess der Zivilisation. Soziogenetische und psychogenetische Untersuchungen*, 2 vols. (Bern 1969); Norbert Elias, *Die höfische Gesellschaft. Eine Untersuchung zur Soziologie des Königtums und der höfischen Aristokratie* (Neuwied and Berlin 1969).

10 Jürgen Freiherr von Kruedener, *Die Rolle des Hofes im Absolutismus*, Forschungen zur Sozial- und Wirtschaftsgeschichte 19 (Stuttgart 1973).

11 Sombart, 'The Kaiser in his Epoch', p. 287.

12 Norman Rich and M. H. Fisher (eds.), *The Holstein Papers. The Memoirs, Diaries and Correspondence of Friedrich von Holstein 1837–1919*, 4 vols. (Cambridge 1955–1963). The original German text of this invaluable source is available in *Die Geheimen Papiere Friedrich von Holsteins*, 4 vols. (Göttingen, Berlin and Frankfurt 1956–63).

13 John C. G. Röhl (ed.), *Philipp Eulenburgs politische Korrespondenz*, 3 vols. (Boppard-am-Rhein 1976–83).

14 Walther Peter Fuchs (ed.), *Grossherzog Friedrich I. von Baden und die Reichspolitik 1871–1907*, 4 vols. (Stuttgart 1968–80); see also chapter 4, below.

15 This is of course the central thesis of John C. G. Röhl, *Germany without Bismarck. The Crisis of Government in the Second Reich, 1890–1900* (London and Berkeley 1967). See also chapter 2, above. For the 'Bülow system', see the important study by Katharine Anne Lerman, *The Chancellor as Courtier. Bernhard von Bülow and the Governance of Germany, 1900–1909* (Cambridge 1990).

16 Isabel V. Hull, *The Entourage of Kaiser Wilhelm II 1888–1918* (Cambridge 1982).

17 Record of a discussion between Grand Duke Peter of Oldenburg and Bernhard von Bülow, 4 March 1899, printed in Fuchs, *Grossherzog von Baden*, IV, no. 1953, appendix.

18 See Karl Ferdinand Werner, 'Fürst und Hof im 19. Jahrhundert: Abgesang oder Spätblüte' in K. F. Werner (ed.), *Hof, Kultur und Politik im 19. Jahrhundert* (Bonn 1985), pp. 1–53.

19 See the detailed information placed before the Reichstag in 1908 in connection with the Reich finance reform plans, *Verhandlungen des Reichstags*, 249, appendix, p. 4.

20 Statement by Hermann von Stengel in Prussian House of Deputies, 9 June 1910.

21 See *Verhandlungen des Reichstags*, 249, Appendix, p. 134.

22 *Entwurf eines Gesetzes betr. die Erhöhung der Krondotation*, Begründung, Prussian House of Deputies, Drucksache nos. 515/516, pp. 4548f.

23 BA Koblenz, Reichshaushaltspläne 1874–1918.

24 See fig. 1 above.

25 Financial provision in the Reich budget for 1908–09 for the Reich Chancellor and the Reich Chancellery was 306,360 marks, for the Foreign Office 17,569,032 marks, for the Colonial Office 1,899,147 marks and for the Reich Justice administration 2,463,930 marks.

26 Stengel calculated that the civil list in 1889 (excluding the Kaiser's *Dispositionsfonds*) amounted to 5% of the outgoings of the Prussian state, while in 1910, *before* the increase of 22%, it had dropped to 2.4% of state expenditure. *Verhandlungen des Hauses der Abgeordneten*, 9 June 1910. Despite the constant increase in the civil list, therefore, the general development in favour of the 'principle of state omnipotence' is unmistakable here too. As a comparison it is worth recalling Theodor Mayer's calculation that the expenditure by the court in France and Austria during the *ancien régime* amounted to between 5% and 8.5% of state expenditure as a whole. Theodor Mayer, *Geschichte der Finanzwirtschaft vom Mittelalter bis zum Ende des 18. Jahrhunderts* (Tübingen 1952), pp. 236–72.

27 A detailed apportioning of the Crown budget for 1910–18 is contained in Kurt Heinig, *Hohenzollern. Wilhelm II. und sein Haus. Der Kampf um den Kronbesitz* (Berlin 1921), pp. 14–16.

28 After the increase in the civil list of 17 June 1910, the members of the Imperial family received the following annual amounts (in marks):

Kaiser Wilhelm II	1,760,000
Kaiserin Auguste Viktoria	210,000
Crown Prince and his child	853,840
Prince Eitel Friedrich	431,000
Prince Adalbert and children	363,780
Prince August Wilhelm and children	331,200
Prince Oskar	170,000
Prince Joachim und children	311,900
Prince Heinrich	340,272
Prince Waldemar und Sigismund	110,000
Prince Friedrich Leopold (father)	30,000

Prince Friedrich Sigismund and children	36,000
Prince Friedrich Leopold (son) and children	30,000
Prince Friedrich Heinrich	30,000
Prince Joachim Albrecht	30,000
Prince Friedrich Wilhelm and children	60,000

See Heinig, *Hohenzollern*, pp. 14f.

29 *Verhandlungen des Hauses der Abgeordneten*, 7 June 1910, p. 6650.

30 Heinig, *Hohenzollern*, p. 39. The wealth of Prince Friedrich Leopold of Prussia (father) was estimated in 1914 to be 40 million marks.

31 August Graf zu Eulenburg to Kaiser Wilhelm II, 30 June 1909, Zentrales Staatsarchiv, Hist. Abt. II, Merseburg, Zivilkabinett 2.2.1, no. 3163, Acta betr. die allgemeine Regelung der Gehälter und des Wohnungsgeldzuschusses der Beamten pp. der Königlichen Haus- und Hof-Verwaltung, fol. 134.

32 Philipp Eulenburg to Axel Freiherr von Varnbüler, 19 May 1896, in *Eulenburgs Korrespondenz*, no. 1227.

33 The Prussian Finance Minister provoked amusement in the Prussian House of Deputies when he stated that the cost of acquiring Corfu was not met from the current accounts of the crown but from 'a small inheritance'. *Verhandlungen des Hauses der Abgeordneten*, 7 June 1910, p. 6658. When Prince Alexander of Prussia died at the beginning of 1896, the members of his entourage received 'in some cases very substantial legacies'. The remainder of the estate 'of still around 2.5 million marks' went 'to the usufruct of Prince Georg and after his death became the property of our little Prince Oskar, who was the deceased's godchild'. August Eulenburg to Philipp Eulenburg, 6 January 1896, *Eulenburgs Korrespondenz*, no. 1186.

34 Ibid., I, p. 646. See also Holstein, *Geheime Papiere*, III, nos. 335 and 336.

35 See Hoffmann's speech in the Prussian House of Deputies of 7 June 1910, *Verhandlungen*, pp. 665of.

36 August Graf zu Eulenburg to Kaiser Wilhelm II, 1 November 1909. Acta betr. die Schatulle Sr. Majestät König Wilhelms II., 1888–1912, Zentrales Staatsarchiv, Hist. Abt. II, Merseburg, Zivilkabinett 2.2.1., no. 3417, fols. 195ff.

37 Rudolf Martin, *Jahrbuch des Vermögens und Einkommens der Millionäre in Berlin* (Berlin 1913), introduction and pp. 115–24. See also the details of Crown possessions in Heinig, *Hohenzollern*, pp. 35–47, where the imperial family's castles, estates and Berlin residences are listed. The SPD estimated the Crown's private annual income, erroneously, at 12–15 million marks, a figure which was immediately rejected by the Prussian Finance Minister as having been 'plucked from their imagination'. See *Verhandlungen*, 7 June 1910, pp. 6644f and p. 6658. The assertion sometimes made even today that the Kaiser had huge sums invested in Krupp shares appears to be groundless. See Bernd Engelmann, *Krupp. Legenden und Wirklichkeit* (Munich 1969), pp. 257–8. In contrast, Heinig, *Hohenzollern*, p. 44; Richard Owen, 'Military-Industrial Relations: Krupp and the Imperial Navy Office' in Richard J. Evans (ed.), *Society and Politics in Wilhelmine Germany* (London and New York 1978), p. 88, note 64. There is no evidence for this in Boelcke's comprehensive documentation. See Willi A. Boelcke, *Krupp und die Hohenzollern in Dokumenten. Krupp-Korrespondenz mit Kaisern, Kabinettschefs und Ministern 1850–1918* (Frankfurt 1970). See especially Hull, *Entourage*, pp. 158–71, who rightly emphasises the role of mediator between the Kaiser and Krupp played by Admiral Hollmann.

38 The *Encyclopaedia Britannica* for 1910 states that the Prussian-German civil list differed from the British one by virtue of the fact that in addition the German monarch owned 'large private property [*Kronfideikommiss und Schatullgäter*] the revenue from which contributed to the expenditure of the court and the members of the royal family'. Kruedener argues that the 'confusion of notionally private-princely and notionally public-state duties and expenditure' is characteristic of the world of courts in general. Kruedener, *Die Rolle des Hofes*, p. 14.

39 For an informative recent account of the complex relationship between the public and private aspects of the finances of the British monarchy, see William M. Kuhn, 'Queen Victoria's Civil List: What did She do with It?', *Historical Journal* 36, 3 (1993), pp. 645–65.

40 See the declaration by the Prussian Minister of Finance Georg von Rheinbaben that the private wealth of the Prussian Crown was 'modest by comparison with that of the Austrian Crown'. *Verhandlungen des Hauses der Abgeordneten*, 7 June 1910, p. 6658.

41 Ibid., p. 6656.

42 *Preussisches Haus der Abgeordneten*, Drucksache, no. 515.

43 *Verhandlungen des Hauses der Abgeordneten*, 7 June 1910, p. 6640.

44 The civil list was increased from £385,000 to £470,000 on the accession of Edward VII. The sum was divided in the following way: '1. Their Majesties' privy purse £110,000; 2. Salaries of H.M.'s Household £125,000; 3. Expenses of H.M.'s Household £193,000; 4. Works (interior repair of Buckingham Palace and Windsor Castle) £20,000; 5. Royal bounty, alms and special services £13,200; 6. Unappropriated £8,000'. Appanage payments to the individual members of the royal family were set out in separate schedules, unlike the practice in Prussia. See the *Encyclopaedia Britannica* (1910) entry under 'Civil List'.

45 The figures are taken from the entry 'Zivilliste' in Meyer's *Konversations-Lexikon* for 1908. Cf. the figures in the *Encyclopaedia Britannica* for 1910. The rate of exchange at that time was £1 to 20 marks.

46 4.5 million marks plus 1.17 million marks appanages.

47 From Meyer's *Konversations-Lexikon* for 1908, 'Zivilliste'.

48 See Max Weber, *Wirtschaft und Gesellschaft. Grundriss der verstehenden Soziologie*, ed. J. Winckelmann (Cologne and Berlin 1964), the chapter 'Politische und hierokratische Herrschaft', especially pp. 875ff and p. 889.

49 When Maximilian Harden learned of the planned increase in the civil list, he prophesied a 'Social Democratic explosion'. See Hans Dieter Hellige, *Walther Rathenau – Maximilian Harden, Briefwechsel 1897–1920* (Munich 1983), p. 612. Hoffmann mocked the fact that in 1910 the Left Liberal Progressive Party voted almost unanimously for the increase in the civil list while in 1889 nine of the members of this party had voted against the increase at that time. A 'Byzantine Block' was now replacing the 'Black-Blue Block' in parliament, he claimed. *Verhandlungen des Hauses der Abgeordneten*, 7 June 1910, p. 6653.

50 Ibid., pp. 6645f.

51 Ibid., p. 6641.

52 Ibid., pp. 6639f, p. 6654.

53 Ibid., p. 6649.

54 Ibid., p. 6652.

55 *Kölnische Volkszeitung*, quoted in Hoffmann's speech in the Prussian Landtag, ibid., p. 6638.

56 Hellmut von Gerlach, quoted in ibid., p. 6646.

57 See the *Handbuch über den königlich-preussischen Hof und Staat für 1900* (Berlin 1899), pp. 1–52.

58 In December 1897 the Master of Heralds received an increase in salary of 600 marks, from 7,500 marks to 8,100 marks, plus a personal bonus of 1,200 marks per year, so that his income would be equal to 'the income of a Counsellor in the central Reich administration in mid-career'. Minister of the Household von Wedell to Kaiser Wilhelm II, Memorandum on 'Gehaltserhöhungen für Hofbeamte und -Offizianten' of 7 December 1897. Zentrales Staatsarchiv Merseburg, 2.2.1., no. 3163.

59 Although none of the court officials and functionaries was a state employee, it was thought desirable to equate the salaries to equivalent grades in the civil service because the 'court offices are forced for the most part to recruit their staff from the civil service and for this reason must offer them salaries at least as high as those which they would earn there'. Minister of the Household von Wedell to Kaiser Wilhelm II, Memorandum on 'Regelung der Beamtengehälter nach Dienstalter, 20 February 1895'. Zentrales Staatsarchiv Merseburg, 2.2.1., no. 3163. The Secretaries of the *Hofkammer* were particularly closely associated with the state bureaucracy and therefore automatically received the salary increase for the civil service (together with an additional 300 marks) announced in the All-Highest Order of 9 December 1885. Salary adjustments for the remaining divisions of the court administration always took longer to come through. See Wedell's memorandum of 7 December 1897.

60 See the memorandum of the Minister of the Household Count August von Eulenburg of 26 April 1909, in which he states: 'I have proposed the same salary increases of 2,000 marks for the Ober-Hof und Hausmarschall ..., the Ober-Stallmeister ... and the General-Intendant of the Royal Theatres ... whose salary levels have been 18,000 marks since 1868 or 1871 in line with those of the Under-Secretaries of State. The Hausmarschall, the Hofmarschall and the Ober-hofmeister ..., the Oberjägermeister ... and the Hofkammer-Präsident ... earn (apart from 3,000 marks pensionable augmentation for the Hausmarschall and 1,000 marks remuneration of the Oberhofmeister) the same salary as the Regierungs-Präsidenten and it should for this reason be appropriate for them to receive the same bonus of 1,000 marks which the latter receive.' August Eulenburg to Kaiser Wilhelm II, 26 April 1909, Zentrales Staatsarchiv Merseburg, 2.2.1., no. 3163.

61 August Graf zu Eulenburg to Kaiser Wilhelm II, 1 November 1909. Acta betr. die Schatulle Sr. Majestät König Wilhelms II., 1888–1912, Zentrales Staatsarchiv, Hist. Abt. II, Merseburg, Zivilkabinett 2.2.1., no. 3417, fols. 195ff.

62 Wedell to Kaiser Wilhelm II, 20 February 1895, Zentrales Staatsarchiv Merseburg, 2.2.1., no. 3163.

63 See note 60 above.

64 The officials of the Ober-Hofmarschall-Amt received a salary increase of 17.37% in 1890 in contrast with the 13% of the civil service, 'as they are even now ... underpaid when their responsibilities and the services required of them are taken into account'. Wedell to Kaiser Wilhelm II, 19 November 1890, Zentrales

Staatsarchiv Merseburg, 2.2.1., no. 3163. In a further memorandum of 20 February 1895, Wedell pointed out the 'unusual position of the Court Secretaries' which makes them 'the chief advisers to their director in all administrative matters'. In 1897, on the other hand, Wedell saw no reason for the Ober-Hofmarschall-Amt Secretaries 'to depart from the analogy with the state administration', as the Ober-Hof-und Haus-Marschall Count Eulenburg wished. Wedell to Kaiser Wilhelm II, 7 December 1897.

65 In Wedell's Memorandum of 7 December 1897, he reports that the Ober-Maschinenmeister of the Garten-Intendantur had been appointed in 1888 with a salary of 2,400 marks. In the meantime, however, the position had gained 'a somewhat greater significance' with the result that an increase of 3,600 marks seemed justified.

66 Plinzner, the Leibstallmeister in the Ober-Marstall-Amt received a salary of 7,500 marks in 1897.

67 The Oberjägermeister, Baron von Heintze, was appointed Chief of the Hof-Jagdamt by All-Highest Order of 16 December 1892. He received at that time a salary of 6,000 marks, 3,000 marks personal augmentation and a salary addition of 1,500 marks, which amounted to an overall income of 10,500 marks. In 1897 a salary of 12,000 marks was attached to this position. Ibid.

68 See the documentation in *Eulenburgs Korrespondenz*, nos. 1461, 1464–72.

69 The Intendantur Secretaries of the General-Intendantur in Berlin as well as the Intendantur secretaries of the three 'outward' theatres were from 1895 aligned with the Regierung secretaries of the state bureaucracy or else the Gericht secretaries of the legal administration. Wedell, memorandum of 7 December 1897, Zentrales Staatsarchiv Merseburg, 2.2.1., no. 3163.

70 The court musicians had received a small increase in salary of 8.3% in 1890 and therefore received on average 2,250 marks per annum. The Generalintendant pleaded for a further increase in 1897. He argued that 'the duties of the court orchestra were now incomparably more onerous than before, that the highest demands were being placed upon each individual and they could only undertake other part-time work by jeopardising their physical and mental powers; and that most court musicians are recruited from the military and are only appointed after a certain age.' Wedell therefore suggested a further increase of 4.44%. The musicians in the 'outward' theatres received on average an annual salary of 1,750 marks. Ibid.

71 In 1909 there were 128 people employed in the cathedral choir, 599 in the Royal Theatre in Berlin, 204 in the theatre in Hanover, 156 in Kassel and 127 in Wiesbaden. August Eulenburg to Kaiser Wilhelm II, 26 April 1909, Appendix 20, ibid.

72 See the memoirs of Mathilde Gräfin von Keller, *Vierzig Jahre im Dienst der Kaiserin. Ein Kulturbild aus den Jahren 1881–1921* (Leipzig 1935).

73 From 1897 the Ober-Hofmeister of the Kaiserin received not 9,000 but – like the Hausmarschall and the Hofmarschall – 12,000 marks per annum, i.e. more than a Vortragender Rat. In consequence the post of Cabinet Secretary, which he had also occupied until then, was abolished. Wedell to Kaiser Wilhelm II, 7 December 1897.

74 The Kaiserin's first Kammerherr was Count Keller, a cousin of Countess Mathilde Keller. He received an income of 7,200 marks rising to 8,400 marks with a personal addition of 900 marks. Ibid.

75 Brauchitsch rose to become Commander-in-Chief of the army from 1938 to 1941.
76 Wilmowski was the son of the Chief of the Reich Chancellery under Prince Chlodwig zu Hohenlohe-Schillingsfürst.
77 At the beginning of 1896 Prince Friedrich Leopold of Prussia's residence in Klein-Glienicke was put under guard on the orders of the Kaiser by men from the First Regiment of Guards; the princess, a sister of the Kaiserin, was also put under house arrest for fourteen days. Philipp Eulenburg noted: 'Friedrich Leopold and his wife had many rows, quickly threw every Flügeladjutant and Hofmarschall out of the house and behaved in an unacceptable manner.' With each such conflict in the Imperial family, 'the whole of Potsdam and Berlin ... was provoked into a state of high excitement'. Eulenburg thought it inconceivable that an 'arrest under military guard' had 'taken place in the Prussian royal family after the time of Frederick the Great'. *Eulenburgs Korrespondenz*, III, p. 1634. After numerous further crises the prince's Hofmarschall Count Henckel von Donnersmarck finally had printed in March 1904 a twenty-page pamphlet with the title 'Dienst-Vorschriften für die Hofdienerschaft Seiner Königlichen Hoheit des Prinzen Friedrich Leopold von Preussen'. Hausarchiv des vormals regieren-den preussichen Königshauses, Burg Hohenzollern. The prince's family was the first to take the opportunity presented by the collapse of the monarchy in 1918 to free themselves from the strict Hohenzollern house law. Details in Heinig, *Hohenzollern*, pp. 12f, pp. 150–6.
78 The diaries and memoirs of Hofmarschall Count Robert Zedlitz-Trützschler appeared in 1924 under the title *Zwölf Jahre am deutschen Kaiserhof* and, though incomplete, are one of the best sources on court society in the Wilhelmine epoch.
79 The military entourage of Wilhelm II can only be treated briefly here. See Hull, *Entourage*, pp. 175–306, and Wilhelm Deist, 'Kaiser Wilhelm II in the context of his military and naval entourage' in Röhl and Sombart, Kaiser Wilhelm II, pp. 169–92.
80 When August Mackensen was appointed Flügeladjutant in 1895, he received numerous telegrams of congratulation and letters. Typical of many was the letter of the later Prussian Minister of War von Einem: 'Just yesterday ... I heard of your appointment as Flügeladjutant. I give you my most heartfelt congratulations and I express my joy that you have been accorded this so well-deserved recogni-tion and honour, and that in your person virtue has found its reward. I do not doubt that you will receive the good will of His Majesty, and hope that out of this great benefit and advantage will derive.' Einem to Mackensen, 21 September 1895, BA-MA Freiburg, Mackensen Papers N 39/154. Mackensen was promoted on 21 January 1898 to Diensttuender Flügeladjutant and was ennobled a few weeks later.
81 See Hull, *Entourage*, p. 184. In his unpublished memoirs, the later General Karl Baron von Plettenberg explained: 'The Leib-Compagnie was composed mainly of recruits from the Garde-du-Corps who were over 1.87 meters tall.' When in 1899 he together with some other adjutants accompanied Prince Albrecht and his son Prince Friedrich Heinrich to Madrid to confer the Order of the Black Eagle on the King of Spain, they were 'with few exceptions ... all exceptionally tall, so that we would appear in a good light by comparison with the degenerate Spaniards'. Karl Baron von Plettenberg, 'Erinnerungen', p. 27, p. 85.
82 Even the Flügeladjutanten not on active service were constantly in demand for

court duties. Plettenberg writes that after his appointment as Flügeladjutant on 2 May 1899 'alongside my very demanding guard duties, I had to do a great deal in terms of court duties'. He remembers that 'in the last year when at the head of my regiment, I had to go to Berlin in one month – January – on twenty-seven occasions, of which on five days it was twice and on two days even three times'. Ibid., p. 82, p. 84.

83 Rudolf Count von Stillfried-Alcantara, *Ceremonial-Buch für den Königlich-Preussischen Hof*, sections I-XII (Berlin 1871–8), p. iv.

84 The Flügeladjutant Gustav von Neumann-Cosel, who at every opportunity kissed the Kaiser's hand, found service in the Schloss so stressful that on returning to his bachelor apartment he 'first shouted a very realistic and strong expression three times across the room and then retired to bed for twenty-four hours'. Walter Görlitz (ed.), *Der Kaiser ... Aufzeichnungen des Chefs des Marine-kabinetts Admiral Georg Alexander von Müller über die Ära Wilhelms II.* (Göttingen 1965), pp. 188f.

85 Ibid.

86 Eulenburg to Bülow, 8 June 1896, *Eulenburgs Korrespondenz*, no. 1233.

87 Ibid., III, p. 1945. See above, p. 20.

88 Karl Alexander von Müller, 'An Preussen!' in *Süddeutsche Monatshefte*, special number, September 1914, pp. 826ff.

89 See below, p. 90.

90 See section II 2 (b) in Kruedener, *Die Rolle des Hofes*, which carries the title 'Suspendierung des Abstammungsranges – das Gegenprinzip: "Nähe zum Thron"', pp. 57–65.

91 For the influence of the Chief of the Naval Cabinet Admiral Gustav Freiherr von Senden-Bibran, see Jonathan Steinberg, *Yesterday's Deterrent. Tirpitz and the Birth of the German Battle Fleet* (London and New York 1965); Volker R. Berghahn, *Der Tirpitz-Plan*; Hull, *Entourage*, pp. 97–9, 178–80. Philipp Eulenburg was complaining as early as the summer of 1896 that Senden was giving him 'headaches – and indeed *terrible* ones. The man is a monstrosity!' Eulenburg to Holstein, 16 July 1896, Holstein Papers, Politisches Archiv des Auswärtigen Amtes, Bonn. In November 1896 Eulenburg made a vain attempt to get Senden out of the Kaiser's entourage. Senden, as he wrote to Wilhelm II, had loudly cursed in a club in front of foreign diplomats and parliamentarians about 'the unbelievable feebleness of Prince Hohenlohe', with the result that the Saxon Military Plenipotentiary felt compelled to counter the attack. 'A Saxon to one of Your Majesty's Flügeladjutanten!' Eulenburg to Kaiser Wilhelm II, 12 November 1896, *Eulenburgs Korrespondenz*, no. 1273. The Chief of the Naval Cabinet von Müller had, in contrast to Senden, a very good relationship with the 'responsible government' and in particular with Bethmann Hollweg. See Hull, *Entourage*, p. 246.

92 Characteristic of the growing 'courtierisation' of the Prussian bureaucracy were the conflicts between Holstein and Eulenburg in the 1890s over the position of Lucanus, whose father was an apothecary. In September 1895 Holstein complained: 'I am shocked that you sign yourself to Lucanus "most obediently": that is enough to make all the apothecaries in the Prussian monarchy wild.' *Eulenburgs Korrespondenz*, III, p. 1579. On 27 January 1897 we read in a letter from Holstein: 'Well now, Lucanus has the Black Eagle. How can one still speak of a Prussian

tradition? Do you understand that?' Cited ibid., p. 1784. Eulenburg on the other hand recognised very quickly that Lucanus was not only gaining more and more influence over the Kaiser but was also – precisely because he came from a lower middle-class background – very amenable to flattery. Thus Eulenburg wrote to Lucanus (just at the moment when he himself was raised to the rank of prince): 'Highly honoured Excellency! You *cannot imagine* what joy your letter, which I have just received, has given me! I am devoted to you in true reverence; I feel how the most *real* love binds us to our beloved master – the *caring* love for him! ... I shudder at the thought of the Kaiser being without you! ... I hope that you will continue to address me in a simple manner, as is the wish of Your heartfelt and sincerely devoted Eulenburg-Hertefeld.' *Eulenburgs Korrespondenz*, no. 1412.

93 Valentini was the successor to Lucanus as Chief of the Civil Cabinet. See Bernhard Schwertfeger (ed.), *Kaiser und Kabinettschef. Nach eigenen Aufzeichnungen und dem Briefwechsel des Wirklichen Geheimen Rats Rudolf von Valentini* (Oldenburg 1931).

94 Röhl, *Germany without Bismarck*, p. 273.

95 This development has been described in detail in Rudolf Schmidt-Bückeburg, *Das Militärkabinett der preussischen Könige und deutschen Kaiser* (Berlin 1933).

96 See the statement of ambassador General Hans Lothar von Schweinitz, cited ibid., pp. 157f.

97 The Grand Duke complained that the evening of his life had been 'changed into joyless work' by the rejection of his wish. The decision had 'touched him most painfully'. The Grand Duchess Luise, the Kaiser's aunt, informed the Prussian Envoy in Karlsruhe: 'The blow has been more painful for the Grand Duke and me than I can describe.' See Fuchs, *Grossherzog von Baden*, IV, nos. 2179, 2187 and 2190.

98 See above p. 69.

99 August Eulenburg to Kaiser Wilhelm II, 26 April 1909, Appendix 20, Zentrales Staatsarchiv Merseburg, Zivilkabinett, 2.2.1., no. 3163. This figure referred exclusively to the administration of the Kaiser's court; the administrations of the various princely households were expressly excluded.

100 August Eulenburg to Kaiser Wilhelm II, 30 June 1909, ibid.

101 Heinig, *Hohenzollern*, p. 24.

102 Ibid., p. 164.

103 Obstfelder to Kaiser Wilhelm I, 4 October 1873, Zentrales Staatsarchiv Merseburg, Zivilkabinett, 2.2.1., no. 3136.

104 The new posts were made necessary by the 'lengthy sea cruises' of Wilhelm II, as well as by 'the fact that Your Majesty's residence for the winter months in the Schloss here is transferred for the summer to the Neues Palais, both castles are therefore used more often, and this comes on top of the expansion of the household in general'. Wedell to Kaiser Wilhelm II, 19 November 1890, ibid.

105 August Eulenburg to Kaiser Wilhelm II, 30 June 1909, ibid.

106 A detailed listing of the 'court' of the Crown Prince after 1918 is contained in the papers of Karl von Plettenberg, in the private possession of the family.

107 Heinig, *Hohenzollern*, pp. 162–8.

108 Reproduced from Stillfried, *Ceremonial-Buch für den Königlich-Preussischen Hof*, section x, 'Hof-Rang-Reglement'.

109 The military character of the Court Ranking is clear from Stillfried's commentary. Proudly he writes: 'As two hundred years ago, so still today the military
ranks form the mileposts of the Ranking, which sets down those presentable at
the royal court, and as each lieutenant, even those of common birth, is so
presentable, so the hierarchy goes down to the rank of lieutenant.' Ibid., p. 8.

110 Count Paul Vasili (pseudonym), *La Société de Berlin* (Paris 1884), quoted here
from the English edition (London 1885), p. 125. Katharina Radziwill, née
Countess Rzewuska, (1858–1911) was married to Prince Wilhelm von Radziwill.
Also attributed to her are: *Memories of Forty Years*, (London 1914) and *Secrets
of Dethroned Royalty* (New York 1920). Her sister-in-law, Marie Radziwill, the
wife of the Generaladjutant Prince Anton Radziwill, depicted Berlin court life
in the most informative way in her letters. See *Lettres de la Princesse Radziwill
au Général de Robilant 1889–1914: Une grande dame d'avant guerre*, 4 vols.
(Bologna 1933–4).

111 K. A. Lerman, *The Chancellor as Courtier. Bernhard von Bülow and the
Governance of Germany, 1900–1909* (Cambridge 1990), p. 146. Bülow had
declined a princely title in December 1902 because he was not sufficiently
wealthy. Only after he had inherited several million marks in 1905 did he accept
the elevation. See Bülow, *Denkwürdigkeiten*, I, pp. 594f, II, p. 121; Lerman,
Chancellor as Courtier, pp. 97f. See below, pp. 101f.

112 Eulenburg, memorandum of 12/13 October 1895, *Eulenburgs Korrespondenz*, II,
p. 1568.

113 Karl Baron von Plettenberg, 'Erinnerungen', p. 44 and p. 72.

114 *Eulenburgs Korrespondenz*, no. 1078 and no. 1294. See above, note 92.

115 *Eulenburgs Korrespondenz*, III, p. 1470.

116 Ibid., no. 1088.

117 Kaiser Wilhelm II to Eulenburg, 12 February 1895, ibid., no. 1083.

118 Stolberg and Wedell to Kaiser Wilhelm II, 5 March 1889, Zentrales Staatsarchiv Merseburg, Zivilkabinett, 2.2.1., no. 3162, 'Acta betr. die Kompetenzver-
hältnisse der Königlichen Hofbehörden sowie die Regelung des Geschäfts-
ganges bei denselben'.

119 See Eulenburg's amusing letter describing a ball at the Munich court, *Eulenburgs Korrespondenz*, no. 897. See the memoranda in Philipp Eulenburg, *Erlebnisse an deutschen und fremden Höfen* (Leipzig 1934).

120 Stillfried, *Ceremonial-Buch*, VI, p. 31.

121 Ibid., p. 33.

122 Ibid., p. 37.

123 Ibid., p. 41.

124 Ibid., p. 61.

125 See above, pp. 90f. Good-looking officers were also in demand at other balls.
Thus in 1894 the Kaiser's brother Prince Heinrich invited August Mackensen
'and three dancing gentlemen from the regiment to a ball in Kiel on 10 January'.
The officers' travel costs were all reimbursed. Seckendorff to Mackensen, 4
January 1894. BA-MA Freiburg, Mackensen Papers N 39/44, fol. 54.

126 Stillfried, *Ceremonial-Buch*, sections VII, pp. 60f.

127 Helmuth von Moltke, *Erinnerungen, Briefe, Dokumente 1877–1916* (Stuttgart
1922), p. 316.

128 See Stillfried, *Ceremonial-Buch*, sections VII, VIII and IX.

129 Keller, *Vierzig Jahre im Dienst der Kaiserin*, pp. 51f. See also the detailed descriptions of the various balls in Fedor von Zobeltitz, *Chronik der Gesellschaft unter dem letzten Kaiserreich*, 2 vols. (Hamburg 1922).

130 Eulenburg to Bülow, 24 September 1900, *Eulenburgs Korrespondenz*, III, p. 1994.

131 Kaiser Wilhelm II to Lady Mary Montagu, 1 May 1910, cited in John C. G. Röhl, 'The Emperor's new clothes' in Röhl and Sombart, *Kaiser Wilhelm II*, p. 42.

132 Fuchs, *Grossherzog von Baden*, III, p. 120.

133 Brauer to Turban, 16 February 1892, ibid., no. 1154.

134 Brauer to Turban, 6 March 1892, ibid., no. 1163.

135 See the exact details of the Kaiser's annual programme of events in Thomas A. Kohut, *Wilhelm and the Germans. A Study in Leadership* (Oxford 1991), pp. 235–247. Cf. Hull, *Entourage*, pp. 38f. She too speaks of the Liebenberg Circle as 'an alternate court'. Ibid., p. 68.

136 Hull, *Entourage*, p. 39. Harry F. Young, *Prince Lichnowsky and the Great War* (Athens, Georgia, 1977), p. 28.

137 See the detailed commentary on the House law in Hermann Rehn, *Modernes Fürstenrecht* (Munich 1904), pp. 352–78. An anonymous book of the time speaks of the 'tyranny' of the monarch over the other members of the Hohenzollern family. The latter were 'exposed to every caprice and every whim of the head of their family'. See Anon., *The Private Life of two Emperors. Wilhelm II of Germany and Francis-Joseph of Austria*, 2 vols. (London 1905), I, pp. 59ff.

138 Marginal comment by Wilhelm II on a letter of Prince Friedrich Wilhelm of 26 December 1907, Hausarchiv des vormals regierenden preussischen Königshauses, Burg Hohenzollern.

139 Oswald Freiherr von Richthofen to Minister of the Household von Wedell, 31 December 1902, ibid.

140 Kaiser Wilhelm II to Prince Friedrich Wilhelm of Prussia, 25 December 1909, ibid.

141 Eulenburg to Varnbüler, 25 May 1896, *Eulenburgs Korrespondenz*, no. 1230.

142 Eulenburg to Varnbüler, 28 March 1896, ibid., no. 1231. It is interesting to note how many princely marriages were brought to an abrupt end as soon as the Hohenzollern House law became inoperable in November 1918. See Heinig, *Hohenzollern*, pp. 12f.

143 Directive from Kaiser Wilhelm II to Minister of the Household von Wedell, May 1902, Hausarchiv, Burg Hohenzollern.

144 See Brauer's comprehensive reports in Fuchs, *Grossherzog von Baden*, III, pp. 56ff.

145 *Eulenburgs Korrespondenz*, II, p. 1568. The Kaiser's brother Heinrich was married to Alexandra's sister Irene.

146 See Stephan Kekule von Stradonitz, 'Ueber die Zuständigkeit des preussischen Heroldsamts' in *Archiv für öffentliches Recht*, edited by Paul Laband, Otto Mayer and Felix Stoerk, 18 (1903), p. 195.

147 See Eulenburg's letter of 15 November 1898 to the Kaiser with the postscript: 'I know only too well what Your Majesty wished to convey by placing my picture – the old face! – on your desk (which I feel myself is almost too much!). I have understood the *love* which in deep human sympathy you wanted to show

to an old friend suffering inwardly to death.' *Eulenburgs Korrespondenz*, III, p. 1931.

148 See chapter 5, below.

149 Georg von Hülsen to Hermann von Lucanus, 14 June 1892 and 6 September 1892, Zentrales Staatsarchiv Merseburg, Zivilkabinett, 2.2.1., no. 21 260/1.

150 Werner Graf von Alvensleben-Neugattersleben to Kaiser Wilhelm II, 5 October 1903, Zentrales Staatsarchiv Merseburg, Hausarchiv, Rep. 53 J, Lit. A, no. 3.

151 Bernhard Graf von Bülow to Eulenburg, 11 December 1902, *Eulenburgs Korrespondenz*, no. 1492.

152 Eulenburg to Kaiser Wilhelm II, 10 December 1902, ibid., no. 1491.

153 Prince Wilhelm of Prussia to Kaiserin Augusta, 27 June 1886, Zentrales Staatsarchiv Merseburg, Hausarchiv, Rep. 53 J, Lit. P, no. 14.

154 See Fritz Friedmann, *Der deutsche Kaiser und die Hofkamarilla. I. Der Fall Kotze II. Wilhelm II. und die Revolution von oben* (Zürich 1896). Friedmann was a schoolfriend and the lawyer of Master of Ceremonies von Kotze, who was arrested on suspicion of being the author of the letters. Friedmann too was later arrested.

155 See above, p. 227. Hull, *Entourage*, pp. 109–45; Hull, 'Kaiser Wilhelm II and the "Liebenberg Circle"' in Röhl/Sombart, *Kaiser Wilhelm II*, pp. 193–220.

156 See pp. 61ff above.

157 Maximilian Harden to Friedrich von Holstein, 15 November 1908, Holstein, *Geheime Papiere*, IV, no. 1151. See above p. 63.

158 Maurice Baumont, *L'Affaire Eulenburg*, revised edition (Geneva 1973), p. 249.

159 Friedmann, *Der deutsche Kaiser und die Hofkamarilla*, pp. 86f. The Hohenau brothers were the product of the morganatic marriage of Prince Albrecht of Prussia. The elder brother Wilhelm was married to a Princess zu Hohenlohe-Oehringen.

160 Eulenburg to Kaiser Wilhelm II, 5 December 1899, *Eulenburgs Korrespondenz*, no. 1406.

161 Bülow to Eulenburg, 24 December 1899, ibid., no. 1409. See ibid., p. 1971, note 1.

162 Ibid., p. 1977, note 1.

163 Alexander Prince zu Hohenlohe-Schillingsfürst to his father, 2 and 12 January 1900, BA Koblenz, Hohenlohe Papers 1615.

164 Rudolf Vierhaus (ed.), *Das Tagebuch der Baronin Spitzemberg*, pp. 392f.

165 Szögyény's report of 19 February 1904, cited in Isabel V. Hull, 'Prussian Dynastic Ritual at the End of Monarchy' in C. Fink, I. V. Hull and M. Knox (eds.), *German Nationalism and the European Response 1890–1945* (Norman and London 1985), pp. 13–41, note 82.

166 Szögyény's report of 15 January 1898, cited ibid., note 65.

167 Fedor von Zobeltitz, *Chronik der Gesellschaft unter dem letzten Kaiserreich*, I, p. 139.

168 Spitzemberg, *Tagebuch*, pp. 436f.

169 Ibid., p. 393.

170 For Holstein's comment, see above, note 92; Moltke, *Erinnerungen, Briefe, Dokumente*, p. 353.

171 *Eulenburgs Korrespondenz*, no. 1511.

172 Agnes Gräfin Pourtalès to Axel Varnbüler, 11 April 1906, cited ibid., p. 2122.

173 Moltke, *Erinnerungen, Briefe, Dokumente*, pp. 337f.

174 Quoted by Adolph Hoffmann in his speech of 7 June 1910. *Verhandlungen des Hauses der Abgeordneten*, 21. Legisl., III. Session 1910, pp. 6648f.

175 Heinig, *Hohenzollern*, p. 18.

176 Informative on this point: Thomas Nipperdey, 'Nationalidee und Nationaldenkmal in Deutschland im 19. Jahrhundert' in Thomas Nipperdey (ed.), *Gesellschaft, Kultur, Theorie. Gesammelte Aufsätze zur neueren Geschichte* (Göttingen 1976), p. 169.

177 See Nicolaus Sombart, '"Ich sage, untergehen". Zum zweiten Band von Philipp Eulenburgs Politischer Korrespondenz' *Merkur*, 385 (June 1980), pp. 542–54.

178 Eulenburg to Kuno Moltke, 15 June 1895, *Eulenburgs Korrespondenz*, III, no. 1112, p. 1506.

179 Bülow to Eulenburg, 9 January 1893, ibid., II, no. 758, cited in Röhl, *Germany without Bismarck*, pp. 103f.

180 See the devastating criticism of the Prussian Envoy in Munich, Count Anton Monts, after Wilhelm's 'lackey speech' 1897, quoted above, p. 22.

181 On the social composition of the higher civil service in the Kaiserreich, see below, chapter 5.

182 Siegfried Sommer, memorandum of 23 December 1903. I am grateful to Professor Lewis Elton of Guildford for making his grandfather's papers available to me.

183 Cited by Lamar Cecil, 'History as family chronicle: Kaiser Wilhelm II and the dynastic roots of the Anglo-German antagonism' in Röhl and Sombart, *Kaiser Wilhelm II*, p. 107.

184 See Dominic Lieven's excellent study of the Tsarist court in *Russia's Rulers under the Old Regime* (New Haven and London 1989).

185 Hans-Ulrich Wehler, *Das deutsche Kaiserreich 1871–1918* (Göttingen 1973), pp. 69–72. See the critique of Wehler's influential view in Röhl and Sombart, *Kaiser Wilhelm II*, pp. 1–22 and, more recently, in Isabel V. Hull, 'Persönliches Regiment' in John C. G. Röhl (ed.), *Der Ort Kaiser Wilhelms II. in der deutschen Geschichte* (Munich 1991), pp. 3–23.

186 See Röhl, *Germany without Bismarck*, pp. 175ff.

4 THE 'KINGSHIP MECHANISM' IN THE KAISERREICH

1 Hermann Oncken (ed.), *Grossherzog Friedrich I. von Baden und die deutsche Politik von 1854 bis 1971. Briefwechsel, Denkschriften, Tagebücher*, 2 vols. (Stuttgart 1927).

2 Walther Peter Fuchs (ed.), *Grossherzog Friedrich I. von Baden und die Reichspolitik 1871–1907* (hereafter Fuchs). 4 vols.: I: 1871–9 (Stuttgart 1968); II: 1879–90 (Stuttgart 1975); III: 1890–7 (Stuttgart 1980); IV: 1898–1907 (Stuttgart 1980).

3 Documents from the Kaiser's Military Cabinet were for instance taken to the prisoner-of-war camp at Bad Aibling/Bavaria during the relocation of the army personnel office from Berlin in 1945. In the camp the officers decided not to allow these historically valuable documents 'to fall into the hands of the Americans' but to divide them amongst themselves until 'better times' returned.

Whether General Hans von Plessen's diary survived the Second World War in a similar fashion, or whether it was destroyed out of fear of the 'enemy' is still not clear. Especially regrettable in this respect is the destruction – apparently in the 1960s – of the pre-war diaries of Kurt Riezler, Bethmann Hollweg's closest assistant. See Karl Dietrich Erdmann (ed.), *Kurt Riezler, Tagebücher, Aufsätze, Dokumente* (Göttingen 1972). On the destruction of the diaries for the period before 15 August 1914 and the closely related question of the authenticity of the surviving entries from the July crisis of 1914 see Wilhelm Deist's discussion in *Militärgeschichtliche Mitteilungen* 2 (1973); Adolf Gasser, 'Erster Weltkrieg und "Friedensforschung"' in *Allgemeine Schweizerische Militär-Zeitschrift* (May 1974), p. 237; Fritz Fellner's discussion in *Mitteilungen des Oesterreichischen Staatsarchivs* (1973), pp. 490–5; Bernd Sösemann, 'Die Erforderlichkeit des Möglichen'. Kritische Bemerkungen zu der Edition Kurt Riezler, Tagebücher, Aufsätze, Dokumente' in *Blätter für deutsche Landesgeschichte* 110 (1974), pp. 261–75. See also F. Fischer, *Juli 1914: Wir sind nicht hineingeschlittert. Das Staatsgeheimnis um die Riezler-Tagebücher* (Frankfurt am Main, 1983), and especially Bernd Sösemann, 'Die Tagebücher Kurt Riezlers. Untersuchungen zu ihrer Echtheit und Edition', *Historische Zeitschrift* 236 (1983), pp. 327–69. The vehement tone of Erdmann's reply (ibid., pp. 371–402) cannot disguise the poverty of his arguments. See also chapter 7, note 10.

4 Report of Oberhofmeister von Chelius on the burning of the letters of Grand Duchess Luise, November–December 1918, Zentrales Staatsarchiv Merseburg, Rep. 51W, no. 2a.

5 Letters of Grand Duchess Luise von Baden to Kaiser Wilhelm II, 1874–1922, Zentrales Staatsarchiv Merseburg, Rep. 51W, no. 2a.

6 On the nationalism of the German history professors in the inter-war years, see Bernd Faulenbach, *Ideologie des deutschen Weges. Die deutsche Geschichte in der Historiographie zwischen Kaiserreich und Nationalsozialismus* (Munich 1980).

7 At the time this chapter was written, no fewer than three American historians – Lamar Cecil, Thomas A. Kohut and Robert G. L. Waite – were working on biographies of Kaiser Wilhelm II. The first volume of Cecil's biography, *Wilhelm II Prince and Emperor 1859–1900* (Chapel Hill and London 1989), has now appeared, as has Kohut's psychological investigation *Wilhelm II and the Germans. A Study in Leadership* (New York and Oxford 1991). The American historian Isabel Hull has published a definitive examination of the Kaiser's entourage based on years of archival study: see Isabel V. Hull, *The Entourage of Kaiser Wilhelm II, 1888–1918* (Cambridge 1982). In Britain three biographies of Kaiser Wilhelm II have been published in the last two decades; they are however of variable quality. See Michael Balfour, *The Kaiser and his Times* (London 1964); Tyler Whittle, *The Last Kaiser. A Biography of William II, German Emperor and King of Prussia* (London 1977); Alan Palmer, *The Kaiser, Warlord of the Second Reich* (London 1978). A good overview of the state of international research on Wilhelm II and his court is provided by the twelve essays in John C.G. Röhl and Nicolaus Sombart (eds.), *Kaiser Wilhelm II – New Interpretations* (Cambridge 1982). Willibald Gutsche's brief study *Wilhelm II. Der letzte Kaiser des Deutschen Reiches* (Berlin 1991) cannot rank as a scholarly biography, nor can Franz Herre's recent *Wilhelm II. Monarch zwischen den Zeiten* (Cologne 1993) which was written without footnotes for the popular market. British studies of

British kings, princes and courts are of course too numerous to be listed here.

8 The conference organised by the German Historical Institute in Paris in September 1982 on the history of courts in France and Germany, offered a good opportunity to survey the state of French research on this theme. See Karl Ferdinand Werner (ed.), *Hof, Kultur und Politik im 19. Jahrhundert* (Bonn 1985).

9 Nicolaus Sombart, 'Der letzte Kaiser was so, wie die Deutsche waren' in *Frankfurter Allgemeine Zeitung*, 27 January 1979.

10 See Walter Goetz, 'Kaiser Wilhelm II und die deutsche Geschichtsschreibung', *Historische Zeitschrift*, 179 (1955), pp. 21f. On 23 January 1926 Friedrich von Berg told the ex-Kaiser in Doorn that he had, on the basis of an All-Highest Order, 'set up a special propaganda office here [in Berlin] with the express purpose of influencing the whole press extending far to the left'. The purpose of the propaganda office was 'to create a dam against the unfettered agitation of the left-wing parties'. The Professors Spahn, Bornhak, Hötzsch, Zorn and Hellfritz had declared themselves ready, along with Carl Schmitt, 'to use their authority and their work in professional journals etc., to support the cause of the royal house'. Berg had also ensured that the files of the Hohenzollern house archive could only be examined with the express consent of the Hohenzollern family. Berg to Kaiser Wilhelm II, 23 January 1926, Hausarchiv des vormals regierenden preussischen Königshauses, Burg Hohenzollern, Hechingen.

11 Otto Pflanze, 'Bismarcks Herrschaftstechnik als Problem der gegenwärtigen Historiographie' in *Historische Zeitschrift* 234 (1982), pp. 561–99.

12 Hans-Ulrich Wehler, *Das Deutsche Kaiserreich 1871–1918* (Göttingen 1973), pp. 60ff, especially pp. 63–9.

13 Friedrich Naumann, *Demokratie und Kaisertum* (Berlin 1900), pp. 167f.

14 Jonathan Steinberg, 'Kaiser Wilhelm II and the British' in Röhl and Sombart, *Kaiser Wilhelm II*, p. 127.

15 J.W. Wheeler-Bennett, *Three Episodes in the Life of Kaiser Wilhelm II* (Cambridge 1956), p. 1, see also p. 26. Interestingly the American expert on Friedrich von Holstein, Norman Rich, also came to the conclusion after years of close study of the archival record that it was Wilhelm II who possessed 'the ultimate authority' in the Reich and who 'insisted on exercising this authority'. It was he 'far more than Bismarck who fostered the quality of grovelling servility in the German administration and who would tolerate only sycophants or mediocrities in his immediate entourage and in the highest position of the German government – including the German army'. Norman Rich, *Friedrich von Holstein: Politics and Diplomacy in the Era of Bismarck and Wilhelm II*, 2 vols. (Cambridge 1965), II, p. 847.

16 Brauer, report of 12 January 1906. Fuchs, no. 2538.

17 See Fuchs, nos. 2358, 2359, 2376, 2380, 2400. See also below, p. 126.

18 Jagemann, 7 May 1898. Fuchs, no. 1851.

19 Jagemann, 17 June 1898. Fuchs, no. 1659. See Geoff Eley, 'Sammlungspolitik, Social Imperialism and the Navy Law of 1898', *Militärgeschichtliche Mitteilungen* 15 (1974).

20 See Fuchs, nos. 1143, 2188 and 2270. See also Derek M. Bleyberg, 'Government and Legislative Process in Wilhelmine Germany: The Reorganisation of the Tariff Laws under Reich Chancellor von Bülow, 1897–1902' (unpublished Ph.D. dissertation, University of East Anglia 1980).

21 Tirpitz to Grand Duke, 31 March 1903, Fuchs, no. 2407.
22 See Fuchs, no. 1386.
23 Adolf Freiherr Marschall von Bieberstein, diary entry of 29 March 1898, cited in Fuchs, III, p. 532. The Russian proposal was immediately and forcefully rejected by Berlin.
24 Bodman, 4 December 1895, Fuchs, no. 1498.
25 Brauer, 10 May 1893, Fuchs, no. 1268.
26 Grand Duke to Brauer, 21 June 1898, Fuchs, no. 1863.
27 See Nicolaus Sombart, '"Ich sage, untergehen"'. Zum zweiten Band von Philipp Eulenburgs Politischer Korrespondenz', *Merkur* 385 (June 1980), pp. 542–54. Reprinted in Nicolaus Sombart, *Nachdenken über Deutschland. Vom Historismus zur Psychoanalyse* (Munich and Zürich 1987), pp. 96–113.
28 See chapter 2, above.
29 The original German text of the Holstein Papers is published in Norman Rich and M.H. Fisher (eds.), *Die geheimen Papiere Friedrich von Holsteins*, 4 vols. (Göttingen, Berlin and Frankfurt 1956–63).
30 Eulenburg to Bülow, 23 September 1905, *Eulenburgs Korrespondenz*, no. 1508.
31 Bodman, 18 June and 26 July 1895, Fuchs, nos. 1464 and 1467.
32 Jagemann, 12 May 1899, Fuchs, no. 1981.
33 Brauer, 16 June 1890, Fuchs, no. 1058.
34 Brauer, 7 December 1890, Fuchs, no. 1088.
35 Brauer, 26 February 1891, Fuchs, no. 1106.
36 Jagemann, 26 October 1898, Fuchs, no. 1905.
37 Jagemann, 22 April 1896, Fuchs, no. 1536. The statement referred directly to the controversial matter of duelling.
38 Grand Duke to Kaiser Wilhelm II, 1 November 1897, Fuchs, no. 1766.
39 Grand Duke, declaration of 19 September 1897, Fuchs, no. 1737.
40 Grand Duke Peter von Oldenburg, record of a conversation with Bülow, 4 March 1899, Fuchs, IV, pp. 122f.
41 Erich Eyck, *Das Persönliche Regiments Wilhelms II. Politische Geschichte des Deutschen Kaiserreichs von 1890 bis 1914* (Erlenbach and Zürich 1948).
42 Fritz Hartung, 'Das persönliche Regiment Kaiser Wilhelms II.' in *Sitzungsberichte der deutsche Akademie der Wissenschaften zu Berlin*, no. 3 (1952); Ernst Rudolf Huber, 'Das persönliche Regiment Wilhelms II.', *Zeitschrift für Religions- und Geistesgeschichte* 3 (1951). See Huber's comments on this complex of themes in his *Deutsche Verfassungsgeschichte seit 1789*, IV, *Struktur und Krisen des Kaiserreichs* (Stuttgart, Berlin, Cologne and Mainz 1969), pp. 329–47. Cf. the thoughtful observations on this difficult subject in Isabel V. Hull, 'Persönliches Regiment', in John C. G. Röhl (ed.), *Der Ort Kaiser Wilhelms II. in der deutschen Geschichte* (Munich 1991), pp. 3–23.
43 Ernst Rudolf Huber, *Deutsche Verfassungsgeschichte*, IV, p. 333 and p. 342. According to this definition there could have been no 'personal rule' in Prussia, especially with regard to the power of military command, as the Prussian constitution was open in the upward direction. When Huber states that Wilhelm II acted in agreement with the 'responsible channels', he glosses over the fact that the leaders of these offices were appointed by Wilhelm and could be dismissed by him. The question whether the Kaiser's measures were undertaken 'with the agreement of the majority of the population' (p. 341) or not cannot be valid as a

criterion for the existence of a 'personal rule' in the sense of 'precise constitutional law'. Huber's statements on the responsibility of diplomacy and the other authorities for the Kaiser's 'displays of superiority' (*Auftrumpfen*) have an unmistakable air of apologia about them. 'It was often the departments', he writes, 'which built up the façade of "personal rule" in order to hide behind it' (pp. 342ff). A more helpful concept – even if it does not go far enough – is the distinction which Huber makes between 'institutionalised personal rule' on the one hand, in which 'political initiative' resides 'not with the ministers but with the monarch' and in which decisions are 'not taken by the cabinet and sanctioned by the monarch' but on the contrary 'taken by the monarch and carried out by the ministers'; and on the other hand 'improvised personal rule' in which the intervention of the monarch in the affairs of government can take on 'a chronic character' (pp. 333ff). Huber denies the existence of both forms of rule.

44 On the inner connection between absolutist strivings and administrative chaos, Jonathan Steinberg has written: 'Now the real source of the chaos lay not in the personality of the monarch but in the Frederician tradition of the genius statesman, in the notion that one man, be he king, emperor, quartermaster-general or "Führer", ought to be the soul fount of decision-making.' Jonathan Steinberg, 'The Tirpitz Plan', *The Historical Journal* 16.1 (1973), p. 198.

45 See for example the role of Ministerialdirektor Friedrich Althoff in the matter of appointments to the Prussian universities, to which Bernhard vom Brocke has drawn attention. Bernhard vom Brocke, 'Hochschul- und Wissenschaftspolitik in Preussen und im Deutschen Kaiserreich 1882–1907: Das "System Althoff"' in Peter Baumgart (ed.), *Bildungspolitik in Preussen zur Zeit des Kaiserreichs* (Stuttgart 1980), pp. 9–118. For a similar case in the area of painting, see Peter Paret, 'The Tschudi Affair', *Journal of Modern History* 53 (1981), pp. 589–618.

46 Norbert Elias, *Über den Prozess der Zivilisation. Soziogenetische und psychogenetische Untersuchungen*, 2 vols. (Bern 1969), II, pp. 236ff. The idea of applying the concept developed by Elias to the Wilhelmine system of government stems from Nicolaus Sombart. In the following pages I have slightly widened the concept in order to show the social and personal effects of the 'kingship mechanism' in the Kaiserreich.

47 Hull, *Entourage*, pp. 4ff *et passim*. See also Röhl, 'Introduction', in Röhl and Sombart, *Kaiser Wilhelm II*, pp. 11ff.

48 Brauer, 29 October 1891, Fuchs, no. 1137.

49 Brauer, 7 December 1890, Fuchs, no. 1088.

50 See Fuchs, III, p. 150.

51 See Fuchs, no. 1143 and no. 2118. See also Rolf Weitowitz, *Deutsche Politik und Handelspolitik unter Reichskanzler Leo von Caprivi, 1890–1894* (Düsseldorf 1978).

52 Jagemann, 10 March 1902, Fuchs, no. 2270.

53 Fuchs, no. 1559 and no. 1981. See above, pp. 114f.

54 Fuchs, no. 1559.

55 Fuchs, no. 1142.

56 Fuchs, no. 1340a and no. 1341.

57 Fuchs, no. 1354; see also nos. 1472, 1474 and also III, p. 453.

58 Fuchs, no. 1914.

59 See John C.G. Röhl, *Germany without Bismarck*, pp. 262f.

60 Fuchs, no. 1983.

61 Fuchs, no. 1526.
62 Fuchs, no. 1548; see also no. 2026. Jonathan Steinberg rightly emphasises the key role of the Kaiser and Senden-Bibran as initiators of the 'boundless' fleet plans. See J. Steinberg, *Yesterday's Deterrent. Tirpitz and the Birth of the German Battle Fleet* (London 1965).
63 Adolf Freiherr Marschall von Bieberstein, diary entry for 5 February 1895, quoted in Fuchs, III, p. 390.
64 Jagemann, 9 January 1895, Fuchs, no. 1407. See also Alfred von Tirpitz, *Erinnerungen* (Leipzig 1919), p. 80. See in addition the pathfinding works of Volker R. Berghahn, 'Zu den Zielen des deutschen Flottenbaus unter Wilhelm II.', *Historische Zeitschrift* 210 (February 1970), pp. 34–100, especially pp. 61f; Volker R. Berghahn, *Der Tirpitz-Plan. Genesis und Verfall einer innenpolitischen Krisenstrategie unter Wilhelm II.* (Düsseldorf 1971).
65 Fuchs, no. 1751.
66 Fuchs, no. 2025.
67 Fuchs, no. 2034.
68 Fuchs, no. 1999.
69 Fuchs, no. 2009.
70 Maximilian Harden, *Die Zukunft*, no. 40 (1902), p. 340. See also Fuchs, no. 1713.
71 Fuchs, no. 2042.
72 Fuchs, no. 2027.
73 See Ekkehard-Teja P.W. Wilke, *Political Decadence in Imperial Germany: Personal-political Aspects of the German Government Crisis 1894–1897* (Urbana, Chicago and London 1976); Hans Wilhelm Burmeister, *Prince Philipp Eulenburg-Hertefeld (1847–1921). His Influence on Kaiser Wilhelm II and his Role in the German Government, 1888–1902* (Wiesbaden 1981); G. David Fraley, 'Government by procrastination. Chancellor Hohenlohe and Kaiser Wilhelm II, 1894–1900', *Central European History* 7 (1974), pp. 159–83.
74 On Eulenburg's role in preparing Bülow's rise to power see chapter 2, above.
75 General Wilhelm von Hahnke to Carl Count von Wedel, January 1894, in the private possession of Count Gustav von Wedel, Frankfurt am Main.
76 Bülow's handwritten letter is reproduced in facsimile in Friedrich Thimme (ed.), *Front wider Bülow. Staatsmänner, Diplomaten und Forscher zu seinen Denkwürdigkeiten* (Munich 1931); see also Röhl, *Germany without Bismarck*, p. 194.
77 Brauer, 17 December 1890, Fuchs, no. 1089.
78 Brauer, 22 May 1892, Fuchs, no. 1184.
79 Jagemann, October 1895, Fuchs, no. 1486.
80 Marschall von Bieberstein, diary entry for 25 January 1896, cited in Fuchs, III, p. 497.
81 Bülow to Lindenau, 20 November 1897. Quoted in Kathy Lerman, 'The Decisive Relationship. Kaiser Wilhelm II and Chancellor Bernhard von Bülow 1900–1905' in Röhl and Sombart, *Kaiser Wilhelm II*, p. 223. See also K. A. Lerman, *The Chancellor as Courtier. Bernhard von Bülow and the Governance of Germany, 1900–1909*, (Cambridge 1990), p. 28.
82 Bülow to Holstein, 24 November 1899, quoted in Lerman, 'The Decisive Relationship', p. 227.
83 Fuchs, no. 2182.
84 Fuchs, no. 2366.

85 Fuchs, no. 2370.
86 Brauer, 2 December 1904, Fuchs, no. 2490.
87 Berckheim, 10 November 1906, Fuchs, IV, p. 662.
88 Berckheim, 14 December 1906, Fuchs, no. 2593.
89 Brauer, 26 February 1892, Fuchs, no. 1159.
90 Brauer, 4 June 1892, Fuchs, no. 1187.
91 Brauer, 17 and 20 November 1892, Fuchs, nos. 1210, 1211.
92 Brauer, 5 January 1893, Fuchs, no. 1218.
93 Brauer, 6 November 1892, Fuchs, no. 1207.
94 Brauer, 20 August 1896, Fuchs, no. 1576.
95 Tirpitz to Grand Duke, 14 November 1897, Fuchs, no. 1775; see above, p. 122.
96 Brauer, 1 April 1892, Fuchs, no. 1178.
97 Jagemann, 29 October 1894, Fuchs, no. 1377.
98 Jagemann, 26 October 1898, Fuchs, no. 1905.
99 Brauer, 3 February 1891, Fuchs, no. 1099.
100 Marschall von Bieberstein, diary entry for 11 June 1895, Fuchs, III, p. 526.
101 Ibid., 15 August 1896, Fuchs, III, p. 549.
102 Fuchs, no. 1631.
103 Jagemann, 5 May 1901, Fuchs, no. 2181.
104 Jagemann, 18 April 1899 and 18 May 1903, Fuchs, no. 1975a and no. 2415.
105 Bülow to Eisendecher, 12 March 1903, Fuchs, no. 2400.
106 Berckheim, 26 June 1907, Fuchs, no. 2640.
107 Berckheim, 13 October 1905, Fuchs, no. 2524.
108 Jagemann, 11 March 1901, Fuchs, no. 2157.
109 Holstein to Eulenburg, 21 February 1895, *Eulenburgs Korrespondenz*, no. 1093.
110 Jagemann, 5 May 1901, Fuchs, no. 2181.
111 Brauer, 16 February 1892, Fuchs, no. 1154.
112 Ibid.
113 Brauer, 10 January 1893, Fuchs, no. 1219.
114 Brauer, 6 March 1892, Fuchs, no. 1163. See above p. 96.
115 See chapter 3, above.
116 Hull, *Entourage*, pp. 15ff *et passim*.
117 *Eulenburgs Korrespondenz*, II, p. 953.
118 See Fritz Friedman, *Der Deutsche Kaiser und die Hofkamarilla*. I. *Der Fall Kotze*. II. *Wilhelm II. und die Revolution von oben* (Zürich 1896).
119 Philipp Eulenburg, 'Aufzeichnungen', I, pp. 55f, Haus Hertefeld; see also John C.G. Röhl, 'The Emperor's New Clothes. A Character Sketch of Kaiser Wilhelm II' in Röhl and Sombart, *Kaiser Wilhelm II*, p. 45.
120 Hohenlohe to Lucanus, 28 May 1897. See now John C.G. Röhl, *Wilhelm II. Die Jugend des Kaisers 1859–1888* (Munich 1993), p. 467.
121 Berckheim, 8 November 1906, Fuchs, no. 2583; Bodman, 15 November 1906, Fuchs, no. 2584.
122 Eisendecher, 12 May 1901, Fuchs, no. 2187.
123 Grand Duke to Bülow, 18 May 1901, Fuchs, no. 2190.
124 Kaiser Wilhelm II to Max Egon Fürst zu Fürstenberg, 5 October 1907, Fürstlich Fürstenbergisches Archiv, Donaueschingen.
125 When news of the death of the Grand Duke reached The Hague, Marschall von Bieberstein noted in his diary (28 September 1907): 'Deeply saddened. He was a

wonderful man.' At the time of writing the diary was in the possession of Marschall's daughter, Frau von Seyfried, of Oberkirch in Baden.

126 Brauer, 9 March 1892, Fuchs, no. 1164.

127 Bodman, 4 March 1897, Fuchs, no. 1654. See also the impressive letter which Monts wrote to Philipp Eulenburg on 20/21 March 1897 on the evident mental illness of the Kaiser, cited above, p. 22.

128 Bodman, 7 March 1897, Fuchs, no. 1657.

129 Jagemann, 18 May 1897, Fuchs, no. 1694.

130 Bülow, memorandum of 7 April 1897 on discussions with Eulenburg; Bülow to Eulenburg, 22 November 1900. Both documents are printed in *Eulenburgs Korrespondenz*, nos. 1312 and 1439. It is clear from Marschall's diary that the Grand Duke entirely shared the fears about the Kaiser's mental condition. On 24 March 1897 he wrote: 'He [the Grand Duke] sees things very clearly and he too has psychological worries.' Fuchs, III, p. 626; see above, p. 22.

131 See Nicolaus Sombart, 'The Kaiser in his epoch' in Röhl and Sombart, *Kaiser Wilhelm II*, pp. 287–311.

132 Bülow's speech of 21 January 1903, quoted from the stenographic reports of the Reichstag debates by Elisabeth Fehrenbach, *Wandlungen des deutschen Kaisergedankens, 1871–1918* (Munich and Vienna 1969), p. 130. Bülow expressed himself in a very similar vein in a speech in the Reichstag on 14 November 1906.

5 HIGHER CIVIL SERVANTS IN WILHELMINE GERMANY

1 Approximately a quarter of the candidates failed the simple writing and mathematical examination which was introduced in Great Britain by an 'Order in Council' in 1855. See W.A. Robson (ed.), *The Civil Service in Britain and France* (London 1956), p. 35.

2 Heinrich von Treitschke, *Aufsätze, Reden und Briefe*, IV (Merseburg 1919), pp. 54–8.

3 Quoted in R.J. Lamer, *Der englische Parlamentarismus in der politischen Theorie im Zeitalter Bismarcks 1857–1890* (Lübeck and Hamburg 1963), p. 79.

4 Alfred von Tirpitz, *Erinnerungen* (Leipzig 1919), p. 34.

5 Gustav von Schmoller, *Zwanzig Jahre Deutscher Politik 1897–1917. Aufsätze und Vorträge* (Munich, Leipzig 1920), p. 188.

6 See Hans-Jürgen Puhle, *Agrarische Interessenpolitik und preussischer Konservatismus* (Hanover 1967).

7 Zentrales Staatsarchiv (ZStA) Merseburg, Rep. 89H, XXI, Deutsches Reich, 1.

8 Max Weber, 'Parlament und Regierung im neugeordneten Deutschland' in J. Winkelmann (ed.), *Gesammelte politische Schriften* (Tübingen 1958), pp. 328–30.

9 According to the census of 1907, over one million state servants had the right to use the title 'official' (*Beamte*) but this included policemen, teachers and post and railway officials. Officials in the narrower sense, including judges and public prosecutors, numbered 390,000. See Otto Hintze, 'Der Beamtenstand' in *Soziologie und Geschichte* (Göttingen 1964), p. 68. The number of higher officials in the central departments in Berlin, i.e. those carrying the rank of Vortragender Rat or above, was by comparison very small: approximately 200 in the Prussian

Ministries and 120 in the Reich Offices in the 1890s. This chapter is concerned primarily with this group of no more than 400.

10 Rudolf Morsey, *Die oberste Reichsverwaltung unter Bismarck 1867–1890* (Münster 1957), p. 251.

11 ZStA Merseburg, Minutes of the Prussian Ministry of State meeting of 29 June 1895.

12 Commission Reports of 31 July 1898 and 3 September 1900. ZStA Potsdam, Reichskanzlei, no. 1903.

13 Herman Finer, *The Theory and Practice of Modern Government* (London 1947), p. 1261.

14 According to.the Northcote–Trevelyan Reforms of the British civil service (1870), all candidates had to be between twenty-two and twenty-four years of age. In Britain it did not matter what subject had been studied at university. A useful introduction to the contemporary debate is Valerie Cromwell, 'Interpretations of Nineteenth-Century Administration. An Analysis' in *Victorian Studies* (March 1966), pp. 245–55. See also Zara S. Steiner, *The Foreign Office and Foreign Policy, 1898–1914* (Cambridge 1969).

15 In the Bismarck era five of the 23 secretaries of state and 26 of the 167 Vortragende Räte had law doctorates (Morsey, *Reichsverwaltung*, p. 250). Of the 113 Vortragende Räte in the Reich administration, 30 had this academic rank in 1895. Almost a half of the officials in the Reich Justice Office, a third in the Foreign Office and in the Reich Office of the Interior, and a quarter in the Reich Treasury Office, Reich Navy Office and Reich Railway Office had law doctorates. See G. von Schmoller, 'Zur Frage der Einrichtung des akademischen Studiums, hauptsächlich der Juristen' (1886) in *Zwanzig Jahre*, pp. 191ff.

16 Anon., Die *Zukunft des preussischen Staatseisenbahn- und Staatsbauwesens und ihrer höheren Beamten, von Einem Freunde Derselben* (Leipzig 1892), p. 17.

17 Chlodwig Fürst zu Hohenlohe-Schillingsfürst, *Denkwürdigkeiten der Reichskanzlerzeit* (Stuttgart 1931), p. 290.

18 B.W. von König, *Handbuch des Deutschen Konsularwesens* (Berlin 1896), pp. 45ff.

19 ZStA Potsdam, Reichskanzlei, no. 1903. Memorandum of 8 May 1908.

20 Morsey, *Reichsverwaltung*, p. 246.

21 Brauer, report no. 71, 13 November 1891. Generallandesarchiv (GLA) Karlsruhe, 49/8. The Kaiser had the right to dismiss anyone who married a foreigner. Under Bismarck no use was made of this right, but in 1891 Kaiser Wilhelm II dismissed Baron von Mentzingen, Counsellor of Legation in Brussels, as he had married the Belgian Countess Liedekerke. It was only in 1895 that he lifted his Order and so allowed Mentzingen to be appointed to Buenos Aires. A similar case is described by G.W.F. Hallgarten, *Imperialismus vor 1914* (Munich 1951), I, p. 414.

22 Morsey, *Reichsverwaltung*, p. 246. The diplomat Alfred von Kiderlen-Wächter received a letter in 1895 from a fellow member of his student corporation with the question whether – if one wished to enter the consular service – it was advisable to go to any particular university, whether substantial private means or a doctorate were necessary and whether this career would be a difficult one without connections. The diplomat's reply has unfortunately not survived. Curt Weinert to Kiderlen, 28 March 1895, ZStA Merseburg, Kiderlen Papers.

23 Eulenburg to Herbert Graf von Bismarck, 9 October 1887; Herbert Bismarck to

Eulenburg, 11 October 1887, Bundesarchiv (BA) Koblenz, Eulenburg Papers, 2, 60–2.

24 G.W.F. Hegel, *Grundlinien der Philosophie des Rechts*, (Berlin, 1821) § 291.

25 ZStA Merseburg, Rep. 89H, VII Deutsches Reich I, vol. 1. The comment referred to Dr Paul Ernst von Koerner, 1881–91 in the Saxon Finance Ministry, 1891–5 Deputy Saxon Plenipotentiary in the Bundesrat, from 1895 Ministerial Director in the Reich Treasury Office.

26 Oelschläger to Caprivi, 29 March 1892, ZStA Potsdam, Reichskanzlei, no. 1616.

27 Jagemann's report no. 133, 30 November 1895. GLA Karlsruhe, 49/14; Brauer's report no. 3, 16 November 1890, ibid., 49/7; Jagemann's report no. 144, 30 September 1897, ibid., 49/16.

28 Berchem to Caprivi, 10 March 1894. ZStA Potsdam, Reichskanzlei, no. 1443.

29 See John C.G. Röhl, 'Friedrich von Holstein' *Historical Journal* 9 (1966), p. 354.

30 Eugen von Jagemann, *75 Jahre des Erlebens und Erfahrens* (Heidelberg 1925), p. 146.

31 Eulenburg to Herbert Bismarck, 20 March 1888, BA Koblenz, Eulenburg Papers 3, 98–9.

32 Oelschläger to Caprivi, 29 February 1892, ZStA Potsdam, Reichskanzlei, no. 1616.

33 Rudolf Vierhaus (ed.), *Das Tagebuch der Baronin Spitzemberg* (Göttingen 1960), p. 327.

34 Hohenlohe, *Denkwürdigkeiten der Reichskanzlerzeit*, p. 474.

35 Julius Bachem, *Erinnerungen eines alten Publizisten und Politikers* (Cologne 1913), p. 38; J. Bachem, *Die Parität in Preussen* (Cologne 1899).

36 Karl Bachem, *Vorgeschichte, Geschichte und Politik der deutschen Zentrumspartei*, 9 vols., IX (Cologne 1932), pp. 67f. Bachem mistakenly states that Brefeld was a Catholic and he fails to mention either Maybach or Hanauer.

37 ZStA Merseburg, Rep. 89H, II Preussen I, vol. III; VII Preussen I, vols. X and XI.

38 Ibid., IX Gen. I, vols. VI, VII and VIII.

39 P.G.J. Pulzer, *The Rise of Political Anti Semitism in Germany and Austria* (London 1964), p. 12.

40 Robert Graf von Zedlitz-Trützschler, *Zwölf Jahre am deutschen Kaiserhof* (Berlin 1924), pp. 187f.

41 F. von Holstein, *Die Geheimen Papiere Friedrich von Holstein*, 4 vols. (Göttingen, Berlin and Frankfurt 1956–63), IV, p. 472.

42 Alexander von Hohenlohe, *Aus meinem Leben* (Frankfurt am Main. 1925), p. 328.

43 Walter Frank, 'Der Geheime Rat Paul Kayser', *Historische Zeitschrift*, 168 (1943), p. 326.

44 Chlodwig Fürst zu Hohenlohe-Schillingsfürst, *Denkwürdigkeiten*, 2 vols. (Stuttgart 1907), II, p. 440. See however Hohenlohe, *Denkwürdigkeiten der Reichskanzlerzeit*, p. 481.

45 Robert Bosse, diary entry for 5 December 1895, BA Koblenz; Marschall, diary entry for 27 May 1896, Politisches Archiv des Auswörtigen Amtes (PA) Bonn. Bitter became Director in the Prussian Ministry of the Interior in 1898 and *Oberpräsident* of Posen in 1899.

46 *Eulenburgs Korrespondenz*, no. 625; Holstein, *Geheime Papiere*, I, p. 148.

47 Eulenburg to Holstein, 9 February 1892, *Eulenburgs Korrespondenz*, no. 584; Oelschläger to Caprivi, 29 March 1892, ZStA Potsdam, Reichskanzlei, no. 1616.

48 Hohenlohe, *Denkwürdigkeiten*, II, p. 449.

49 ZStA Merseburg, minutes of the Prussian Ministry of State, 12 December 1895.

50 Maximilian Harden, *Köpfe: Porträts, Briefe und Dokumente*, new ed., H.-J. Fröhlich (Hamburg 1963), p. 42; see also Tirpitz, *Erinnerungen*, p. 34.

51 See above, p. 106.

52 E. Heilborn, *Zwischen zwei Revolutionen* (Berlin 1929), II, pp. 214f.

53 See above pp. 236f.

54 ZStA Merseburg, Rep. 89H, XXI, Appendix; Beistücke zu Büroakten no. 101.

55 Holstein, *Geheime Papiere*, III, p. 511.

56 ZStA Potsdam, Reichskanzlei, no. 1630. As he feared that 'von Schulz' would sound strange, he added his wife's maiden name to his own and from then on called himself 'von Schulz-Hausmann'. See in general Lamar Cecil, 'The Creation of Nobles in Prussia, 1871–1918' *American Historical Review* 75 (1970), pp. 757–95.

57 ZStA Merseburg, Rep. 89H, XXI, Gen. I, vol. XI.

58 Wilmowski's personal file, BA Koblenz, R43/I 3627; Lysbeth W. Muncy, *The Junkers in the Prussian Administration under William II, 1888–1914* (Providence, Rhode Island 1944), p. 97; Hallgarten, *Imperialismus*, I, p. 422. See also Tilo Freiherr von Wilmowski, *Rückblickend möchte ich sagen ...* (Oldenburg and Hamburg 1961).

59 Ludwig Raschdau, *Unter Bismarck und Caprivi* (Berlin 1939), p. 87.

60 Peter Rassow and Karl-Erich Born (eds.), *Akten zur staatlichen Sozialpolitik in Deutschland* (Wiesbaden 1959), p. 134.

61 On the question whether Holstein speculated on the stock exchange, see Norman Rich, *Friedrich von Holstein*, 2 vols. (Cambridge 1965), I, pp. 49–59. Hatzfeldt would no doubt have become secretary of state in the Foreign Office in 1890 if his finances had been in a more healthy condition. See Raschdau, *Unter Bismarck und Caprivi*, p. 207. Boetticher would have resigned when his father-in-law Berg suffered financial embarrassment after borrowing a large sum of money had not Bismarck helped him out with money from the Guelph fund. In 1891 Bismarck made this public and thereby almost brought about Boetticher's fall. Caprivi observed that Boetticher had acted properly 'as a man' but not 'as a civil servant'. BA Koblenz, Bosse Diary, 24 March, 25 April, 24 and 27 May 1891.

62 ZStA Merseburg, Rep. 89H, II Preussen I, vol. III. See Minutes of the Prussian Ministry of State, 26 January 1897, 16 April 1898 and 28 April 1900.

63 This policy was sharpened still further after the appointment of Robert von Puttkamer as Prussian Minister of the Interior in 1881. When Kleist-Retzow heard that Bismarck was considering appointing a Liberal to this post, he wrote: 'Dear Otto! ... Please, don't do that. The Ministry of the Interior must have an Old Prussian who is respected as a Conservative and who will favour the aristocracy.' Kleist-Retzow to Bismarck, 28 February 1881, ZStA Potsdam, Reichskanzlei, no. 1457. See Helmut Böhme, *Deutschlands Weg zur Grossmacht* (Cologne 1966), p. 567; Eckart Kehr, 'Das soziale System der Reaktion in Preussen unter dem Ministerium Puttkamer', reprinted in Kehr, *Der Primat der Innenpolitik*, ed. Hans-Ulrich Wehler (Berlin 1965), pP. 64ff. See also John Gillis, 'Aristocracy and Bureaucracy in Prussia', *Past and Present* 41 (1968), pp. 105–29.

64 Herrfurth to Lucanus, 20 June 1891, ZStA Potsdam, Reichskanzlei, no. 1445; Böhme, *Deutschlands Weg*, p. 582.

65 Fritz Hartung, 'Studien zur Geschichte der preussischen Verwaltung' in *Staats-bildende Kräfte der Neuzeit* (Berlin 1961), p. 336; Peter Molt, *Der Reichstag vor der improvisierten Revolution* (Cologne 1963), p. 143; Morsey, *Reichsverwaltung*, p. 246.

66 Seven of the twelve worked in the Reich Office of the Interior, three in the small Reich Justice Office. There were no nobles at all in the Reich Navy Office or the Reich Post Office. In Prussia the Ministry of the Interior had the highest percentage of aristocrats: a third of the higher officials there were nobles. The Ministries of Finance, Public Works and Justice were almost totally manned by commoners.

67 Quoted in Molt, *Reichstag*, p. 142.

68 Rassow and Born, Akten, p. 146; see also P. Duggan, 'Stimoli di riforma nell'am-ministrazione prussiana durante la coalizione Buelow (1907–1909)', *Rivista Storica Italiana*, 81/2.

69 Hartung, *Staatsbildende Kräfte*, pp. 248ff; Molt, *Reichstag*, pp. 139ff; James J. Sheehan, 'Political Leadership in the German Reichstag, 1871–1918' *American Historical Review* 74/2 (1968), p. 518.

70 ZStA Merseburg, Minutes of the Prussian Ministry of State, 16 October 1891; Caprivi to state secretaries of the Reich Offices, 31 October 1891, based on Goering's memorandum of 20 October 1891, ZStA Potsdam, Reichskanzlei, no. 1423. The Reich Justice Office warned the Chancellor that the prohibition was unconstitutional. BA Koblenz, Bosse Diary, 29 October 1891.

71 ZStA Merseburg, Minutes of the Prussian Ministry of State, 18 December 1893 and 26 May 1894; see also Duggan, 'Stimoli di riforma', p. 336.

72 ZStA Merseburg, Minutes of the Prussian Ministry of State, 25 February 1896, 2 April 1898, 20, 21, 28, 31 August, 21 September 1899, 28 February 1900. The case of Dr Schilling is interesting. He lost his post as Landrat in Liegnitz because, as a Conservative, he cast his vote against the Canal Bill in 1899. In June 1900 Hammerstein, with the agreement of the Prussian Ministry of State, proposed him as a Vortragender Rat in the Prussian Ministry of Agriculture. Wilhelm II was not impressed by the fact that Schilling had given up his post as Landrat, and insisted on hearing more about his conduct. When Hammerstein and Rheinbaben replied that it could be assumed that Schilling 'would be loyal to the throne', the Kaiser wrote: 'I very much advise him to be, because otherwise the devil will take him! ... The Ministers must not simply assume, as their superiors they must ensure that those gentlemen who through My Royal Grace are reappointed avoid all such impertinences in future. I hold them responsible for that on pain of losing their heads.' ZStA Merseburg, Rep. 89H, Gen. I, vol. v.

73 In the course of the colonial scandals of 1906 it became known that Podbielski was closely involved with the firm of Tippelskirch and had transferred 10,000 marks to his wife's bank account. Lerchenfeld's Report, no. 531, 9 November 1906, Bayerisches Hauptstaatsarchiv Munich, B 4 MA III. 2684. Podbielski was forced to resign.

74 Hans Hermann Freiherr von Berlepsch (Trade), Wilhelm von Heyden-Cadow (Agriculture), Robert Graf von Zedlitz-Trützschler (Ecclesiastical Affairs and Education), Botho Graf zu Eulenburg (Prussian Minister-President and Inter-ior), Eberhard Freiherr von der Recke von dem Horst (Interior), Georg Freiherr von Rheinbaben (Interior) und Konrad von Studt (Ecclesiastical Affairs and Education).

75 Holstein's memorandum of 10 November 1890, printed in *Eulenburgs Korrespondenz*, no. 318. See also Röhl, *Germany without Bismarck*, p. 43.
76 The most blatant case was the appointment of Count von Zedlitz-Trützschler as Prussian Minister of Education in 1891; he had not even passed the *Abitur*. Siegfried von Kardorff, *Wilhelm von Kardorff* (Berlin 1936), p. 237.
77 Hohenlohe, *Denkwürdigkeiten*, p. 524.

6 THE SPLENDOUR AND IMPOTENCE OF THE GERMAN DIPLOMATIC SERVICE

1 Bülow to Eulenburg, 7 February 1895, in *Eulenburgs Korrespondenz*, II, pp. 1454f.
2 Hans von Herwarth, *Zwischen Hitler und Stalin. Erlebte Zeitgeschichte 1931–1945* (Frankfurt 1982), pp. 239f.
3 See Kurt Doss, 'Vom Kaiserreich zur Weimarer Republik. Das deutsche diplomatische Korps in einer Epoche des Umbruchs'; Peter Krüger, 'Struktur, Organisation und aussenpolitische Wirkungsmöglichkeiten der leitenden Beamten des Auswärtigen Dienstes 1921–1933' in Klaus Schwabe (ed.), *Das Diplomatische Korps 1871–1945* (Boppard-am-Rhein 1985), pp. 81–100 and pp. 101–69.
4 See Lamar Cecil, *The German Diplomatic Service 1871–1914* (Princeton 1976), pp. 30, 42.
5 *Eulenburgs Korrespondenz*, III, no. 1582.
6 Valerie Cromwell and Zara Steiner, 'Reform and Retrenchment: The Foreign Office between the Wars' in Roger Bullen (ed.), *The Foreign Office. A Bicentennial Study* (London 1985).
7 Cecil, *German Diplomatic Service*, p. 42. Hans-Jürgen Döscher, *Das Auswärtige Amt im Dritten Reich. Diplomatie im Schatten der 'Endlösung'* (Berlin 1987), pp. 44ff.
8 See the tables presented by Lamar Cecil and Peter Krüger, in Schwabe, *Das Diplomatische Korps*, pp. 23f and p. 167.
9 Hans-Adolf Jacobsen, 'Zur Rolle der Diplomatie im 3. Reich' in Schwabe, *Das Diplomatische Korps*, p. 182. According to the testimony of L. von Keller, 122 of the 611 diplomats in the Third Reich were nobles. See Jacobsen, 'Rolle der Diplomatie', note 22. The German Foreign Office and diplomatic service of the National Socialist era has now been closely investigated on the basis of captured German documents in American archives. See Hans-Jürgen Döscher, *Das Auswärtige Amt im Dritten Reich. Diplomatie im Schatten der 'Endlösung'* (Berlin 1987).
10 Quoted in Doss, 'Vom Kaiserreich zur Weimarer Republik', p. 100.
11 See in particular Walter Bussmann (ed.), *Graf Herbert von Bismarck. Aus seiner politischen Privatkorrespondenz* (Göttingen 1974); Norman Rich and M.H. Fisher (eds.), *The Holstein Papers. The Memoirs, Diaries and Correspondence of Friedrich von Holstein*, 4 vols. (Cambridge 1955–63); Ernst Deuerlein (ed.), *Briefwechsel Hertling-Lerchenfeld 1912–1917*, 2 vols. (Boppard-am-Rhein 1973); Gerhard Ebel (ed.), *Botschafter Graf Paul von Hatzfeldt. Nachgelassene Papiere 1838–1901*, 2 vols. (Boppard-am-Rhein 1976); Walther Peter Fuchs (ed.), *Grossherzog Friedrich I von Baden und die Reichspolitik 1871–1907*, 4 vols. (Karlsruhe 1968–80); John C. G. Röhl (ed.), *Philipp Eulenburgs Politische Korrespondenz*, 3 vols. (Boppard-am-Rhein 1976–83).

12 Krüger, 'Struktur, Organisation und aussenpolitische Wirkungsmöglichkeiten der leitenden Beamten', p. 120. Of eighty-six diplomats recruited during the Weimar Republic for whom Döscher found evidence, seventy-two (83.7%) were Lutheran and eleven (12.8%) Roman Catholic. See Döscher, *Das Auswärtige Amt*, p. 42.

13 Cecil, *German Diplomatic Service*, pp. 72, 99f, 103.

14 Ibid., pp. 177ff.

15 Lamar Cecil provides a detailed analysis of these recruitment criteria. Ibid., pp. 21–78.

16 See Lamar Cecil, 'Der diplomatische Dienst im Kaiserlichen Deutschland' in Schwabe, *Das Diplomatische Korps*, p. 29.

17 Krüger, in Schwabe, ibid., p. 120.

18 See chapter 3, above.

19 See especially Karl Demeter, *Das deutsche Offizierskorps in Gesellschaft und Staat 1650–1945*, 4th edn (Frankfurt 1965).

20 See chapter 5, above.

21 See Holger H. Herwig, *The German Naval Officer Corps. A Social and Political History 1890–1918* (Oxford 1973).

22 Quoted in Doss, 'Vom Kaiserreich zur Weimarer Republik', p. 86. See also Döscher, *Das Auswärtige Amt*, pp. 18–50.

23 Cecil, *German Diplomatic Service*, p. 67.

24 On this controversial issue, see the study by David Blackbourn and Geoff Eley, *Mythen deutscher Geschichtsschreibung. Die gescheiterte bürgerliche Revolution von 1848* (Frankfurt am Main 1980), now expanded and translated as *The Peculiarities of German History: Bourgeois Society and Politics in Nineteenth-Century Germany* (Oxford and New York 1984).

25 See Cromwell and Steiner, *Foreign Office*.

26 The memoirs of Axel Varnbüler, which are still in private possession, are highly revealing in this respect.

27 Cecil, *German Diplomatic Service*, p. 34.

28 *Eulenburgs Korrespondenz*, II, p. 845.

29 See above, note 11.

30 Doss, 'Vom Kaiserreich zur Weimarer Republik', pp. 89f.

31 See for example Andrew Sinclair, *The Other Victoria* (London 1981). Also John C. G. Röhl, *Wilhelm II. Die Jugend des Kaisers* (Munich 1993), p. 542.

32 Quoted in Cecil, *German Diplomatic Service*, p. 230.

33 *Eulenburgs Korrespondenz*, II, p. 953. See above, p. 16.

34 Robert Graf von Zedlitz-Trützschler, *Zwölf Jahre am deutschen Kaiserhof*, 2nd edn (Stuttgart 1924), pp. 216ff. See above, p. 16.

35 Quoted in John C. G. Röhl, *Germany without Bismarck. The Crisis of Government in the Second Reich 1890–1900* (London 1967), p. 194.

36 See the evidence presented in chapter 1 above.

37 Walter Görlitz (ed.), *Der Kaiser ... Aufzeichnungen des Chefs des Marinekabinetts Admiral Georg Alexander von Müller über die Aera Wilhelms II.* (Göttingen 1965), p. 109.

38 See chapter 4, above.

39 See John C. G. Röhl, *1914 – Delusion or Design? The Testimony of Two German Diplomats* (London 1973), pp. 41ff.

40 Cecil, 'Der diplomatische Dienst im Kaiserlichen Deutschland', pp. 15f.
41 Quoted in Cecil, *German Diplomatic Service*, p. 245.
42 Helmuth Rogge, 'Die Kladderadatschaffäre' in *Historische Zeitschrift* 195 (1962), pp. 90–130.
43 *Eulenburgs Korrespondenz*, no. 966 and no. 1007. See above, pp. 42f.
44 See Karl Dietrich Erdmann, 'Zur Echtheit der Tagebücher Kurt Riezlers. Eine Antikritik', *Historische Zeitschrift* 236 (1983), pp. 371–402.
45 See Jacobsen, 'Zur Rolle der Diplomatie im 3. Reich', p. 178. Döscher, *Das Auswärtige Amt im Dritten Reich, passim*.
46 Jacobsen, 'Zur Rolle der Diplomatie im 3. Reich', pp. 189f. Döscher, *Das Auswärtige Amt im Dritten Reich*, pp. 103ff.
47 Christopher R. Browning, *The Final Solution and the German Foreign Office. A Study of Referat D III of Abteilung Deutschland 1940–43* (New York 1978); Browning, 'Unterstaatssekretär Martin Luther and the Ribbentrop Foreign Office', *Journal of Contemporary History* 12 (1977), pp. 313–44. Döscher, *Das Auswärtige Amt im Dritten Reich*, pp. 213ff. Jacobsen, 'Zur Rolle der Diplomatie im 3. Reich', p. 180.

7 DRESS REHEARSAL IN DECEMBER: MILITARY DECISION-MAKING IN GERMANY ON THE EVE OF THE FIRST WORLD WAR

1 On the controversy on the so-called 'war council' of 8 December 1912, see: Fritz Fischer, *Krieg der Illusionen* (Düsseldorf 1969), pp. 231ff; Adolf Gasser, 'Der deutsche Hegemonialkrieg von 1914' in Imanuel Geiss and Bernd-Jürgen Wendt (eds.), *Deutschland in der Weltpolitik des 19. und 20. Jahrhunderts. Festschrift für Fritz Fischer* (Düsseldorf 1973), pp. 307ff; Adolf Gasser, 'Erster Weltkrieg und "Friedensforschung"', *Allgemeine Schweizerische Militärzeitschrift* 140 (1974), pp. 235ff; Adolf Gasser, *Preussischer Militärgeist und Kriegsentfesselung 1914. Drei Studien zum Ausbruch des Ersten Weltkrieges* (Basel and Frankfurt 1985); Imanuel Geiss, *German Foreign Policy 1871–1914* (London 1976), pp. 142ff; John C.G. Röhl, *1914: Delusion or Design? The Testimony of Two German Diplomats* (London 1973), pp. 28ff; John C. G. Röhl, 'Admiral von Müller and the Approach of War, 1911–1914' *The Historical Journal* 12 (1969), pp. 651ff; John C. G. Röhl, 'An der Schwelle zum Weltkrieg: Eine Dokumentation über den "Kriegsrat" vom 8. Dezember 1912' *Militärgeschichtliche Mitteilungen* (1977), pp. 77–134; John C. G. Röhl, 'Die Generalprobe. Zur Geschichte und Bedeutung des "Kriegsrates" vom 8. Dezember 1912' in D. Stegmann, B.-J.Wendt and P.-C. Witt (eds.), *Industrielle Gesellschaft und politisches System* (Bonn 1978), pp. 357–73; L.C.F. Turner, 'The Edge of the Precipice. A Comparison between November 1912 and July 1914' *Royal Military College Historical Journal* 3 (1974), p. 18; L.C.F. Turner, in *The Australian Journal of Politics and History*, 20 (1974), pp. 121ff; L.C.F. Turner, *Origins of the First World War* (London 1970), p. 49; Klaus Hildebrand, in *Historische Zeitschrift* 223 (1976), p. 478; see also Klaus Hildebrand, 'Imperialismus, Wettrüsten und Kriegsausbruch 1914', *Neue Politische Literatur* 20 (1975), pp. 160ff; Winfried Baumgart, in *Historisches Jahrbuch der Görres-Gesellschaft* 93 (1973), pp. 471ff; Wolfgang J. Mommsen, 'Domestic Factors in German Foreign Policy before

1914', *Central European History* 6 (1973), pp. 12f; Wolfgang J. Mommsen, 'Die latente Krise des Deutschen Reiches 1909–1914' in *Handbuch zur Deutschen Geschichte. Deutsche Geschichte der neuesten Zeit von Bismarcks Entlassung bis zur Gegenwart*, part 1. *Von 1890–1933.* Section 1a (Frankfurt 1973), pp. 56f; Wolfgang J. Mommsen, 'The Topos of Inevitable War in Germany in the Decade before 1914' in Volker R. Berghahn and Martin Kitchen (eds.), *Germany in the Age of Total War. Essays in Honour of Francis Carsten* (London 1981); Wolfgang J. Mommsen, 'Kaiser Wilhelm II and German Politics', *Journal of Contemporary History* 25, nos. 2–3 (May–June 1990), pp. 307f.; Egmont Zechlin, 'Die Adriakrise und der "Kriegsrat" vom 8. Dezember 1912' in *Krieg und Kriegsrisiko. Zur deutschen Politik im Ersten Weltkrieg* (Düsseldorf 1979), pp. 115–59; Erwin Hölzle, *Die Selbstentmachtung Europas. Das Experiment des Friedens vor und im Ersten Weltkrieg* (Göttingen 1975), pp. 180ff; Willibald Gutsche, 'Probleme des Verhältnisses zwischen Monopolkapital und Staat in Deutschland vom Ende des 19. Jahrhunderts bis zum Vorabend des Ersten Weltkrieges' in Fritz Klein (ed.), *Studien zum deutschen Imperialismus vor 1914* (Berlin 1976), p. 66; Volker R. Berghahn, *Germany and the Approach of War in 1914* (London 1973), pp. 165ff; Bernd-Felix Schulte, *Die Deutsche Armee 1900–1914. Zwischen Beharren und Verändern* (Düsseldorf 1977); Bernd-Felix Schulte, *Vor dem Kriegsausbruch 1914. Deutschland, die Türkei und der Balkan* (Düsseldorf 1980), pp. 8ff, pp. 75–122; Bernd-Felix Schulte, *Europäische Krise und Erster Weltkrieg. Beiträge zur Militärpolitik des Kaiserreichs, 1871–1914* (Frankfurt and Bern 1983), *passim*; Bernd-Felix Schulte, 'Zu der Krisenkonferenz vom 8. Dezember 1912', *Historisches Jahrbuch* 102 (1982), pp. 183–97; Isabel V. Hull, *The Entourage of Kaiser Wilhelm II, 1888–1918* (Cambridge 1982), pp. 248–53; Ivo Nikolai Lambi, *The Navy and German Power Politics 1862–1914* (Boston 1984), pp. 382ff; Stig Förster, *Der Doppelte Militarismus. Die Deutsche Heeresrüstungspolitik zwischen Status-quo-Sicherung und Aggression 1890–1913* (Stuttgart 1985), pp. 252–7; Wilhelm Deist, 'Kaiser Wilhelm II. als Oberster Kriegsherr' in John C. G. Röhl, *Der Ort Kaiser Wilhelms II. in der deutschen Geschichte* (Munich 1991), pp. 34ff; Terence F. Cole, 'German Decision-Making on the Eve of the First World War: The Records of the Swiss Embassy in Berlin' in Röhl, *Der Ort Kaiser Wilhelms II.*, pp. 62ff; R.J.W. Evans and Hartmut Pogge von Strandmann (eds.), *The Coming of the First World War* (Oxford 1988), pp. 6, 112f *et passim*.

2 Müller, diary entry for 8 December 1912, BA-MA Freiburg. Printed in Röhl, 'An der Schwelle', document no. 4. Cf. the previously published version in Walter Görlitz (ed.), *Der Kaiser ... Aufzeichnungen des Chefs des Marinekabinetts Admiral Georg Alexander von Müller über die Ära Wilhelms II.* (Göttingen 1965), pp. 124f.

3 The words 'the sooner the better' were inserted by Müller in his own hand between the original lines. It is not clear from the manuscript when this insertion was made.

4 Görlitz, *Der Kaiser*, pp. 124f. For a critical assessment of the Görlitz edition of the Müller diary in general, see John C. G. Röhl, 'Admiral von Müller and the Approach of War, 1911–1914', *The Historical Journal* 12 (1969), pp. 651–73.

5 Müller to Bethmann, 8 December 1912, Röhl, 'An der Schwelle', document no. 5.

6 Röhl, 'An der Schwelle', document no. 14. Leuckart's report was first discovered

by Volker R. Berghahn in the Staatsarchiv, Dresden, and was first published in Röhl, 'Admiral von Müller', p. 662.

7 Röhl, 'An der Schwelle', document no. 22.

8 Albert Hopman, diary entry for 9 December 1912, BA-MA Freiburg, Hopman Papers, N326/12. Printed in Schulte, 'Zu der Krisenkonferenz vom 8. Dezember 1912 in Berlin', *Historisches Jahrbuch der Görres-Gesellschaft* 102 (1982), p. 196. It is quite probable that the Chief of the Military Cabinet von Lyncker was present at the meeting. In Wenninger's Report of 15 December 1915, on the other hand, it is expressly stated that the Prussian War Minister Josias von Heeringen was *not* invited.

9 Bethmann to Eisendecher, 29 December 1912, Röhl, 'An der Schwelle', document no. 36.

10 See Karl Dietrich Erdmann (ed.), *Kurt Riezler, Tagebücher, Aufsätze, Dokumente* (Göttingen 1972), pp. 7ff. Cf. Bernd Sösemann, 'Die Tagebücher Kurt Riezlers. Untersuchungen zu ihrer Echtheit und Edition', *Historische Zeitschrift* 236 (1983), pp. 327–369; Erdmann's reply in ibid., pp. 371–402; Fritz Fischer, *Juli 1914: Wir sind nicht hineingeschlittert. Das Staatsgeheimnis um die Riezler-Tagebücher* (Frankfurt 1983); Bernd-Felix Schulte, *Die Verfälschung der Riezler-Tagebücher. Ein Beitrag zur Wissenschaftsgeschichte der 50er und 60er Jahre* (Frankfurt, Bern and New York 1985).

11 Müller, diary entry for 19 October 1912, BA-MA Freiburg.

12 Ibid., 1 and 5 November 1912. See John C. G. Röhl, 'Admiral von Müller', p. 659.

13 Lichnowsky to Kaiser Wilhelm II, 6 November 1912, ZStA Merseburg, Rep. 53J, Lit. L. no. 5, quoted in Röhl, *1914 – Delusion or Design?*, p. 43.

14 Kaiser Wilhelm II to Kiderlen-Wächter, 7 November 1912, *Die Grosse Politik der europäischen Kabinette*, XXXIII, no. 12339.

15 Müller, diary entry for 8 November 1912, BA-MA Freiburg.

16 Kaiser Wilhelm II to Kiderlen-Wächter, 9 November 1912, *Grosse Politik*, XXXIII, no. 12348.

17 Müller, diary entry for 8 November 1912, BA-MA Freiburg.

18 Bethmann Hollweg to Kiderlen-Wächter, 9 November 1912, *Grosse Politik*, XXXIII, p. 302, note.

19 Müller, diary entry for 8/9 November 1912, BA-MA Freiburg. Röhl, 'Admiral von Müller', pp. 659f.

20 Kaiser Wilhelm II, memorandum, *Grosse Politik*, XXXIII, no. 12349.

21 BA-MA, RM 2/1775.

22 Kaiser Wilhelm II to Kiderlen-Wächter, 21 November 1912, *Grosse Politik*, XXXIII, no. 12405.

23 Schemua, 'Bericht über meinen Aufenthalt in Berlin am 22 d.M.', printed in E. C. Helmreich, 'An Unpublished Report on Austro-German Military Conversations of November 1912', *Journal of Modern History* 5 (1933), pp. 205ff.

24 Archduke Franz Ferdinand's reports from Berlin are printed in *Österreich-Ungarns Aussenpolitik 1908–1914*, 8 vols. (Vienna 1930) IV, no. 4559 and no. 4571.

25 Müller, diary entry for 22/23 November 1912, BA-MA Freiburg. Röhl, 'Admiral von Müller', p. 660.

26 Kiderlen-Wächter to Pourtalès, 19 November 1912, PA Bonn, Pourtalès Papers, quoted in Gutsche, 'Probleme', p. 65.

27 Müller, diary entry for 26/27 November 1912, BA-MA Freiburg.
28 *Grosse Politik*, XXXIII, no. 12474. See Ernst Jäckh, *Kiderlen-Wächter. Der Staatsmann und der Mensch*, 2 vols. (Berlin 1924), II, p. 192; E. C. Helmreich, *The Diplomacy of the Balkan Wars 1912–1913* (New York 1938), p. 244.
29 Reichstag Debates, vol. 286 (Berlin 1913), Column 2472ff.
30 Müller, diary entry for 14 December 1912, BA-MA Freiburg.
31 *Grosse Politik*, XXXIX, no. 15634.
32 Printed in *Kriegsrüstung und Kriegswirtschaft*, prepared in the Reichsarchiv. Appendix to vol. 1 (Berlin 1930), no. 48.
33 Dieter Groh, '"Je eher, desto besser!" Innenpolitische Faktoren für die Präventivkriegsbereitschaft des Deutschen Reiches 1913/14', *Politische Vierteljahresschrift* 13 (1972), p. 506.
34 Printed in *Kriegsrüstung und Kriegswirtschaft*, Appendix, no. 50.
35 *Grosse Politik*, XXXIX, no. 15634.
36 Kaiser Wilhelm II, marginal comment of 21 November 1912, *Grosse Politik*, XXXIII, no. 12404.
37 *Grosse Politik*, XXXIII, no. 12405.
38 Lichnowsky to Kaiser Wilhelm II, 23 November 1912, ZStA Merseburg, Rep. 53 J, Lit. L, no. 5, quoted in Röhl, *1914 – Delusion or Design?*, p. 44. See also Eisendecher to Kaiser Wilhelm II, 20 November 1912, BA-MA Freiburg, RM 2/1765.
39 Müller, diary entry for 3 December 1912, BA-MA Freiburg. Röhl, 'Admiral von Müller', p. 660.
40 August von Heeringen, memorandum of 29 November 1912, presented to the Kaiser on 3 December 1912. BA-MA Freiburg, RM 5/v898.
41 Heeringen, memorandum of 28 November 1912, approved by the Kaiser on 3 December 1912, ibid.
42 Heeringen, memorandum of 28 November 1912, 'Falls S.M. auf die Transportfrage näher eingehen', ibid.
43 *Norddeutsche Allgemeine Zeitung*, 5–7 December 1912.
44 On the Franco-British conversations, see S. R. Williamson Jr., *The Politics of Grand Strategy. Britain and France Prepare for War, 1904–1914* (Cambridge, Mass. 1969), pp. 294ff. In a memorandum of 24 September 1912, Grey had defined the British point of view in the words: 'If Germany dominated the policy of the Continent it would be disagreeable to us as well as to others for we should be isolated', *British Documents on the Origins of the War*, vol. 9/I, no. 805.
45 Lichnowsky's Report of 3 December 1912, *Grosse Politik*, XXXIX, no. 15612.
46 Lichnowsky's Report of 4 December 1912, *Grosse Politik*, XXXIII, no. 12481. See also his Report of 9 December 1912, *Grosse Politik*, XXXIII, no. 12489.
47 Prince Heinrich of Prussia, diary entry for 6 December 1912, printed in Röhl, 'An der Schwelle', document no. 2.
48 King George V to Grey, 8 December 1912, printed in Sir Harold Nicolson, *King George the Fifth. His Life and Reign* (London 1952), p. 206.
49 Kaiser Wilhelm II, marginal comments on Lichnowsky's report of 3 December 1912, *Grosse Politik*, XXXIX, no. 15612.
50 Kaiser Wilhelm II to Bethmann Hollweg, 30 September 1912, ZStA Merseburg, Rep. 53J, Lit. B, no. 7, quoted in Röhl, *1914 – Delusion or Design?*, p. 42.
51 Kaiser Wilhelm II to Kiderlen-Wächter, 8 December 1912, *Grosse Politik*, XXXIX, no. 15613.

52 See the four documents on the 'war council' of 8 December 1912 quoted at the beginning of this chapter, above pp. 162–5.

53 Kaiser Wilhelm II to Archduke Franz Ferdinand, 9 December 1912, printed in Röhl, 'An der Schwelle', document no. 8. See R. A. Kann, 'Emperor William II and Archduke Francis Ferdinand in their Correspondence', *American Historical Review* 57 (1952), pp. 344f. See also R. A. Kann, *Erzherzog Franz Ferdinand. Studien* (Munich 1967), pp. 74f.

54 Kaiser Wilhelm II to Prince Heinrich of Prussia, 12 December 1912, printed in Röhl, 'An der Schwelle', document no. 12.

55 Kaiser Wilhelm II to Karl von Eisendecher, 12 December 1912, ibid., document no. 13. See also Fischer, *Krieg der Illusionen*, pp. 236f.

56 Count Hugo von Lerchenfeld to Count Georg von Hertling, 14 December 1912, in Ernst Deuerlein (ed.), *Briefwechsel Hertling-Lerchenfeld. Dienstliche Privatkorrespondenz zwischen dem bayerischen Ministerpräsidenten Georg Graf von Hertling und dem bayerischen Gesandten in Berlin Hugo Graf von und zu Lerchenfeld* (Boppard-am-Rhein 1973), part I, pp. 189ff. See also Karl Alexander von Müller in *Süddeutsche Monatshefte* (July 1921), pp. 294f.

57 Klaus Meyer, *Theodor Schiemann als politischer Publizist* (Frankfurt 1956), p. 181, note 537.

58 Alfred de Claparède, report of 10 December 1912, printed in Terence F. Cole, 'German Decision-Making on the Eve of the First World War. The Records of the Swiss Embassy in Berlin' in John C. G. Röhl (ed.), *Der Ort Kaiser Wilhelms II. in der deutschen Geschichte* (Munich 1991), pp. 62f.

59 Bernhard Huldermann, *Albert Ballin* (Oldenburg 1922), pp. 273f.

60 Alfred von Kiderlen-Wächter to Karl von Eisendecher, 19 December 1912, printed in Röhl, 'An der Schwelle', document no. 35.

61 Müller, diary entry for 8 December 1912, see above pp. 162f.

62 Bethmann Hollweg to Eisendecher, 20 December 1912, Röhl, 'An der Schwelle', document no. 36.

63 Ibid., document no. 14. See above, pp. 163f.

64 Ibid., document nos. 15, 20, 21 and 22. See above, p. 164.

65 Bethmann Hollweg, memorandum of 20 December 1912, ibid., Document no. 34; *Grosse Politik*, XXXIII, no. 12496.

66 Müller, diary entry for 14 December 1912, BA-MA Freiburg.

67 Erwin Hölzle, *Die Selbstentmachtung Europas*, pp. 180ff.

68 Mommsen, 'Domestic Factors in German Foreign Policy', pp. 12f.

69 Müller to Bethmann Hollweg, 8 December 1912, printed in Röhl, 'An der Schwelle', document no. 5. See Imanuel Geiss, *Julikrise und Kriegsausbruch 1914*, 2 vols. (Hanover 1963/4), I, p. 45.

70 Röhl, 'An der Schwelle', document no. 9, appendix, with the Kaiser's marginal comment.

71 Bethmann Hollweg to Kaiser Wilhelm II, 10 December 1912, ibid., document no. 9.

72 Kiderlen-Wächter to Müller, 11 December 1912, ibid., document no. 10.

73 Mommsen, 'Domestic Factors in German Foreign Policy', pp. 12f.

74 Karl Freiherr von Bienerth to Franz Graf Conrad von Hötzendorf, 18 December 1912, Österreichisches Kriegsarchiv, Vienna, Generalstab 1912, 25–1/58. This document was generously brought to my attention by Isabel V. Hull.

75 Röhl, 'An der Schwelle', document no. 28.
76 Ibid., document no. 5.
77 Ibid., document no. 16.
78 See ibid., document no. 28, appendix.
79 Ibid., document no. 28.
80 Ibid., document no. 17.
81 Ibid., document no. 28.
82 Ibid., document no. 17.
83 Alfred von Tirpitz, *Der Aufbau der deutschen Weltmacht* (= *Politische Dokumente*, vol. 1) (Stuttgart 1924), pp. 369f.
84 Röhl, 'An der Schwelle', document no. 30.
85 In his Report of 9 December 1912, Lichnowsky expressed the hope that England 'will only attack us if we march into France and have won the first battle'. *Grosse Politik*, XXXIII, no. 12489, pp. 463ff.
86 Röhl, 'An der Schwelle', document no. 31.
87 The Kaiser's marginal comments on ibid., document no. 31; see also document no. 32.
88 Ibid., document no. 33.
89 Ibid., document no. 34. See also p. 164.
90 See Röhl, *1914 – Delusion or Design?*, p. 41.
91 Röhl, 'An der Schwelle', document no. 36; see also Lichnowsky's Report of 20 December 1912 in *Grosse Politik*, 34, no. 12561, pp. 70ff.
92 Röhl, 'An der Schwelle', document no. 35.
93 Ibid., document no. 39. See also Eisendecher's (unsent) letter to the British Colonial Secretary Harcourt, document no. 26b.
94 Bethmann and Lichnowsky were invited to breakfast with the Kaiser on 31 December 1912. Müller, diary, BA-MA Freiburg.
95 Röhl, 'An der Schwelle', document no. 2.
96 Müller, diary entry for 1 January 1913, BA-MA Freiburg.
97 Müller to Tirpitz, 4 January 1913, BA-MA Freiburg, RM2/1731. Printed in part in Tirpitz, *Aufbau*, p. 370.
98 Müller, diary entry for 4 January 1913, BA-MA Freiburg.
99 Ibid., entry for 5 January 1913.
100 Ibid., entry for 6 January 1913. Müller to Tirpitz, 6 January 1913, BA-MA Freiburg, RM2/1731. Tirpitz, *Aufbau*, pp. 370f.
101 Müller, diary entry for 6 January 1913, BA-MA Freiburg.
102 Wenninger's report, 24 December 1912, printed in Röhl, 'An der Schwelle', document no. 38.
103 Reinhold Zilch, 'Zur wirtschaftlichen Vorbereitung des deutschen Imperialismus auf den Ersten Weltkrieg. Das Protokoll der Sitzung des "Wirtschaftlichen Ausschusses" vom Mai 1914', *Zeitschrift für Geschichtswissenschaft* 24 (1976), pp. 202ff.
104 Wenninger's report, 24 December 1912, printed in Röhl, 'An der Schwelle', document no. 38.
105 Ibid.
106 Politisches Archiv des Auswärtigen Amtes Bonn, Deutschland 121, vol. 12.
107 Sir Edward H. Holden, 'The World's Money Markets', speech of 23 January 1914, printed in *The Statist. A Journal of Practical Finance and Trade*, 24

January 1914, supplement. I am grateful to Professor Paul Kennedy for bringing this important source to my attention. Cf. the figures in Fischer, *Krieg*, pp.
280–4.
108 Röhl, 'An der Schwelle', document nos. 14,15 and 21.
109 Leuckart's Report, 12 December 1912, ibid., document no. 14.
110 The Krümper system was adopted by Prussia in the years 1808 to 1812 as a
means of quickly increasing the size of the army with partially trained reservists.
111 My italics. Wenninger's Report, 14 December 1912, ibid., document no. 21.
112 Dieter Groh, 'Je eher, desto besser', pp. 501ff.
113 See Adolf Gasser, 'Deutschlands Entschluss zum Präventivkrieg 1913/14' in
Discordia Concors. Festschrift für Edgar Bonjour (Basel 1968), p. 173; Dieter
Groh, *Negative Integration und revolutionärer Attentismus. Die deutsche Sozialdemokratie am Vorabend des 1. Weltkrieges, 1909–1914* (Berlin 1973), pp. 406–14.
114 Groh, 'Je eher, desto besser', p. 506. See the important new study by Stig
Förster, *Der Doppelte Militarismus*, pp. 247ff.
115 Groh, 'Je eher, desto besser', p. 503.
116 Memorandum on a conversation between Reich Chancellor von Bethmann
Hollweg and Field Marshal Baron von der Goltz, in the Mudra Papers, BA-MA
Freiburg, printed in Bernd-Felix Schulte, *Vor dem Kriegsausbruch 1914*, p. 156.
The memorandum carries the note by Mudra: 'Goltz said more or less this to me
on 10.12.[19]12.'

8 KAISER WILHELM II AND GERMAN ANTI-SEMITISM

1 The author of these vicious broadsheets was Max Bewer, a Bismarckian fanatic
born of Catholic parents in the Düsseldorf area but working from 1891 until his
death in 1921 in Laubegast near Dresden. See the telling account of his life by
Barbara Suchy, 'Antisemitismus in den Jahren vor dem ersten Weltkrieg' in
Jutta Bohnke-Kollwitz (ed.), *Köln und das Rheinische Judentum* (Cologne 1985),
pp. 252–83. Bewer's ideology and propaganda are now usefully analysed in
Matthew Paul Stibbe, 'Anti-Semitic Publicists and Agitators in Imperial
Germany 1871–1900', unpublished M.A. dissertation, University of Sussex,
1993.
2 See the outraged correspondence on this issue in the *Frankfurter Allgemeine
Zeitung*, 5 September 1991.
3 The original contributions to the much-discussed 'Historikerstreit' are collected
together in a volume of that title published by Piper (Munich 1987).
4 Friedrich Schmitt-Ott, *Erlebtes und Erstrebtes, 1860–1950* (Wiesbaden 1952),
p. 195; Kaiser Wilhelm II to George Sylvester Viereck, 29 January 1926, Lamar
Cecil, 'Wilhelm II. und die Juden', in Werner E. Mosse and Arnold Paucker
(eds.), *Juden im Wilhelminischen Deutschland 1890–1914* (Tübingen 1976),
p. 344; Wolfgang Pfeiffer-Belli (ed.), *Harry Graf Kessler, Tagebücher 1918–1937*
(Frankfurt am Main 1961), p. 383.
5 Thomas Nipperdey, 'Wilhelm II. – Verkannt oder nur vergessen?' Norddeut-
scher Rundfunk (NDR), Das Montagsthema, 13 June 1988.
6 Indeed, at Bonn Wilhelm met a young Jewish officer, Walter Mossner, whom he
later ennobled and appointed as his adjutant.
7 Bismarck, *Die gesammelten Werke*, XV, p. 553.

8 *Politischer Bilderbogen* Nr. 20, 'Der Teufel in Deutschland'.
9 *Politischer Bilderbogen* Nr. 33, 'Der Weltboxer'. As early as 1892, Hermann Ahlwardt had published his book *Der Verzweiflungskampf der arischen Völker mit dem Judentum*, alleging a Jewish world conspiracy.
10 Ernst Graf zu Reventlow, *Der Vampir des Festlandes* (Berlin 1915).
11 For Stoecker's first 'Judenrede' of 19 September 1879, 'Unsere Forderung an das Moderne Judentum', see Kurt Wawrzinek, *Die Entstehung der deutschen Antisemitenparteien 1873–1890* (Berlin 1927), pp. 26–8. Stoecker's speech of 22 November 1880 is printed in *Die Judenfrage im preussischen Abgeordnetenhaus, Wörtlicher Abdruck der stenographischen Berichte v. 20. und 22. November 1880* (Breslau 1880), p. 115. Stoecker's speech 'Die Bedeutung der christlichen Weltanschauung für die brennenden Fragen der Gegenwart', 21 July 1881, is printed in A. Stoecker, *Christlich-Sozial, Reden und Aufsätze* (Berlin 1885), p. 381. His speech 'Das Judentum im öffentlichen Leben – eine Gefahr für das Deutsche Reich', 1882, is in Stoecker, *Christlich-Sozial*, pp. 210f., 215f. Stoecker's speech 'Die Berliner Juden und das öffentliche Leben', 2 July 1883, is printed in Stoecker, *Christlich-Sozial*, p. 228. Of fundamental importance is Werner Jochmann, 'Stoecker als nationalkonservativer Politiker und antisemitischer Agitator' in Günter Brakelmann, Martin Greschat and Werner Jochmann, *Protestantismus und Politik, Werk und Wirkung Adolf Stoeckers* (Hamburg 1982), pp. 148–61.
12 *Die Judenfrage im preussischen Abgeordnetenhaus*, p. 106.
13 Werner Jochmann, *Gesellschaftskrise und Judenfeindschaft in Deutschland 1870–1945* (Hamburg 1988), p. 47.
14 Werner Jochmann, 'Stoecker als nationalkonservativer Politiker und antisemitischer Agitator', pp. 152f. See Peter G. J. Pulzer, *Die Entstehung des politischen Antisemitismus in Deutschland und Österreich 1867 bis 1914* (Gütersloh 1966), p. 85; Walter Frank, *Hofprediger Adolf Stoecker und die christlichsoziale Bewegung* (Hamburg 1935), p. 93.
15 Norbert Kampe, *Studenten und 'Judenfrage' im Deutschen Kaiserreich. Die Entstehung einer akademischen Trägerschicht des Antisemitismus*, Göttingen 1988.
16 Crown Princess to Crown Prince, 9 January 1880, in John C. G. Röhl, *Wilhelm II. Die Jugend des Kaisers* (Munich 1993), p. 414.
17 Crown Princess to Crown Prince, 4 January 1880, ibid.
18 Crown Princess to Crown Prince, 23 April 1880, ibid.
19 Crown Prince to Baron Ernst von Stockmar, 18 November 1880, ibid., p. 415.
20 Queen Victoria to Crown Princess, 22 January 1881, Roger Fulford (ed.), *Beloved Mama. Private Correspondence of Queen Victoria and the German Crown Princess 1878–1885* (London 1981), p. 95.
21 Crown Princess to Crown Prince, 16 March and 17 December 1879, Röhl, *Die Jugend des Kaisers*, p. 419.
22 Crown Princess to Queen Victoria, 5 August 1880, Fulford, *Beloved Mama*, p. 85.
23 Brigitte Hamann, 'Das Leben des Kronprinzen Rudolf von Österreich-Ungarn nach neuen Quellen', unpublished doctoral dissertation in University of Vienna 1977, pp. 619f.
24 Prince Wilhelm of Prussia to Gustav Kardinal zu Hohenlohe-Schillingsfürst, 18 April 1884, Röhl, *Die Jugend des Kaisers*, p. 422.

25 Frank, *Hofprediger Adolf Stoecker*, pp. 167f.
26 Peter Broucek, 'Kronprinz Rudolf und k. u. k. Oberstleutnant im Generalstab Steininger', in *Mitteilungen des österreichischen Staatsarchivs* 26 (1973), pp. 446f.
27 Waldersee, diary entry for 27 December 1885, ZStA Merseburg, Nl. Waldersee. The version of the Waldersee diary published by Meisner in the early 1920s is scandalously unreliable. See Heinrich Otto Meisner (ed.), *Denkwürdigkeiten des General-Feldmarschalls Alfred Grafen von Waldersee*, 3 vols. (Stuttgart and Berlin 1922–3).
28 Frank, *Hofprediger Adolf Stoecker*, pp. 124–43.
29 Prince Wilhelm of Prussia to Kaiser Wilhelm I, 5 August 1885, ZStA Merseburg, Brand.-Preuss. Hausarchiv, Rep. 53T Preussen: An Kaiser Wilhelm I. Cf. Frank, *Hofprediger Adolf Stoecker*, pp. 145f., 310.
30 Waldersee, diary entry for 15 October 1885, ZStA Merseburg, Nl. Waldersee; cf. Meisner, *Waldersees Denkwürdigkeiten*, I, p. 263.
31 Waldersee, diary entry for 27 March 1886, ZStA Merseburg, Nl. Waldersee; cf. Meisner, *Waldersees Denkwürdigkeiten*, I, p. 286.
32 Waldersee, diary entry for 15 February 1886, ZStA Merseburg, Nl. Waldersee; cf. Meisner, *Waldersees Denkwürdigkeiten*, I, pp. 274f.
33 Waldersee, diary entry for 20 December 1886, ZStA Merseburg, Nl. Waldersee; not in Meisner, *Waldersees Denkwürdigkeiten*, I, p. 308.
34 Alfred Graf von Waldersee to Prince Wilhelm of Prussia, 21 November 1887, Röhl, *Die Jugend des Kaisers*, p. 717.
35 Herbert Graf von Bismarck to Otto Fürst von Bismarck, 19 September 1895, Nl. Bismarck, BA Koblenz.
36 Waldersee, diary entry for 23 December 1887, ZStA Merseburg, Nl. Waldersee.
37 Waldersee, diary entry for 15 December 1887. Ibid.
38 Prince Wilhelm of Prussia to Philipp Graf zu Eulenburg, 19 February 1888, in John C. G. Röhl (ed.), *Philipp Eulenburgs Politische Korrespondenz*, 3 vols. (Boppard-am-Rhein 1976–83), I, no. 153.
39 Prince Wilhelm of Prussia to Philipp Eulenburg, 12 April 1888, *Eulenburgs Korrespondenz*, I, no. 169.
40 Georg Ritter von Schönerer, 'Unverfälschte Deutsche Worte', 1. Oktober 1888, quoted in Brigitte Hamann, *Rudolf, Kronprinz und Rebell* (Vienna and Munich 1978), p. 362. On Lueger see ibid., pp. 408f., on Drumont's book *La fin du monde* see ibid., pp. 397ff.
41 Kaiser Wilhelm II to Crown Prince Gustav of Sweden, 25 July 1895, in Karl Alexander von Müller (ed.), *Fürst Chlodwig zu Hohenlohe-Schillingsfürst, Denkwürdigkeiten der Reichskanzlerzeit* (Munich 1931), pp. 102–5. See the interesting study of the Kaiser's 'Nordic' passions by Birgit Marschall, *Reisen und Regieren. Die Nordlandfahrten Kaiser Wilhelms II.* (Heidelberg 1991).
42 Kaiser Wilhelm II to Archduke Franz Ferdinand, 12 February 1909, Cecil, 'Wilhelm II. und die Juden', p. 332.
43 See above pp. 173ff.
44 See Heinz Gollwitzer, *Die Gelbe Gefahr. Geschichte eines Schlagworts. Studien zum imperialistischen Denken* (Göttingen 1962), pp. 206ff. See also the chapter on the Kaiser and the 'yellow peril' in Arthur N. Davis, *The Kaiser I Knew. My Fourteen Years with the Kaiser* (London 1918), pp. 107ff.
45 The speech is quoted on pp. 13f above.

46 Bernhard Fürst von Bülow, *Denkwürdigkeiten*, 4 vols. (Berlin 1930–1), II, pp. 63f.
47 Kaiser Wilhelm II to Tsar Nicholas II, 28 December 1907, in Walter Goetz (ed.), *Briefe Wilhelms II. an den Zaren 1894–1914* (Berlin 1920), pp. 393f.
48 See Ute Mehnert, 'Deutschland, Amerika und die "Gelbe Gefahr". Zur Karriere eines Schlagworts in der grossen Politik 1905–1917', unpublished doctoral dissertation, University of Cologne 1992; Ragnhild Fiebig-von Hase, 'Die Rolle Kaiser Wilhelms II. in den deutsch-amerikanischen Beziehungen', in John C. G. Röhl (ed.), *Der Ort Kaiser Wilhelms II. in der deutschen Geschichte* (Munich 1991), pp. 223–57.
49 Werner E. Mosse, 'Wilhelm II and the Kaiserjuden. A Problematical Encounter', in Jehuda Reinharz and Walter Schatzberg (eds.), *The Jewish Response to German Culture* (Hanover and London 1985), pp. 164–94. The Kaiser's bitter statement of 1940 is revealing in this context: 'I have invited Jews to my table, have supported *Judenprofessoren* and helped them, their answer was: scorn, ridicule, World War, betrayal, Versailles and *Revolution!*' Kaiser Wilhelm II to Alwina Gräfin von der Goltz, 7 August 1940, printed in Willibald Gutsche, 'Illusionen des Exkaisers. Dokumente aus dem letzten Lebensjahr Kaiser Wilhelms II. 1940/41', *Zeitschrift für Geschichtswissenschaft* 19 (1991), pp. 1029ff.
50 Kaiser Wilhelm II to Friedrich I Grossherzog von Baden, 29 September 1898, Hermann and Bessi Ellern, *Herzl, Hechler, the Grand Duke of Baden and the German Emperor 1898–1904* (Tel-Aviv 1961), pp. 48ff.
51 Ibid. See also Alexander Bein, 'Erinnerungen und Dokumente über Herzls Begegnung mit Wilhelm II.', in *Zeitschrift für die Geschichte der Juden* (1964), p. 44ff; Walther Peter Fuchs (ed.), *Grossherzog Friedrich I. von Baden und die Reichspolitik 1871–1907*, 4 vols. (Stuttgart 1968–80), IV, no. 1891 *et passim*; *Philipp Eulenburgs Korrespondenz*, III, pp. 1920–27. See Egmont Zechlin, *Die deutsche Politik und die Juden im Ersten Weltkrieg* (Göttingen 1969), p. 285ff.
52 Kaiser Wilhelm II, speech of 3 February 1899. Printed in Johannes Penzler (ed.), *Die Reden Kaiser Wilhelms II. in den Jahren 1896–1900* (Leipzig 1904), pp. 144ff. See Gisela Brude-Firnau, 'Preussische Predigt. Die Reden Wilhelms II.', in Gerald Chapple and Hans H. Schulte (eds.), *The Turn of the Century. German Literature and Art, 1890–1915* (Bonn 1981), pp. 149–70.
53 See Geoffrey G. Field, *Evangelist of Race. The Germanic Vision of Houston Stewart Chamberlain* (New York 1981).
54 Kaiser Wilhelm II to H. S. Chamberlain, 31 December 1901, in Chamberlain, *Briefe 1882–1924*, II (Munich 1928), pp. 142f.
55 Kaiser Wilhelm II to H. S. Chamberlain, 21 December 1902, in Chamberlain, *Briefe*, II, p. 166f.
56 H. S. Chamberlain to Kaiser Wilhelm II, 20 February 1902, Chamberlain, *Briefe*, II, p. 161.
57 Lady Susan Townley, *Indiscretions* (New York 1922), p. 45.
58 M. V. Brett (ed.), *Journals and Letters of Reginald Viscount Esher*, 2 vols. (London 1934), II, p. 255.
59 Davis, *The Kaiser I Knew*, p. 174.
60 N. M. Butler, *Across the Busy Years*, 2 vols. (New York and London 1940), II, p. 63.
61 Kaiser Wilhelm II to Tsar Nicholas II, 29 January 1906 in W. Goetz (ed.), *Briefe Wilhelms II. an den Zaren 1894–1914* (Berlin 1920), pp. 386–388.

62 Kaiser Wilhelm II to H. S. Chamberlain, 23 December 1907, *Briefe*, II, p. 226f.

63 Kaiser Wilhelm II to G. S. Viereck, 29 January 1926, Cecil, 'Wilhelm II. und die Juden', p. 344.

64 Bülow's note, 29 December 1908, quoted in Cecil, 'Wilhelm II. und die Juden', p. 336.

65 Bülow's note, 14 December 1908, Kaiser Wilhelm II to Archduke Franz Ferdinand, 16 December 1908, Cecil, 'Wilhelm II. und die Juden', p. 337.

66 Kaiser Wilhelm II to Max Egon Fürst zu Fürstenberg, 11 January 1909, Fürstlich Fürstenbergsches Archiv Donaueschingen.

67 Hartmut Pogge von Strandmann, 'Staatsstreichpläne, Alldeutsche und Bethmann Hollweg', in Hartmut Pogge von Strandmann and Imanuel Geiss, *Die Erforderlichkeit des Unmöglichen* (Frankfurt 1965).

68 Admiral Georg Alexander von Müller, diary entry for 4 September 1914, BA-MA Freiburg. This entry was omitted in Walter Görlitz (ed.), *Regierte der Kaiser? Kriegstagebücher, Aufzeichnungen und Briefe des Chefs des Marine-Kabinetts Admiral Georg Alexander von Müller 1914–1918* (Göttingen 1959), pp. 54f. See Isabel V. Hull, *The Entourage of Kaiser Wilhelm II* (Cambridge 1982), p. 267; John C. G. Röhl, 'The Emperor's New Clothes: A Character Sketch of Kaiser Wilhelm II' in John C. G. Röhl and Nicolaus Sombart (eds.), *Kaiser Wilhelm II, New Interpretations. The Corfu Papers* (Cambridge 1982), p. 31.

69 Charles Seymour (ed.), *The Intimate Papers of Colonel House*, 4 vols. (Boston and New York 1926–8), II, p. 139.

70 H. S. Chamberlain, 'Kaiser Wilhelm II.', in *Deutsches Wesen* (Munich 1916).

71 Chamberlain, 'Deutscher Friede', in *Kriegsaufsätze* (Munich 1915), pp. 87–90.

72 Chamberlain, *Die Zuversicht* (Munich 1915), pp. 11–12. Cf. Richard Wagner, *Das Judentum in der Musik* (1850). See Wagner's statements on the Jews, as recorded in Cosima Wagner's diaries: he referred to them as 'Ratten', 'Mäuse', 'Fliegen', 'Trichinen', 'Warzen' und 'Gewürm'. Cosima Wagner, *Tagebücher*, 2 vols. (Munich 1976–7), I, p. 135; II, pp. 293, 454, 460, 599, 888. See the important new study by Hartmut Zelinsky, 'Kaiser Wilhelm II, die Werk-Idee Richard Wagners and der Weltkampf', in Röhl, *Der Ort Kaiser Wilhelms II. in der deutschen Geschichte*, pp. 297–356.

73 H. S. Chamberlain to Kaiser Wilhelm II, 20 January 1917, *Briefe*, II, pp. 251–3.

74 Kaiser Wilhelm II to H. S. Chamberlain, 15 January 1917, Chamberlain Papers, Richard Wagner Museum Bayreuth. The version of this letter printed in Chamberlain, *Briefe*, II, p. 250, has been heavily edited and abbreviated.

75 Max Bewer, *Beim Kaiser und Hindenburg im Großen Hauptquartier* (Dresden 1917). Here the Kaiser is reported to have declared: 'Hindenburg is our Wotan and Ludendorff is the Siegfried of our time!', ibid., p. 34. Bewer claimed that he had met the Kaiser 'for several hours' once before, in Norway in July 1913, ibid., p. 29. In his diary, the Chief of the Civil Cabinet, Rudolf von Valentini, recorded his disgust that the Kaiser had received 'das Ekel' – that horror – Max Bewer. Valentini, diary entry for 24 August 1917, BA Koblenz, Thimme Papers, No. 26.

76 See *Semi-Imperator 1888–1918. Eine genealogisch-rassengeschichtliche Aufklärung zur Warnung für die Zukunft* (Munich 1919). The book, published in the form of the 'Gotha', bore the emblem of the swastika.

77 See the recent study by Willibald Gutsche, *Ein Kaiser im Exil. Der letzte deutsche Kaiser Wilhelm II. in Holland* (Marburg 1991).

78 Sigurd von Ilsemann, diary entry for 22 August 1934, omitted in Harald von Königswald (ed.), *Sigurd von Ilsemann, Der Kaiser in Holland*, 2 vols. (Munich 1967–8). Quoted in Röhl, 'The Emperor's New Clothes', p. 32.

79 Ilsemann, diary entry for 12 November 1923, *Der Kaiser in Holland*, I, p. 303.

80 These ravings are examined at some length in Gutsche, *Ein Kaiser im Exil*.

81 Schmitt-Ott, *Erlebtes und Erstrebtes, 1860–1950*, p. 195.

82 Kaiser Wilhelm II, 'Vatikan und Völkerbund', June 1926, Gutsche, *Ein Kaiser im Exil*, p. 78.

83 Kaiser Wilhelm II to H. S. Chamberlain, 12 March 1923, *Briefe*, II, pp. 265–73.

84 Kaiser Wilhelm II to H. S. Chamberlain, 3 June 1923, *Briefe*, II, pp. 273f.

85 Kaiser Wilhelm II, 'The Sex of Nations', *The Century Magazine* 116, no. 2 (June 1928), pp. 129–39.

86 Ilsemann, diary entry for 7 October 1923, *Der Kaiser in Holland*, I, p. 287; Kaiser Wilhelm II, 'The Sex of Nations', pp. 138f.

87 Kaiser Wilhelm II to George Sylvester Viereck, 20 February and 18 June 1925, Cecil, 'Wilhelm II. und die Juden', p. 346.

88 Kaiser Wilhelm II to G. S. Viereck, 20 December 1923, Cecil, 'Wilhelm II. und die Juden', p. 346.

89 Kaiser Wilhelm II to G. S. Viereck, 27 April 1925, Cecil, 'Wilhelm II. und die Juden', p. 345. See Gutsche, *Ein Kaiser im Exil*, p. 78.

90 Kaiser Wilhelm II to G. S. Viereck, 20 February and 18 June 1925, Cecil, 'Wilhelm II. und die Juden', p. 346.

91 Kaiser Wilhelm II to G. S. Viereck, 26 October 1926, Cecil, 'Wilhelm II. und die Juden', p. 345.

92 Kaiser Wilhelm II to Poultney Bigelow, 14 April 1927. Bigelow Papers, New York Public Library.

93 Quoted in chapter 1, above p. 14.

94 Kaiser Wilhelm II to Poultney Bigelow, 18 October 1927. Bigelow Papers, New York Public Library.

95 Kaiser Wilhelm II to Poultney Bigelow, 15 August 1927. Bigelow Papers, New York Public Library. Two months earlier, Wilhelm had instructed a member of his entourage to ask Fritz Haber whether the *Totalvergasung* of large cities had become a practicable possibility. Wilhelm von Dommes to Fritz Haber, 14 June 1927, Gutsche, *Ein Kaiser im Exil*, p. 92.

96 Cf. Friedrich Wilhelm Prinz von Preussen, *Das Haus Hohenzollern 1918–1945* (Munich 1985), p. 185. On Himmler and 9 November 1938, see Richard Breitman, *The Architect of Genocide. Himmler and the Final Solution* (London 1991), pp. 53f.

97 Kaiser Wilhelm II to Poultney Bigelow, 14 September 1940, quoted in Röhl, *Kaiser Wilhelm II, 'Eine Studie über Cäsarenwahnsinn'* (Munich 1989), p. 7.

98 Kaiser Wilhelm II to Alwina Gräfin von der Goltz, 28 July 1940 and 7 August 1940, printed in Willibald Gutsche, 'Illusionen des Exkaisers. Dokumente aus dem letzten Lebensjahr Kaiser Wilhelms II. 1940/41', *Zeitschrift für Geschichtswissenschaft*, 10 (1991), pp. 1028–32.

99 Kaiser Wilhelm II to Margarethe Landgräfin von Hessen, 3 November 1940, quoted in Röhl, *Kaiser Wilhelm II, 'Eine Studie über Cäsarenwahnsinn'*, p. 7. Cf. Kaiser Wilhelm II to Alfred Niemann, 24 December 1940, GStA HA Rep. 192, Nr. 16, now printed in Gutsche, 'Illusionen des Exkaisers', pp. 1032–34.

INDEX

Kaiser Wilhelm II has not been included in the index. Members of royal families are listed by their first name. German aristocratic titles have been left in the original